Resources for Teaching   7/04

THE STORY
AND ITS WRITER

An Introduction to Short Fiction

Fourth Edition

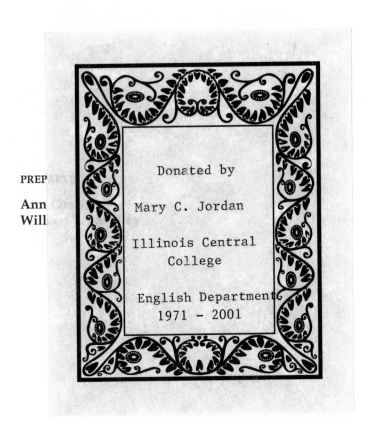

PREP

Ann
Will

Bedford Books *of* **St. Martin's Press**

BOSTON

Copyright © 1995 by Bedford Books *of* St. Martin's Press
All rights reserved.
Manufactured in the United States of America.

9 8 7 6 5
f e d c b a

For information, write: St. Martin's Press, Inc.
175 Fifth Avenue, New York, NY 10010

Editorial Offices: Bedford Books *of* St. Martin's Press
29 Winchester Street, Boston, MA 02116

ISBN: 0–312–10340–9

Cover Design: Hannus Design.

Cover Painting: Henry Varnum Poor, *The Writer at the Window,* c. 1930. Bornick
Fine Art.

Instructors who have adopted *The Story and Its Writer,* Fourth Edition, as a
textbook for a course are authorized to duplicate portions of this manual for their
students.

PREFACE

The entries in this manual include commentaries on each story in the anthology, along with questions for discussion, writing assignments, and suggested readings. The commentaries offer brief critical analyses of the stories and suggest ways to approach them in class. Like the questions that follow, the commentaries aim to promote a lively exchange of responses and perceptions without insisting on any particular interpretation or critical methodology.

Following the Topics for Writing are Connections questions, which ask students to link selections in the book. These questions promote critical thinking and are designed to provide both stimulating topics for writing assignments and material for fruitful class discussions. Instructors using these resources will readily see ways to rephrase, restructure, and reapply these assignments to suit their own purposes and the needs of their students. Some writing topics may serve equally well as discussion questions, and vice versa.

The suggested reading lists that conclude most entries are neither exhaustive nor highly selective; they simply cite interesting and, when possible, readily available criticism that proved useful in preparing the manual or that contains information and approaches to the stories that could not be incorporated in the commentaries. Thanks are due to the authors mentioned, to whose insights and scholarship these resources are generally indebted.

At the end of these resources is a chronological listing of authors and titles, a thematic index of stories, a list of films from some of the stories in *The Story and Its Writer*, and a list of film distributors and their addresses.

CONTENTS

Contents

PART ONE

THE STORIES

CHINUA ACHEBE

Civil Peace (p. 10)

Achebe narrates this story about the "civil peace" prevailing in war-torn Nigeria after the Biafran war with an ironic control that provides a strong contrast to the human suffering portrayed in the story. When the story opens, we learn that the protagonist, Jonathan Iwegbu, considers himself lucky to have survived the war with his wife and three of their four children. The terms of his survival, and the price he continues to pay for his own and his family's safekeeping despite the official end to the civil war, are dramatized in the events of the story.

Jonathan Iwegbu is an excellent example of what the critic Frank O'Connor called "the little Man" in short story literature, a figure projecting a distinctive aura of human dignity despite his all-too-apparent vulnerability and isolation. Like the clerk in Gogol's story "The Overcoat," Jonathan Iwegbu is tormented by the people around him (the soldiers who threaten to shoot up his house and force him to give up his money), yet his fundamental decency speaks so directly to us that we seem to hear him say, as in Gogol's story, "Why do you [bother] me? . . . I am your brother."

Achebe's story can be compared with Ben Okri's "In the Shadow of War" in this anthology, since both are contemporary stories about life in war-torn Nigeria. Students may be struck by the differences resulting from each author's choice of point of view. Achebe's "Civil Peace" is narrated by an omniscient author ostensibly sharing his reliable adult protagonist's perspective: Jonathan Iwegbu is a kindhearted man completely devoted to his family, hard-working, resourceful, and patient in adversity. On the other hand, Okri narrates "In the Shadow of War" from the perspective of an unreliable witness, the young boy Omovo (see discussion of this story on page 194 of this manual).

Questions for Discussion

1. Is "Civil Peace" a fully developed short story or an anecdote? What qualities in the narrative — characterization, setting, plot — lead you to your answer?
2. Explain the irony in the title of the story.
3. Jonathan Iwegbu acts as a self-reliant head of his family throughout the narrative. Why then does Achebe emphasize the "miracle" of his family's survival and the "monumental blessing" of his house's survival, and why does he repeat the phrase "nothing puzzles God" at the end of the story?

Topics for Writing

1. Translate into conventional English the words of the leader of the group who knocks on the door of Jonathan's house and demands money from him in the middle of the night. Analyze the dramatic effect of this dialogue as the climax of the story.
2. **CONNECTIONS** Compare and contrast the narrative elements of realism and surrealism in "Civil Peace" and "In the Shadow of War."

Suggested Readings

Achebe, Chinua. *Girls at War and Other Stories.* New York: Ballantine, 1973.
Chargois, J. A. *Two Views of Black Alienation: A Comparative Study of Chinua Achebe and Ralph Ellison.* Bloomington: Indiana UP, 1973.
Wren, R. W. *Achebe's World.* Washington, DC: Three Continents, 1980.

ALICE ADAMS

The Last Lovely City (p. 14)

"The Last Lovely City" is constructed on contrasts: the differences between young and old, past and future, rich and poor, Mexico and the United States, the living and the dead. The story is set at a luncheon party in Stinson Beach, California, but the protagonist, Dr. Benito Zamora, finds the nearby city of San Francisco—which Zamora considers "the last lovely city" and which Adams has called a "more or less offstage character"—nearly always present in his thoughts. It encapsulates his life, beginning nearly a half-century before with his ambitious dreams as an indigent student of medicine from Oaxaca, Mexico, and ending with the memories of his harmonious marriage to his wealthy wife Elizabeth, recently deceased. Canny investment in San Francisco real estate, not his practice as a cardiologist, has made Dr. Zamora rich enough to fund clinics for the poor people of his native state of Chiapas in Mexico.

San Francisco has fulfilled Dr. Zamora's dreams, but as a lonely widower he realizes that "the tall, pale city, lovely and unreal," has never become his home. Avoiding the "rich and crazily corrupt population" at the luncheon, the doctor returns to San Francisco, dreading "the first pale, romantic view" of the city from the Golden Gate bridge, having resolved to spend his remaining years working in his clinic and living with his old mother in Mexico.

This narrative can be read as a bittersweet "rags-to-riches" immigrant's success story, using San Francisco as a paradoxical symbol of America — essentially cold and rootless. Although beautiful, it is as remote and inhuman as the pear tree in Mansfield's "Bliss." Despite Dr. Zamora's success, he feels alien and alone in the United States, still a stranger after a lifetime in his adopted country.

Questions for Discussion

1. Why is Doctor Benito Zamora so self-conscious about his name? Why does he also dislike his nickname, Dr. Do-Good? What does this suggest about his self-esteem?
2. Why does Dr. Zamora think of marrying Carla, and not Posey Pendergast or Dolores Gutierrez, who are both much closer to him in age? Does Carla's statement, "Get real," when Dr. Zamora complains about real estate corruption in San Francisco, tell you anything important about her?
3. Why is Dr. Zamora so critical of Herman Tolliver's starched white embroidered shirt?
4. How does Alice Adams suggest the rootlessness of life in California by the details of the crumbling sand castle on the beach and Carla's comment that Posey had put her house up for sale?

Topics for Writing

1. Using a place or setting as "an offstage character," write a story in which a person achieves a new and perhaps unwelcome understanding of him- or herself.
2. **CONNECTIONS** "The Last Lovely City" and James Joyce's "Araby" are both suffused with a sense of longing and a sense of place. Explore these and other parallels you might note between the stories in a comparison-contrast essay.

Suggested Readings

Adams, Alice. *After You've Gone: Stories.* New York: Knopf, 1989.

———. "The American Short Story in the Cybernetic Age." *Journal of the Short Story in English* 17 Autumn (1991): 9–22.

Chell, Cara. "Succeeding in Their Times: Alice Adams on Women and Work." *Soundings: An Interdisciplinary Journal* Spring 68:1 (1985): 62–71.

Holt, P. "Publisher's Weekly Interviews: Alice Adams." *Publisher's Weekly* 16 (Jan. 1978): 8–9.

"On Turning 50." *Vogue* 173 (1983): 230.

Upton, Lee. "Changing the Past: Alice Adams's Revisionary Nostalgia." *Studies in Short Fiction* Winter 26:1 (1989): 33–41.

Jack Agueros

Dominoes (p. 26)

The action of this story erupts as suddenly as does the murderous street fight Agueros describes. What begins as a game of dominoes between four Puerto Rican men in New York City deteriorates into open warfare between two of the players whose cultural background has instilled in them the belief that their destiny lies in being *macho*. As Wilson explains the philosophy to Alma, "Men who are real men can live their lives anyway they like—because their destiny is clear. To be a *macho* is the destiny." With his large hands wrapped around the other's throat, Paco intends to strangle Ebarito, who in turn pulls out a pair of scissors and stabs Paco a dozen times between the ribs. Ebarito survives with his vocal chords permanently damaged, while Paco staggers off to a fire hydrant and crumbles "into a pile like a pneumatic tire that had a blow out." Alma, hysterical, screaming over Ebarito's body on the sidewalk, doesn't even realize her uncle Paco is dead. Her grief is misdirected, Agueros tells the reader: "She screamed at everyone. She screamed at no one."

While Agueros is careful to sketch in the individual personalities of the four domino players in order to motivate the action, he does so without sentimentality or sensationalism. Ebarito can't play the game as skillfully as the other three players, and he is unable to concede defeat gracefully, although he knows he should. He tries to cheat instead, and he gets caught immediately. Tito is kinder but weak, unlike Wilson and Paco, best friends, who both left Puerto Rico at sixteen to join the merchant marine. Agueros shows sympathy for their poverty-stricken background: Wilson and Paco had been "country boys suddenly [placed in the merchant marine] with mean men and dangerous work and thirty years at sea always looking to see who was standing behind you."

Poverty and hardship have toughened both men, but Agueros is critical of the lessons their difficult lives have taught them. His placement of Alma in the story provides a moral frame of reference to contrast with the amorality of the other characters' brutal behavior. The orderly game of dominoes, explained as Paco taught it to Alma, is another steadfast reference point, a contrast to the impulsive and destructive behavior the men display when not playing the game.

Questions for Discussion

1. "Dominoes seemed to Alma a ridiculous game." Explain how to play it, and analyze its appeal for Paco, Wilson, Tito, and Ebarito.
2. Why do Wilson and Paco break into laughter at Wilson's response to Alma after she asks him, "What is the fate for a woman?"
3. Why does Wilson keep Tito from stopping the fight between Paco and Ebarito?
4. What is the effect of Agueros's organization of the story into sections paralleling the doubled numbers ranging from six to zero (blank) on the face of the dominoes?

Topics for Writing

1. Instead of using Agueros's omniscient point of view, rewrite the story from the first-person point of view of Alma or one of the other characters.
2. Analyze the social and cultural background of the Puerto Rican community in New York City as it appears in "Dominoes."

Suggested Readings

Agueros, Jack. *Correspondence Between the Stonehaulers.* Brooklyn: Hanging Loose, 1991.

———. *Dominoes and Other Stories from the Puerto Rican.* Willimantic, CT: Curbstone, 1993.

Woody Allen

The Kugelmass Episode (p. 32)

Like most works of fiction based on impossible or unlikely suppositions, "The Kugelmass Episode" entertains us with the device on which it is grounded. Rather than developing the intellectual puzzles of science fiction, however, Allen mainly offers gently satiric jokes made possible by the incongruities arising from his donnée. When her class notices that on page 100 "a bald Jew is kissing Madame Bovary," the teacher in South Dakota, without consulting her desk copy, blames the problem on a mass-media stereotype, drug-crazed students; a professor at Stanford sees in the incredible instability of the text a confirmation of a mindless academic cliché: "Well, I guess the mark of a classic is that you can reread it a thousand times and always find something new." Thus we transform what is unfamiliar into bricks for the wall of presupposition that barricades us from the truth. Meanwhile, Allen delights in collapsing the distance between "good literature" and everyday banality. Emma admires Kugelmass's leisure suit; he thrills her with black panties and designer slacks; and, like every other good-looking girl who goes to New York, she dreams of a career on the stage.

But the fantasy on which Allen bases his tale has deeper roots. Like Faust, Kugelmass dreams of transcending human limitations, of living for a while free from the constraints of time and ordinary causation. He abandons human science and philosophy, here represented by his shrink, and turns to magic. Although Persky resembles an auto mechanic more than Mephistopheles, he offers an equally dangerous and meaningful temptation to Kugelmass. If the professor lacks the poetry and grandeur of his Faustian predecessors, he is motivated by parallel desires. Bored with his life and unable to love the people he shares it with (who can blame him?), he bargains for something he expects will be better. Appropriately, given the diminished scale of modern heroism, he signs away not his soul but merely a "double sawbuck." As happens especially with Marlowe's Dr. Faustus, for his reward Kugelmass gets only what he is capable of imagining. Emma Bovary as he experiences her talks and acts like any woman he could have picked up at Elaine's — exactly what he wanted, and what he turns her into by bringing her out of the novel and into the Plaza Hotel.

After the near-disaster of his affair with Emma, Kugelmass swears off philandering, but of course he has not learned his lesson. When he asks Persky to use the wondrous machine to send him for a date with "The Monkey" of *Portnoy's Complaint*, Kugelmass reveals the utter emptiness of spirit that hides behind his glib pop-culture romanticism, and it is fitting that he ends up scrambling through a desert inhabited by predatory words without meaning.

The intellectual and moral universe that Kugelmass inhabits even before his final translation is no less devoid of meaning. Allen's fantasy shows how the sophistication of modern life can drain the spirit out of human language, desires, and relationships. Kugelmass claims to have "soul," but his needs are quoted from advertisements in *The New Yorker*. The language of commercial psychology debases even his dreams, whose imagery is third hand and probably phony: "I was skipping through a meadow holding a picnic basket and the basket was marked 'Options.' " Kugelmass picks his mistress as from a menu; he decides to plunge into the supernatural (but for exceedingly *natural* reasons) more easily than he chooses between red and white wine (as if those were the only possibilities); significantly, he is most comfortable minimizing the importance of what he is doing: "'Sex and romance,' Kugelmass said from inside the box. 'What we go through for a pretty face.' "

Through the fantastic device of Persky's box, Allen achieves the small dislocation necessary to reveal that remark of Kugelmass's as a pitifully inadequate cliché. The story is full of such instances, and the technique embodies its larger vision. We choose the things we say to describe our lives to ourselves because they have been purged of discomforting truths. Allen shows that these statements are illusions. Kugelmass regards his life as a novel that has turned out badly. Rather than seeking to understand why he has come to a second marital dead end burdened with financial obligations and bored with his family, he tries to escape from the present and reenact the past. He wants only to enter *Madame Bovary* before page 120, and he dreams of starting life over in Europe, selling the (long defunct) *International Herald Tribune* "like those young girls used to."

The story leaves us with an implicit question: What redemption is possible for Kugelmass and the culture — our culture — that he represents? Is there an alternative to the Hobson's choice between desperation and meaninglessness?

WILLIAM E. SHEIDLEY

Questions for Discussion

1. Comment on the situation of Kugelmass as described in the first two paragraphs. Do you think his circumstances are unusual? Where should we lay blame for his predicament?
2. Kugelmass "had soul." What does that term seem to mean in this context?
3. Interpret Kugelmass's dream. Is it profoundly symbolic?
4. How effective is Dr. Mandel? Why does Kugelmass need a magician?
5. Discuss Persky. What might be Allen's basis for this character? How important is Persky to the story?
6. What factors enter into Kugelmass's choice of a mistress? What does this event suggest about his attitude toward literature? toward women?
7. Explore the implications of this quip: "She spoke in the same fine English translation as the paperback."
8. Review the first conversation between Kugelmass and Emma. Has Kugelmass really been transported into *Madame Bovary*? Does it resemble the novel as you read it or as you imagine it to be?
9. What does Allen achieve by noting the effect of the sudden appearance of the Kugelmass episode in the novel on various readers?

10. "By showing up during the correct chapters, I've got the situation knocked," Kugelmass says. Consider the implications of that idea. Would you like to live only certain chapters of your life?
11. Why does Emma want to come to New York? Why does Kugelmass want to take her there? Are the ensuing problems entirely the result of her being a character in a novel?
12. As Persky struggles to repair his box and Emma consumes "Dom Pérignon and black eggs," Kugelmass becomes more and more agitated. Finally, he contemplates suicide ("Too bad this is a low floor") or running away to Europe to sell the *International Herald Tribune*. How serious is he? Explain why those ideas accord with his character.
13. Why does it take Kugelmass only three weeks to break his resolution, "I'll never cheat again"?
14. *Portnoy's Complaint* examines, among other things, masturbation and adolescent sexual fantasies. What does it imply about Kugelmass that he chooses that book for his next adventure?
15. Do you think the ending of the story is appropriate? Why should Allen choose a remedial Spanish grammar for Kugelmass's hell rather than, say, a book in which adulterers are punished or in which none of the characters is a good-looking young woman?

Topics for Writing

1. Analyze how Allen crosses the border between life and art in "The Kugelmass Episode" and in his film *The Purple Rose of Cairo*.
2. Discuss the theme of meaningless language in "The Kugelmass Episode."
3. Study the use of language in Allen's story. List familiar phrases. What are their sources? Examine the conversations between characters. How much communication is taking place?
4. People often wish aloud for something they know to be impossible or speak of what they would do *if only*: "If only I had her looks and his money." "If only I were in charge." Imagine a character — yourself or someone you know, perhaps — whose impossible wish comes true. Then what? Follow Allen's lead by using the device to express the real truth in a surprising new way.
5. **CONNECTIONS** Compare and contrast the responses to marvels in Allen's "The Kugelmass Episode" and García Márquez's "A Very Old Man with Enormous Wings."

Suggested Readings

Gianetti, L. "Ciao, Woody." *Western Humanities Review* 35 (1981): 157–61.

Jacobs, Diane. *Magic of Woody Allen*. London: Robson, 1982.

Reisch, M. S. "Woody Allen: American Prose Humorist." *Journal of Popular Culture* 17 (1983): 68–74.

Rose, L. "Humor and Nothingness." *Atlantic* 255 (1985): 94–96.

Shechner, Mark. "Woody Allen: The Failure of the Therapeutic." *From Hester Street to Hollywood*. Ed. Sarah B. Cohen. Bloomington: Indiana UP, 1983. 231–44.

"Woody Allen on the American Character." *Commentary* 76 (1983): 61–65.

Isabel Allende

And of Clay Are We Created (p. 42)

"And of Clay Are We Created" is the last story in Allende's *The Stories of Eva Luna*, published after her third novel, *Eva Luna*, about a woman who "defeats the odds of her fate with generosity and candor." Rolf Carlé, the television journalist in the story who befriends Azucena, the thirteen-year-old girl caught in the mudpit after the volcano's eruption destroys her village, also writes the prologue to *The Stories of Eva Luna*. There Carlé comments on Allende the storyteller: "You think in words; for you, language is an inexhaustible thread you weave as if life were created as you tell it."

In Allende's hands, a story about the tragedy of a natural disaster is the occasion for a celebration of life. In an essay entitled "Writing as an Act of Hope," Allende has said that writing *clearly* is the first duty of the storyteller: "Not simply — that only works with soap advertising; we don't have to sacrifice aesthetics for the sake of ethics. On the contrary, only if we are able to say it beautifully can we be convincing. Most readers are perfectly able to appreciate subtleties and poetic twists and symbols and metaphors." In "And of Clay Are We Created," the volcano's eruption elicits the young girl's heroism, which in turn frees the journalist who befriends her so that he is able to confront his own deeply repressed fears about his traumatic youth in Austria thirty years before.

One aspect of "And of Clay Are We Created" that could stimulate discussion in the classroom is how Allende suggests the difference between a television reporter's coverage of a story and a short story writer's handling of the same event. Rolf Carlé has at his disposal an expensive arsenal of technical equipment: helicopter, video camera and microphone, "spools of cable, tapes, film, videos, precision lenses, recorders, sound consoles, lights, reflecting screens, auxiliary motors, cartons of supplies, electricians, sound technicians, and camera men." Allende, on the other hand, has only her words and the blank page. Yet she is able to get beneath the surface of the natural disaster and tell the story in depth, so that we learn of the impact of the girl's heroism on Rolf Carlé. Allende's handling of the sequence of events communicates a moral lesson as well as a historical one.

Questions for Discussion

1. Analyze how the opening paragraph of the story foreshadows the events to come in the narrative.
2. What is the effect of Allende's description of the girl's "head budding like a black squash from the clay" after we are told that her name is *Azucena*, meaning "Lily"?
3. In the second paragraph of the story, Allende employs irony to describe the events leading up to the volcano's eruption. How does her tone establish her emotional control over her material?
4. What other examples of irony can you find in the story?
5. Discuss the significance of the title of the story.

Topics for Writing

1. Write a book review of Allende's novel *Eva Luna*.
2. Allende has said that "it's hard for a book to stand against the message of the mass media; it's an unfair battle. Writers should therefore look for other forms of expressing their thoughts, avoiding the prejudice that only in books can they make literature. All means are legitimate, not only the cultivated language of academia but also the direct language of journalism, the mass language of radio, television and the movies, the poetic language of popular songs and the passionate language of talking face to face with an audience. These are all forms of literature." Agree or disagree with her statement.
3. **CONNECTIONS** Compare and contrast Allende's description of a disaster in this story with the disaster described by Bharati Mukherjee in "The Management of Grief."

Suggested Readings

Allende, Isabel. *The Stories of Eva Luna*. Trans. Margaret Sayers Peden. New York: Atheneum, 1991.

Zinsser, William, ed. *Paths of Resistance: The Art and Craft of the Political Novel.* Boston: Houghton, 1989. Contains Isabel Allende's "Writing as an Act of Hope."

SHERWOOD ANDERSON

Death in the Woods (p. 51)

"Death in the Woods" presents a religious image of the earth mother, the principle of connectedness by which life is fostered and sustained. Anderson's depiction of the woman whose job it is to feed animal life, "in cows, in chickens, in pigs, in horses, in dogs, in men," congeals in the visionary revelation of her death scene. To the men and boys who stand around her, the moonlit glimpse of her naked breast—effectively foreshadowed in the incident in which, as a girl, she had her dress ripped open by the German farmer she was bound to—conveys a sense of wonder: They look upon a marble statue of a beautiful young woman in the snow. Near her, or perhaps around her, lies the oval track left by the dogs, at once a prayer ring and a symbol of the interdependence and endless continuity of the life she has served.

It is appropriate that the basis of Mrs. Grimes's scant economy is eggs, whose various connotations are obvious enough. As the nurse of living things, Mrs. Grimes establishes bonds and fosters community. The world with which she must deal, however, corrodes those bonds. When we first see her she is struggling alone: "People drive right down a road and never notice an old woman like that." The men she feeds are rapacious and cruel — to her and, as in the fight between Jake and the German farmer, to each other. The town treats them all with cold suspicion. Even the butcher who loads her grain bag out of pity would deny the food to Mrs.

9

Grimes's husband or son: "He'd see him starve first." Not Mrs. Grimes, who tacitly reaffirms her theme: "Starve, eh? Well things had to be fed. . . . Horses, cows, pigs, dogs, men." When she dies the forces for harmony and union that she embodies achieve a momentary victory, as the townspeople fall into a ragged communal procession to witness her death — a ceremony as instinctive as the ring running of the dogs, if somewhat less orderly and beautiful.

Anderson's story progresses from an apprehension of drab poverty and ugliness to a discovery of wonder and beauty. The agency that distills religious and aesthetic emotion out of the profane world of the story is the inquiring imagination of the narrator, who muses over his recollections, reconstructs his story from fragments, and in doing so explains the process of synthesis that takes place as he writes. In its progress from the ordinary to the mystical, from ugliness and privation to a soul-nourishing beauty, the story records a triumph of the creative imagination, which penetrates the surfaces of things to find within them their inherent mythic truth.

What makes that triumph possible is the narrator's subtly expressed identification with Mrs. Grimes. The fascination that causes him to cling to his recollections and finally to work them through may arise, as William J. Scheick argues, from the shock of his initiation into an awareness "of the relation between feeding, sex, and death" that blocks his sexual development; or it may arise from a sense of the hitherto unexpressed mythic implications of the scene in the woods. In either case, the narrator recognizes that the death of Mrs. Grimes has meaning for him — as one who has worked for a German farmer, who has himself watched dogs run in a ring, and who has kept silent; as one who is fed by women; and as one who must die. The story's circular structure, like the ring of dogs and the ring of men around the corpse, transforms compulsion into worship, just as Anderson's art transforms the report of a frightening death into a celebration of life and of the power of the sympathetic imagination to render its beauty.

WILLIAM E. SHEIDLEY

Questions for Discussion

1. Discuss the style of the opening paragraph. What qualities of the old woman's life are reflected in the syntax and rhythms of the prose?
2. How does Anderson modulate from generalization through recollection to specific narration? What change in narrative mode takes place in section II with the paragraph that begins "One day in Winter"? Does the story ever return to its original mode? Where?
3. "Her name was Grimes" — appropriately?
4. What does the narrator mean when he calls the Grimes men "a tough lot"? Are they alone in this in the story?
5. Describe the woman's life with the German farmer. How important to the story is the farmer's having torn "her dress open clear down the front"?
6. How big a part does love play in the relations between people in this story? What other factors are prominent — exploitation? mistrust? violence?
7. Does the butcher's generosity seem a welcome change? How does the butcher compare with Mrs. Grimes as a nurturer of life?
8. How does Anderson prepare us to accept it as probable that Mrs. Grimes would sit down under a tree and freeze to death?

9. Describe the behavior of the dogs. How does Anderson explain it? How does the narrator know it took place?

10. Comment on the tonal effect of the passage "It had been a big haul for the old woman. It was a big haul for the dogs now."

11. What does the corpse look like in the moonlight? Why does Anderson give a concise description of the corpse near the beginning of section IV rather than saving the whole revelation until the men and boys arrive on the scene at the end of that section?

12. Comment on the implications of this line: "Either mother or our older sister would have to warm our supper."

13. Explain the possible meanings of the word "everything" in the first sentence of section V.

14. Discuss the narrator's remarks about why he has told the story. What is "the real story I am now trying to tell"? To what extent is it a story about the narrator himself? About stories and storytelling?

Topics for Writing

1. In an essay, describe Anderson's circular notion of image and structure in "Death in the Woods."

2. Discuss the narrator's struggle "to tell the simple story over again."

3. Write an essay analyzing the role of the community in "Death in the Woods."

4. Describe Mrs. Grimes and the mythic roles of woman in "Death in the Woods."

5. On a second reading, make notes about the narrator. Rearrange his activities, experiences, and concerns into chronological order. What is the narrator's story? What is his conflict? What does he achieve? What does he learn?

6. Read several myths from Ovid's *Metamorphoses*. Rewrite the story of Mrs. Grimes as an Ovidian myth. What changes of tone are necessary? What important themes have you had to abandon? What have you had to invent?

Related Commentary

Sherwood Anderson, Form, Not Plot, in the Short Story, p. 1379.

Suggested Readings

See page 13.

SHERWOOD ANDERSON

Hands (p. 60)

Anderson's story "Hands" might be called a portrait. Like a formal painted portrait, it depicts Wing Biddlebaum not only as he exists at a given moment but also in conjunction with certain props in the background that reveal who he is by recalling his past and defining his circumstances. The focal image of the portrait is Wing's hands, around which the other elements of the picture are organized and to which they lend meaning. Further, the story depends for a portion of its effect upon a series of painterly tableaux, from the sunset landscape with berry pickers with which it begins to the silhouette of Wing as a holy hermit, saying over and over the rosary of his lonely years of penance for a sin he did not commit.

In keeping with this achronological narration (which William L. Phillips has shown may in part result from Anderson's thinking his way through the story as he wrote it), neither Wing nor George Willard experiences any clear revelation or makes any climactic decision. Wing never understands why he was driven out of Pennsylvania, and George is afraid to ask the questions that might lead them both to a liberating understanding of Wing's experience.

The reader, however, is not permitted to remain in the dark. With the clear understanding of how the crudity and narrow-minded suspicion of his neighbors have perverted Wing's selfless, "diffused" love for his students into a source of fear and shame comes a poignant sorrow for what is being wasted. Wing's hands may be the pride of Winesburg for their agility at picking strawberries, but the nurturing love that they betoken is feared by everyone, including George, including even Wing himself, whose loneliness is as great as his capacity to love — from which, by a cruel irony, it arises.

WILLIAM E. SHEIDLEY

Questions for Discussion

1. Define Wing Biddlebaum's relationship to his community as it is implied in the first paragraph. To what extent is the impression created here borne out?
2. Why does Wing hope George Willard will come to visit? Does George ever arrive?
3. Wing's name, which refers to his hands, was given to him by "some obscure poet of the town," and telling the full story of those hands "is a job for a poet." What connotations of "wings" are appropriate? Why is "Wing" a better name for Biddlebaum than, say, "Claw," or "Hook," or "Picker"?
4. Could Wing himself have been a poet? Why does he tell his dreams only to George?
5. Why did the people of the town in Pennsylvania nearly lynch Adolph Myers? Why was he unable to defend himself?
6. Are the people in Ohio any different from those in Pennsylvania? Explain. What about George Willard? Evaluate his decision not to ask Wing about his hands.
7. What other hands do we see in the story? Compare them with Wing's.
8. Explain the implications of our last view of Wing. What is the pun in the last line?

Topics for Writing

1. Write an essay analyzing the crucifixion of Wing Biddlebaum.
2. Consider Anderson's comments in "Form, Not Plot, in the Short Story" (included in Part Two, p. 1379) as a key to his art in "Hands."

3. After reading the story once, jot down your response, including your feelings about Wing, George, the townspeople, and the narrator. Also write, in one or two sentences, a summation of the story's theme as you understand it. Then reread the paragraphs in the order they would have followed had Anderson told the story in chronological order. Would your responses differ? Would the story have an identical theme? Explain.

4. Anderson claimed to have written this story at a sitting and to have published it without rearrangements or major additions or deletions of material. Imitating his process, write a vignette about a person unknown to you whom you see in a photograph. Start with the scene in the photo and end with the same, interpolating previous incidents and background information as they occur to you.

5. **CONNECTIONS**   Compare and contrast Anderson's Wing and Flaubert's Félicité.

Related Commentary

Sherwood Anderson, Form, Not Plot, in the Short Story, p. 1379.

Suggested Readings

Anderson, David, ed. *Critical Essays on Sherwood Anderson.* Boston: G. K. Hall, 1981.

Anderson, Sherwood. *A Story Teller's Story.* Cleveland: The UP of Case Western Reserve, 1968.

———. *The Portable Sherwood Anderson.* New York: Viking, 1972.

———. *The Teller's Tales.* Introduction by Frank Gado. Schenectady, NY: Union College P, 1983.

Burbank, Rex. *Sherwood Anderson.* Twayne's United States Authors Series 65. New York: Twayne, 1964. 64–66.

Crowley, John W., ed. *New Essays on* Winesburg, Ohio. New York: Cambridge UP, 1990.

Joselyn, Sister Mary. "Some Artistic Dimensions of Sherwood Anderson's 'Death in the Woods.'" *Studies in Short Fiction* 4 (1967): 252–59.

Phillips, William L. "How Sherwood Anderson Wrote *Winesburg, Ohio.*" *The Achievement of Sherwood Anderson.* Ed. Ray Lewis White. Chapel Hill: U of North Carolina P, 1966. 62–84, esp. 74–78. Originally published in *American Literature* 23 (1951): 7–30.

Rideout, Walter B., ed. *Sherwood Anderson.* Englewood Cliffs, NJ: Prentice, 1974.

Scheick, William J. "Compulsion toward Repetition: Sherwood Anderson's 'Death in the Woods.'" *Studies in Short Fiction* 11 (1974): 141–46.

Townsend, Kim. *Sherwood Anderson.* Boston: Houghton, 1987.

White, Ray Lewis. Winesburg, Ohio: *An Explanation.* Boston: Twayne, 1990.

Margaret Atwood

Happy Endings (p. 66)

Atwood's story can be read profitably in conjunction with Grace Paley's "A Conversation with My Father." In both, the authors use humor to suggest a certain impatience with the traditional short-story form. Both stories can be read as "metafictions," fictions that comment on the art of telling stories. Atwood's piece is harsher than Paley's in its insistence that happy endings are impossible in stories; Atwood tells us clearly that death is "the only authentic ending" to everyone's story. Paley, in contrast, clearly values both her relationship with her dying father and her own imagination, allowing (even half-jokingly) her fictional heroine the possibility of rehabilitation after her drug addiction and a valued place in society as a counselor in a center for young addicts.

The first time students read "Happy Endings," they may miss the way Atwood connects the stories from "A" to "F." "B" is the first unhappy ending (as Atwood warns us in the third sentence), with the "worst possible scenario" worked out in John and Mary's love affair. Atwood's vocabulary here is deliberately harsh and unromantic, unlike the sentimental clichés of the "A" scenario.

As Atwood continues her permutations of the couples' possible relationships, her stories get shorter and more perfunctory. Her language becomes more elemental, preparing the reader for her summary dismissal of all plots, since they all end in death. In the final three paragraphs, Atwood drops all pretense that she is telling stories and directly addresses her readers, revealing that her true subject is not the emotional life she is creating for her characters but her awareness of the elements of fiction. She defines plot as "what" or "just one thing after another." Then, like the instructor's manual of a short-story anthology, she leaves the rest up to her reader: "Now try How [character] and Why [theme.]"

Questions for Discussion

1. Atwood's authorial presence is the strongest element in "Happy Endings" — does this make the text closer to an essay than a short story? Explain.
2. How does Atwood elicit your curiosity, so that you continue to read this short story? Would you say that she has proven that plot is the most essential element in a story? Is there also an underlying, coherent theme to "Happy Endings"?
3. Would the story still be effective if Atwood omitted her direct address to the reader ("If you want a happy ending, try A.")? Explain.

Topics for Writing

1. Rewrite the story inventing additional outcomes for John and Mary's relationship.
2. In "Reading Blind," (p. 1381), Atwood gives her criteria for judging whether a story is "good." Using these criteria, how would you rate "Happy Endings"?

3. Ray Bradbury, in his book *Zen in the Art of Writing: Essays on Creativity* (Capra, 1990) writes, "The writer must let his fingers run out the story of his characters, who, being only human and full of strange dreams and obsessions, are only too glad to run. . . . Remember: *Plot* is no more than footprints left in the snow after your characters have run by on their way to incredible destinations. *Plot* is observed after the fact rather than before. It cannot precede action. It is the chart that remains when an action is through." Apply Bradbury's analysis to "Happy Endings."

Related Commentary

Margaret Atwood, Reading Blind, p. 1381.

Suggested Readings

Atwood, Margaret. *Murder in the Dark.* Toronto: Coach House, 1983.
———. *Second Words.* Toronto: Anansi, 1982.
Grace, Sherrill E., and Lorraine Weir. *Margaret Atwood: Language, Text and System.* Vancouver: U of British Columbia P, 1983.
Rigney, Barbara Hill. *Margaret Atwood.* Totowa, NJ: Barnes & Noble, 1987.
Stouck, David. *Major Canadian Authors.* Lincoln: U of Nebraska P, 1988.

Isaac Babel

My First Goose (p. 70)

The narrator in this story is an outsider, a lonely and hungry intellectual who wins a meal and the acceptance of the Cossacks by killing the old peasant woman's goose. He does it roughly, demonstrating that he will "get on all right" at the front. The act is portrayed partly as a rape, partly as a crucifixion. The quartermaster tells him, "you go and mess up a lady, and a good lady too, and you'll have the boys patting you on the back," and that is what he does, trampling her goose under his boot and plunging his sword into it while she repeats, "I want to go and hang myself," and he says, "Christ!" But the narrator recoils from his self-debasement: The night that enfolds him resembles a prostitute; the moon decorates it "like a cheap earring." Lenin says there is a shortage of everything, and though Surovkov believes that Lenin strikes straight at the truth "like a hen pecking at a grain," the narrator uses the spectacles of his learning to discern "the secret curve of Lenin's straight line," the hidden purpose of the speech. The narrator, too, has taken an apparently bold and forthright step in killing the goose, but the secret curve of his straight line has been to gain acceptance by the Cossacks and a share of *their* dinner, which reminds him of his home. As he sleeps with his new friends he dreams of women, just as he saw female beauty in the long legs of Savitsky. But in taking his first goose he has messed up a good lady and stained his heart with bloodshed, and his conscience is not at peace.

Questions for Discussion

1. Describe Savitsky. What is the narrator's attitude toward him? Why does Babel begin the story with this character, who never reappears?
2. What advice does the quartermaster give? Does the narrator follow it?
3. Why are the narrator's "specs" an object of derision? Who else in the story wears glasses?
4. Why does the Cossack throw the narrator's trunk out at the gate?
5. When the narrator first tries to read Lenin's speech, he cannot concentrate. Why?
6. How does the narrator win the respect of the Cossacks?
7. Discuss the difference between Surovkov's understanding of Lenin's speech and the narrator's.
8. Explain the last sentence. What is the narrator's feeling about himself? about the situation he is in?
9. "Lenin writes that there's a shortage of everything." Of what is there a particular shortage in the story?

Topics for Writing

1. Write an essay analyzing the function of sexual imagery in "My First Goose."
2. Explain why the narrator stains himself in "My First Goose."
3. What is the effect of Babel's extreme brevity in "My First Goose?" Describe the way it is achieved.
4. Before beginning to read "My First Goose," write your prediction of what its subject might be on the basis of its title alone. Write a second guess as well. After reading the story, review your predictions. To what extent were the expectations aroused by the title — even if they were not confirmed — relevant to an understanding of Babel's narrative?

Suggested Readings

Carden, Patricia. *The Art of Isaac Babel.* Ithaca: Cornell UP, 1972. 97, 100, 110, 130–31.

Falen, James E. *Isaac Babel: Russian Master of the Short Story.* Knoxville: U of Tennessee P, 1974. 142–45.

JAMES BALDWIN

Sonny's Blues (p. 74)

The marvel of this story is the way the narrator — Sonny's older brother — narrows the physical and emotional distance between himself and Sonny until Sonny's plight is revealed and illuminated in a remarkable moment of empathy and insight. This story of drug addiction in the inner city's black ghetto is as valid today as it was when it was written. By juxtaposing the two brothers — a straight high school math teacher and a heroin addict blues pianist — Baldwin makes it possible for readers to enter the world of the story regardless of their racial background or their opinions about drugs. The author doesn't judge Sonny's plight. Instead, through the brother, he helps us understand it, sympathize with it, and transcend it in a brief shared experience of Sonny's inspired musical improvisation.

This is a long story, and its plot consists mostly of flashbacks, more "told" than "shown" in the reminiscences of Sonny's older brother. Yet the power of Baldwin's sympathy for his characters and his eloquent style move the reader along. Baldwin captures the African American culture of strong family allegiances in the face of American racism. Both Sonny and his brother are trying to survive, and we respect them for their courage.

One of the ways to discuss the story is through an analysis of the narrator's growing sympathy for Sonny. Baldwin tells us that the narrator thinks, after the death of his little daughter Grace from polio, "My trouble made his real." This realization motivates the first scene with the two brothers in which Baldwin begins to build the bridge between them. Separately they watch three sisters and a brother hold a revival meeting on the sidewalk opposite the narrator's apartment, and after they hear the gospel music, the silence between Sonny and his brother begins to give way to shared sound. The scene leads directly to the two brothers going to the bar where Sonny plays and creates an opportunity for the narrator (and the reader) to enter Sonny's world and satisfy his anguished need to share his music with someone who will listen to it and understand.

Questions for Discussion

1. Analyze the following speech, in which Sonny explains to his brother how he has survived (however tenuously) the experience of racism in America:

   "It's terrible sometimes, inside," he said, "that's what's the trouble. You walk these streets, black and funky and cold, and there's not really a living ass to talk to, and there's nothing shaking, and there's no way of getting it out — that storm inside. You can't talk it and you can't make love with it, and when you finally try to get with it and play it, you realize *nobody's* listening. So *you've* got to listen. You got to find a way to listen." .

   How does this explanation make Sonny a sympathetic character?

2. Discuss Baldwin's comment on the blues Sonny plays with Creole and the two other musicians at the end of the story:

   Creole began to tell us what the blues were all about. They were not about anything very new. He and his boys up there were keeping it new, at the risk of ruin, destruction, madness, and death, in order to find new ways to make us listen. For, while the tale of how we suffer, and how we are delighted, and how we may triumph is never new, it always must be heard. There isn't any other tale to tell, it's the only light we've got in all this darkness.

   Baldwin's subject is the music, of course, but he is also talking about other forms of creation. What might they be?

Topics for Writing

1. Chinua Achebe describes Baldwin as having brought "a new sharpness of vision, a new energy of passion, a new perfection of language to battle the incubus of race" in his eulogy titled "Postscript: James Baldwin (1924–1987)" (*Hopes and Impediments*, 1990). How does "Sonny's Blues" embody these qualities?

2. **CONNECTIONS** Baldwin's commentary "Autobiographical Notes" (p. 1385) states that he found it difficult to be a writer because he was forced to become a spokesman for his race: "I have not written about being a Negro at such length because I expect that to be my only subject, but only because it was the gate I had to unlock before I could hope to write about anything else." Yet Baldwin's depiction of the life lived by African Americans is unique and very different from Richard Wright's or Ralph Ellison's, Toni Cade Bambara's or Alice Walker's accounts. Compare and contrast "Sonny's Blues" with a story by one or more of these writers to describe how each finds his or her own way to dramatize what Baldwin calls "the ambiguity and irony of Negro life." Could "Sonny's Blues" be set in an Italian-American or Jewish-American family?

3. **CONNECTIONS** Compare and contrast "Sonny's Blues" with Willa Cather's "Paul's Case."

Related Commentary

James Baldwin, Autobiographical Notes, p. 1385.

Suggested Readings

Bloom, Harold, *James Baldwin*. New York: Chelsea House, 1986.

Burt, Nancy. *Critical Essays on James Baldwin*. Boston: G. K. Hall, 1986.

Campbell, James. *Talking at the Gates: A Life of James Baldwin*. New York: Viking, 1991.

Chametzky, Jules, ed. *A Tribute to James Baldwin: Black Writers Redefine the Struggle*. Amherst: U of Massachusetts P, 1989.

Kinnamon, Kenneth, ed. *James Baldwin*. Englewood Cliffs, NJ: Prentice, 1974.

Macebuh, Stanley. *James Baldwin: A Critical Study*. New York: Third, 1973.

Pratt, Louis H. *James Baldwin*. Twayne's United States Authors Series 290. Boston: G. K. Hall, 1978.

Standley, F. L., ed. *Conversations with James Baldwin*. Jackson: U of Mississippi P, 1989.

Toni Cade Bambara

The Lesson (p. 99)

Relationships are an organizational key to this story. "The Lesson" is narrated by Sylvia, one of a group of eight African American children living in an uptown slum in New York City who are "treated" by their neighborhood guide Miss Moore to an educational visit to the F.A.O. Schwartz toy store at Fifth Avenue and Fifty-Seventh Street. The group consists of four girls (Sylvia and her best friend Sugar, the relatively affluent Mercedes and her friend Rosie Giraffe) and four boys (Big Butt [Ronald] and Junebug, and Little Q.T. and Flyboy).

The "lesson" of the story is learned first by Sugar and then by Sylvia. All along Sylvia has assumed Sugar to be her ally, sharing her hostility to all adults as authority figures and to the idea of education. There's a suggestion of foreshadowing when the girls pay the taxicab driver outside F.A.O. Schwartz and Sugar steps in when Sylvia can't figure out the 10 percent tip on the 85-cent fare — "Give him a dime." (This is a taxi fare from twenty-five years ago, when the story was written.) But Sugar plays dumb as usual in her next appearance in the story, when she asks Miss Moore outside the toy store, "Can we steal?"

After the children learn about the high prices of the luxury toys at F.A.O. Schwartz, they return to their homes uptown. Sugar's remark to Miss Moore before they disperse reveals that the afternoon's lesson in economics hasn't been wasted: "this is not much of a democracy if you ask me. Equal chance to pursue happiness means an equal crack at the dough, don't it?" Bambara doesn't tell us whether Sugar intends to begin studying hard in school or to begin dealing drugs (this is the early 1970s), but the blinders formed by her life in the inner-city ghetto have fallen away, and she's clearly dissatisfied with her customary smart-aleck role. In her first response Sylvia is dumbfounded by her friend's betrayal, but within a few minutes she awakens to a sense of rivalry: "But ain't nobody gonna beat me at nuthin." Again Bambara leaves the lesson unspecified, and the reader must imagine *how* Sylvia intends to win the new game she's playing.

Questions for Discussion

1. What is the effect of the inner-city ghetto language in the story?
2. Is Sylvia a reliable or an unreliable narrator?
3. How does Bambara evoke a sense of sympathy for the people enduring the poverty and filth in Sylvia's neighborhood through her descriptions of the relationship of the winos and the newly arrived families from the South?
4. Describe the eight children and their relationships within the neighborhood group. How dependent is Sylvia on her friend Sugar?
5. Who is Miss Moore? Why does she personify the hostile force of "education" to the ghetto children?
6. Why does Sylvia keep the four dollars' change from the taxi fare? What does she do with the money? Is this a convincing ending to the story?

Topics for Writing

1. Write a story using a special dialect that you have learned from your family or friends.
2. **CONNECTIONS** Compare and contrast the authors' uses of African American speech in this story and in Richard Wright's "The Man Who Was Almost a Man." Analyze the different ways the two writers keep the dialect from distracting readers and causing them to lose interest in the stories.

Suggested Readings

Bambara, Toni Cade. *The Sea Birds Are Still Alive: Stories*. New York: Vintage, 1982.

Bell, Roseann P., Bettye J. Parker, and Beverly Guy-Sheftall, eds. *Sturdy Black Bridges: Visions of Black Women in Literature*. New York: Anchor, 1979.

Butler-Evans, Elliot. *Race, Gender, and Desire: Narrative Strategies in the Fiction of Toni Cade Bambara, Toni Morrison, and Alice Walker*. Philadelphia: Temple UP, 1989.

Cartwright, Jerome. "Bambara's 'The Lesson.'" *Explicator* Spring 47:3 (1989): 61–63.

Evans. Mari. ed. *Black Women Writers (1950–1980): A Critical Evaluation*. New York: Anchor, 1984. 41–71.

Giddings, P. "Call to Wholeness from a Gifted Storyteller." *Encore* 9 (1980): 48–49.

Lyles, Lois F. "Time, Motion, Sound and Fury in *The Sea Birds Are Still Alive*." *College Language Association Journal* December 36:2 (1992): 134–44.

Morrison, Toni. "City Limits, Village Values: Concepts of the Neighborhood in Black Fiction." *Literature and the Urban Experience: Essays on the City and Literature*. Ed. Ann Chalmers Watts and Michael C. Jaye. New Brunswick: Rutgers UP, 1981.

Tate, Claudia, ed. *Black Women Writers at Work*. New York: Continuum, 1983. 12–38.

Vertreace, Martha M. "A Bibliography of Writings about Toni Cade Bambara." *American Women Writing Fiction: Memory Identity, Family and Space*. Ed. Mickey Pearlman. Lexington: U of Kentucky P, 1989.

———. "Toni Cade Bambara: The Dance of Character and Community." *American Women Writing Fiction: Memory, Identity, Family, Space*. Ed. Mickey Pearlman. Lexington: U of Kentucky P, 1989.

JOHN BARTH

Lost in the Funhouse (p. 105)

In a brief comment written for the collection *Writer's Choice*, edited by Rust Hills (New York: McKay, 1974), Barth describes this story as occupying a medial position in a development from conventional to less conventional techniques and from youthful and presumably more personal versions of Ambrose in the earlier stories in the volume *Lost in the Funhouse* to later "more mythic avatars of the narrator." He goes on to repudiate "merely cerebral inventions, merely formalistic tours de force," and to declare his hope that the story is "accessible, entertaining, perhaps moving." Just as Ambrose is portrayed "at that awkward age," so the narrator who portrays him (a being hard to distinguish from Ambrose on the one hand and Barth on the other) appears in a transitional stage, the adolescence of his art. Quoting to himself the supposedly infallible principles of composition that he seems to have learned in a creative writing course, he struggles forward self-consciously, complaining that what is supposed to be happening as he writes does not seem to be taking place. Just as for Ambrose in the toolshed or at his baptism, observation of the proper forms does not necessarily bring the expected results. Yet, just as Ambrose is capable of experiencing unusual transports at inopportune moments, so the story, in spite of or apart from the conventions, renders a poignant account of the time and place in which it is set, of its protagonist's initiation into the mysteries of life and art, and of the narrator's unexpected triumph over the difficulties he confronts.

Readers may compare their experience of the story to the difficult progress through a funhouse, with its sudden surprises, its maddening reflections, its obvious contrivances, and the heavy atmosphere of sexuality. We enter perhaps violently yawning in the nervous anticipation that shocks are in store, but surely few readers are prepared for the upending of expectation that takes place even in the first paragraph. We stagger forward with the narrator, bumping into the pasteboard screens of his contrivance, glimpsing the pulleys and levers by which the story is operated but nonetheless responding to the images thrust before us. When the narrator complains, "We haven't even reached Ocean City yet: we will never get out of the funhouse," the reader knows he is referring to the story itself as well as to the boardwalk attraction.

Fiction is traditionally supposed to be an imitation of life, made the more credible, as the narrator remarks, by the artifice of illusion. By extension, then, the funhouse can be called an imitation of life, and of that part of life called art (the commentator wanders in these mazes too). While the funhouse may be fun for lovers, for Ambrose and the narrator it begins as *a place of fear and confusion*, mastered only by the fantasy of control with which the story concludes. Life, too, which resembles the funhouse in having seduction, coupling, and propagation as its central purpose, appears to the sensitive adolescent a frightening labyrinth that he must enter. The realities of war, death, and suffering — masked by the diversions of the funhouse or glimpsed behind them — lie in wait, and perhaps the Operator of the whole show is dozing at the controls. Although Ambrose has theoretical access in Magda to the "fun" life has to offer, he recoils with nausea from his visions of the universal copulation, can bear only the lightest contact with her body, and recalls their precocious experience in the toolshed mainly by reference to the image of a muselike woman with a lyre printed on a cigar box, her lower parts peeled away. When he loses Magda in the funhouse, Ambrose feels relief, and although he finds his name, with its suggestions of enlightenment (or vision) and divinity, he loses *himself* in the multiple reflections of the mirrors.

The narrator knows that a conventionally structured story would reach its climax in Ambrose's escape from the funhouse, but what would this story become if its culminating image were the emergence of Ambrose from the funhouse in uneasy companionship with a blind, black Ariadne? Barth's self-regarding experimental narrative technique enables him to beg the question of his protagonist's escape from the literal funhouse and to leave him lost in the figurative one, blocked from enjoying the "fun" but assured of his ability to create through his art even better "funhouses for others."

The discovery of this assurance constitutes a victory for Ambrose over his initial *"fear and confusion,"* and it proclaims the narrator's triumph over the problems of his art with which he has struggled throughout the story. It is a triumph gained in large measure by means of acknowledging the struggle. Like Joyce's *A Portrait of the Artist as a Young Man,* to which Barth alludes more than once, "Lost in the Funhouse" combines a nostalgic realization of the circumstances that determine the protagonist's vocation with the assertion of a provisional theory according to which he intends to carry it out. Just as Stephen Dedalus's resolution to take wing is subject to an ironic interpretation that sees it as an expression of his emotional immaturity, so Ambrose's decision to *substitute* the detached manipulation of the funhouse for living his life might be regarded as an expression of adolescent neuroses that he will outgrow. Barth makes clear, however, that the combined sensitivity to and detachment from his experience that make Ambrose an artist do not simply result from a trauma in the toolshed; rather, as existing qualities of his personality (perhaps inherited from his father, whom he resembles as Peter resembles Uncle Karl), they have conspired to render that occasion a tangible memory for Ambrose while for Magda it remains, if it lingers at all, an aspect of her vague but condescending warmth to Peter's little brother. Barth's handling of the double *pas de trois* that evolves its intricate parallels and contrasts in the front and back seats of the La Salle and along the boardwalk at Ocean City demonstrates that the artist's way of revealing the hidden realities of life does not have to follow the repellent naturalism of Ambrose's flashlight view below the boardwalk or the oversimplifications of his fantasies about the essential activities of his ancestors and the world at large. No less than *A Portrait,* Barth's story is a tour de force whose own principles of composition criticize the conclusions reached by its protagonist.

WILLIAM E. SHEIDLEY

Questions for Discussion

1. How are italics used most frequently in this story?
2. Examine the remarks about nineteenth-century realistic fiction in the second paragraph. If Barth's story seeks to convey an illusion of reality, what reality does it represent? A family's trip to Ocean City, or a writer's effort to narrate that trip? or to narrate his effort to narrate that trip?
3. Starting with the fourth sentence in the story, trace all references to American history, society, and current events, including World War II. How important are these concerns? What do you think Barth intends to accomplish by bringing them up?
4. Describe the seating arrangements in the car. What parallels do you notice between the two rows of people? Later, as they walk on the boardwalk similarly disposed, the narrator remarks, "Up front the situation was reversed." Explain. The name Peter means "rock." What objects and qualities are associated with Uncle Karl?
5. The narrator worries that "if one imagines a story called 'The Funhouse,' or 'Lost in the Funhouse,' the details of the drive . . . don't seem especially relevant." What does Barth accomplish on this drive with his characters, setting, and theme?
6. What does Barth succeed in communicating about Ambrose by tracing the chain of associations involving cigars, the banana, and Magda?

7. Immediately after chiding himself for having "nothing in the way of a *theme*," the narrator produces the account of Ambrose's visit to the toolshed with Magda. Explain the thematic implications of that passage. Do they account for Ambrose's moving away his hand as Magda sits down?

8. Why does Uncle Karl warn the young people to "stay out from under the boardwalk"? How are the various elements of this and the next few paragraphs related? Trace the associations in Ambrose's mind; in the narrator's.

9. Who asks, "How long is this going to take?"

10. Why does the narrator remark, "Nobody likes a pedant"? Is his attention to language part of what separates Ambrose from Magda?

11. If diving is a literary symbol, what does it symbolize? Judging from his choice of words, what is Ambrose thinking of as he talks to Magda about Peter's diving?

12. The next two paragraphs leap ahead to the funhouse and back to the toolshed, ending with another grammatical error. What does Barth achieve by thus manipulating chronology, here and elsewhere?

13. Analyze the paragraph that begins, "Let's ride the old flying horses!" Whose thoughts are transcribed there? What kinds of alternative plots are envisioned? In the next paragraph, the narrator contemplates still other ways of ending his story. What is the effect of our discovery that one of these endings may be more or less what "actually" happened?

14. Why do Ambrose's initiations — toolshed, baptism, Boy Scouts — all leave him cold?

15. Is Ambrose correct in his insight about the point of the funhouse?

16. One effect of Barth's manner of narration is to put off Ambrose's entry into the funhouse until the last possible moment. What does he gain by doing so?

17. Referring to the second diagram, a variant of "Freitag's Triangle," what event or events in the story of Ambrose should be represented by *C*? by *CD*? And what events in the story of the narrator's effort to tell the story?

Topics for Writing

1. Write an essay describing Barth's use of realistic narration in "Lost in the Funhouse."

2. Discuss the meaning of nausea in Barth's story.

3. Analyze Barth's funhouse technique — obvious imagery, abrupt changes, and surprising drafts from below.

4. "Lost in the Funhouse" resembles an author's journal or an early draft of a traditional story coming into existence on the page. Outline that story as it finally emerges, and outline the story of the process by which it develops. Do you believe that this is an accurate account of how stories are written?

Suggested Readings

Beinstock, Beverly Gray. "Lingering on the Autognostic Verge: John Barth's *Lost in the Funhouse*." *Critical Essays on John Barth*. Ed. Joseph J. Waldmeir. Boston: G. K. Hall, 1980. 201–09. Esp. 206–09. (Originally published in *Modern Fiction Studies* 19 (1973): 69–78.)

Knapp, Edgar H. "Found in the Barthhouse: Novelist as Savior." *Critical Essays on John Barth*. Ed. Waldmeir, cited above. 183–89. (Originally published in *Modern Fiction Studies* 14 [1968–69]: 446–51.)

Morrell, David. *John Barth: An Introduction.* University Park: Pennsylvania State UP, 1976. 87–90.

Schulz, Max F. *Black Humor Fiction of the Sixties: A Pluralistic Definition of Man and His World.* Athens: Ohio UP, 1973. 34–36, 129–30.

Seymour, Thom. "One Small Joke and a Packed Paragraph in John Barth's 'Lost in the Funhouse.'" *Studies in Short Fiction* 16 (1979): 189–94.

DONALD BARTHELME

The Indian Uprising (p. 123)

This story was occasioned by the 1968 student uprisings in Paris, when radical young people took to the streets in an attempt to bring about revolution in what the historian Todd Gitlin described as "the Year of the Barricade." Barthelme equates the French students' attempts to bring down "the Establishment" with the futile struggles of Native Americans against the white settlers on their land a hundred years earlier. A further level of irony and incongruity results from the fact that the narrator is an active participant in the Establishment rather than a sympathizer with the radical cause.

Probably Barthelme's medium is more easily identified by student readers than his message, and yet of course the author's medium here — a verbal collage of apparently disjointed impressions of a situation rapidly spinning out of control — *is* his message. Nothing presented in the story makes any sense or adds up to much. The self-serving, anarchistic rhetoric of the revolutionaries is as suspect as the capitalistic, exploitive values of the conservative mainstream that the narrator represents. The revolutionaries' "kicking ass" in street-fighting is matched by the narrator's acceptance of Third World methods of terrorism ("we attached wires to the testicles of the captured Comanche") and faddish consumerism ("a Comanche flint arrowhead ... in an elegant gold chain and congratulations"). The underlying tone of melancholy in Barthelme's narrative contrasts ironically with the brutal actions he describes.

Questions for Discussion

1. Barthelme's narrative presents neither well-defined characters nor a cause-and-effect plot. Do you think that "The Indian Uprising" is a story or an example of a "New Journalism" essay? Could it be placed in both literary genres?
2. Is the presence of the narrator of "The Indian Uprising" or the collage method of exposition in itself sufficient to turn Barthelme's text into a story?
3. How does Barthelme elicit sympathy for the Comanches? Does he also succeed in presenting his narrator sympathetically?
4. At the end of the story, the narrator has been captured by "the Clemency Committee." What is this committee, and how does its appearance affect

your understanding of Barthelme's point of view concerning the events described?

Topics for Writing

1. Research the background of the radical student uprisings in Paris in 1968 and relate the historical events to Barthelme's fictional presentation.
2. Analyze Barthelme's recurrent use of the image of the heroic Native American in the story. Is he presenting this image as a cliché or as a genuine historical model? What does the recurrence of the image suggest about the narrator's frame of mind?

Suggested Readings

Barthelme, Donald. "Not-Knowing." *Voicelust.* Ed. Allen Wier and Dan Hendrie, Jr. Lincoln: U of Nebraska P, 1985.

Couturier, Maurice, and Regis Durand. *Donald Barthelme.* New York: Methuen, 1982.

Gitlin, Todd. *The Sixties: Years of Hope, Days of Rage.* New York: Bantam, 1987.

Gordon, Lois. *Donald Barthelme.* Twayne's United States Authors Series 416. Boston: G. K. Hall, 1981

Klinkowitz, Jerome. *Donald Barthelme: An Exhibition.* Durham, NC: Duke UP, 1991.

Leitch, Thomas M. "Donald Barthelme and the End of the End." *Modern Fiction Studies* 28.1 (1982): 129–43.

Molesworth, Charles. *Donald Barthelme's Fiction: The Ironist Saved from Drowning.* Columbia: U of Missouri P, 1982.

O'Hara, J. D. "Art of Fiction: Donald Barthelme." *Paris Review* 80 (1981): 181–210.

Stengel, Wayne B. *The Shape of Art in the Short Stories of Donald Barthelme.* Baton Rouge: Louisiana State UP, 1985.

Trachtenberg, Stanley. *Understanding Donald Barthelme.* Columbia: U of South Carolina P, 1990.

Wilde, Alan. *Middle Grounds: Studies in Contemporary American Fiction.* Philadelphia: U of Pennsylvania P, 1987. Contains "Barthelme, His Garden."

Ann Beattie

Janus (p. 129)

Webster's Dictionary tells us that Janus was a Roman god identified with doors, gates, and all beginnings. Classical artists represented the god as having two opposite faces, so the term "Janus-faced" has come to mean "duplicitous" or "two-faced."

It isn't until the end of Beattie's story that the reader learns that the protagonist, Andrea, a real estate agent who uses her "perfect" bowl to help her sell houses, received the bowl as a present from a previous lover. Long and securely married to her stockbroker husband, she has refused to leave her husband for this lover, so he has left her. If students take adultery to be the theme of this short story, they will be quick to call Andrea duplicitous. Yet she regards herself as an honorable woman, possessing what she considers "intransigent ideas about honoring previous commitments."

Instead of obsessing about the absent lover, she obsesses about the bowl. It is beautiful, and she has no scruples about using it to enhance the atmosphere of houses that she is trying to sell. The bowl seems to possess its own aura; besides being beautiful, it is also mysterious, like something out of a fairy tale, and it brings her luck. She dreams about it, and during the day she has an irrepressible desire to thank the bowl as if it were an animate being. She finds that she never talks to her husband about the bowl. "He had no more interest in the bowl than she had in his new Leica," yet she feels "guilty that she had such a constant secret."

As time goes on, Andrea's anxieties increase, she becomes more possessive, fearing that an accident will befall the bowl. Her world consists of strategies to sell real estate, and so she becomes doubly cautious: "Why not, in a world where people set plants where they did not belong, so that visitors touring a house would be fooled into thinking that dark corners got sunlight — a world full of tricks?"

In thinking about the story, a reader might at this point remember Anton Chekhov's words in the commentary section about his use of objectivity in writing short stories: "You would have me, when I describe horse-thieves, say: 'Stealing horses is an evil.' But that has been known for ages without my saying so. Let the jury judge them; it's my job simply to show what sort of people they are." Beattie's character is a realtor who is very good at convincing people to buy houses. Her husband feels that "he [is] fortunate to be married to a woman who had such a fine aesthetic sense and yet could also function in the real world." Like Chekhov, Beattie makes a fictional character come alive by speaking and thinking in her tone and feeling in her spirit; otherwise — as Chekhov knew — "the image becomes blurred and the story will not be as compact as all short stories ought to be."

Questions for Discussion

1. Why does Beattie introduce Andrea's dog Mondo early in the story? Does her care for her dog suggest anything about why she and her husband do not have any children?
2. What does Andrea think of the "tricks" that realtors use to convince a client to buy a house? What are some of the "tricks" she uses?
3. Why does she lie to her client about where the bowl had been bought?
4. How do you know that Andrea has been married to her husband for a long time?
5. What do we learn about Andrea's marriage when Beattie tells us that both she and her husband liked details, but "while ironies attracted her, he was more impatient and dismissive when matters became many-sided or un-clear"?
6. How does Beattie add a dimension of the irrational to the story?
7. How does she build suspense into the story? Are you surprised by the ending?

Topics for Writing

1. Analyze how Beattie uses the bowl in "Janus" as a tangible object through which to communicate her protagonist's unstated deeper feelings without using internal monologue. Be sure to include a full explication of the last paragraph of the story.

2. **CONNECTIONS** Compare and contrast Beattie's story with Raymond Carver's "Cathedral." How has each author's choice of protagonist shaped his or her narrative about contemporary marriage?

Suggested Readings

Beattie, Ann. *What Was Mine: Stories.* New York: Random, 1991.
———. *Where You'll Find Me and Other Stories.* New York: Simon, 1986.
Montresor, Jaye Berman. *The Critical Responses to Ann Beattie.* Westport, CT: Greenwood, 1993.
Murphy, Christina. *Ann Beattie.* Boston: Twayne, 1986.

AMBROSE BIERCE

An Occurrence at Owl Creek Bridge (p. 134)

What is the reason for the enduring interest of this contrived and improbable tale? Surprise endings frequently draw groans similar to those that greet bad puns, but Bierce's final twist is more likely to elicit shock and recoil. Perhaps the story's success results more from its realization of an intimate and familiar fear than from its sharp, vivid style or its tense pacing. The idea of continued life is all that the human mind, unable to imagine mere "darkness and silence," can propose in view of impending death. By narrating a fantasy of escape so persuasively that we succumb to it, and then by revealing it with the snap of a neck to have been only a fantasy, Bierce forces us to recognize once again the reality of our mortal situation.

If, out of the desire to evade that recognition, the reader seeks to repudiate the story as a piece of literary chicanery, he or she will not succeed. A clearheaded review of section III reveals that the exciting tale of escape could not have been real. Even before Farquhar enters the nightmare forest with its strange constellations and peculiar, untraveled roadway, he has experienced a preternatural heightening of sensory awareness that happens only when one sees with the eyes of the mind, and he has undergone sensations better explained by reference to a slow-motion expansion of a hanging than to his imagined plunge into Owl Creek. The images of his dream emerge from Farquhar's instinctual desire to live, and Bierce renders them with such clarity that the reader can cherish them as well. The same intensity of sensory awareness marks Bierce's conjecture about what it must be like when the noose jerks tight. We feel the constriction, see the flash of nervous discharge, and hear the cracking vertebrae.

Our close participation in the imaginary and real sensations of dying countervails the doomed man's symbolic isolation, which is the burden of section I. While the executioners enact the formal rituals that establish distance from the victim, who is being expelled from the human community (even the sentinels are turning their backs on him), Bierce leads the reader into an empathic communion with him. The agency of this imaginative projection is the coolly exact observational style, which carries us across the plank — Farquhar's first thought to which we are privy is his approval of this device — and into the psyche of the condemned.

Before launching into Farquhar's dying fantasy, however, Bierce goes back, in section II, to narrate the events leading up to the execution. Besides establishing for Farquhar an identity with which we can sympathize, this passage presents him as active rather than acted upon, and so generates a momentum that continues into the story of his escape. The section ends with one of several stark, one-line revelations that conclude passages of uncertainty, illusion, or false conjecture in the story: "He was a Federal scout"; "What he heard was the ticking of his watch"; "Peyton Farquhar was dead." This device of style expresses Bierce's major theme: whatever we dream of, life is entrapment by death, and time is running out.

WILLIAM E. SHEIDLEY

Questions for Discussion

1. In what ways does section I suggest a psychological time much slower than actual time?
2. Why is it appropriate that the execution take place on a bridge over a river?
3. What is the function of Farquhar's conjectures about escape at the end of section I?
4. In what ways does Bierce try to gain the reader's sympathy for Farquhar? Why does he need to do this?
5. Which events in section III might be read as dislocations of sensations experienced by a man in the process of being hanged?
6. Contrast the descriptive style of a passage from section III with that of a passage from section I.
7. What would be the result if Farquhar's imagined reunion with his wife took place *after* the snapping of his neck?

Topics for Writing

1. Analyze Bierce's handling of time and chronology in "An Occurrence at Owl Creek Bridge."
2. **CONNECTIONS** Discuss the fiction of effect as a fiction of despair in the works of Bierce, Gogol, and Poe.

Suggested Readings

Bierce, Ambrose. *The Complete Short Stories of Ambrose Bierce.* Lincoln: U of Nebraska P, 1984.

Davidson, Cathy N. *The Experimental Fictions of Ambrose Bierce*. Lincoln: U of Nebraska P, 1984.

Grenander, Mary E. *Ambrose Bierce*. New York: Twayne, 1971.

Stoicheff, Peter. "'Something Uncanny': The Dream Structure in Ambrose Bierce's 'An Occurrence at Owl Creek Bridge.'" *Studies in Short Fiction* Summer 30:3 (1993): 349–58.

Wolotkiewicz, Diana. "Ambrose Bierce's Use of the Grotesque Mode: The Pathology of Society." *Journal of the Short Story in English* Spring 16 (1991): 81–92.

AMY BLOOM

Silver Water (p. 141)

This story was included in *The Best American Short Stories 1992*, in which Bloom, a practicing psychotherapist, explained her motivation for writing it in the Contributors' Notes: "The grief, love, exhaustion of life with schizophrenics is so close to unbearable that I can only admire, and want to sing for, the afflicted and their families."

"Silver Water" is a story of a young woman with mental illness whose life, despite the loving care of her family, ends in suicide. The events in the story occur over a period of more than a decade, beginning before the onset of Rose's clinical depression with a flashback describing her beautiful voice at the age of fourteen. The next year she has what the narrator, her younger sister Violet, calls "her first psychotic break." After ten years of hospitalization and countless sessions with therapists, Rose is sent home from the halfway house where she regresses after showing improvement under the care of the sympathetic Dr. Thorne, who dies unexpectedly. Rose's father, a psychiatrist himself, obtains a new insurance policy for her with improved psychiatric coverage, but it won't go into effect for forty-five days. After caring for Rose at home for three chaotic weeks, Rose's exhausted parents, David and Galen Silverstein, consider sending Rose back to a private hospital, but it would cost a thousand dollars a day, and her new policy does not permit hospitalization prior to coverage. Violet comes home on Sunday to visit her sister and her parents and witnesses Rose's unpredictable mood swings and her painful efforts to control herself. Later that night, seized with remorse after injuring her mother, Rose takes an overdose of sleeping pills and dies in the woods near the house while Violet sits with her.

Bloom's extensive experience with mentally disturbed patients lends authenticity to her description of Rose's behavior, but readers of her story are affected as much by the author's compassion for all of her fictional characters as by the accuracy of her account of Rose's symptoms and treatment. By selecting Violet to tell the story of her older sister's decline, Bloom succeeds in evoking a witness who is both close to Rose and her contemporary, who shares her idiomatic language and her experience of teenage American culture. Rose's last words, "Closing time," are both brave and pathetic; she has summoned the courage to swallow a bottle of pills, even as she communicates a forced bravado that is completely understood by her sister. Violet's calm heroism, sitting by her dying sister until dawn and watching "the stars fade," is equally brave and not at all pathetic. Unlike

Rose, she is a survivor, even if she regresses to an infantile response when her mother appears on the porch. "I could picture my mother slapping me, shooting me for letting her favorite die." Instead, her mother hugs and kisses her, saying, "Warrior queens. I raised warrior queens."

Questions for Discussion

1. How does the narrator's language in the opening paragraph of the story convince you that she both admires and is protective of her sister?
2. How does the second paragraph deal concisely with past events bearing on the story?
3. What is the clinical diagnosis of Rose's illness?
4. Violet believes that Rose is her mother's favorite daughter. Do Galen's words to Violet ("It won't happen to you, honey. Some people go crazy and some people never do. You never will") support Violet's belief? Is there another explanation for how Violet feels about her mother?
5. Why does Dr. Thorne succeed with Rose when other therapists have failed to reach her?
6. How does the detail about the broken piano bench prepare you for the scene that follows in the kitchen, when Rose hurts herself and her mother?

Topics for Writing

1. "Silver Water" is one of three linked stories about David Silverstein in Amy Bloom's story collection *Come to Me,* the other two being "Hyacinths" and "The Sight of You." Read the three stories making up this cluster in *Come to Me.* Analyze whether or not you think that, like the other two stories, "Silver Water" is an independent piece of short fiction. Do those readers acquainted with the first two parts of the story cluster experience a more acute sense of closure at the end of "Silver Water"?
2. **CONNECTIONS** In an essay, explore the nature of the relationships between the narrators and their troubled siblings in "Silver Water" and James Baldwin's "Sonny's Blues."

Suggested Readings

Bloom, Amy. *Come to Me.* New York: Harper, 1993.
Stone, Robert, ed. *The Best American Short Stories 1992.* Boston: Houghton, 1992.

JORGE LUIS BORGES

The Garden of Forking Paths (p. 150)

Most students will find this story very difficult to follow, because few of Borges's tangible clues as to setting or characterization are what they seem to be on first reading. The opening reference to Liddell Hart's *History of World War I*; the statement by Dr. Yu Tsun, with the missing first two pages, that describes the actual plot to follow; and the footnote about Hans Rabener, alias Viktor Runeberg, will mystify many readers. Students should be urged to read the story at least twice before attempting a discussion. In fact, some class time might profitably be given to a guided reading of the story, with students explaining their comprehension as they go along.

The two commentaries on the story in Part Two should also prove helpful. Borges's explanation of his fascination with the image of the labyrinth as "a symbol of bewilderment, a symbol of being lost in life" (p. 1391) explains the motivation behind Yu Tsun's desperate effort to complete his spy mission before he is killed by Captain Richard Madden. Knowledge of his impending death sharpens his concentration on his last action in life. His dilemma might be compared with Flannery O'Connor's dramatization of the final moments of her fictional characters' lives.

Peter Brooks's analysis of "The Garden of Forking Paths" (p. 1393) reveals an interpretation that might clarify the story for some students. Brooks summarizes the plot and explains the story as a metafiction, a story whose meaning is an insight about the significance of fiction itself. In Brooks's reading, "The labyrinth is ultimately that of narrative literature, which is ever replaying time, subverting and perverting it, in order to claim that it is not simply 'time lost,' always in the knowledge that this loss is the very condition of the meanings that narrative claims to relate."

Borges's story is different things to different readers, but some highlights to examine are his skill in pacing the narrative to extract maximum suspense from the confrontation between Yu Tsun and Stephen Albert, Yu Tsun's emotional dilemma in his conflicting loyalties, and the inexorable approach of Richard Madden. Borges's description of the labyrinth, with its "high-pitched, almost syllabic music" audible as Yu Tsun approaches Albert's house, is also a tour de force, not likely to be forgotten if one has read the story carefully.

Questions for Discussion

1. Why does Borges begin this story in such an indirect manner?
2. Who is Yu Tsun? Richard Madden? Stephen Albert?
3. Why is Stephen Albert's last name important?
4. Why is Yu Tsun so loyal to his German chief in Berlin?
5. How does Borges establish this as a war story? How do wartime conditions contribute to the narrative?
6. Are there racist overtones in the statement "I wanted to prove to him [the chief] that a yellow man could save his armies"?

7. Borges describes the meeting between Stephen Albert and Yu Tsun very simply: "We sat down — I on a long, low divan, he with his back to the window and a tall circular clock." Why is this description particularly appropriate?

8. Explain the "ivory labyrinth" in Albert's possession and the "chaotic manuscripts" left by Ts'ui Pen.

Topics for Writing

1. Research the Greek legends about labyrinths and relate them to Borges's story.

2. **CONNECTIONS** Compare Borges's description of Ts'ui Pen's manuscript with the metafictions of Margaret Atwood and John Barth in this anthology.

Related Commentaries

Jorge Luis Borges, The Labyrinth in "The Garden of Forking Paths," p. 1391.

Peter Brooks, A Narratological Analysis of Borges's "The Garden of Forking Paths," p. 1393.

Suggested Readings

Agheana, Ion Tudro. *The Meaning of Experience in the Prose of Jorge Luis Borges.* New York: P. Lang, 1988.

Alazraki, Jaime. *Critical Essays on Jorge Luis Borges.* Boston: Twayne, 1987.

Borges, Jorge Luis. *The Book of Fantasy.* New York: Carroll and Graf, 1990.

————. *The Book of Sand.* New York: NAL-Dutton, 1979.

————. *Dream Tigers.* Austin: U of Texas P, 1984.

————. *A Personal Anthology.* New York: Grove Weidenfeld, 1961.

Christ, Ronald J. *The Narrow Act: Borges's Art of Allusion.* New York: New York UP, 1969.

Lindstrom, Naomi. *Jorge Luis Borges: A Study of Short Fiction.* Boston: Twayne, 1990.

McMurray, George R. *Jorge Luis Borges.* Modern Literature Monographs. New York: Ungar, 1980.

Stabb, Martin S. *Borges Revisited.* Boston: Twayne, 1991.

TADEUSZ BOROWSKI

This Way for the Gas, Ladies and Gentlemen (p. 159)

Borowski's story can be taught with another Holocaust story in this anthology, Cynthia Ozick's "The Shawl." "The Shawl" is told by an omniscient narrator describing the ordeal of a woman victim of the concentration camps. "This Way for the Gas, Ladies and Gentlemen" has a more complex point of view, since the narrator is a Polish political prisoner (indeed, he is the writer), and he voluntarily helps the Nazis unload and brutalize the newly arrived Polish Jews.

The thoughtful comments of the Italian concentration camp survivor Primo Levi are helpful here. In *The Drowned and the Saved* (Summit, 1988), Levi explores the situation of the prisoners of war who, like Borowski, survived to tell their tales. According to Levi, the survivors who wrote about their experiences were often political prisoners like Borowski. The camps held three categories of prisoners — political, criminal, and Jewish — and the political prisoners had "a cultural background which allowed them to interpret the events they saw; and because precisely inasmuch as they were ex-combatants or antifascist combatants even now, they realized that testimony was an act of war against fascism."

Furthermore, according to Levi, "the network of human relationships inside the Lagers [camps] was not simple: it could not be reduced to the two blocs of victims and persecutors." The context of the "prisoner-functionary" (like Borowski) is poorly defined, "where the two camps of masters and servants both diverge and converge. This gray zone possesses an incredibly complicated internal structure and contains within itself enough to confuse our need to judge."

Levi continues,

> The arrival in the Lager was indeed a shock because of the surprise it entailed. The world into which one was precipitated was terrible, yes, but also indecipherable: it did not conform to any model; the enemy was all around but also inside. . . . One entered hoping at least for the solidarity of one's companions in misfortune, but the hoped for allies, except in special cases, were not there; there were instead a thousand sealed off monads, and between them a desperate covert and continuous struggle. This brusque revelation, which became manifest from the very first hours of imprisonment, often in the instant form of a concentric aggression on the part of those in whom one hoped to find future allies, was so harsh as to cause the immediate collapse of one's capacity to resist. For many it was lethal, indirectly or even directly; it is difficult to defend oneself against a blow for which one is not prepared.

"This Way for the Gas, Ladies and Gentlemen" is one of many stories in this anthology that are based on personal experience, meticulously observed, remembered, and re-created as a "story" or work of autobiographical fiction, or "autofiction." Borowski, the narrator, was interned at Birkenau with Communists and Jews from France, Russia, Poland, and Greece. He survived the camp because he cooperated with his jailers in the persecution of victims less fortunate than himself. How does he present his story so that the reader is forced to sympathize with him, even while realizing that this sympathy is itself a faint mirror image of the prisoner's moral dilemma?

A highly rational structure holds together this totally irrational nightmare. The unities of place, time, and point of view are strictly observed. The passage of time is orderly, paralleling the organization of the transport of human beings from train to trucks to crematoria. The narrator is new to his job, and we learn it as he does. As train follows train through the stifling August afternoon and into the evening, we grow exhausted with him. The only variety is the ever-changing stream of prisoners who leave the train, take their brief walk on the platform, and disappear onto the trucks or are sorted out for the work camps. Occasionally an individual achieves humanity, like the young blonde who is so beautiful that she appears to descend "lightly" from the packed train, or the calm, tall, gray-haired woman who takes the bloated infants' corpses from the narrator, whispering to him, "My poor boy." For the narrator, such moments of grace are withheld: He hangs on to his self-control by concentrating on sheer physical endurance.

Questions for Discussion

1. How did the narrator become a storyteller? (The headnote might be helpful here, but students should be encouraged to talk about the cathartic process in the creation of fiction.)
2. What elements of narrative — plot, character, setting, language, theme — are most striking in this story?
3. Is it necessary to know the historic context of the Nazi atrocities in World War II to understand the story? Explain.

Topics for Writing

1. Report on a documentary film or a book about the Holocaust, such as Primo Levi's *The Drowned and the Saved*.
2. **CONNECTIONS** Compare Borowski's story with another example of Holocaust or prison literature you have read, Cynthia Ozick's "The Shawl," or Anne Frank's diary, or Alexander Solzhenitzyn's *One Day in the Life of Ivan Denisovich*.
3. **CONNECTIONS** Compare the psychology of prisoners in Borowski's story and in Frank O'Connor's "Guests of the Nation."

Suggested Readings

Borowski, Tadeusz. *This Way for the Gas, Ladies and Gentlemen*. Trans. Barbara Vedder. New York: Penguin, 1976.
Kuhiwczak, Piotr. "Beyond Self: A Lesson from the Concentration Camps." *Canadian Review of Comparative Literature* September 19:3 (1992): 395–405.
Walc, Jan. "When the Earth Is No Longer a Dream and Cannot Be Dreamed Through to the End." *The Polish Review* 32:2 (1987): 181–94.

PAUL BOWLES

The Eye (p. 172)

As Bowles wrote in his autobiography *Without Stopping*, he believes that stories are dramatic because they depict struggle. "The Eye" is the story of a power struggle between a naive Canadian man named Duncan Marsh and the superstitious Moroccan woman named Meriam whom he employs as a cook after he moves to Tangier. After frightening Meriam's daughter by frowning so fiercely at her that the little girl becomes hysterical and comes down with a fever, Marsh is first poisoned by Meriam and then made the victim of a ritual blood-letting ceremony, as Meriam tries to lift what she believes to be the curse that her employer's "evil eye" has put on her daughter.

In "The Eye" a secondary struggle is played out in the process of narration itself. The nameless storyteller, who has originally heard Marsh's story told as gossip on the cocktail party circuit, is curious to learn the details of Marsh's unfortunate experience in Tangier, an experience that ultimately led to his death after his return to Canada. But the narrator must bribe Marsh's Moroccan night watchman Larbi in order to find out what happened to Marsh twelve years earlier.

The narrator tells us that he becomes interested in Marsh's story after he learns that the soles of Marsh's feet had been cut in "crude patterns." This detail makes "the story take on life" for him. Bowles is skillfully evoking the tactile in his description, however painful the suggestion. In fact, the sadistic flavor of the narrative adds to its fascination for some readers.

Complementing this sadism is the hint of an undisclosed sexual relationship between Marsh and his teenaged Moroccan night watchman in the opening paragraphs of the story, when we learn that until he died Marsh provided financial aid for the boy. This lead is undeveloped, and when the narrator meets the young man ten years later and bribes him to tell him Marsh's story in more detail, Larbi no longer possesses his earlier sexual appeal.

Bowles's skill at telling Marsh's story twice — first in a brief summary at the beginning of the story, second in a more leisurely account of how the narrator ferrets out the details from Marsh's night watchman — results in a narrative that displays some of the qualities of detective fiction, holding the reader captive to complete the puzzle while exploring unknown, mysterious, somehow forbidden territory. The narrator functions as a detective trying to solve a case, hoping "to find someone on whom the guilt might be fixed." But the world of Bowles's fiction is devoid of "criminal intent." Instead, in "The Eye" he dramatizes a power struggle where there are no guilty people, only innocent ones who suffer at the hands of those who wish to exploit them.

Questions for Discussion

1. What atmosphere does Bowles evoke in his opening sentence?
2. How does Bowles establish the sophistication of his narrator? How do you know he's a European resident of Tangier?
3. Is the narrator reliable or unreliable?
4. Why does Marsh's cook know so much about poisons?
5. Why didn't Marsh's night watchman Larbi protect him? Why didn't they call the police?
6. Of what kind of ceremony was Marsh the subject? Was it successful?

Topics for Writing

1. In the 1950s Paul Bowles became one of the earliest American writers to create fiction set in a Third World country. Analyze his description of life in Tangier in "The Eye." Was Bowles being "politically correct" in his depiction of the behavior of the natives of Morocco?

2. **CONNECTIONS**   Compare and contrast "The Eye" with Camus's "The Guest," a story written by a European that was also set in a Third World country.

Suggested Readings

Al-Ghalith, Asad. "Paul Bowles's Portrayal of Islam in His Moroccan Short Stories." *International Fiction Review* 19:2 (1992): 103–8.

Bailey, J. "Art of Fiction: Paul Bowles." *Paris Review* 23 (1981): 63–98.

Bowles, Paul. *Collected Stories, 1939–1976.* Ed. Gore Vidal. Santa Barbara: Black Sparrow, 1979.

———. *Too Far From Home: The Selected Writings of Paul Bowles.* Hopewell, NJ: Ecco, 1993.

———. *Without Stopping: An Autobiography.* New York: Ecco, 1985.

Halpern, D. "Interview with Paul Bowles." *Triquarterly* 33 (1975): 159–77.

Hibbard, Allen E. "Expatriation and Narration in Two Works by Paul Bowles." *West Virginia University Philological Papers* 32 (1986–87): 61–71.

Patteson, R. F. *A World Outside: The Fiction of Paul Bowles.* Austin: U of Texas P, 1987.

Pounds, Wayne. *Paul Bowles: The Inner Geography.* New York: Lang, 1985.

Wolff, T. "A Forgotten Master." *Esquire* 103 (1985): 221–22.

KAY BOYLE

Black Boy (p. 179)

Kay Boyle included "Black Boy" among the stories she called "Early Group 1927–1934" in the first section of her volume *Fifty Stories.* The other groups were "Austrian Group 1933–1938," "English Group 1935–1936," "French Group 1939–1966," "Military Occupation Group 1945–1950," and "American Group 1942–1966." The organization of the volume emphasizes Boyle's formative years as an expatriate writer in the first half of her life, when she was closely involved with other experimental writers in Europe during the first half of the century.

"Black Boy" is an impressionistic story, beautifully organized around recurrent images of the physical setting of sea, sand, and boardwalk. With an almost hypnotic, rhythmic insistence, the first-person narrator remembers a friendship with a "black boy" when she was ten years old. Although her skin color is never described, we infer that she is white and privileged. He is variously called "Charlie," "Sonny," or "Big Boy," depending on the whim of the narrator's grandfather, who hires the boy to wheel him up and down the boardwalk in an upholstered chair. To the little girl, the boy is at first fascinating, although he seems barely human. Sitting in the chair with her grandfather, she sees her friend's face out of the corner of her eye, "hanging black as a bat's wing, nodding and nodding like a dark heavy flower."

The boy offers companionship when the girl comes to the beach at odd hours. In the early morning they sit and eat dog biscuits together, and he tells her his dreams. They also meet at night, when they sit on the sand while he tells her stories. The girl's grandfather grows suspicious, and she is uneasy about his warning that the boy could steal money from her or knock her down. One morning, trying to please her grandfather, she saddles her horse instead of meeting her friend, but when she sees the black boy sitting "idle" and "heedless" on the beach eating peanuts in the shell, she lets him ride the horse, charmed by his skill and grace. A few minutes later she rides the horse under the boardwalk. The horse shies when startled by dogs, and the little girl is badly hurt. The boy soothes her pain, and she (along with the reader) feels "rocked in a cradle of love, cradled and rocked in sorrow" as if she had her "own kin" about her. But when the black boy carries her home at the end of the story, the reader shares the girl's shock when her grandfather, not knowing about the accident, strikes him brutally in the face.

Like James Joyce, Virginia Woolf, and William Faulkner, Boyle sugggested an impressionistic stream of consciousness in her fiction that juxtaposed the narrator's emotional state with the physical world in which she lived. The girl in the story is sensitive to her grandfather's racial prejudice, but powerless to change it. The critic and novelist Vance Bourjaily found that Boyle's stories exhibit a virtuosic range of literary techniques: "grammatical simplification, rhythmic repetition, the mixing in of vernacular, stream of consciousness, density of impressions, radical imagery and experiments with surrealism." In "Black Boy," the fluid but carefully controlled texture of Boyle's fiction is played against the rock-solid conviction of her moral purpose in exposing the injustice of racial prejudice. Her story is both symbolic and real, as complex as life itself.

Questions for Discussion

1. Why doesn't Boyle explain why the ten-year-old girl is living with her grandfather instead of with her mother and father?
2. Why doesn't Boyle set the story in a specific beach resort with a boardwalk, such as Atlantic City?
3. Why does the grandfather treat the black boy so impolitely?
4. What are the feelings of the girl toward the black boy? Does he reciprocate her feelings?
5. How does Boyle build suspense in the story? Were you surprised by the ending?

Topics for Writing

1. Use Boyle's impressionistic style to write a story that you make up or base on your own life about your first encounter with racial prejudice in childhood.
2. **CONNECTIONS** Compare and contrast the literary styles of the two early American modernists Kay Boyle and Katherine Anne Porter in their stories "Black Boy" and "He" (included in this anthology).

Suggested Readings

Boyle, Kay. *Fifty Stories.* New York: Doubleday, 1980.

McAlmon, Robert, and Kay Boyle. *Being Geniuses Together 1920–1930.* San Francisco: North Point, 1984.

Mellen, Joan. *Kay Boyle: Author of Herself.* New York: Farrar, 1994.

T. CORAGHESSAN BOYLE

Stones in My Passway, Hellhound on My Trail (p. 185)

For some instructors and students this story by T. Coraghessan Boyle will seem more like a retelling of a familiar story than a literary composition. The "Robert" of the story is the Mississippi blues singer Robert Johnson. In history, Boyle follows the events of Johnson's life very closely, changing only names and in some instances localities.

It will be useful for students to be familiar with the names and locations that Boyle has used in his narrative. Robert Johnson did grow up in the northern Mississippi delta, outside of the small town of Robinsonville, which Boyle mentions in the text. When a teenager he left the town for a time to live with a sister in another small town. When Johnson returned he was carrying a guitar, and he went to the club where an older singer named Son House, who had given him some instruction, was performing. The name Boyle gives him in history is "Walter Satter." It was Son House who told researchers what happened that night when Johnson returned to Robinsonville.

Johnson's contacts with the recording industry occurred in Jackson, Mississippi, not New Orleans, as in Boyle's story, and he was taken Dallas to record for Vocalion Records — not "Victrix," which is Boyle's reworking of "Victor," the name of the most popular recording company of the period. The man responsible for Johnson during the sessions was Don Law — Boyle's name for the similar character is "Walter Fagan" — and the anecdotes about Johnson's problems before the session were first quoted in the liner notes of a 1968 reissue of Johnson's songs. It is interesting to compare the original notes with Boyle's use of the same material in his story.

Throughout the story, almost as a reward for readers with a special knowledge of Johnson's recording, the author has included names of and references to well-known figures, as well as references to the events and places of Johnson's life. For instance, the name "Huddie Doss" in the second paragraph combines the first name of the Louisiana singer Huddie Ledbetter — better known as Leadbelly — with the last name of the Alabama blues singer Willie Doss, who performed at the Newport Folk Festival in the 1960s.

As Boyle relates, Johnson was poisoned over a woman, but it occurred in Greenwood, Mississippi, not in Dallas where Boyle situates the climax of the story. The events of that night are related in Samuel Charters's *The Bluesmakers:*

He was playing in a road house called Three Forks outside of Greenwood and he became involved with the wife of the man who ran the local juke joint. One Saturday night, August 13, 1938, he was playing at the road house with Sonny Boy Williamson, and when they were taking a break somebody sent him an opened half pint of whiskey. Sonny Boy had some idea what was happening and he knocked the bottle out of Robert's hand. Robert protested, and when somebody handed him a second bottle, already opened like the first, he went ahead and drank it.

The bottle had been laced with poison, probably strychnine, which was commonly used to kill rats. He tried to go on playing, but he was in too much pain, and he was taken back to Greenwood in the middle of the night. He managed to survive the poisoning, but he was too weak to fight off a sudden attack of pneumonia. He died in the stifling heat a few days later, on August 16, 1938. If the May, 1911 date for his birth is correct, he was 27.

If Boyle has taken liberties with the details of Johnson's life, he has quoted the songs accurately, and he has used the power of their imagery with imagination and sensitivity. There will certainly be students who will understand the author's reference to "a song about a train station, a suitcase, and the eyes of a woman." The song is "Love in Vain," one of Johnson's last recordings, which was popularized by The Rolling Stones. In light of Boyle's story it is perhaps ironic that a recent CD reissue of Robert Johnson's songs sold almost a half million copies and — more than fifty years after the session in Dallas — won Johnson a Grammy Award.

Questions for Discussion

1. Why does Boyle change some names and locations in his retelling of Robert Johnson's story?
2. In the third paragraph of the story, Boyle describes events outside of the world of the central figure. What is his intention in doing this?
3. Does the description of the dance at which Johnson is playing seem like a representation of an actual event, or does it seem that Boyle is exaggerating the overt sexual tension of such a dance? If it seems like an exaggeration, what might the writer's purpose be?
4. Is it necessary for the reader to be familiar with Robert Johnson's recordings in order for the story to be effective, or can the reader feel what the author is describing without these references?
5. "[A] Greek chorus gone mad." "Agamemnon, watch out!" What is the author suggesting with his references to classical literature?

Topics for Writing

1. In an essay, analyze Boyle's attitude toward his protagonist, Robert, paying close attention to Boyle's language and imagery and supporting your thesis.
2. Write a story in which you narrate an important episode in the life of an artist, musician, or other entertainer whom you admire and of whom you have some biographical knowledge. (You may want to do some additional research.) Try, as Boyle tries, to communicate a particular mood to your readers.

Suggested Readings

Boyle, T. Coraghessan. *Greasy Lake and Other Stories.* New York: Viking, 1985.
———. *If the River Was Whiskey: Stories.* New York: Viking, 1989.
———. *Without a Hero: Stories.* New York: Viking, 1994.
Pope, Dan. "A Different Kind of Post-Modernism." *The Gettysburg Review* Autumn 3:4 (1990): 658–69.
Stanton, David. "T. Coraghessan Boyle." *Poets and Writers* Jan.–Feb. 18:1 (1990): 29–34.

ROBERT OLEN BUTLER

A Good Scent from a Strange Mountain (p. 191)

Butler tells several stories in "A Good Scent from a Strange Mountain," as befits the many layers of accumulated experience and present consciousness of his first-person narrator Dao, the Vietnamese Buddhist immigrant now residing with his family in New Orleans, who is nearly one hundred years old.

Students may find it difficult to keep track of the different stories within the story as flashbacks merge with present plot action, so it might be a good idea to separate and clarify them at the start of class. On the most basic level, Dao, who feels death approaching, has on the previous night had a visit from his old friend Ho Chi Minh, whom he knew in 1917 when both were working in the kitchen of the Carlton Hotel in London. Ho has a problem that he hopes Dao can solve: what went wrong with a dessert recipe he had learned from the great French chef Escoffier, to whom he was apprenticed at the hotel? This visitation and the two that follow, we are told, are no dream fantasies. Dao is clearly possessed of supernatural powers, as well as the unusual distinction of being the confidante of Ho Chi Minh (1890–1969), who went on to become the mighty Communist leader of North Vietnam.

In the morning, after a second nocturnal visit from his old friend, Dao meets other visitors, some family members who are with him in New Orleans. Besides his eldest daughter, who is his caretaker, Dao receives his son-in-law Thang, a former army colonel in South Vietnam. With Thang is his wife Lam, another of Dao's daughters, and his son Loi. Pretending to drift off into sleep, Dao overhears Thang and Loi discuss murder in which they apparently know the killers: A member of the Vietnamese community in New Orleans has been shot to death after advocating that South Vietnam accept the reality of the communist government in North Vietnam, insisting, "We [have] to work now with those who [control] our country."

Other stories told in flashback are those of Dao's marriage and of a night when he and his wife made love in Saigon "soon after the terrible fighting in 1968." His wife is now dead, and the memory reminds him of other deaths, including the death of his firstborn son when only a child. This leads him to another memory, that of holding Loi when he was a nursing baby and how the child smelled sour to him.

Finally, another important story-within-a-story is the memory of Dao's instruction in Buddhism in Paris in 1918, while his friend Ho turned in a different direction and began to involve himself in politics. The central meaning of the story is tied to Dao's choice of Buddhism instead of Communism. He, not Ho Chi Minh, survives, because Dao has taken the broader view: he "knew you had to understand everything or you would be incomplete forever."

Questions for Discussion

1. Retell the events in "A Good Scent from a Strange Mountain" in chronological order, beginning with the friendship between Dao and Ho in Escoffier's kitchen at the Carolton Hotel in London.
2. What does the story lose by being narrated in chronological order?
3. Why was it important for Ho to use granulated sugar instead of confectioner's sugar in the dessert recipe?
4. Why does Dao pretend to be asleep when his son-in-law and grandson talk about the murder in the Vietnamese community?
5. How does the fact that when Loi was a baby Dao thought he smelled sour foreshadow Dao's later suspicion of his grandson's involvement in a murder?
6. Explicate the last sentences of the story. Where else is Dao's Buddhism expressed in "A Good Scent from a Strange Mountain"?

Topics for Writing

1. It is unusual for a writer to introduce a historical figure into a fictional story. Research the person who was Ho Chi Minh. How has Butler woven the facts of this famous man's life into a short story? Why does the narrator say he accepts the reality of his nighttime visitor "because he did not appear as he was when I'd known him [in 1917] but as he was when he'd died"?
2. Smells play an important role in "A Good Scent from a Strange Mountain," beginning with the second paragraph, when the narrator notices "a sweet smell" about his nighttime visitor. Analyze how Butler introduces and uses different smells throughout the story. What do they tell us about the inner feelings of his narrator?

Suggested Reading

Butler, Robert Olen. *A Good Scent from a Strange Mountain.* New York: Penguin, 1992.

ITALO CALVINO

The Feathered Ogre (p. 200)

For the two years that Italo Calvino immersed himself in preparing *Italian Folktales* (1956; English translation 1980), he pored over folktale collections edited by previous scholars, discovering that "the very essence of the Italian folktale is unparalleled grace, wit, and unity of design." He found that folktales survive as a vital tradition in every culture because they offer

> a general explanation of life preserved in the slow ripening of rustic consciences; these folk stories are the catalog of the potential destinies of men and women, especially for that stage in life when destiny is formed, i.e., youth, beginning with birth, which itself often foreshadows the future; then the departure from home, and, finally, through the trials of growing up, the attainment of maturity and the proof of one's humanity. This sketch, although summary, encompasses everything: the arbitrary division of humans, albeit in essence equal, into kings and poor people . . . the common fate of having one's existence predetermined by complex and unknown forces. This complexity pervades one's entire existence and forces one to struggle to free oneself, to determine one's own fate; at this same time we can liberate ourselves only if we liberate other people, for this is a *sine qua non* of one's own liberation. There must be fidelity to a goal and purity of heart, values fundamental to salvation and triumph. There must also be beauty, a sign of grace . . . and above all, there must be present the infinite possibilities of mutation, the unifying element in everything: men, beasts, plants, things.

Working with the raw material of tales transcribed from the oral tradition in different regions of Italy, Calvino rewrote the tales, trying to preserve "a language never too colloquial, yet colorful and as derivative as possible of a dialect . . . an Italian sufficiently elastic to incorporate from the dialect images and turns of speech that were the most expressive and unusual." He was always aware that although part of a tradition, "the folktale must be re-created each time. At the core of the narrative is the storyteller, a prominent figure in every village or hamlet, who has his or her own style and appeal. And it is through this individual that the timeless folktale is linked with the world of its listeners and with history."

Calvino also speculated on the moral aspect of folktales, which he ingeniously linked to the moral function implicit in the act of storytelling. He considered that the suspense of the story keeps the fascinated listener from transgression." For the storyteller, the moral function of narrative consists of his or her fidelity both to the tradition's conventions and to "a free inventiveness." The narrator must organize his or her materials creatively, producing not only variations on a traditional theme but also "what is in [the] heart."

In the scholarly note at the end of *Italian Folktales,* Calvino states that "The Feathered Ogre" was a tale of generosity:

> This curious and lively Tuscan tale is the triumph of the obliging man who knows that helping others is a small matter and need not originate above. The title "Feathered Ogre" is my own invention; the original

speaks of a vague "beast" (whose traits are nonetheless the ogre's). Also the ending with the retention of the ogre on the ferry is mine, but it does not strike me as arbitrary, since the same thing happens in the Grimms' tale no. 29.

In the Commentary section of *The Story and Its Writer*, Calvino goes further in his analysis of this Italian folktale, pointing out that the stylistic qualities of "economy, rhythm, and hard logic" characterize the construction of such tales. Students might find it profitable to analyze the effect of these specific qualities on listeners as the tale is read aloud in class.

Economy is shown in the rapid exposition of the conflict in the story in the introductory paragraph. Not only is the problem stated early in the story — the king is sick and needs one of the ogre's feathers to recover — but the moral of the story is also suggested in the description of the attendant who says he'll take on the task at the risk of losing his life: he is loyal and courageous. Thus this is a story of virtue tested and rewarded; even the youngest listener in the audience will get the point.

Rhythm is exemplified in the hero's adventures as he goes on his way to meet the ogre. His encounters with the innkeeper, the ferryman, the two noblemen, and the friars have the same structure, and they underscore the seriousness and magic ritual of what he has undertaken. On the other hand, hard logic demands a direct solution to his problem, and this comes when he obeys the ogre's wife and hides under the bed. The wife lies to the ogre about the hiding man, feeds the ogre, pretends to sleep beside him, and steals one feather after another when he falls asleep. She does it so cleverly that she also learns the answers to the riddles that have been put to the hero. He and the wife run off together, and the remainder of the tale is a repetition of economy, rhythm, and logic, concluding with the elegant solution to the problem of what to do with the angry ogre: trap him on a ferry in the middle of a river, so he can do no harm to anyone.

Questions for Discussion

1. In fairy tales and folklore, an ogre is a monstrous giant who eats human beings. How does the addition of feathers make the giant more (or less) of a monster?
2. The men in this story are portrayed as heroes or people in charge of the secular and spiritual worlds: king, innkeeper, ferryman, nobleman, friar. The woman in "The Feathered Ogre" is portrayed as a daughter and a wife, albeit a clever one. How does this story reflect sex roles in the Italian peasant society in which the folktale evolved?
3. What religious background is taken for granted in the story?
4. How does the attendant's generosity play an important role in the story? Are any other characters generous as well?

Topic for Writing

1. **CONNECTION** Compare and contrast Calvino's editing of a folktale from a patriarchal tradition with Angela Carter's feminist retelling of the story of the Erl-King.

Related Commentary

Italo Calvino, On "Quickness" in Narrative, p. 1396.

Suggested Readings

Calvino, Italo, ed. *Italian Folktales.* New York: Pantheon, 1980.
Calvino, Italo. *Six Memos for the Next Millennium.* London: Jonathan Cape, 1992.

ALBERT CAMUS

The Guest (p. 206)

One of the key questions raised by Camus's narrative is, Who is the true guest in the story — the Algerian Arab prisoner or the Algerian French schoolteacher? Daru, the schoolteacher, thinks of the prisoner as his guest, but at the end of the story, after watching the freed Arab choose the path to prison, the schoolteacher returns to his classroom to find he has been judged an enemy by the Arabs — on the blackboard is the message, "You handed over our brother. You will pay for this." Daru, who feels at home in the landscape, learns that he is only a temporary guest there. Its Arab inhabitants have found him lacking.

Daru's fairness and impartiality are never in question; the Arab prisoner doesn't want to leave him and doesn't kill him when he falls deeply asleep. But Daru's sense of isolation and solitude is a false one. Camus tells the story in such a way that there is never a time when the schoolteacher is unaware of the presence of both Arabs and French in his environment, beginning with the opening sentence and continuing to the last sentence, when ironically Daru feels himself truly alone, caught between opposing hostile forces.

Given the history of political strife in Algeria, the reader may well ask if Daru hasn't recognized before the story opens that he cannot remain neutral after war is declared as a result of Algeria's struggle to break free of French rule. The story takes place shortly before the French-Algerian war (1954–1962). The schoolmaster's friend Balducci, the old gendarme, warns, "Things are brewing, it appears. There is talk of a forthcoming revolt. We are mobilized, in a way." Then he goes even further, telling Daru, "If there's an uprising, no one is safe, we're all in the same boat." Daru denies the truth of his friend's words, but they nevertheless foreshadow the hostile message on the schoolmaster's blackboard the next day. Daru is unable to continue what Balducci refers to as the soothing routine of the "comfortable life" he has enjoyed, caring for the poverty-stricken Islamic schoolchildren and tacitly endorsing the status quo.

To be sure, Daru seems to have earned the right to his peaceful life after his service in World War II. After what he has been through he feels anger toward "all men with their rotten spite, their tireless hates, their blood lust." His love for his Arab charges and for the barren, arid landscape of the country of his birth is what sustains him. Denying the political reality of his situation, carefully drawing maps of the distant rivers of France on the blackboard of his one-room schoolhouse, he has retreated to a dream world, until the advent of his uninvited guest brings him back to the world of bloodshed and civil war.

Questions for Discussion

1. Why does Balducci have a different attitude than Daru toward the Arab prisoner?
2. How does the Arab show that he shares Daru's respect for the ancient rule of hospitality — that a guest is never to be harmed?
3. Why has Daru drawn the four rivers of France on the blackboard of his Algerian schoolroom? Why does his action turn out to have ironic implications at the end of the story?
4. How does the scorched landscape of the story contribute to its theme? What is the story's theme?
5. What crime did the Arab commit? Why doesn't he tell Daru he is sorry for what he has done?
6. Why does Daru let the Arab go free?
7. Why do the Arabs watching Daru leave their message on his blackboard?

Topics for Writing

1. Camus once wrote in an essay entitled "The Wager of Our Generation" (1957), "No great work has ever been based on hatred or contempt. On the contrary, there is not a single true work of art that has not in the end added to the inner freedom of each person who has known and loved it." Write an essay in which you evaluate "The Guest" in light of Camus's statement.
2. Analyze the story to account for the presence of both a limited omniscient narrator and an omniscient narrator in the narrative.

Suggested Readings

Eberhard, Greim. "Albert Camus's 'The Guest': A New Look at the Prisoner." *Studies in Short Fiction* Winter 30:1 (1993): 95–98.

Knapp, Bettina L., ed. *Critical Essays on Albert Camus.* Boston: G. K. Hall, 1988.

McBride, Joseph. *Albert Camus: Philosopher and Litterateur.* New York: St. Martin's, 1992.

McDermott, John V. "Albert Camus's Flawed Guest." *Notes on Contemporary Literature* May 14:3 (1984): 5–7.

Meagher, Robert E., ed. *Albert Camus. The Essential Writings.* New York: Harper Colophon, 1979.

ANGELA CARTER

The Erl-King (p. 216)

In the introduction to *Italian Folktales,* Italo Calvino notes that the

> natural cruelties of the folktale give way to the rules of harmony [in Italian folktales]. The continuous flow of blood that characterizes the Grimms' brutal tales is absent. The Italian folktale seldom displays unbearable ferocity. Although the notion of cruelty persists along with an injustice bordering on inhumanity, . . . the narrative does not dwell on the torment of the victim, not even under pretense of pity, but moves swiftly to a healing solution. . . .

The English writer Angela Carter writes "The Erl-King" from a different perspective. In 1991 she edited a collection of fairy tales for the Virago Press in London, a feminist press. The stories she chose had, as she said, "only one thing in common — they all center around a female protagonist; be she clever, or brave, or good, or silly, or cruel, or sinister, or awesomely unfortunate, she is center stage, as large as life." In her earlier collection, *The Bloody Chamber* (1981), in which "The Erl-King" appears, Carter also worked in this vein. There she rewrote traditional fairy tales to make the passive women characters assertive participants in the narratives. The result of Carter's re-imaginings usually was a great deal of ferocity.

A quality of the demonic permeates "The Erl-King." In Carter's introduction to *The Virago Book of Fairy Tales,* she recognized that

> The fairy tale, as narrative, has far less in common with the modern bourgeois forms of the novel and the feature film than it does with contemporary demonic forms, especially those "female" forms of romance. Indeed, the elevated rank and excessive wealth of some of the characters, the absolute poverty of others, . . . the tumultuous plethora of events, the violent action, the intense and inharmonious personal relationships, the love of a row for its own sake, the invention of a mystery for its own sake — all these are characteristics of the fairy tale that link it directly to the contemporary television soap opera.

Carter's description of fairy tales holds true for "The Erl-King." Her description of the forest setting is lushly evocative of chaos and decay. The animals and birds trapped in the impenetrable forest parallel the hopeless entrapment of the girl narrating the story, as she is drawn like a sleepwalker or one under a spell into the embrace of her demon lover. Their life together is a parody of nurturing domesticity. Despite the cozy fire carefully tended by the Erl-King and the ingenious and delicious meals he concocts out of mushrooms, dandelions, strawberry leaves, and wild garlic, she feels herself threatened, not loved, by him, and she feels terribly alone.

In one paragraph we are told, "He is an excellent housewife. His rustic home is spick and span. He puts his well-scoured saucepan and skillet neatly on the hearth side by side, like a pair of polished shoes." As the girl realizes, the Erl-King is self-sufficient. He has no need of a wife. Instead he treats her like a trapped, harmless animal: "Skin the rabbit, he says! Off come my clothes." As if in a mirror, she instinctively recognizes herself in the baskets of trapped birds he keeps around him.

How does Carter enable her dizzy little rabbit to turn on he captor? Self-preservation wins over desire. She sees the cage he is building for her, and she plans to strangle the Erl-King with his own hair as he lies asleep before freeing all the caged birds in his house. Every one of them "will change back into young girls, every one, each with the crimson imprint of his love-bite on their throats."

The attentive reader will notice that the narrative shifts to the future tense at the point when the spellbound girl begins to describe how she will kill the Erl-King. As the birds change into young girls, so she also loses her identity in the story, which changes from a first-person to a third-person narration as she asserts herself. The Erl-King, not the girl, has the last word in the story, when the sound of his voice is heard protesting in the strings of the old fiddle strung with his hair: "Mother, mother, you have murdered me!"

Questions for Discussion

1. How has Carter woven a thicket of words in her description of the forest in order to suggest the plight of the young heroine?
2. Can you find humor in the story? Consider Carter's description of the way the Erl-King keeps house for himself.
3. Do you feel sympathy for the girl? Why has she come under the spell of the Erl-King?
4. How has Carter introduced an element of uncertainty into the conclusion of her fairy tale? Is it justified?

Topics for Writing

1. Rewrite your favorite fairy tale so that the heroine is no longer a passive participant in the story.
2. **CONNECTIONS** Apply the criteria for good fairy tales that Italo Calvino lists in his commentary (he believed they should exhibit the qualities of "economy, rhythm, and hard logic") to Carter's story. Then apply her criterion (the women characters should be assertive, not passive) to Calvino's "The Feathered Ogre."

Suggested Readings

Carter, Angela. *Come unto These Yellow Sands.* Newcastle upon Tyne: Bloodaxe, 1985.

——. *Fireworks: Nine Profane Pieces.* New York: Penguin, 1987.

——. *Nothing Sacred: Selected Writings.* London: Virago, 1982.

Fowl, Melinda G. "Angela Carter's 'The Blood Chamber Revisited.'" *Critical Survey* 3(1) (1991): 71–79.

Michael, Magali Cornier. "Feminism and the Postmodernist Impulse: Doris Lessing, Marge Piercy, Margaret Atwood, and Angela Carter." *Dissertation Abstracts International* 51(5) (Nov. 1990): 1609A.

Rushdie, Salman. "Angela Carter, 1940–92: A Very Good Wizard, A Very Dear Friend." *New York Times Book Review* Mar. 8, 1992, p. 5.

Wilson, Robert Rawdon. "SLIP PAGE: Angela Carter, in/out/in the Postmodern Nexus." *Ariel: A Review of International English Literature* 20(4) (Oct. 1989): 96–114.

RAYMOND CARVER

Cathedral (p. 224)

"Cathedral" is a story about alienation, isolation, and the cure for both. The narrator is an insecure, jealous man, more dead than alive — a man who has constructed a virtual prison in which he exists emotionally detached from his wife and cut off from any active participation in what makes life worth living. He anesthetizes his pain with drink and marijuana while making comments that reveal his feelings of inferiority, confusion, and resentment.

When the story opens, the narrator's tone is anecdotal and familiar ("this blind man, an old friend of my wife's, he was on his way to spend the night . . . I wasn't enthusiastic about his visit"); at the conclusion, however, his tone has become one of awe ("'it's really something,' I said"). We are aware that he has undergone an important transformation, an almost mystical experience that comes to him at an unexpected moment from an unexpected source and literally frees him from the prison his life had become. Despite his jealousy of blind Robert, and his professed resistance to the other's intrusion, the narrator unwittingly makes a friend of the blind man and in the process comes to understand something about himself. As he begins, ironically, to see through Robert's eyes, to experience the world through Robert's perceptions, his own horizons are expanded ("my eyes were still closed. I was in my house. I knew that. But I didn't feel like I was inside anything"). Robert contradicts every stereotypical idea the narrator holds about the blind, and with his commanding presence, his vitality, his sensitivity, and his engagement with life, he forces the narrator to see.

Contrasts abound between Robert and the narrator and between their respective relationships with the narrator's wife. The blind man is infinitely more alive than the narrator ("I don't have any blind friends," the narrator tells his wife; "you don't have *any* friends," she replies. "The blind man was also a ham radio operator. He talked in his loud voice about conversations he'd had with fellow operators in Guam, in the Philippines, in Alaska, and even in Tahiti. He said he'd have a lot of friends there if he ever wanted to go visit those places"). Robert and the narrator's wife (whom the narrator never calls by name but refers to, significantly, as "my wife") have a special and long-lasting friendship that involves a level of intimacy conspicuously absent from the narrator's marital relationship, the cause of much jealousy and resentment. An underlying tension is constantly present in the conversations between the couple, but with Robert the woman is a different person: "I saw my wife laughing as she parked the car. I saw her get out of the car and shut the door. She was still wearing a smile. Just amazing." We infer from this observation that she does not laugh much with her husband. His wife and Robert approach the house, "talking all the way." Earlier the narrator had commented, "right then my wife filled me in with more detail than I cared to know." Talking and the emotional sharing that results have played a vital role in the enduring relationship between the woman and the blind man; they are obviously not an integral part of the marital relationship.

"I want you to feel comfortable in this house," the wife says to her friend. "I am comfortable," Robert replies. Oddly, it is the narrator who is uncomfortable, and this discomfort prompts his pathetic attempts to feel superior to the blind man. Offering him marijuana, the narrator observes: "I could tell he didn't know the first thing." But soon he grudgingly acknowledges, "it was like he'd been doing it since he was nine years old," and the dynamics of the relationship slowly begin to change. After his wife falls asleep, the narrator offers to take Robert up to bed, but Robert declines and the narrator comments: "I'm glad for the company" and adds, "and I guess I was." They watch television together, Robert telling his host: "whatever you want to watch is okay. I'm always learning something. Learning never ends. It won't hurt me to learn something tonight," but it is the narrator, not the blind man, who will learn something important tonight. The image of the two men's hands tracing the cathedral together is dramatic, striking, and poignant. Robert asks him if he is religious, and the narrator realizes that he truly does not know how to talk to Robert, but the difference now is that he begins to care that he doesn't ("I guess I don't believe in it. In anything. Sometimes it's hard. You know what I'm saying?" "Sure, I do," Robert Answers. "Right," the narrator replies).

As the two men's hands trace the cathedral, we are reminded of the time when Robert touched the woman's face. Perhaps the connection that has been forged between the men will influence the marriage as well. The narrator's awkward and inadequate attempts at conversation with Robert are a form of engagement, and his hand speeding across the page drawing windows and arches and buttresses is truly a liberating experience. Inspired by the man who cannot see, he has literally drawn himself out of the prison to which his own limited perceptions had restricted him.

Questions for Discussion

1. Is the narrator a sympathetic protagonist? Does our opinion of him change as the story progresses?
2. What does the narrator learn from his encounter with Robert? Do you believe that there will be a significant change in his outlook from this point on?
3. What is the significance of Carver's choice of a cathedral as catalyst for the narrator's learning experience? What added dimension does this symbol bring to our understanding of the story? Can you tie it to any previous detail?
4. Contrast the author's tone and the narrator's mood at the opening of the story with the tone and mood at the end. How does the change in style reflect the change that has occurred in he narrator?
5. What is the narrator's attitude toward his wife? What kind of marriage do they have, and what evidence do you find to support your conclusion? Is the narrator's jealousy of Robert irrational?
6. What are the primary emotions displayed by the narrator throughout, and how can we understand them in terms of the life he leads? What are some adjectives you would use to characterize him? What role does alcohol play in his life?

7. What is it about Robert that unsettles the narrator? How do his appearance and bearing resist every stereotypical image the narrator has about blind people, and why is this so upsetting?

Topics for Writing

1. For Carver, salvation lies in human contact and connection. Comment critically.
2. Create a conversation between Robert and his wife after Robert's departure.
3. Discuss "Cathedral" as a story about "the blind leading the blind."

Related Commentaries

Raymond Carver, "The Ashtray," p. 1531.
Raymond Carver, Creative Writing 101, p. 1528.
Raymond Carver, On Writing, p. 1524.
Tom Jenks, The Origin of *Cathedral*, p. 1537.

Suggested Readings

See page 54.

RAYMOND CARVER

Errand (p. 235)

Raymond Carver's story may be instructively compared with the excerpt from Henri Troyat's biography of Anton Chekhov describing Chekhov's death (included with other commentary in the Carver Casebook in this anthology). In addition to providing a considerable amount of factual background about Chekhov and the last years of his century, this comparison may shed light on a question at could conceivably be asked by students in the course: What is the difference between a short story and an essay?

In comparing the fiction and nonfiction descriptions of Chekhov's last days, students will notice that Carver has based a good deal of his story on Troyat's biography of Chekhov, which Carver read and enjoyed. A knowledgeable and highly skilled literary biographer, Troyat wrote prose that (even in translation) moves briskly along almost like a short story, since Troyat eliminates editorial digressions and commentary in his desire to dramatize his account of Chekhov's last illness.

Carver has absorbed Troyat's style in addition to information about the people and places involved in Chekhov's death. The pace of the narrative is calm and unhurried, the tone unassuming and authoritive. To make "Errand" complete unto itself as a short narrative, Carver includes information about Chekhov's life

— the hemorrhage he suffered while dining with Suvorin, his marriage to the actress Olga Knipper — found in earlier pages in Troyat's biography. These details provide the reader with the information necessary to appreciate the background of the story.

Perhaps most significant, Carver, unlike Troyat, invents details in telling the story of Chekhov's death. "Errand" contains the fictional character of the blond young man who works at the hotel. He brings up the bottle of champagne that Doctor Schwöhrer has ordered for Chekhov in the middle of the night. Later in the morning, the young man reappears at the door of the suite with a vase containing three yellow roses to announce to Olga Knipper that breakfast will be served that day in the garden of the hotel because of the heat wave.

Carver ingeniously introduces this fictional character by having Doctor Schwöhrer summon him from the hotel kitchen by using the telephone in Chekhov's room. This would have been a new-fangled gadget in 1904, and the doctor's meticulous way of following the "instructions for using the device" makes his action believable to the reader, thus preparing the way for a fictional rather than a historical character to enter the story. Carver then tells us everything we need to know to accept the "lie": First we visualize the appearance of the young man, who was awakened from sleep and who dressed so hastily that his jacket is carelessly buttoned. Then we see what he sees when he brings his tray into Chekhov's hotel suite, and hear what he hears — the "dreadful, harrowing sound" of the dying writer's "ratchety breathing."

With the young man's reappearance in the concluding paragraphs of the story, Carver's imagination sets to work dramatizing the way that Chekhov's widow entrusts the waiter with the precious errand of notifying the mortician of Chekhov's death. Olga Knipper was an actress, and her way of explaining the errand is an actress's visualization technique. "If it would help keep his movements purposeful he should imagine himself as someone moving down the busy sidewalk carrying in his arms a porcelain vase of roses that he had to deliver to an important man." Chekhov, of course, is the precious "porcelain vase of roses," but to keep the story from veering off into sentimentality, Carver must keep imagining. He succeeds by balancing the widow's beautiful image of the precious vase with the prosaic fact of the champagne cork in the last paragraph of the narrative. The young servant, totally alive and believable as he functions in the story, has been superbly trained in this elegant Swiss hotel to do his duty. "He leaned over. Without looking down, he reached out and closed it into his hand."

Questions for Discussion

1. Why does Carver begin "Errand" with an account of Chekhov's meeting with Alexei Suvorin in 1897, four years before the writer's death?
2. Why does Carver allow Leo Tolstoy to appear in this story?
3. What have you learned about the difference between Tolstoy and Chekhov from this fictionalized encounter? (Refer to Tolstoy's commentary on Chekhov's "The Darling" in this anthology.)
4. What do Chekhov's efforts to minimize the seriousness of his tuberculosis tell you about him?
5. How effective was the medical treatment of tuberculosis at the turn of the century, judging from Doctor Schwöhrer's prescription for Chekhov's diet?

6. Why does Doctor Schwöhrer try to muffle "the festive explosion" when he uncorks the champagne? Why does he push the cork back into the bottle after he pours three glasses of the wine? Why does the champagne cork reappear in the story?

Topics for Writing

1. Write a short story based on an incident you have read in a biography of a famous person.
2. **CONNECTIONS**   Write an essay comparing and contrasting Carver's treatment of death and dying with Tolstoy's in "The Death of Ivan Ilych."

Related Commentaries

Raymond Carver, "The Ashtray," p. 1531.
Raymond Carver, Creative Writing 101, p. 1528.
Raymond Carver, On *Errand*, p. 1532.
Raymond Carver, On Writing, p. 1524.
Henri Troyat, From *Chekhov*, p. 1534.

Suggested Readings

See page 54.

RAYMOND CARVER

What We Talk About When We Talk About Love (p. 243)

The scarcely veiled animosity between Dr. Mel McGinnis and his wife, Terri, gives tension to this story of three married couples. Through Mel's thoughts and experiences, Carver is investigating the nature of married love. Like the naive boy in Sherwood Anderson's classic short story "I Want to Know Why," Mel insists on asking an impossible question: What is the nature of love? What is the meaning of sharing?

The three pairs of lovers represent different stages of marriage. At one end of a spectrum are Laura and Nick (the narrator), married only a year and a half, still infatuated, glowing with the power of their attraction for each other.

At the other end of the spectrum are the old married pair in the hospital whom Mel and the other doctors have patched up after a catastrophic highway accident. Glad to learn his wife has survived, the old man — as Mel tells the story — is depressed, not because of their physical suffering but because he can't see his wife through the eye holes in his bandages. As Mel says, "Can you imagine? I'm telling you, the man's heart was breaking because he couldn't turn his goddamn head and *see* his goddamn wife."

Between the two extremes of perfect love, Mel and Terri are veterans (four years married to each other), who are past the bliss of their first attraction and not yet two halves of a whole because they've survived the long haul together. Each has been married before, and each is obsessed with the earlier partner. First Terri talks too much about her sadistic ex-husband Ed; then Mel reveals that he hates his first wife because she kept their kids. Terri says, "she's bankrupting us." The talk appears to ramble, but Carver keeps it under control by sticking to his subject — specific examples of the different varieties of love — and organizing the four friends' conversation by chronicling the stages of their drunkenness as they go through two bottles of gin in the afternoon.

The passing of time is brilliantly described, paralleling the waxing and waning of the stages of love. When the story opens, sunlight fills the New Mexico kitchen where the four friends with their gin and tonics are talking around the table. Midway, when the narrator is beginning to feel the drinks, he describes the sun like the warmth and lift of the gin in his body. "The afternoon sun was like a presence in this room, the spacious light of ease and generosity." As the conversation wears on and Mel tells Terri to shut up after she's interrupted one too many times, the light shifts again, the sunshine getting thinner. The narrator is a shade drunker, and his gaze fixes on the pattern of leaves on the windowpanes and on the Formica kitchen counter, as if he's staying alert by focusing deliberately on the edges of the objects around him. "They weren't the same patterns, of course." Finally, mysteriously, the light drains out of the room, "going back through the window where it had come from." The alcoholic elation has evaporated. At the end of the story, the couples sit in darkness on their kitchen chairs, not moving. The only sound the narrator hears is everyone's heart beating, separately.

The person we know least about is the narrator, Nick. Perhaps Carver deliberately echoes the name of Nick Adams, Hemingway's autobiographical narrator in his stories of initiation; or Nick Carraway, the narrator of Fitzgerald's *The Great Gatsby*. The role of Carver's Nick in the story is also like that of Marlow in Conrad's "Heart of Darkness," as Nick voyages through the conversation of Mel and Terri into uncharted, deep waters of the heart. But this Nick is also a participant, through the gin and the sunlight, in the feelings of his troubled, overworked doctor friend.

Questions for Discussion

1   As the story opens, what is the setting in time, place, and situation?
2.   How would you describe Terri? What type of person is Mel?
3.   What was Terri's experience with her first husband, Ed? In what way was Mel involved in this experience? How does Terri's view of Ed contrast with Mel's view of him? What does this contrast reveal about the character of Mel and Terri's relationship?
4.   In the discussion about Ed, what do we discover about the couple with whom Mel and Terri are socializing? What is their relationship both to each other and to Mel and Terri? Compare and contrast their marriage with Terri and Mel's.
5.   What is the point of view in this story? Who is the narrator? How reliable is he?

6. Does Mel view his first wife in the same way he does Terri? What are we told about his first wife?

7. What are some of the questions about love that Carver raises through his characters? Does he offer any answers to these questions?

8. A third couple is introduced in the story. What astonishes Mel about their relationship?

9. What changes in the setting, if any, can you identify over the course of the story? In what way does the setting mirror Carver's message about the stages of love?

10. What does each of the couples represent? What is the significance of the last paragraph?

Topics for Writing

1. Write an essay discussing theme and characterization in "What We Talk About When We Talk About Love."

2. Explore the question posed by the title of this story: What does Carver (and the reader) talk about when he (and we) talks about love?

3. Think about married couples you know and discuss what their views on love might be as well as the quality of their relationships.

4. **CONNECTIONS** Compare and contrast the types of love in Carver's story and Joyce's "The Dead."

Related Commentaries

Raymond Carver, "The Ashtray," p. 1531.
Raymond Carver, Creative Writing 101, p. 1528.
Raymond Carver, On Writing, p. 1524.
Arthur M. Saltzman, A Reading of *What We Talk About When We Talk About Love*, p. 1539.

Suggested Readings

Adelman, Bob. *Carver Country — The World of Raymond Carver*. New York: Scribner's, 1991. A photographic essay with quotations from Carver's writing.

Carver, Raymond. "The Art of Fiction LXXVI." Interview in *The Paris Review*, No. 88 (Summer 1983).

———. *Fires: Essays, Poems, Stories*. Santa Barbara, CA: Capra, 1983.

———. *Where I'm Calling From: New and Selected Stories*. New York: Atlantic Monthly, 1988.

Gentry, Marshall B., and William A. Stull, eds. *Coversations with Raymond Carver*. Jackson, MI: UP of Mississippi, 1990.

Halpert, Sam, ed. *When We Talk About Raymond Carver*. Layton, UT: Gibbs Smith, 1991.

Simpson, M. "Art of Fiction: Raymond Carver." *Paris Review* 25 (1983)193–221.

Stull, W. L. "Beyond Hopelessville: Another Side of Raymond Carver." *Philological Quarterly* 64 (1985): 1–15.

Troyat, Henri. *Chekhov*. Trans. Michael Henry Heim. New York: Dutton, 1986.

WILLA CATHER

Paul's Case (p. 254)

Students may feel repelled by this story and reject its ending as heavy-handed. The structure of the plot, which pits a sensitive adolescent against an ugly and confining bourgeois society, invites us to admire Paul's rebellion and to glamorize his suicide, but Cather takes great pains to make Paul as unattractive in his way as the family, school, and neighborhood he hates. Quite apart from his supercilious mannerisms, which his teachers feel some inclination to forgive, Paul's quest for brightness and beauty in the world of art and imagination is subjected to Cather's devastating criticism, so readers who were ready to make a stock tragic response to his demise may find it difficult to care.

Try meeting this objection directly by examining the implications of the story's concluding passage. The vision presented here comes close to formulaic naturalism. Paul is not only caught in a universal machine, he is himself a machine. The imagination that has sustained him against the ugliness of his surroundings is dismissed as a "picture making mechanism," now crushed. The world against which Paul rebels is plain, gray, narrow, and monotonous. Its combination of saints (Calvin, Washington) and customary homilies precludes all that is in itself beautiful, pleasant, and fulfilling in the present moment. Paul's reaction, however, is merely the obverse. His habitual lies reflect his general resort to the artificial. He may be "artistic," but not in the sense of being creative, and his romantic fantasies involve no more satisfactory relations with others than does his ordinary life. Paul's world is so intolerable to his sensitivity that he is driven to escape from it, even at the cost of sitting in the cellar with the rats watching him from the corners. His escape inevitably becomes a form of self-destruction, as manifested in his criminal act — which to him feels like confronting "the thing in the corner" — and finally in his suicide. Paul passes through the "portal of Romance" for good, into a dream from which "there would be no awakening."

If it could be termed a choice, it would clearly be a bad choice, but Cather presents it rather as a symptom of Paul's "case," a disease of life from which he suffers, has suffered perhaps since his mother died when he was an infant, and for which, at first glance, there seems to be no cure. No wonder readers may be inclined to dismiss the story as unduly negative because unduly narrow. But Cather, at the same time that she meticulously documents the inexorable progress of Paul's illness, defines by implication a condition of health whose possible existence gives meaning to Paul's demise. As Philip L. Gerber explains: "Although [Cather] extolled the imaginative, her definition of imagination is all-important; for rather than meaning an ability 'to weave pretty stories out of nothing,' imagination conveyed to her 'a response to what is going on — a sensitiveness to which outside things appeal' and was an amalgam of sympathy and observation."

Paul's refuge is the product of the first, false kind of imagination, but the reality and the power of an imagination of the second sort is evident throughout the story, in the masterful evocations of Cordelia Street, of the school and its all-too-human teachers, and not least of Paul himself. When Paul's case finally becomes extreme enough to break through the insensitivity of bourgeois Pittsburgh, the world of the street that bears the name of King Lear's faithful daughter at last begins to live up to its name, sympathizing with Paul's plight and offering to embrace him with its love. To Paul, however, whose own unregenerate imagination is still confined to making pretty pictures rather than sympathetic observations, the advances of Cordelia Street seem like tepid waters of boredom in which he is called upon to submerge himself. The potential for growth and change that is reflected in his father's abandoning his usual frugality to pay back the money Paul has stolen and in his coming down from the top of the stairs into Paul's world to reach out to him, escape Paul's notice — but not that of the reader.

WILLIAM E. SHEIDLEY

Questions for Discussion

1. Describe Paul's personality as Cather sets it forth in the opening paragraph of the story. Is this someone we like and admire?
2. Why do Paul's teachers have so much difficulty dealing with him? What does the knowledge that Cather was a teacher in Pittsburgh at the time she wrote this story suggest about her perspective on Paul's case?
3. What techniques does Cather use to establish the reader's sympathy for Paul? What limits that sympathy?
4. Contrast the three worlds — school, Carnegie Hall, and Cordelia Street — in which Paul moves. Why does Cather introduce them in that order?
5. What is the effect of Cather's capitalizing the word "Romance"?
6. Discuss the three decorations that hang above Paul's bed. What aspects of American culture do they refer to? What do they leave out?
7. Explore the allusion embodied in the name "Cordelia Street." Why does Paul feel he is drowning there?
8. Discuss Paul's fear of rats. Why does he feel that he has "thrown down the gauntlet to the thing in the corner" when he steals the money and leaves for New York?
9. Explicate the paragraph that begins "Perhaps it was because, in Paul's world, the natural nearly always wore the guise of ugliness." To what extent does this paragraph offer a key to the story's structure and theme?
10. Describe the effect of the leap forward in time that occurs in the white space before we find Paul on the train to New York. Why does Cather withhold for so long her account of what has taken place?
11. What is admirable about Paul's entry into and sojourn in New York? What is missing from his new life?
12. Why does Paul wink at himself in the mirror after reading the newspaper account of his deeds?
13. On the morning of his suicide, Paul recognizes that "money was everything." Why does he think so? Does the story bear him out?
14. What is the effect of Paul's burying his carnation in the snow? of his last thoughts?

Topics for Writing

1. Analyze "Paul's Case" as an attack on American society.
2. In an essay argue that Cather's commentary on Mansfield (printed in Part Two, p. 1398) is a basis for criticism of "Paul's Case."

3. Cather's story is punctuated by several recurrent images and turns of phrase. Locate as many as you can and take note of their contexts. What does this network of internal connections reveal?
4. **CONNECTIONS** Compare Cather's account of Paul's death with accounts of dying in other stories, such as Tolstoy's "The Death of Ivan Ilych" and Bierce's "An Occurrence at Owl Creek Bridge."

Suggested Readings

Arnold, Marilyn. *Willa Cather: A Reference Guide*. Boston: G. K. Hall, 1986.

———. *Willa Cather's Short Fiction*. Athens: Ohio UP, 1984.

Brown, E. K., and Leon Edel. *Willa Cather: A Critical Biography*. Lincoln: U of Nebraska P, 1987.

Callander, Marilyn B. *Willa Cather and the Fairy Tale*. Ann Arbor, MI: UMI Research P, 1989.

Cather, Willa. *Collected Short Fiction 1892–1912*. Introduction by Mildred R. Bennett. Lincoln: U of Nebraska P, 1965.

———. *Early Novels and Stories*. The Library of America. New York: Viking, 1986.

Daiches, David. *Willa Cather: A Critical Introduction*. Ithaca: Cornell UP, 1951. 144–47.

Gerber, Philip L. *Willa Cather*. Twayne's United States Authors Series 258. Boston: Hall, 1975. 72–73, 101, 141, 163.

Murphy, John J. *Critical Essays on Willa Cather*. Boston: G. K. Hall, 1984.

Thomas, Susie. *Willa Cather*. Savage, MD: Barnes and Noble, 1990.

Wasserman, Loretta. *Willa Cather: A Study of Short Fiction*. Boston: Twayne, 1991.

JOHN CHEEVER

The Swimmer (p. 270)

One way to reconstruct a naturalistic time scheme for the story, so Neddy's "misfortunes," the awareness of which he seems to have repressed, can be dated with regard to the other events in the narrative, is to imagine a gap in time covered by the line "He stayed in the Levys' gazebo until the storm had passed." The authoritative point of view in the opening paragraphs seems to preclude placing the misfortunes before Neddy begins his swim, while the gathering clouds and circling de Haviland trainer assert the continuity of the first phase of his journey. After the storm, however, signs of change appear, and it is possible to reconcile Neddy's subsequent encounters with the proposition that he is continuing his swim on another day or days under quite different circumstances. Before the storm, he visits the Grahams and the Bunkers, who greet him as the prosperous and popular Neddy Merrill described at the beginning of the story, but after the storm Neddy visits only the empty houses of the Lindleys and the Welchers; the public pool where any derelict may swim; the peculiar Hallorans, who mention his troubles; the Sachses, who have problems of their own and refuse him a drink; the socially inferior Biswangers, who snub him; and his old mistress Shirley, who implies that this call is not the first he has paid in this condition.

But Cheever is not interested in a realistic time scheme. If he were, he would not have burned the 250-page novelistic version of the story (mentioned in the headnote) that presumably filled in the blanks. Instead, he has constructed the story so Neddy's recognition of his loss strikes the reader with the same impact it has on Neddy. By telescoping time, Cheever thrusts us forward into a state of affairs that exists only as a dim cloud on the horizon on the day the story begins and at first seems to be entirely taking place.

What accounts for the reversal in Neddy's life? Surely it is possible to tax Neddy for irresponsibility and childishness in turning his back on his friends and family and so casually setting off on an odyssey from which he returns far too late. Neddy's own view of his adventure is considerably more attractive. The only member of his society who seems free from a hangover on this midsummer Sunday, Neddy simply wishes to savor the pleasures of his fortunate life: "The day was beautiful and it seemed to him that a long swim might enlarge and celebrate its beauty." Although he has been (or will be) unfaithful to his wife with Shirley Adams, and although he kisses close to a dozen other women on his journey, Neddy does not construe his departure as infidelity to Lucinda. Rather, to swim the string of pools across the suburban county is to travel along "the Lucinda River." As "a pilgrim, an explorer, a man with a destiny," Neddy plunges into this river of life aware of the gathering storm on the horizon but regarding it with pleasurable anticipation. When it finally breaks over the Levys' gazebo, he savors the exciting release of tension that accompanies the arrival of a thunder shower, but with the explosion of thunder and the smell of gunpowder that ensues, Neddy finds his happy illusions, his world of "youth, sport, and clement weather," lashed by a more unpleasant reality, just as the "rain lashed the Japanese lanterns that Mrs. Levy had bought in Kyoto the year before last, or was it the year before that?"

What Neddy now confronts, though he tries gamely to ignore it, are the twin recognitions that his youth is not eternal and that the pleasant society of the "bonny and lush . . . banks of the Lucinda River" is unstable, exclusive, and cruel. Grass grows in the Lindleys' riding ring, the Welchers have moved away, and the sky is now overcast. Crossing Route 424 in his swimming suit, Neddy is subjected to the ridicule of the public, and at the Recreation Center he finds that swimming does not convey the same sense of elegance, pleasure, and freedom that it does in the pools of his affluent friends. The validity of the society Neddy has previously enjoyed is called further into question by the very existence of the self-contradictory Hallorans, whose personal eccentricity is matched by their political hypocrisy. Neddy's visits to the Biswangers and to Shirley Adams complete the destruction of his illusions, but it is Eric Sachs, disfigured by surgery and (with the loss of his navel) symbolically cut off from the human community, who embodies the most troubling reflection of Neddy's condition. "I'm not alone," Shirley proclaims, but Neddy is, and as this man who "might have been compared to a summer's day" recognizes that his summer is over, it is not surprising that for "the first time in his adult life" he begins to cry. While the reader may relish Cheever's indictment of a society whose values have so betrayed Neddy, it is hard not to feel some admiration for a man who, by executing his plan to swim the county through the now icy autumn waters, has indeed become a legendary figure, an epic hero of a sort.

WILLIAM E. SHEIDLEY

Questions for Discussion

1. Who is referred to by the word "everyone" in the opening sentence? Who is not?
2. How does Neddy Merrill relate to the world in which he moves? Why does he decide to swim home?
3. Why does Neddy name his route "the Lucinda River"? The Levys live on "Alewives Lane." Alewives are a kind of fish that swim up rivers to spawn. Is there a sexual component to Neddy's journey?
4. Is the storm that breaks a surprise? How does Neddy feel about the beginning of the rain?
5. What differences can be noticed between what Neddy experiences before and after the storm? How might they be explained?
6. What new elements enter the story when Neddy crosses Route 424? Why do the drivers jeer at him?
7. Before he dives into the unappealing public swimming pool, Neddy tells himself "that this was merely a stagnant bend in the Lucinda River." How characteristic is this effort to assuage his own doubts and discontents?
8. Based on what the Hallorans, the Sachses, the Biswangers, and Shirley Adams say to Neddy, what is the truth about himself and his life of which he is unaware?
9. Cheever has his hero discover the season by observing the stars. What effect does that choice among various possibilities have on our attitude toward Neddy?
10. It is not difficult to say what Neddy has lost. What has he gained?

Topics for Writing

1. Explain why Neddy Merrill talks only with women.
2. Analyze the characters Rusty Towers, Eric Sachs, and Neddy Merrill.
3. Write an essay discussing Neddy Merrill's voyage of exploration and discovery.
4. Evaluate Cheever's attitude toward the swimmer.

Related Commentary

John Cheever, Why I Write Short Stories, p. 1403.

Suggested Readings

Cheever, John. *The Journals of John Cheever*. New York: Knopf, 1991.

Cheever, Susan. *Home before Dark*. Boston: Houghton, 1984.

Coale, Samuel. *John Cheever*. New York: Ungar, 1977. 43–47.

Collins, R. G., ed. *Critical Essays on John Cheever*. Boston: G. K. Hall, 1982.

O'Hara, James E. *John Cheever: A Study of the Short Fiction*. Boston: Twayne, 1989.

Waldeland, Lynne. *John Cheever*. Twayne, 1979.

Writers at Work, Fifth Series. New York: Penguin, 1981. Interview with John Cheever by Annette Grant, Fall 1976.

Anton Chekhov

The Darling (p. 280)

One of the liveliest discussions about a short story in this anthology could be started by a class debate based on the contradictory interpretations of "The Darling" by Leo Tolstoy and Eudora Welty included in Part Two (pp. 1497 and 1510). Tolstoy was convinced that Chekhov was misguided in satirizing women's tendency to depend on men for meaning and direction in their lives. In Tolstoy's view, Chekhov had allowed himself to become a women's rights advocate under the pernicious influence of his "liberated" wife, the actress Olga Knipper. Welty, in contrast, reveals the subtle emotional tyranny of the protagonist, Olenka. In Welty's interpretation, the schoolboy shows us at the end of the story that men want their "space" too. Students could be assigned Tolstoy's or Welty's interpretation and asked to support or refute it. Certainly neither interpretation is unassailable.

Other critical perspectives can also be applied to this provocative story. A feminist reader could argue that Olenka has been handicapped by the environment around her: uneducated for a profession, she can have no ideas or life of her own. A psychological interpretation could concentrate on the darling's early, possibly traumatic fixation on her father and his long mortal illness just as she reaches manageable age. A formalist approach might look closely at the words the schoolboy uses as he cries out in his sleep: "I'll give it you! Get away! Shut up!" Welty assumes that the boy is dreaming of Olenka. He could just as well be dreaming of his teacher at school, other students fighting with him in the schoolyard, or his own mother, who appears to have abandoned him. He could even be repeating the cruel words his mother might have said to drive him away from her before she left him with Olenka.

The English short story writer H. E. Bates interpreted the story yet another way. Comparing Chekhov's technique with Maupassant's, Bates writes, "Both like to portray a certain type of weak, stupid, thoughtless woman, a sort of yes-woman who can unwittingly impose tragedy or happiness on others. Maupassant had no patience with the type; but in Olenka, in the 'The Darling,' it is precisely a quality of tender patience, the judgment of the heart and not the head, that gives Chekhov's story its effect of uncommon understanding and radiance."

Bates saw Chekhov as subtle: His

> receptivity, his capacity for compassion, are both enormous. Of his characters he seems to say, "I know what they are doing is their own responsibility. But how did they come to this, how did it happen? There may be some trivial thing that will explain." That triviality, discovered, held for a moment in the light, is the key to Chekhov's emotional solution. In Maupassant's case the importance of that key would have been inexorably driven home; but as we turn to ask of Chekhov if we have caught his meaning aright, it is to discover that we must answer that question for ourselves — for Chekhov has gone. . . . Both [Maupassant and Chekhov] knew to perfection when they had said enough; an acute instinct continually reminded them of the fatal

tedium of explanation, of going on a second too long. In Chekhov this sense of impatience, almost a fear, caused him frequently to stop speaking, as it were, in mid-air. It was this which gave his stories an air of remaining unfinished, of leaving the reader to his own explanations, of imposing on each story's end a note of suspense so abrupt and yet refined that it produced on the reader an effect of delayed shock.

Questions for Discussion

1. How does Chekhov characterize Olenka at the beginning of the story?
2. Why does he have the "lady visitors" be the first ones to call her a "darling"?
3. Olenka "mothers" each of her husbands. Could she have been both a good wife and a good mother if she had had children of her own? Why or why not?

Topics for Writing

1. Interpret Sasha's words at the end of "The Darling." Identify the person he is talking to, and find details in the story that justify your interpretation.
2. Continue "The Darling," supposing that the "loud knock at the gate" is a message from Sasha's mother, who wants him to join her in Harkov.

Related Commentaries

Anton Chekhov, Technique in Writing the Short Story, p. 1405.
Leo Tolstoy, Chekhov's Intent in "The Darling," p. 1497.
Eudora Welty, Plot and Character in Chekhov's "The Darling," p. 1510.

Suggested Readings

See page 63.

Anton Chekhov

The Lady with the Pet Dog (p. 289)

Anna Sergeyevna comes to Yalta because she wants "to live, to live!" Gurov begins his affair with her because he is bored and enjoys the freedom and ease of a casual liaison. At the outset both are undistinguished, almost clichés — a philandering bank employee escaping from a wife he cannot measure up to, a lady with a dog and a "flunkey" for a husband. By the end of the story, however, after having been captured and tormented by a love that refuses to be filed away in memory, the two gain dignity and stature by recognizing that life is neither exciting nor easy; and, by taking up the burden of the life they have discovered in their mutual compassion, they validate their love.

Chekhov develops the nature of this true love, so ennobling and so tragic, by testing it against a series of stereotypes that it transcends and by showing a series of stock expectations that it violates. Anna Sergeyevna reacts differently from any of the several types of women Gurov has previously made love to, and Gurov finds himself unable to handle his own feelings in the way he is accustomed to. Anna Sergeyevna proves neither a slice of watermelon nor a pleasant focus of nostalgia. Most important, as the conclusion implies, she will not remain the secret core of his life, bought at the price of falsehood and suspicion of others.

In observing the evolution of the lovers, the reader is led through a series of potential misconceptions. We may want to despise Gurov as a careless breaker of hearts, but it is clear that he has one of his own when he sees Anna Sergeyevna as a Magdalene. Later, when Gurov is tormented by his longings for Anna Sergeyevna, we are tempted to laugh the superior realist's laugh at a romantic fool: Surely when Gurov arrives at S——, disillusionment will await him. And in a sense it does. Just as there was dust in the streets at Yalta, the best room in the hotel at S—— is coated with dust; reality is an ugly fence; and even the theater (where *The Geisha* is playing) is full of reminders of how unromantic life really is. But Anna Sergeyevna has not, as Gurov supposes at one point, taken another lover, nor has she been able to forget Gurov.

The antiromantic tone is but another oversimplification, and the story comes to rest, somewhat like Milton's *Paradise Lost*, at a moment of beginning. The lovers' disillusionment about the nature of the struggle they face creates in them a deep compassion for each other, which finds its echo in readers' final attitude toward them as fellow human beings whose lives are like our own and who deserve a full measure of our sympathy. Or perhaps they draw our pity; surely their fate, which Chekhov so skillfully depicts as probable and true, inspires tragic fear. Gurov and Anna Sergeyevna have met the god of love, and Chekhov awes us by making him seem real.

WILLIAM E. SHEIDLEY

Questions for Discussion

1. Why does Gurov call women "the inferior race"?
2. At the end of section I, Gurov thinks that there is "something pathetic" about Anna Sergeyevna. Is there? What is it?
3. Why is Anna Sergeyevna so distracted as she watches the steamer putting in?
4. How does Anna Sergeyevna differ from other women Gurov has known, as they are described in the paragraph that ends "the lace on their lingerie seemed to him to resemble scales"? Compare this passage with the paragraph that begins "His hair was already beginning to turn gray."
5. In view of what follows, is it appropriate that Gurov should see Anna Sergeyevna as a Magdalene?
6. What is the function of the paragraph that begins "At Oreanda they sat on a bench not far from the church"?
7. What "complete change" does Gurov undergo during his affair with Anna Sergeyevna at Yalta? Is it permanent?
8. Explain Gurov's remark at the end of section II: "High time!"

9. Why is Gurov enraged at his companion's remark about the sturgeon?
10. Discuss the possible meanings of the objects Gurov encounters in S——: the broken figurine, the long gray fence, the cheap blanket, and so on.
11. Seeing Anna Sergeyevna enter the theater, Gurov "understood clearly that in the whole world there was no human being so near, so precious, and so important to him." What is Chekhov's tone in this statement?
12. Explain Anna Sergeyevna's reaction to Gurov's arrival. Why does she volunteer to come to Moscow?
13. Discuss the implications of Gurov's "two lives" as Chekhov explains them in section IV. Do you agree with the generalizations about the desire for privacy with which the paragraph ends? Relate these ideas to the story's ending.
14. What will life be like for Gurov and Anna Sergeyevna? Anna has previously said, "I have never been happy; I am unhappy now, and I never, never shall be happy, never!" Is she right?

Topics for Writing

1. Write an essay describing Chekhov's characterization of the wronged spouse in "The Lady with the Pet Dog."
2. Discuss the meaning of the three geographical locales in "The Lady with the Pet Dog."
3. On your first reading of the story, stop at the end of each section and write down your judgment of Gurov and Anna Sergeyevna and your prediction of what will happen next. When you have finished reading, compare what you wrote with what turned out to be the case and with your final estimate of the protagonists. To the extent that your initial impressions were borne out, what points in the text helped to guide you? To the extent that you were surprised, explain what led you astray. What might Chekhov have wanted to accomplish by making such misconceptions possible?
4. **CONNECTIONS** Explore the themes of geography and adultery in Chekhov's "The Lady with the Pet Dog" and Bessie Head's "Life."

Related Commentaries

Anton Chekhov, Technique in Writing the Short Story, p. 1405.
Vladimir Nabokov, A Reading of Chekhov's "The Lady with the Little Dog," p. 1471.

Suggested Readings

Bates, H. E. *The Modern Short Story*. Boston: The Writer, 1972.
Eekman, Thomas. *Critical Essays on Anton Chekhov*. Boston: G. K. Hall, 1989.
Friedland, Louis S., ed. *Anton Tchekhov's Letters on the Short Story, the Drama, and Other Topics*. Salem, NH: Ayer, 1965.
Kramer, Karl D. *The Chameleon and the Dream: The Image of Reality in Chekhov's Stories*. The Hague: Mouton, 1970. 171.

(text pp. 302–314)

Matlaw, Ralph E., ed. *Anton Chekhov's Short Stories.* New York: Norton, 1979.

Meister, Charels W. *Chekhov Criticism, 1880 through 1986.* New York: St. Martin's, 1990.

Pritchett, V. S. *Chekhov: A Spirit Set Free.* New York: Random, 1988.

Rayfield, Donald. *Chekhov: The Evolution of His Art.* New York: Barnes, 1975. 197–200.

Smith, Virginia Llewellyn. "The Lady with the Dog." Anton Chekhov's Short Stories: Texts of the Stories, Backgrounds, Criticism. Ed. Ralph E. Matlaw. New York: Norton, 1979. Excerpted from Smith, *Anton Chekhov and the Lady with the Dog* (New York: Oxford UP, 1973). 96–97, 212–18.

Troyat, Henri. *Chekhov.* Trans. Michael Henry Heim. New York: Dutton, 1986.

CHARLES CHESNUTT

The Sheriff's Children (p. 302)

Webster's Dictionary defines "melodrama" as a work characterized by the predominance of plot and physical action over characterization. Plot is plentiful in Chesnutt's story; first he begins with leisurely opening paragraphs to set the time and place of the story in the backwoods of North Carolina a decade after the Civil War, and then in a few rapid paragraphs he presents the reader with a murder, the capture of the murder suspect, and the formation of a mob determined to lynch the suspect before he can be brought to trial. The characters in Chesnutt's story are types: the angry, self-righteous members of the lynch mob; the brave white Southern sheriff faithful to his duty who confronts the mob in order to see justice done (rather than to protect the prisoner); his obedient, loving daughter, who courageously saves his life; and the prisoner, the sheriff's unrecognized illegitimate son, who commits suicide rather than face southern justice (or, it might be argued, chooses to become a hero and take his own life rather than compromise his father's respected position in local society by revealing his identity).

Plot may dominate this "old-fashioned" story, but the thoughtful reader may have occasion to reflect upon the manner of Chesnutt's telling of his tale. He delineates wooden, stereotypical characters, but he is passionately involved in dramatizing the tragic legacy of racism flourishing in the United States after the Civil War, and to this end he skillfully suggests subtle undercurrents beneath the surface of the father-son relationship. Writing at the turn of the century, Chesnutt can be categorized as a naturalist like his American contemporaries Theodore Dreiser and Jack London, deeply engaged in the debates of his time over the relative importance of the influences of nature and nurture in the formation of human character.

The sheriff's daughter, unlike his illegitimate son, shares her father's sense of responsibility and bravery. When the sheriff learns he is the prisoner's father, he thinks in terms of the careful nurturing he received, which his own life reflects: "He saw in this mulatto what he himself might have become had not the safeguards of parental restraint and public opinion been thrown around him." Unlike the sheriff's daughter, the mulatto has had none of the opportunities due him by right of birth, namely, the privileges of his father's social class and the protection of his father's position. Instead, race has ruled his life in the United States. Born the son of a black slave mother, his opportunities to succeed in life have been restricted from birth, despite his intelligence. He tells the sheriff that in school "I learned to feel that no degree of learning or wisdom will change the color of my skin and that I shall always wear what in my own country is a badge of degradation."

The mulatto prisoner is thus a "natural" man, his character bereft of the civilizing effects of a nurturing family upbringing. We first see him through the sheriff's eyes as he sits in his cell, a yellow-faced (read cowardly), "cowering wretch," protesting his innocence in a way that evokes the sheriff's contempt. Uppermost in the nameless mulatto's mind is his own survival. When he gets control of the sheriff's gun, his character changes dramatically. The sheriff is overcome with "an involuntary feeling of apprehension. . . . The keen-eyed, desperate man before him was a different being altogether from the groveling wretch who had begged so piteously for life a few minutes before."

Readers may analyze the spirited exchange between father and son in which the son's innate courage and intellectual superiority are apparent in his rational judgment that death is preferable to life as a mulatto in the United States. Like his father, he is also aware of the nature/nurture controversy: "It is the animal in me, not the man, that flees the gallows." He is prepared to kill his father to save his own life, and has "raised his arm to fire," when his half-sister Polly wounds him in the arm with her own pistol. Chesnutt skillfully diverts our attention from the mulatto's feelings at this point by describing Polly's action. When we next see the prisoner, he has changed once again: "His bravado had given place to a stony apathy. There was no sign in his face of fear or disappointment or feeling of any kind." When his father bandages the wound, the son "utter[s] no word of thanks or apology, but [sits] in sullen silence." Chesnutt tells us no more. He lets us put ourselves in the mulatto's situation to imagine what he might have been thinking and feeling locked overnight in his cell, making his decision to tear the bandage from his wound in order to bleed to death.

Questions for Discussion

1. Why does Chesnutt go into such detail in describing the setting of the story? What is the importance of the "sequestered," "conservative" nature of Branson County, North Carolina?
2. Analyze the process by which the lynch mob persuades itself to take justice into its own hands, ending in Chesnutt's simple statement, "a white man had been killed by a negro."
3. Why does the sheriff invite the negro Sam to have some dinner?
4. Why is the sheriff a hero to the people in the town?
5. Analyze the foreshadowing that Chesnutt has written into the passage beginning, "He had sworn to do his duty faithfully, and he knew what his duty was . . ." and continuing to the end of the paragraph.
6. Why is the sheriff able to talk the mob out of lynching the prisoner?
7. Why do you feel the prisoner took his own life? How does his action relate to the statement he made to his father, "You gave me a white man's spirit, and you made me a slave, and crushed it out"?

Topics for Writing

1. Research the history of the changing social position of African Americans in the southern states after the Civil War.
2. Analyze Chesnutt's explanation of why the sheriff hesitates to promise *not* to go after the mulatto after he escapes from jail: "[T]he baleful influence of human slavery poisoned the very foundations of life, and created new standards of right. The sheriff was conscientious: his conscience had merely been warped by his environment."
3. Analyze the racial stereotypes in the story.
4. **CONNECTIONS** Compare and contrast Chesnutt's dramatization of black-white relations in the South with that in the stories by William Faulkner and Zora Neale Hurston.

Suggested Readings

Chesnutt, Charles Waddell. *The Conjure Woman and Other Conjure Tales.* R. Broadhead, ed. Durham, NC: Duke UP, 1993.

———. *The Wife of His Youth, and Other Stories of the Color Line.* Ridgewood, NJ: Gregg, 1967.

Render, Sylvia Lyons. *Charles W. Chesnutt.* Boston: Twayne, 1980.

———. ed. *The Short Fiction of Charles W. Chesnutt.* Washington, DC: Howard UP, 1974.

KATE CHOPIN

Désirée's Baby (p. 316)

It is difficult to imagine a reader who would not be horrified and disgusted by the tragic results of the racism and sexism that permeate this story. No one could believe that Armand Aubigny's inhuman cruelty to his wife Désirée and his child is warranted. The only real uncertainty the reader confronts regards Armand's foreknowledge of his own parentage: Did he know that his mother had "negro blood" before he married Désirée, or did he discover her revealing letter later on? If he *did* know beforehand (and it is difficult to believe that he did not) his courtship of and marriage to Désirée were highly calculated actions, with Désirée chosen because she was the perfect woman to be used in an "experimental" reproduction. If their child(ren) "passed" as white, everything would be fine. If not, Désirée, the foundling, would be the perfect victim to take the blame.

This may seem to be judging Armand too harshly, because the narrator does describe his great passion for Désirée, so suddenly and furiously ignited. Certainly Armand behaves like a man in love. But Chopin inserts a few subtle remarks that allow us to question this, at least in hindsight: "The wonder was that he had not loved her before; for he had known her since his father brought him home from Paris, a boy of eight, after his mother died there." It does seem unlikely that a man of Armand's temperament would conceive this sudden intense desire for "the girl next door," a sweet, naive young woman whom he has known for most of his life. Right from the beginning, Chopin also reveals details about his character that are unsettling, even to the innocent and loving Désirée. The basic cruelty of Armand's nature is hinted at throughout the story, particularly regarding his severe treatment of "his negroes," which is notably in sharp contrast to his father's example.

Armand's reputation as a harsh slavemaster supports the presumption that he has known about his own part-negro ancestry all along. He did not learn this behavior from his father, who was "easy-going and indulgent" in his dealings with the slaves. The knowledge that some of his own ancestor spring from the same "race of slavery" would surely be unbearable to the proud, "imperious" Armand, and the rage and shame that his knowledge brings would easily be turned against the blacks around him. In much the same way, when Armand realizes that his baby is visibly racially mixed, he vents his fury viciously on his slaves, the "very spirit of Satan [taking] hold of him."

Modern readers will find many disturbing aspects to this story. The seemingly casual racism is horrifying. And feminists will be likely to take exception (as they sometimes do to Chopin's "The Awakening") to Désirée's passive acceptance of Armand's rejection of her and his child, and her apparently deliberate walk into the bayou. Suicide is not the strong woman's answer to the situation, but Désirée is definitely not a strong woman. What she does have is wealthy parents who love her and are willing to take care of her and the baby. So why would she feel that she has to end her life? Discussion of this issue will have to focus on the historical period and social setting of the story. Gender and class roles and structures were so rigid that it was impossible for a woman to cross those lines very far. If she tried, what would the cost be to her children? And of course, the most rigid barrier of all was racial. No mixing of black and white blood would ever be condoned in that society (thus, Armand's mother remained in France, keeping her family secrets), so Désirée's baby would never have acceptance anywhere. Désirée isn't able to see any viable way out of her terrifying situation, and her view is not entirely unrealistic, considering her time and place. Once again, Kate Chopin realistically depicts the cruelty and horror of a social structure that totally denies power to women, children, the poor, and most of all, to blacks.

Questions for Discussion

1. Describe your feelings toward Armand at the end of the story. What aspect of this last scene do you find the most shocking? Are you completely surprised by his behavior here? See if you can trace Chopin's gradual building of Armand's character, noting the things she chooses to reveal to us throughout the story.

2. What kind of a person is Désirée? Does she seem to be a good match for Armand? Does your opinion of her change as the story progresses? How consistent is she as a character?

3. How do you feel about Désirée's final choice? Is suicide an understandable choice, or is she simply a weak character? What other options do you think she may have?

4. Should Madame Valmondé have told Désirée of her realization about the baby? When she sees the baby at four weeks of age, she obviously is startled by something in its appearance, but doesn't mention it. Then, she returns

home and seems to wait for disaster to strike, never returning to visit Désirée. How do you explain this behavior, coming from an obviously protective, loving mother?

5. Armand is shown to be a very cruel master to his slaves, a direct contrast to the way in which his father ran the plantation. Does learning his family secret in the last scene suggest any explanation for this?

6. Do you think Armand knew about his own mother's negro ancestry before he courted and married Désirée? Look for evidence from the story to support your opinion.

Topics for Writing

1. Discuss the way the setting affects the action in this story.
2. Should Désirée have returned to her family home with her baby? Consider the pros and cons of her future there.
3. According to the critic Wai-chee Dimock, the racial injustice in "Désirée's Baby" is "only a necessary background against which Chopin stages her deadly dramatic irony. . . . The injustice here is not the injustice of racial oppression but the injustice of a wrongly attributed racial identity." Agree or disagree with this interpretation of the story.
4. **CONNECTIONS** Compare and contrast "Désirée's Baby" and Chesnutt's "The Sheriff's Children," two stories about mulatto offspring.

Suggested Readings

See page 70.

KATE CHOPIN

The Story of an Hour (p. 320)

Does the O. Henryesque trick ending of this story merely surprise us, or does Chopin arrange to have Louise Mallard expire at the sight of her unexpectedly still living husband in order to make a thematic point? Students inclined to groan when Brently Mallard returns "composedly carrying his gripsack and umbrella" may come to think better of the ending if you ask them to evaluate the doctors' conclusions about the cause of Mrs. Mallard's death. Although Richards and Josephine take "great care . . . to break to her as gently as possible the news of her husband's death," what actually kills Mrs. Mallard is the news that he is still alive. The experience of regeneration and freedom that she undergoes in the armchair looking out upon a springtime vista involves an almost sexual surrender of conventional repressions and restraints. As she *abandons herself* to the realization of her freedom that *approaches to possess her*, Mrs. Mallard enjoys a hitherto forbidden physical and spiritual excitement. The presumption that she would be devastated by the death of her husband, like the presumption that she needs to be protected by watchful, "tender" friends, reduces Mrs. Mallard to a dependency from which she is joyful at last to escape. Chopin best images this oppressive, debilitating concern in what Mrs. Mallard thinks she will weep again to see: "the kind, tender hands folded in death; the face that had never looked save with love upon her, fixed and gray and dead." Although had she lived Mrs. Mallard might have felt guilty for, as it were, taking her selfhood like a lover and pridefully stepping forth "like a goddess of Victory," Chopin effectively suggests that the guilt belongs instead to the caretakers, the "travel-stained" Brently, the discomfited Josephine, and Richards, whose "quick motion" to conceal his error comes "too late."

WILLIAM E. SHEIDLEY

Questions for Discussion

1. In view of Mrs. Mallard's eventual reactions, evaluate the efforts of Josephine and Richards to break the news of her husband's death gently.
2. What purpose might Chopin have in stressing that Mrs. Mallard does not block out the realization that her husband has died?
3. What might be the cause or causes of the "physical exhaustion that haunted her body and seemed to reach into her soul" that Mrs. Mallard feels as she sinks into the armchair?
4. Describe your reaction to the view out the window the first time you read the story. Did it change on a second reading?
5. Mrs. Mallard's face bespeaks repression. What has she been repressing?
6. Discuss the imagery Chopin uses to describe Mrs. Mallard's recognition of her new freedom.
7. What kind of man is Brently Mallard, as Mrs. Mallard remembers him? In what ways does he resemble Josephine and Richards?
8. Describe your feelings about Mrs. Mallard as she emerges from her room. Is the saying "Pride goeth before a fall" relevant here?
9. In what way is the doctors' pronouncement on the cause of Mrs. Mallard's death ironic? In what sense is it nonetheless correct?

Topics for Writing

1. Discuss the imagery of life and the imagery of death in "The Story of an Hour."
2. Write a paper analyzing "The Story of an Hour" as a thwarted awakening.
3. Describe the tragic irony in "The Story of an Hour."
4. On a second reading of "The Story of an Hour," try to recall how you responded to each paragraph or significant passage when you read it the first time. Write short explanations of any significant changes in your reactions. To what extent are those changes the result of knowing the story's ending? What other factors are at work?
5. Can falsehood be the key to truth? Narrate a personal experience in which your own or someone else's reaction to misinformation revealed something meaningful and true.
6. How long is a turning point? Tell a story covering a brief span of time — a few minutes or an hour — in which the central character's life is permanently changed. Study Chopin's techniques for summarizing and condensing information.

(text pp. 323–331)

Suggested Readings

Bender, B. "Kate Chopin's Lyrical Short Stories." *Studies in Short Fiction* 11 (1974): 257–66.

Chopin, Kate. *The Complete Works of Kate Chopin.* Baton Rouge: Louisiana State UP, 1970.

Dimock, Wai-chee. "Kate Chopin." *Modern American Women Writers.* Ed. Elaine Showalter et al. New York: Collier, 1993.

Fluck, Winifred. "Tentative Transgressions: Kate Chopin's Fiction as a Mode of Symbolic Action." *Studies in American Fiction* 10 (1982): 151–71.

Miner, Madonne M. "Veiled Hints: An Affected Stylist's Reading of Kate Chopin's 'Story of an Hour.' " *Markham Review* 11 (1982): 29–32.

Seyersted, Per. *Kate Chopin: A Critical Biography.* Baton Rouge: Louisiana State UP, 1969. 57–59.

Skaggs, Peggy. *Kate Chopin.* Boston: Twayne, 1985.

Toth, Emily. *Kate Chopin.* New York: Morrow, 1990.

Sandra Cisneros

Little Miracles, Kept Promises (p. 323)

Knowledge of the Hispanic background of this story would enrich interpretation, clarifying Spanish terms and religious references for students unfamiliar with this culture. The first part of the story consists of a series of brief letters to saints that have been left by petitioners before religious statues in towns along the border between Texas and Mexico. These letters are like miniature true-life anecdotes, revealing a good deal about the trials and difficulties of Hispanic families living along the border.

Students should be encouraged to read the letters carefully. Despite their brevity, they convey in their details a sense of the petitioners' lives. For example, Arnulfo Contreras's letter to the Virgin of Guadalupe (the tenth letter in the series) reveals that he was paid less than two dollars an hour after taxes when he worked his two-week job — and he has been waiting three weeks to get paid. He has been exploited for his labor much as the fictional character Dave, the seventeen-year-old son of a Mississippi tenant farmer in Richard Wright's story of thirty years before "The Man Who Was Almost a Man," has been.

Some Spanish terms used in the story include *Exvoto,* an offering in fulfillment of a vow; *retablo,* altarpiece; *La Virgencita,* the little Virgin, a familiar form of address to the Virgin of Guadalupe, a patron saint of Mexico; and *Santo Niño de Atocha,* Blessed child of Atocha. The last third of "Little Miracles, Kept Promises" is one long letter that becomes a story in itself, describing the "little miracle" of a rebellious young woman's coming of age in Austin, Texas. She learns to recognize the power in the women in her family, instead of being fixated on their passivity, and comes to understand the spirituality of the female goddess to whom she writes her letter:

> When I could see you in all your facets, all at once the Buddha, the Tao, the true Messiah, Yahweh, Allah, the Heart of the sky, the Heart of the

Earth, the Lord of the Near and Far, the spirit, the Light, the Universe,
I could love you, and, finally, learn to love me.

The rhythm of Cisneros's prose is undeniable, even if some readers might have difficulty understanding how the series of brief notes and personal letters in "Little Miracles, Kept Promises" cohere as a short story. Lacking a central character, a dramatic conflict, a well-developed plot, or a carefully described setting, the separate pieces of Cisneros's narrative nevertheless communicate a sense of emotional unity through the prose rhythms of her remarkable lyrical voice. Her narrative is as much a prose poem as it is a story.

Questions for Discussion

1. The background of this story is the Texas-Mexico border, but are the experiences of the impoverished Mexican settlers who are new to the United States unique, or are they similar to the experiences of other immigrant groups new to this country?
2. What are the recurrent problems described in the letters to the saints?
3. What are the specific "little miracles, kept promises" mentioned in the letters?
4. Why does Rosario cut off her hair?

Topic for Writing

1. Write a short story composed of a series of letters, formed either out of individual letters written by a series of people, as in this story, or out of correspondence between two people.

Suggested Reading

Cisneros, Sandra. *Woman Hollering Creek.* New York: Random, 1991.

JOSEPH CONRAD

Heart of Darkness (p. 333)

At the center of the concentric layers out of which Conrad constructs this story lies a case of atavism and the collapse of civilized morality. Kurtz casts aside all restraint and becomes as wild as his surroundings; or rather, the darkness around him calls out the darkness within his innermost being. Kurtz is a man of heroic abilities and exemplary ideals, yet at the end of the story, he explodes, unable to control his own strength.

Conrad does not provide an intimate inside view of Kurtz. To do so would destroy the aura of mystery and special significance that marks the story's theme as a profound revelation, the "culminating point of [Marlow's] experience," gained at "the farthest point of navigation." Instead, Conrad positions Kurtz in the midst of an impenetrable jungle, at "the very heart of darkness," as far from home and as remote from familiar frames of reference as possible. Then he causes the reader to approach Kurtz through a series of identifications that make the revelation of his debasement a statement not just about Kurtz, but about us all.

Conrad creates this effect mainly through his use of Marlow as narrator, and no discussion of the story can avoid exploring his function. He is on the one hand a kind of prophet — his pose resembles that of an idol or Buddha — whose wisdom arises from his having looked beyond the veil that screens the truth from common view ("the inner truth is hidden — luckily, luckily"), and on the other hand an adventurer like the heroes of epic poems, descending into Hades and emerging shaken with his dark illumination. But Marlow's vision is neither of heaven nor of hell. His journey up the Congo River is in fact a descent into the inner reaches of the human soul. Forced by a combination of circumstances and preconceptions into a special association with Kurtz, Marlow recognizes in that "shadow" the intrinsic darkness of human nature, in which he shares. When he plunges into the jungle to redeem Kurtz, who has crawled away on all fours to rejoin the "unspeakable rites" of his worshipers, Marlow embraces what Kurtz has become no less than what he once was or might have been, acknowledging his own kinship with the deepest depravity. Kurtz dies crying, "The horror!' The horror!" — apparently having regained from his rescuer enough of his moral bearings to recoil from his own behavior. Marlow, who judges the truth "too dark — too dark altogether," preserves the innocence of Kurtz's "Intended," leaving her "great and saving illusion" intact.

Conrad may be suggesting that only by a conscious lie or by willful blindness can we avoid sinking into the savagery that surrounds us, that dwells under externally maintained restraint within us, and that animates our civilization in various guises, such as the "flabby, pretending, weak-eyed devil of a rapacious and pitiless folly." The conquest of the earth, which is what the civilized society portrayed in the story is engaged in, "is not a pretty thing when you look into it too much," Marlow says. "What redeems it is the idea only . . . an unselfish belief in the idea — something you can set up, and bow down before, and offer sacrifice to." But such idolatry of our own idea is not far from its horrible perversion into the worship of himself that the would-be civilizer Kurtz sets up. It leads to a civilization aptly portrayed in Kurtz's symbolic painting of a blindfolded woman carrying a torch through darkness. If Conrad offers a glimmer of light in the dark world he envisions, it is in the sympathetic understanding that enables Marlow to befriend Kurtz and to lie for Kurtz and his Intended, even at the cost of having to taste the "flavor of mortality" he finds in lies, which he detests like the death it suggests to him.

WILLIAM E. SHEIDLEY

Questions for Discussion

1. What does Conrad gain by having his story told by Marlow to a group of important Londoners on a yacht in the Thames estuary? What is implied by the association of the Thames with the Congo? by Marlow's assertion, "And this also . . . has been one of the dark places on the earth"?

2. Marlow enters on his adventure through a city he associates with "a whited sepulcher"; he passes old women knitting who remind him of the Fates; the Company office is "as still as a house in a city of the dead." Locate other indications that Marlow's journey is like a trip into the underworld. What do they suggest about the story's meaning?
3. In what ways is the French warship "shelling the bush" an apt image of the European conquest of Africa? What does this historical theme contribute to our understanding of Marlow and Kurtz?
4. Discuss the Company's chief accountant. Why is it appropriate that Marlow first hears of Kurtz from him?
5. Marlow calls the men waiting for a post in the interior "pilgrims." Explain the irony in his use of the term.
6. Marlow is associated with Kurtz as a member of "the gang of virtue." Explain the resonance of that phrase.
7. Describe the journey up the Congo as Marlow reports it in the pages that follow his remark, "Going up that river was like traveling back to the earliest beginnings of the world." In what ways does Conrad make it a symbolic journey as well as an actual one?
8. Discuss Marlow's attitudes toward the natives. What do they mean to him?
9. As the boat draws near Kurtz's station, people cry out "with unrestrained grief" from the jungle. Why?
10. After the attack of the natives is repulsed and the narrative seems at the point of reaching the climax toward which so much suspense has been built — the meeting with Kurtz — Conrad throws it away by having Marlow stop to light his pipe and speak offhandedly and abstractly about what he learned. Why? Does this passage actually destroy the suspense? Is the story rendered anticlimactic? Or is the climax changed? What is the true climax of the story?
11. Why do you think the heads on stakes are facing Kurtz's house?
12. Discuss the Russian and his attitude toward Kurtz. Why does Conrad trouble to add this European to Kurtz's train of cultists?
13. Marlow is astonished that the Manager calls Kurtz's methods "unsound." Why? What does this passage reveal about each of them?
14. Explain what happens to Marlow when he goes into the bush after Kurtz. Explain what happens to Kurtz. Why does Marlow call Kurtz "that shadow"?
15. Marlow claims to have "struggled with a soul"; he tells Kurtz that if he does not come back he will be "utterly lost." Is Marlow a savior for Kurtz? Is Kurtz saved?
16. Why does Marlow lie to Kurtz's "Intended"?
17. Contrast the last paragraph of the story with the opening.
18. Comment on the title of Kurtz's pamphlet, about the "Suppression of Savage Customs," and on the significance of its scrawled postscript, "Exterminate all the brutes."

Topics for Writing

1. In an essay, explore Conrad's use of foreshadowing.
2. Discuss traditional symbolism and literary allusion as a way of universalizing the theme of "Heart of Darkness."
3. Analyze the function of the frame in this novella.

4. Marlow frequently concludes a segment of his narrative with a generalization that sums it up and takes on a quality of special significance, such as, "I
felt as though, instead of going to the center of a continent, I were about to
set off for the center of the earth"; or, "It was like a weary pilgrimage among
hints for nightmares." Locate as many such passages as you can. What do
they reveal about the mind of the narrator?

5. Conrad frequently uses an impressionist technique that Ian Watt has called
"delayed decoding." When the steamboat is attacked, for example, Marlow
first sees "little sticks" flying about, and only later recognizes them as
arrows. Find other instances of delayed decoding in the story, and then write
a narrative of your own using a similar method.

6. **CONNECTIONS** Analyze the journey into madness in Conrad's "Heart of
Darkness" and Gilman's "The Yellow Wallpaper."

Related Commentaries

Chinua Achebe, An Image of Africa: Conrad's "Heart of Darkness," p. 1373.
Lionel Trilling, The Greatness of Conrad's "Heart of Darkness," p. 1501.

Suggested Readings

Bender, Todd K. *Concordances to Conrad's "The Shadow Line" and "Youth": A
Narrative*. New York, Garland, 1980.

Bennett, Carl D. *Joseph Conrad*. New York: Continuum, 1991.

Berthoud, Jacques. *Joseph Conrad: The Major Phase*. New York: Cambridge UP, 1978.
41–63.

Billy, Ted. *Critical Essays on Joseph Conrad*. Boston: G. K. Hall, 1987.

Cohen, Michael. *Sailing through "The Secret Sharer": The End of Conrad's Story*.
Studies in English 10(2) (Fall 1988): 102–09.

Conrad, Joseph. *Heart of Darkness: An Authoritative Text, Backgrounds and Sources,
Criticism*. Ed. Robert Kimbrough. Rev. ed. New York: Norton, 1971.

Conrad, Joseph. *Portable Conrad*. New York: Penguin, 1991.

Gekoski, R. A. *Conrad: The Moral World of the Novelist*. New York: Barnes,
1978. 72–90.

Gillon, Adam. *Joseph Conrad*. Boston: Twayne, 1982.

Graver, Lawrence. *Conrad's Short Fiction*. Berkeley: U of California P, 1969.

Hynes, Samuel, ed. *The Complete Short Fiction of Joseph Conrad. The Stories, Volume
I*. New York: Ecco, 1991.

Page, Norman. *A Conrad Companion*. New York: St. Martin's, 1986.

JULIO CORTÁZAR

Axolotl (p. 397)

Webster's Dictionary defines *axolotl* (pronounced ak-so-letl) as a type of
salamander living and breeding without metamorphosing in the lakes of Mexico
and the western United States. The joke of Cortázar's fantastic story, of course, is

that he dramatizes the inverse metamorphosing that occurs when his obsessed first-person narrator suddenly turns into a salamander and begins a life inside a tank in the Paris aquarium.

In giving his story a sense of closure and enclosure, Cortázar has constructed it so that it appears to be as water-tight as an aquarium tank. The remarkably self-contained narrative structure might seem to the attentive reader to stand in marked contrast to the tone of the narrator in relating the events of the story, which seems relaxed and casual. Consider the opening sentence: "There was a time when I thought a great deal about the axolotls." The understated quality of this statement disarms the casual reader into thinking, perhaps, that nothing much is going on here. Yet two sentences later, concluding the first paragraph, we read a simple assertion of fact, "Now I am an axolotl," and think to ourselves, "How can this be true?" Thus are we caught up in the story in much the same manner as Franz Kafka disarms us in the opening paragraph of "The Metamorphosis."

The narrator's sympathy for the "silent and immobile figures" of the axolotls is perhaps similar to the reader's sympathy for Kafka's Gregor Samsa, a sensitive, caring human soul who upon awakening one morning finds himself trapped inside the body of a monstrous insect. Cortázar's nameless narrator is fascinated by the "diaphanous interior mystery" of the axolotls' lidless eyes, so unlike the "simple stupidity of the handsome eyes" of fishes in nearby tanks that strike him as "so similar to our own." He cannot tear himself away from "the presence of a different life, of another way of seeing" in the axolotls, who seem to him to possess "a mysterious humanity."

Empathizing with their pain, "that stiff torment at the bottom of the tank" where they suffer their timeless immobility, the narrator presses his face against the glass of the tank. Suddenly his reflection is on the other side of the glass, and he is one with the axolotls. He has committed an irreversible act, and his reward is his instant understanding that communication is no more possible between the different creatures living inside and outside the aquarium tank than between the living and the dead.

One possible interpretation of the story is that Cortázar has dramatized a human being's awareness of the common link between different animal species and written a fantasy story about it. "Axolotl" ends like a Zen koan, or puzzle about the nature of existence. The human narrator metamorphosized into a salamander is now obsessed with thoughts about the human being outside the aquarium tank who used to visit in order to gaze upon the life inside the tank, so he imagines that person at home "making up a story, he's going to write all this about axolotls."

In his essay "On the Short Short Story and Its Environs," Cortázar developed his idea that the best contemporary stories followed Edgar Allan Poe's rule, as Cortázar presented it, that a short story should demonstrate "the maximum economy of means . . . that implacable race against time. . . . It seems to me that the archetypal stories of the last hundred years have come out of a merciless elimination of . . . editorializing, circumlocutions, gradual unfoldings and other narrative devices. . . . [T]he astonishing thing about race-against-time stories is that they draw a lightning charge out of a minimum of elements."

Cortázar also stated that he believes that first-person narration like that in "Axolotl" and Poe's "The Cask of Amontillado" gives the writer the best means of achieving the dramatic compression of his materials because the first-person perspective "plops us right inside" the fantasy that obsesses the writer. Writing for

Cortázar is a process of exorcism, "rejecting invading beings by casting them out into a condition that paradoxically gives them a universal existence at the same time it sets them at the other end of the bridge. . . . [E]very top-flight short story, and especially fantastic stories, come out of neurosis, nightmares and hallucinations neutralized by being objectified and moved to a medium away from the neurotic terrain." Writing a story is the way an author can rid himself of an obsession, "exorcising it the only way he could: by writing it."

Questions for Discussion

1. What sort of man is the narrator of "Axolotl"? Why does he have so much free time to spend at the aquarium? What does his visit to the library tell you about him?
2. What is the effect of the narrator's casual way of speaking, for example his statement in the second paragraph, "I hit it off with the axolotls." (Remember that this is a translation from the Spanish.)
3. What is the effect of the narrator's shift to first person plural in the middle of the story: "It's that we don't enjoy moving a lot, and the tank is so cramped. . . . The time feels like it's less if we stay quietly"?
4. How does the narrator convince you that the axolotls are intelligent creatures?
5. How does he convince you that he has become an axolotl?

Topics for Writing

1. Is writing a short story "dreaming while awake," as Cortázar maintained? Write an essay in which you explore this definition, referring to the events in "Axolotl" for your examples.
2. **CONNECTIONS** Compare and contrast the elements of fantasy in "Axolotl" and Octavio Paz's "My Life with the Wave," paying particular attention to what Cortázar called "the tension, rhythm, and inner beat" that he valued most in poetry, jazz, and short fiction.

Suggested Readings

Alazraki, Jaime, and Ivar Ivask, eds. *The Final Island: The Fiction of Julio Cortázar.* Norman: U of Oklahoma P, 1978.

Cortázar, Julio. *Around the Day in Eighty Worlds.* Tr. Thomas Christensen. San Francisco: North Point, 1986. Esp. 17–23, 158–67.

———. *Blow Up and Other Stories.* London: Panther, 1967.

STEPHEN CRANE

The Open Boat (p. 402)

Crane's story fictionalizes an actual experience. A correspondent himself, Crane happened to be aboard the *Commodore* when it went down, and he included in his newspaper report of the event this passage (as quoted by E. R. Hagemann):

> The history of life in an open boat for thirty hours would no doubt be instructive for the young, but none is to be told here now. For my part I would prefer to tell the story at once, because from it would shine the splendid manhood of Captain Edward Murphy and of William Higgins, the oiler, but let it suffice at this time to say that when we were swamped in the surf and making the best of our way toward the shore the captain gave orders amid the wildness of the breakers as clearly as if he had been on the quarter deck of a battleship.

It is good that Crane did not write "at once" but let his experience take shape as a work of art which, instead of celebrating the "splendid manhood" of two or four individuals, recognizes a profound truth about human life in general — about the puniness of humankind in the face of an indifferent nature and about the consequent value of the solidarity and compassion that arise from an awareness of our common fate. Crane's meditation on his experience "after the fact" enables him to become not simply a reporter but, as he puts it in the last line of the story, an *interpreter* of the message spoken to us by the world we confront.

Crane portrays the exertions of the four men in the boat without glamorizing them. His extended and intimate account of their hard work and weariness wrings out any false emotion from the reader's view of the situation. By varying the narrative point of view from a coolly detached objective observer to a plural account of all four men's shared feelings and perceptions to the correspondent's rueful, self-mocking cogitations, Crane defeats our impulse to choose a hero for adulation, at the same time driving home the point that the condition of the men in the dinghy — their longing, their fear, and their powerlessness before nature and destiny —reflects our own. By the end, what has been revealed is so horrible that there can be no triumph in survival. The good fortune of a rescue brings only a reprieve, not an escape from what awaits us. Billie the oiler drowns, but there is no reason it should have been he, or only he. His death could be anybody's death.

Crane's narration builds suspense through rhythmic repetition, foreshadowing, and irony. We hear the surf periodically: Our hopes for rescue are repeatedly raised and dashed; night follows day, wave follows wave, and the endless struggle goes on. The correspondent's complaint against the cruelty of fate recurs in diminuendo, with less whimsy and self-consciousness each time.

These recurrences mark the men's changes in attitude — from the egocentric viewpoint they start with, imagining that the whole world is watching them and working for their survival, to the perception of the utter indifference of nature with which the story ends. Some stages in this progression include their false sense of security when they light up the cigars; their isolation from the people on shore, epitomized by their inability to interpret the signal of the man waving his coat (whose apparent advice to try another stretch of beach they nonetheless inadvertently follow); their experience of aloneness at night; their confrontation with the hostility of nature in the shark; and, finally, their recognition that death might be a welcome release from toil and suffering. They respond by drawing together in a communion that sustains them, sharing their labor and their body heat, huddled together in their tiny, helpless dinghy. Even their strong bond of comradeship, however, cannot withstand the onslaught of the waves. When the boat is swamped, it is every man for himself: Each individual must face death alone. Because of the fellowship that has grown up among them, however, when Billie dies, each of the others feels the oiler's death as his own. The reader, whom Crane's narrative has caused to share thirty hours at sea in an open boat, may recognize the implication in what is spoken by "the sound of the great sea's voice to the men on shore."

WILLIAM E. SHEIDLEY

Questions for Discussion

1. Contrast the imagery and the tone of the first paragraph with those of the second. Why does Crane continually seek to magnify nature and to belittle the men who are struggling with it? Find other instances of Crane's reductive irony, and discuss their effects.
2. How does Crane convey the men's concentration on keeping the boat afloat?
3. Explain Crane's use of the word "probably" in the first paragraph of section II.
4. Why does the seagull seem "somehow gruesome and ominous" to the men in the boat? Compare and contrast the seagull with the shark that appears later.
5. Comment on the imagery Crane uses to describe changing seats in the dinghy (stealing eggs, Sèvres).
6. What is it that the correspondent "knew even at the time was the best experience of his life"? Why is it best?
7. What is the purpose of Crane's understatement in the line "neither the oiler nor the correspondent was fond of rowing at this time"?
8. What is the effect on the reader of the men's lighting up cigars?
9. Discuss the meaning of the correspondent's question "Was I brought here merely to have my nose dragged away as I was about to nibble the sacred cheese of life?"
10. What do you think the man waving a coat means? Why is it impossible for him to communicate with the men in the boat?
11. "A night on the sea in an open boat is a long night," says Crane. How does he make the reader feel the truth of that assertion?
12. At one point the correspondent thinks that he is "the one man afloat on all the oceans." Explain that sensation. Why does the wind he hears sound "sadder than the end"? Why does he later wish he had known the captain was awake when the shark came by?
13. Why does the correspondent have a different attitude toward the poem about the dying soldier in Algiers from the one he had as a boy?
14. Examine the third paragraph of section VII. How important are the thoughts of the correspondent to our understanding of the story? What would the story lose if they were omitted? What would the effect of this passage have been if Crane had narrated the story in the first person? If he had made these comments in the voice of an omniscient third-person narrator?

15. Define the correspondent's physical, mental, and emotional condition during his final moments on the boat and during his swim to the beach.
16. Characterize and explain the tone of Crane's description of the man who pulls the castaways from the sea.
17. Why does Crane make fun of the women who bring coffee to the survivors?

Topics for Writing

1. Consider Crane's handling of point of view in "The Open Boat."
2. Discuss the importance of repetition in Crane's narrative.
3. Analyze imagery as a key to tone in "The Open Boat."
4. After reading the story once rapidly, read it again with a pencil in hand, marking every simile and metaphor. Then sort them into categories. What realms of experience does Crane bring into view through these devices that are not actually part of the simple boat-sea-sky-beach world in which the story is set? Why?
5. Write an eyewitness account of some experience you have undergone that would be suitable for newspaper publication. Then note the changes you would make to turn it into a fictional narrative with broader or more profound implications — or write that story.

Related Commentary

Stephen Crane, The Sinking of the *Commodore*, p. 1408.

Suggested Readings

Adams, Richard P. "Naturalistic Fiction: 'The Open Boat.' " *Stephen Crane's Career: Perspectives and Evaluations.* Ed. Thomas A. Gullason. New York: New York UP, 1972. 421–29. Originally published in *Tulane Studies in English* 4 (1954): 137–46.

Cady, Edwin H. *Stephen Crane.* Twayne's United States Authors Series 23. Rev. ed. Boston: G. K. Hall, 1980. 150–54.

Colvert, James B. *Stephen Crane.* New York: Ungar, 1987.

Follett, Wilson, ed. *The Work of Stephen Crane.* New York: Knopf, 1925.

Fryckstedt, O. W., ed. *Stephen Crane: Uncollected Writings.* Uppsala: Studia Anglistica Upsaliensia, 1963.

Hagemann, E. R. " 'Sadder than the End': Another Look at 'The Open Boat.' " *Stephen Crane in Transition: Centenary Essays.* Ed. Joseph Katz. DeKalb: Northern Illinois UP, 1972. 66–85.

Johnson, Glen M. "Stephen Crane." *American Short-Story Writers, 1880–1910. Dictionary of Literary Biography,* vol. 78. Detroit: Gale, 1989.

Katz, Joseph, ed. *The Portable Stephen Crane.* New York: Viking, 1985.

Kissane, Leedice. "Interpretation through Language: A Study of the Metaphors in Stephen Crane's 'The Open Boat.' " Gullason, cited above. 410–16. Originally published in *Rendezvous* (Idaho State U) 1 (1966): 18–22.

Knapp, Bettina L. *Stephen Crane.* New York: Ungar, 1987.

Stallman, R. W. *Stephen Crane: A Critical Bibliography.* Ames: Iowa State UP, 1972.

————. *Stories and Tales/Stephen Crane.* New York: Vintage, 1955.

Wolford, Chester L. *Stephen Crane: A Study of the Short Fiction.* Boston: Twayne, 1989.

Isak Dinesen

The Sailor-Boy's Tale (p. 421)

Dinesen's fantasy story is for the young-at-heart and incorrigibly romantic. Students will probably enjoy the adventures of a young man who starts off believing, after his narrow experience of life, "that in this world everyone must look after himself and expect no help from others," but who learns in the course of the story that life is neither quite so predictable nor quite so grim as he believed it to be.

"The Sailor-Boy's Tale" might have begun "Once upon a time," for a sense of wonder is at its center. This is generated by Simon's acting on his "higher feelings" — first the sense of brotherhood or "common tragedy" he feels onboard the Mediterranean barque when he decides to rescue the trapped peregrine falcon caught in the tackle-yarn at the top of the mast; then his sense of "a new benevolence in the world" in the magic northern light that he notices shining on the April sea and sky in the seaport on the coast of Norway, not far from the Arctic Circle. Once he shows pity and rescues the bird, he is a charmed man, although he doesn't know it. Dinesen suggests that fate operates in the world like a balancing scale: one favor deserves another.

But if the lives of all creatures intersect and are joined by fate, life isn't necessarily simple or easy in Dinesen's model of the world. Creatures also have their own space, a separate "aura" that must be respected. When Ivan, the burly, drunken Russian sailor, hugs Simon, insisting they spend the evening together despite Simon's protests, crushing the boy "like a bear that carries off a sheep," Simon's personal space has been violated and Dinesen suggests he is within his rights to kill Ivan. Tender-hearted Simon feels great remorse, but the flirtatious yet sensible Nora, with whom he has fallen in love, doesn't renounce him. Instead, appropriately, she distances herself from him. "No, I do not hate you," she says, when he tells her of the stabbing. "But do put your hands at your back."

Dinesen constructs the beautifully proportioned plot of her tale as elegantly as she does her world-view. After a one-page introduction describing Simon's rescue of the falcon that establishes the sailor-boy's generous if immature character, Dinesen takes a page to set the sun-drenched Norwegian scene and introduce Nora, whom Simon loves at first sight. Two more pages introduce complications that threaten the development of this love, resolved by Simon's impetuous knifing of Ivan. Next come two additional pages of complications to the homicide, when the old Lapp woman Sunniva (whom we met previously incarnated in the body of the falcon) takes Simon into her home and saves him from the mob that is searching for Ivan's killer. The final page is the story's conclusion, when Sunniva releases Simon at daybreak so he can return to his ship and tells him, "Now we are quits."

A generous act of mercy has been reciprocated, and Dinesen's fabulous world has returned to balance.

Questions for Discussion

1. Why are Simon's youth and small size emphasized in the story?
2. Why does the bird bite Simon's thumb? What is his response?
3. What do we learn about Simon after he brings the falcon down from the mast?
4. How do you explain the miraculous light in the sky "high up on the coast of Norway"?
5. Why does Simon give Nora an orange? Why does she agree to give him a kiss for it?
6. Why is it significant that Nora's father is the parson in the seacoast village?
7. Why does Nora agree to marry Simon after she's kissed him?

Topics for Writing

1. Write a paper analyzing the character of Sunniva after you have researched Norse mythology for information about the sun god. How does her metamorphosis into a falcon relate to her existence as Sunniva? Which is the "true" form of this character?
2. How does Dinesen introduce humor into "The Sailor-Boy's Tale"? For example, why does Sunniva tell Simon that she turned herself into a falcon in order to visit her younger sister and her children in Africa?
3. **CONNECTIONS** Compare and contrast the role of the generous hero in "The Sailor-Boy's Tale" and Calvino's "The Feathered Ogre."

Suggested Readings

Dinesen, Isak. *Winter's Tales.* New York: Random, 1942, 1970.

Hannah, Donald. "In Memoriam Karen Blixen: Some Aspects of Her Attitude to Life." *Sewanee Review* 71 (1963): 585–604.

Landry, M. "Anecdote as Destiny: Isak Dinesen and the Story-Teller." *Massachusetts Review* 19 (1978): 389–406.

RALPH ELLISON

Battle Royal (p. 430)

In the headnote to his comments on "Battle Royal" reprinted in Part Two (p. 1411), Ellison is quoted expounding on the importance of "converting experience into symbolic action" in fiction. One of the major triumphs of "Battle Royal" (and of *Invisible Man* as a whole) is Ellison's success in the realistic rendering of experiences that are in themselves so obviously significant of larger social, psychological, and moral truths that explication is unnecessary. From the small American flag tattooed on the nude dancer's belly to the "rope of bloody saliva forming a shape like an undiscovered continent" that the narrator drools on his new briefcase, Ellison's account of the festivities at the men's smoker effectively symbolizes the condition of blacks in America while remaining thoroughly persuasive in its verisimilitude. Both the broader structure of the evening and the finer details of narration and description carry the force of Ellison's theme. The young blacks are tortured first by having the most forbidden of America's riches dangled before them, then by being put through their paces in a melee in which their only victims are their fellows and the whites look on with glee, and finally by being debased into groveling for money (some of it counterfeit) on a rug whose electrification underlines their own powerlessness. In one brief passage, the nightmare of such an existence appears in a strange subaqueous vision of primitive life: "The boys groped about like blind, cautious crabs crouching to protect their midsections, their heads pulled in short against their shoulders, their arms stretched nervously before them, with their fists testing the smoke-filled air like the knobbed feelers of hypersensitive snails."

Because his actual experience forms itself into such revealing images, the narrator's dream of his grandfather seems all the more credible as a statement of his position. "Keep This Nigger-Boy Running," he dreams the message of his briefcase says — not far from "You've got to know your place at all times." The narrator's grandfather knew his place and played his role, but he never believed a word of it. It is this assurance of an inner being quite different from the face he turned toward the world that makes him so troubling to his descendants. In his effort to please the white folks and in so doing to get ahead, the narrator seeks alliance rather than secret enmity with his antagonists. As a result he subjects himself to the trickery and delusions the white community chooses to impose on him. Dependent for his sense of himself on his ability to guess what they want him to do, the narrator finds himself groping in a fog deeper than the swirls of cigar smoke that hang over the scene of the battle royal. When the smoke clears and the blindfold comes off, he will recognize, as he puts it at the start, that he is invisible to the whites and may therefore discover his own identity within himself.

The first episode of a long novel does not accomplish the narrator's enlightenment, but it constitutes his initiation into the realities of the world he must eventually come to understand. Ellison says (in the Commentary in Part Two, p. 1412) that the battle royal "is a ritual in preservation of caste lines, a keeping of taboo to appease the gods and ward off bad luck," and that "it is also the initiation ritual to which all greenhorns are subjected." This rite of initiation bears a revealing relation to the primitive initiation ceremonies known to anthropologists. The battle royal, for example, separates the boys from their families, challenges them to prove their valor, and subjects them to instruction by the tribal elders in a sort of men's house. The boys are stripped and introduced to sexual mysteries. But the hazing of women that is a frequent feature of such initiations is not carried on here by the boys but by the gross elders, whose savagery is barely under control; the ritual ends not with the entry of the initiates into the larger community but with their pointed exclusion; and the sacred lore embodied in the narrator's recital of his graduation speech makes explicit the contradictions inherent in the society it describes. To cast down his bucket where he is forces him to swallow his own blood. The narrator is delighted with the scholarship to "the state college for Negroes" that he wins by toeing the line and knowing his place, and he does not object that the "gold" coins he groveled for are fraudulent. His education in the meaning of his grandfather's troubling injunctions will continue, but the reader has already seen enough to recognize their validity.

WILLIAM E. SHEIDLEY

Questions for Discussion

1. In the opening paragraph the narrator says, "I was naïve." In what ways is his naiveté revealed in the story that follows?
2. Why does the narrator feel guilty when praised?
3. What is the message to the narrator behind the suggestion "that since I was to be there anyway I might as well take part in the battle royal"? Explain his hesitation. What is the most important part of the evening for the whites?
4. Who is present at the smoker? Discuss the role of the school superintendent.
5. What techniques does Ellison use to convey to the reader the impact that seeing the stripper has on the boys?
6. What does the stripper have in common with the boys? Why are both a stripper and a battle royal part of the evening's entertainment?
7. During the chaos of the battle, the narrator worries about how his speech will be received. Is that absurd or understandable?
8. Does the deathbed advice of the narrator's grandfather offer a way to handle the battle royal?
9. Why does Tatlock refuse to take a dive?
10. Explain the narrator's first reaction to seeing the "small square rug." In what sense is his instinct correct?
11. What is the meaning of the electric rug to the whites? What do they wish it to demonstrate to the blacks?
12. Explain Mr. Colcord's reaction when the narrator tries to topple him onto the rug.
13. Analyze the narrator's speech. What is the implication of his having to deliver it while swallowing his own blood?
14. Why is the school superintendent confident that the narrator will "lead his people in the proper paths"?
15. Why does the narrator stand in front of his grandfather's picture holding his briefcase? Who gets the better of this confrontation?

Topics for Writing

1. Make a study of seeing and understanding in "Battle Royal."
2. Analyze the role of sex, violence, and power in Ellison's "Battle Royal."
3. Write an essay exploring the battle royal and black experience in America.
4. Describe the "permanent interest" of "Battle Royal." (See Ellison's Commentary in Part Two, p. 1412).
5. Examine the blonde, the gold coins, and the calfskin briefcase in "Battle Royal."
6. Select a passage of twenty lines or less from this story for detailed explication. Relate as many of its images as possible to others in the story and to the general ideas that the story develops. To what extent does the passage you chose reflect the meaning of the story as a whole?

7. Recall an experience in which you were humiliated or embarrassed. What motives of your own and of those before whom you were embarrassed put you in such a position? Narrate the incident so these underlying purposes become evident to the reader.

8. Write a description of a game or ceremony with which you are familiar. What set of principles or relationships (not necessarily malign) does it express?

Related Commentary

Ralph Ellison, The Influence of Folklore on "Battle Royal," p. 1412.

Suggested Readings

See page 85.

RALPH ELLISON

King of the Bingo Game (p. 441)

In contrast to the realistic story "Battle Royal," Ellison's early story "King of the Bingo Game" is an impressionistic, even surrealistic narrative about the ghettoization of African Americans in the United States at mid-century, before the Civil Rights movement of the 1960s changed social attitudes in this country. When the nameless protagonist of "King of the Bingo Game" fills in his card in the movie theater and wins the chance to go onstage and press the button to stop the wheel of fortune, he thinks he is in control of his fate for the first time in his life.

Then, instead of winning the "big money" jackpot of $36.90, he loses control of himself in his excitement and is knocked unconscious by the theater police. Ellison's compassion for the unemployed man driven to desperation by his hunger and his thoughts of his sick wife Laura " 'bout to die 'cause we got no money for a doctor" makes the reader a participant in the story. At the beginning of the story we smell the delicious roasted peanuts with the man in the audience; at the end we feel the "dull pain exploding in his skull" from the crushing blow administered to him from behind and share his ironic sense before losing consciousness that "his luck had run out on the stage" although he saw that he'd stopped the wheel at double zero.

Ellison's account of how the man feels holding the button of the wheel of fortune is the main event in the story, comprising nearly half of the narrative. Ellison's pacing here is leisurely, more like the extended description of a novelist creating a chapter of a long work than the compression of a writer fashioning a short story. At first the man seems to be aware that he's losing control as his thoughts race on. He interacts with the crowd, but he is discouraged when he is unable to communicate his ecstatic discovery that "This is God!" as he clutches the electric button wired to the whirling wheel of fortune.

When the white master of ceremonies tries to stop him, the man tries to explain what he's feeling and is overwhelmed by his thoughts. "Most of the time he was ashamed of what Negroes did himself. Well, let them be ashamed for something this time. Like him. He was like a long thin black wire that was being stretched and wound upon the bingo wheel." Ellison describes his collapse onstage in his anguish over his inability to help Laura, his fear of losing her, and his terror of living without her. By the time the uniformed guards come to get him, he is screaming in panic, feeling "that the whole audience had somehow entered him and was stamping its feet in his stomach and he was unable to throw them out." The visceral despair is unbearable, and unconsciousness in the form of the blow to his head comes as a relief.

Questions for Discussion

1. Ellison published this story in 1944, a period close to the Depression of the 1930s, when bingo games were presented in movie theaters to entice the customers. Why were they so eager to win the prizes?
2. What is the background of Ellison's nameless protagonist?
3. What kind of people are in the audience of the movie theater? Why does the protagonist think they are different from "folks down South"?
4. What details of the man's behavior during the movie make you sympathetic or unsympathetic to him?
5. What does the bingo wheel represent to him after he pushes the button?
6. Are the people in the audience in sympathy with the black protagonist or with the white master of ceremonies? How do their indifference and hostility contribute to the nameless protagonist's frustration at feeling himself invisible in the movie theater?
7. In what way is the ending of the story ironic? What does this suggest about Ellison's control over his presentation of the nightmarish experience of his protagonist?

Topic for Writing

1. Richard Wright's novel *Native Son*, published shortly before Ellison wrote "King of the Bingo Game," also contains a scene in a movie theater where his African American protagonist and his friends watch a double feature. Compare and contrast Wright's presentation of racial and sexual stereotypes in American popular entertainment and its effect on his characters with Ellison's description of the Hollywood film and the theater audience in this story.

Suggested Readings

Blake, Susan L. "Ritual and Rationalization: Black Folklore in the Works of Ralph Ellison." *PMLA* 94 (1979): 121–26, esp. 122–23.

Horowitz, Ellin. "The Rebirth of the Artist." *Twentieth-Century Interpretations of "Invisible Man."* Ed. John M. Reilly. Englewood Cliffs, NJ: Prentice, 1970. 80–88, esp. 81. (Originally published in 1964.)

O'Meally, Robert G. *The Craft of Ralph Ellison*. Cambridge, MA: Harvard UP, 1980. 12–14.

Vogler, Thomas A. *"Invisible Man*: Somebody's Protest Novel." *Ralph Ellison: A Collection of Critical Essays*. Ed. John Hersey. Englewood Cliffs, NJ: Prentice, 1974. 127–50, esp. 143–44.

Louise Erdrich

The Red Convertible (p. 448)

The story takes place in 1974, when Henry Junior comes back to the Chippewa Indian reservation after more than three years as a soldier in Vietnam. He is mentally disturbed by his experiences in the war, and, as his brother Lyman (who narrates the story) says laconically, "the change was no good."

Erdrich has structured her story in a traditional manner. It is narrated in the first person by Lyman, who uses the past tense to describe the finality of what happened to his brother and the red Oldsmobile convertible they once shared. The plot moves conventionally, after a lengthy introduction giving the background of the two brothers and their pleasure in the car. They are Indians who work hard for what they earn, but they also enjoy their money. As Lyman says, "We went places in that car, me and Henry." An atmosphere of innocence pervades this part of the story. They enjoy sightseeing along the western highways, going when and where they please, spending an entire summer in Alaska after they drive a female hitchhiker with long, beautiful hair home.

The story moves forward chronologically (although it is told as a flashback after the opening frame of four paragraphs), organized in sections usually several paragraphs long. Its structure is as loose and comfortable as the brothers' relationship. Then, midway, the story darkens when Henry goes off to Vietnam. For three sections, Lyman describes Henry's disorientation after the war. Then Henry fixes the convertible, the boys get back behind the wheel, and it seems briefly as if the good times are again starting to roll. But Henry feels internal turmoil similar to that of the flooded river they park alongside. The story reaches its climax when Henry suddenly goes wild after drinking several beers, deteriorating into what he calls a "crazy Indian." Lyman stares after him as he jumps into the river, shouting, "Got to cool me off!" His last words are quieter, "My boots are filling," and then he is gone.

The last paragraph of the story is its final section, Lyman describing how he drove the car into the river after he couldn't rescue Henry. It has gotten dark, and he is left alone with the sound of the rush of the water "going and running and running." This brings the story full circle, back to the beginning, where Lyman told us that now he "walks everywhere he goes." His grief for his brother is as understated as the rest of his personality. Erdrich has invented a natural storyteller in Lyman. We feel his emotional loss as if it were our own.

Questions for Discussion

1. In the opening paragraph, Lyman says that he and Henry owned the red convertible "together until his boots filled with water on a windy night and he bought out my share." When does the meaning of this sentence become clear to you? What is the effect of putting this sentence in the first paragraph?

2. Also in the opening paragraph, Erdrich writes: "his youngest brother Lyman (that's myself), Lyman walks everywhere he goes." If Lyman is narrating this story, why does he name himself? Does speaking of himself in the third person create any particular effect?

3. What is the function of the third section of the story? Why does the narrator tell us about their wandering, about meeting Susy? What associations does the red convertible carry?

4. Watching Henry watching television, Lyman says, "He sat in his chair gripping the armrests with all his might, as if the chair itself was moving at a high speed and if he let go at all he would rocket forward and maybe crash right through the set." How would you describe the diction in this sentence? What effect does the sentence's length — and its syntax — create? What is the tone? What does this line, and the paragraphs around it, tell you about Lyman's reaction to Henry's change?

5. Where do Lyman and Henry speak directly to each other in this story? Where do they speak indirectly? How do they communicate without speech? Describe how Erdrich presents the moments of emotion in this story.

6. Why is Lyman upset by the picture of himself and his brother? When does the picture begin to bother him? Do we know if it's before or after Henry's death? Does it make a difference to our interpretation of the story? What burden of memory does this picture carry?

7. Consider the tone of the final paragraph, in which Lyman is describing how he felt when he gave his car to his dead brother. Look at the diction surrounding the red convertible here: It plows into the water; the headlights "reach in . . . go down, searching"; they are "still lighted. . . ." What attribute does the diction give the car? How is the car different now from the way it's been in the rest of the story? Does this transformation of the car invoke a sense of closure in the story?

8. The closing sentence says "And then there is only the water, the sound of it going and running and going and running and running." How does this statement comment on the relationship between the two brothers?

Topics for Writing

1. Write an essay considering brotherhood in "The Red Convertible."
2. Discuss Erdrich's use of setting to determine tone.
3. Rewrite the story from the third person point of view.
4. **CONNECTIONS** Compare and discuss Lyman's initiation into maturity with that of Julian in Flannery O'Connor's "Everything That Rises Must Converge."

Suggested Readings

Erdrich, Louise. "Excellence Has Always Made Me Fill with Fright When It Is Demanded by Other People, but Fills Me with Pleasure When I Am Left to Practice It Alone." *Ms.* 13 (1985): 84.

———."Where I Ought to Be: A Writer's Sense of Place." *New York Times Book Review* 28 July 1985: 1+.

Howard, J. "Louise Erdrich." *Life* 8 (1985): 27+.

WILLIAM FAULKNER

A Rose for Emily (p. 457)

Few stories, surely, differ more on a second reading than does "A Rose for Emily," which yields to the initiate some detail or circumstance anticipating the ending in nearly every paragraph. But Faulkner sets the pieces of his puzzle in place so coolly that the first-time reader hardly suspects them to fit together into a picture at all, until the curtain is finally swept aside and the shocking secret of Miss Emily's upstairs room is revealed. Faulkner makes it easy to write off the episodes of the smell, Miss Emily's denial of her father's death, the arsenic, and the aborted wedding (note the shuffled chronology) as the simple eccentricities of a pathetic old maid, to be pitied and indulged. The impact of the final scene drives home the realization that the passions of a former generation and its experience of life are no less real or profound for all their being in the past — whether we view them through the haze of sentimental nostalgia, as the Confederate veterans near the end of the story do, or place them at an aesthetic distance, as the townspeople do in the romantic tableau imagined in section II.

In his interviews with students at the University of Virginia (excerpted in Part Two, p. 1416), Faulkner stressed Miss Emily's being "kept down" by her father as an important factor in driving her to violate the code of her society by taking a lover, and he expressed a deep human sympathy for her long expiation for that sin. In the narrative consciousness of the story, however — the impersonal "we" that speaks for the communal mind of Jefferson — Miss Emily Grierson is a town relic, a monument to the local past to be shown to strangers, like the graves of the men slain at the battle of Jefferson or the big houses on what long ago, before they put the sidewalks in, was the "most select street." Because all relics are to a degree symbolic, one should not hesitate to take up the challenge found in Faulkner's ambiguous claim quoted in the headnote, that "the writer is too busy . . . to have time to be conscious of all the symbolism that he may put into what he does or what people may read into it." Miss Emily, for example, may be understood to express the part of southern culture that is paralyzed in the present by its inability to let go of the past, even though that past is as dead as Homer Barron, and even though its reality differed from the treasured memory as greatly as the Yankee paving contractor — "not a marrying man" — differs from the husband of Miss Emily's desperate longings. Other details in Faulkner's economical narration fit this reading: the prominence of Miss Emily's iconic portrait of her father; her refusal to acknowledge changing laws and customs; her insistence that the privilege of paying no taxes, bestowed on her by the chivalrous Colonel Sartoris, is an inalienable right; her dependence on the labors of her Negro servant, whose patient silence renders him an accomplice in her strange crime; and, not least, her relationship of mutual exploitation with Homer, the representative of the North — a relationship that ends in a morbid and grotesque parody of marriage. In this context, the smell of death that reeks from Miss Emily's house tells how the story judges what she stands for, and the dust that falls on everything brings the welcome promise of relief.

But Faulkner will not let it lie. Seen for what she is, neither romanticized nor trivialized, Miss Emily has a forthright dignity and a singleness of purpose that contrast sharply with those representatives of propriety and progress who sneak around her foundation in the dark spreading lime or knock on her door in the ineffectual effort to collect her taxes. And as the speechless townsfolk tiptoe aghast about her bridal chamber, it is Miss Emily's iron will, speaking through the strand of iron-gray hair that lies where she has lain, that has the final word.

WILLIAM E. SHEIDLEY

Questions for Discussion

1. The story begins and ends with Miss Emily's funeral. Trace the chronology of the intervening sections.
2. Emily is called "a fallen monument" and "a tradition." Explain.
3. Why does the narrator label Miss Emily's house "an eyesore among eyesores"?
4. Define the opposing forces in the confrontation that occupies most of section I. How does Miss Emily "vanquish them"?
5. Discuss the transition between sections I and II. In what ways are the two episodes parallel?
6. Apart from her black servant, Miss Emily has three men in her life. What similarities are there in her attitudes toward them?
7. Why is Homer Barron considered an inappropriate companion for Miss Emily?
8. Consider Faulkner's introduction of the rat poison into the story in section III. What is the narrator's avowed reason for bringing it up?
9. At the beginning of section IV, the townspeople think Emily will commit suicide, and they think "it would be the best thing." Why? What is the basis of their error regarding her intentions?
10. Why do you think Miss Emily gets fat and develops gray hair when she does?
11. Why does Miss Emily's servant disappear after her death?
12. Describe Miss Emily's funeral before the upstairs room is opened. In what way does that scene serve as a foil to set off what follows?
13. Discuss the role of dust in the last few paragraphs of the story.
14. Why does Faulkner end the story with "a long strand of iron-gray hair"?

Topics for Writing

1. Contrast the various attitudes toward the past in "A Rose for Emily."
2. Discuss the meaning of time and Faulkner's handling of chronology in "A Rose for Emily."

3. Construct a profile of Emily Grierson — Is she a criminal, a lunatic, or a heroine?
4. Explain the title of "A Rose for Emily."
5. Consider the relationship between "A Rose for Emily" and the history of the South.
6. What can you discern about the narrator of "A Rose for Emily"?
7. Were you surprised by the story's ending? On a second reading, mark all the passages that foreshadow it.
8. Imitate Faulkner by telling the events that lead up to a climax out of chronological order. What new effects do you find it possible to achieve? What problems in continuity do you encounter?

Related Commentary

William Faulkner, The Meaning of "A Rose for Emily," p. 1416.

Suggested Readings

See page 91.

WILLIAM FAULKNER

That Evening Sun (p. 464)

That Evening Sun is one of a handful of American short stories that have been so frequently anthologized and discussed that they almost define the style and the method of American short fiction. For the instructor the question may not be so much presenting the story for its literary qualities, but in seeing how well the story still relates to the political and social attitudes of students today, more than sixty years since it was first published. It isn't as acceptable now for a white writer to deal with themes of African American life, and for many feminists there can be questions about a white male author's presentation of a black woman's experience. Does the story still have the powerful effect on its readers that it had in the harsh years of the Great Depression and the cruelest decades of legalized segregation?

The answer is that the narrative device that gave the story so much of its first impact still is as effective today. By weaving through the story the uncomprehending chorus of children's voices, Faulkner succeeds in making the brutal violence of the story frighteningly real. There is no more desperate moment in American literature than when Nancy's attempt to keep the children amused in her lonely cabin ends with the broken popcorn popper. The reader's realization that the children don't understand what is happening only sharpens the effect. For women readers the story perhaps will reflect some of their own emotions and responses as the society is ready now to listen to the stories of battered wives and of women threatened by lovers or friends. The terror that is stalking Nancy is no different from the fear that a woman feels when she knows that a restraining order issued by a distant judge won't protect her from the rage of a disturbed ex-husband.

From the perspective of sixty years, it is also possible to see the racial dimensions of the story in a different way. Perhaps part of what gave Faulkner his great international reputation — and his Nobel Prize — was an understanding that what he was describing was the bitter reality of life for any underclass. The black underclass outside the white neighborhoods of this southern town has been forced into the way of life of the peasants of the older European societies. Faulkner's Nancy could have been a servant in a renter's cottage outside the manor walls in nineteenth-century England, or a woman forced outside the social framework — as she would be by her unwed pregnancy — in any European small town before the First World War. Faulkner's story still forces us to face this very real inhumanity in a world we realize has not left this legacy of violence behind.

Questions for Discussion

1. Compare the ages of the children with the responses to Nancy's fear. How much more awareness do the older children have?
2. How does Faulkner describe the small town's ability to help someone like Nancy?
3. Why is Jesus still able to go free, despite the awareness of the children's father of what is happening?

Topics for Writing

1. Faulkner describes the uneasy boundary where the white and the black societies of this small town meet. What are the real effects of this boundary?
2. Compare the situation Nancy faces with a similar situation today.
3. The children's father acts in a way that he would consider sympathetic and protective but would be considered paternalistic today. Discuss his character and role in the story.

Suggested Readings

Basset, John E. *Vision and Revisions: Essays on Faulkner.* West Cornwall, CT: Locust Hill, 1989.

Bloom, Harold. *William Faulkner.* New York: Chelsea House, 1986.

Blotner, Joseph. *Faulkner: A Biography.* New York: Random, 1991.

Brooks, Cleanth. *A Shaping Joy.* New York: Harcourt, 1971.

Gwynn, Frederick, and Joseph Blotner, eds. *Faulkner in the University.* Charlottesville: U of Virginia P, 1959.

Hall, Donald. *To Read Literature: Fiction, Poetry, Drama.* New York: Holt, 1981. 10–16.

Heller, Terry. "The Telltale Hair: A Critical Study of William Faulkner's 'A Rose for Emily.' " *Arizona Quarterly* 28 (1972): 301–18.

Hoffman, Frederick J. *William Faulkner, Revised.* Boston: Twayne, 1990.

Howe, Irving. *William Faulkner: A Critical Study.* 2nd ed. New York: Vintage, 1962. 265.

Leary, Lewis. *William Faulkner of Yoknapatawpha County*. Twentieth-Century American Writers. New York: Crowell, 1973. 136.

Millgate, Michael. *The Achievement of William Faulkner*. New York: Random, 1966.

F. Scott Fitzgerald

Babylon Revisited (p. 478)

"Babylon Revisited" develops a paradox about the past: It is irretrievably lost, but it controls the present inescapably. Charlie Wales revisits the scenes of "the big party" carried on by stock-market rich Americans in Paris during the 1920s — a party at which he was one of the chief celebrants — and shakes his head over how much things have changed. His memories of those times come into focus only gradually, and as they do his nostalgia modulates to disgust. His guilt-ridden desire to repudiate his past behavior reaches a peak *not* when his negotiations to get his daughter back remind him that he brought on his wife's pneumonia by locking her out in the snow, but only when Lorraine's *pneumatique* reminds him that for several years his life was given over to trivial foolishness. For a man trying to reestablish himself as a loving and responsible father, the memory of harming his wife in wild anger at her flirtation with "young Webb" is less embarrassing than the memory of riding a stolen tricycle all over the Étoile with another man's wife.

The problem for Charlie Wales is that his past — for the moment embodied in the pathetic relics Duncan and Lorraine — clings to him despite his efforts to repudiate it. The reader (like Marion) is inclined to fear that Charlie might return to his past ways, but Charlie is not tempted by Lorraine or by the lure of alcohol. His lesson has been learned, but that does not prevent the past from destroying his plans for the future. Or perhaps, as David Toor argues, it is Charlie who clings to the past; perhaps he ambivalently punishes himself out of a guilt he refuses to acknowledge, as when he sabotages his campaign to get Honoria from the Peterses by leaving their address for Duncan with the bartender at the Ritz. As the story ends, history is repeating itself. Just as Charlie caused Helen's sickness, the inopportune arrival of his old friends has sickened Marion. As a result he loses Honoria, at least for six months of her fast-waning and irretrievable childhood — just as he has lost Helen for good.

William E. Sheidley

Questions for Discussion

1. Why does Fitzgerald begin the story with what seems to be the end of a conversation that then begins when Charlie walks into the bar in the next paragraph?

2. As Charlie rides through Paris on his way to see his daughter, he thinks, "I spoiled this city for myself." What reason might Fitzgerald have for treating this subject so mildly and in such vague terms here?

3. Characterize the Peters family. To what extent are we to approve of their attitudes?
4. What is the effect of Charlie's repeatedly taking "only one drink every afternoon"? Does the reader expect him to regress into alcohol abuse?
5. What does Charlie's brief encounter with the woman in the *brasserie* contribute to the story?
6. Why does Charlie identify the fine fall day as "football weather"?
7. Discuss the impact of the appearance of Duncan and Lorraine after Charlie's lunch with Honoria.
8. Why is Marion reluctant to release Honoria to her father? Why is Charlie able to win her consent, temporarily?
9. When Marion suggests that Charlie may have caused Helen's death, "an electric current of agony surged through him," but Lincoln says, "I never thought you were responsible for that." Was he? What does Charlie himself think? Explain his reaction.
10. Explain Charlie's reaction to Lorraine's *pneumatique*. Why does he ignore it? Why does that tactic fail?
11. Why does Fitzgerald introduce the arrival of Duncan and Lorraine precisely where he does, and in the way he does?
12. What does Paul mean when he supposes that Charlie "lost everything [he] wanted in the boom" by "selling short"? What does Charlie mean when he replies, "Something like that"?
13. Explain the irony of Charlie's present financial success, apparently unique among his old friends.
14. What does the title mean?

Topics for Writing

1. Analyze Fitzgerald's use of recurring motifs and foreshadowing in "Babylon Revisited."
2. Consider Charlie Wales as a study of remorse.
3. Write an essay describing the techniques of characterization in "Babylon Revisited" of the secondary characters.
4. Consider Charlie's daughter's name as the key to his underlying motives.
5. After reading each of the five sections of the story, write a paragraph giving your assessment of Charlie Wales and your prediction of what will happen to him. Is there consistency, or a progression, in your judgments?

Suggested Readings

Gallo, Rose Adrienne. *F. Scott Fitzgerald*. Modern Literature Monographs. New York: Ungar, 1978. 101–05.

Gross, Seymour. "Fitzgerald's 'Babylon Revisited.'" *College English* 25 (1963): 128–35.

Male, Roy R. "'Babylon Revisited': The Story of the Exile's Return." *Studies in Short Fiction* 2 (1965): 270–77.

Toor, David. "Guilt and Retribution in 'Babylon Revisited.'" *Fitzgerald/Hemingway Annual 1973*. Ed. Matthew J. Bruccoli and C. E. Frazer Clark, Jr. Washington, DC: Microcard Eds., 1974. 155–64.

GUSTAVE FLAUBERT

A Simple Heart (p. 495)

Students may find Flaubert's long narrative boring and pointless, its central character too narrow and insignificant for such extended treatment, and its plot lacking the qualities of conflict, suspense, and climax customary in well-structured fiction. Rather than assuring them of the work's recognized perfection or quoting Ezra Pound's judgment that "A Simple Heart" embodies "all that anyone knows about writing," you might try placing the work in contexts that will make it more interesting and accessible.

That the tale is an autobiographically intimate recollection of the people and places of Flaubert's childhood, some of them revisited while it was being written, underlines the degree to which his objective narration controls strong personal feelings. Add that Félicité is run down by the mail coach at precisely the same spot on the road where Flaubert suffered the first onset of the epilepsy that led him to choose a life of retirement and dedicated labor at his art — a life in many ways comparable to Félicité's own obscure and laborious existence — and students may find themselves ready to give the story a second look.

Flaubert wrote "A Simple Heart" during the last years of his life as one of three interrelated tales, the *Trois Contes*, on religious themes. By this time Flaubert had suffered the humiliation of seeing Normandy and his own home occupied by the invading Prussians; he had lost most of his money through misguided generosity to the husband of an ungrateful niece; and he had watched his friends die off. One of them was the novelist George Sand, for whom he was writing "A Simple Heart" in response to her chiding him for insensitivity in his detached style of fiction. The *Trois Contes* each in a different way, embody Flaubert's reaction to these losses. Each subjects pride and worldliness to a devastating confrontation with humility and self-abnegation.

The genre of "A Simple Heart" is the saint's life; its deceptively simple chronological structure traces the stages by which the protagonist throws off selfishness and worldly desires and, in the process, attains the spiritual purity requisite for miracles, martyrdom, and assumption into bliss. With the loss of Théodore, Félicité leaves ordinary erotic love behind her and enters upon a lifelong devotion to selfless labor. She does this not as a self-conscious and would-be heroic rejection of the world but only because she knows of nothing else to do. The love she feels subsequently, however, is as selfless as her labor. It goes virtually unrewarded by Paul, Virginie, and Victor, but it is in a sense its own reward, for it enables Félicité to experience a vicarious life of the imagination seemingly more real than her own, as in Virginie's first communion or Victor's trip to Havana. As the world relentlessly strips her of each beloved person and finally even of the very senses by which to apprehend them, Félicité can resort to the power of her imagination, unrestrained by any conventional critical intellect. Imagination blooming into faith allows her not only to find the answer to her loneliness in a parrot but also to endow the dead, stuffed bird with spiritual life and to experience her final beatific vision of the parrotlike Holy Ghost spreading over her from heaven.

Flaubert worried that his tale would seem ironic and Félicité's confusion of the parrot Loulou with the deity absurd. On the contrary, he insisted, "it is in no way ironic, as you may suppose, but . . . very serious and very sad" (quoted by Stratton Buck, p. 105). The question of tone should lead a class discussion straight to the fundamental issues raised by the story. Félicité's utter lack of pretension, as Jonathan Culler argues, defeats the impulse toward irony because it allows nothing for irony to deflate, while Flaubert, by avoiding commentary and committing himself to the pure and precise rendering of the facts of the case, presents the reader with the necessity, in order to give meaning to Félicité's life, of imagining a sacred order in which her vision of the parrot is not a mockery but a divine blessing and a fit reward.

WILLIAM SHEIDLEY

Questions for Discussion

1. One critic (Peter Cortland) remarks that in a way Félicité's life is "entirely covered" by Flaubert's opening sentence. How is that so? In what sense does that sentence miss everything?
2. Why does Flaubert introduce his second section by defeating any excitement or special interest the reader might feel about Félicité's affair with Théodore?
3. What is the effect of Flaubert's detailed descriptions of the Norman countryside as well as the other settings and circumstances of the story?
4. Explain the purpose of Félicité's musings about the Holy Ghost in the third section.
5. Why is Virginie's first communion more meaningful to Félicité than her own reception of the sacrament?
6. Compare the reactions of Félicité and Mme Aubain to the death of Virginie. What do the differences reveal about their characters?
7. What is the effect on the reader's attitude toward Félicité of the passage that begins when she is whipped by the coachman?
8. Why does Flaubert have Mère Simon tell herself, as she sponges the sweat from the dying Félicité's temples, "that one day she would have to go the same way"?
9. *Félicité* means happiness, good fortune, or bliss. Is the name of Flaubert's heroine ironic?

Topics for Writing

1. Examine the episode of Loulou's disappearance and return, and the consequences of Félicité's search for him as an epitome of the story.
2. Discuss the circumstances of Félicité's death as a key to Flaubert's theme.
3. Analyze the function of the brief, one-sentence paragraphs that punctuate the text at certain points.
4. Review the story and make a list of everything Félicité loses. Is it possible to make a corresponding list of things she gains?
5. Study Flaubert's description of Mme Aubain's house in the first section and write a similar description of a house you know.
6. Write an obituary for Félicité such as might have been published in the Pont-l'Évêque newspaper. Are you satisfied with the result?

(text pp. 519–523)

Suggested Readings

Buck, Stratton. *Gustave Flaubert*. Twayne's World Authors Series 3. New York: Twayne, 1966. Esp. 103–08.

Cortland, Peter. *A Reader's Guide to Flaubert*. New York: Helios, 1968. 127–46.

Cross, Richard K. *Flaubert and Joyce: The Rite of Fiction*. Princeton: Princeton UP, 1971. 17–25.

Culler, Jonathan. *Flaubert: The Uses of Uncertainty*. Ithaca: Cornell UP, 1974. Esp. 11–19, 208–11.

Mavis Gallant

1933 (p. 519)

Mavis Gallant, in her essay "What Is Style?" (p. 1418 of this anthology), makes an arresting analogy between fiction and life:

> Style is inseparable from structure, part of the conformation of whatever the author has to say. What he says — this is what fiction is about — is that something is taking place and that nothing lasts. Against the sustained tick of a watch, fiction takes the measure of a life, a season, a look exchanged, the turning point, desire as brief as a dream, the grief and terror that after childhood we cease to express. The lie, the look, the grief are without permanence. The watch continues to tick where the story stops.

Gallant's story "1933" is an evocation of a distant time and place, the first of several linked stories about the French-Canadian widow Mme. Carette and her daughters Berthe and Marie published in *Across the Bridge.* The opening pages of the story have a stillness so quiet that the ticking of Gallant's watch is hardly noticed as she skillfully and swiftly sketches in the background of her narrative. The widow's financial situation, her decision to move to a smaller and less expensive apartment, the careful disposition of the furniture, the fatherless family's cautious adjustment to the new neighborhood — all the details proceed at a funereal pace in the story, as stylized as in an early Ingmar Bergman film. We know that nothing lasts, because death is behind all the decisions being made: the widow and her children are survivors, but in their Catholic Quebeçois world, death is just a matter of time.

What makes Gallant's story so poignant is that the act of imagination creating it, rather than the austere religion shaping its every detail, is what resurrects the life being described. Like the fiction of Isaac Bashevis Singer, Gallant's presentation of a distant and lost past preserves its memory for posterity. The author's narrative is alive. It breathes in the accuracy of its details and the passion of its telling. The spirit of the mother's stern renunciation of life in her widowhood moves on the page in sentences such as "Mme. Carette told Berthe that her days of entertaining and cooking for guests were over. She was just twenty-seven." Later her exhaustion and sense of humiliation at being forced to earn money for her children by sewing in other people's houses leads her to express spiteful thoughts about the marriage of the couple downstairs who have taken care of Berthe and Marie overnight, and she is appalled at herself: "No sooner had she said this than she covered her mouth and spoke through her fingers: 'God forgive my unkind thoughts.' She propped her arms on each side of her plate, as the girls were forbidden to do, and let her face slide into her hands."

As Gallant says, "The watch continues to tick where the story stops," reminding us that nothing in life is permanent. Memories can keep the past alive, and stories are as close to permanent as we get.

Questions for Discussion

1. Where does the story take place? How does Gallant suggest the French-Canadian background of her characters?
2. How does the death of M. Carette affect his family?
3. What is the symbolic significance of the location of the family's new apartment near the Institute for the Deaf and Dumb?
4. How religious is Mme. Carette? What does the narrator imply about the role of religion in the children's daily life?
5. Why are so few English words needed between Rue Saint-Denis and Parc Lafontaine?
6. Why can't Mme. Carette become friends with M. Grosjean's Irish wife?

Topic for Writing

1. Write a story about a death in your family, and describe how it affected your life.

Related Commentary

Mavis Gallant, What Is Style? (p. 1418).

Suggested Readings

Gallant, Mavis. *Across the Bridge.* New York: Random, 1933.
———. *Paris Notebooks.* Toronto: Macmillan, 1985.

Gabriel García Márquez

A Very Old Man with Enormous Wings (p. 525)

The word "allegories" in the headnote presents a challenge to readers of this story, and the inevitable failure of any simple scheme of interpretation to grasp fully the mystery at its heart, reflects García Márquez's central theme exactly. Like the crabs, which come into the human world from an alien realm, the "flesh-and-blood angel" constitutes an intrusion of something strange and unfathomable into the comfortable world of reality as we choose to define it. Everybody, from the "wise" woman next door to the pope, takes a turn at trying to find a slot in which to file the winged visitor, but no definition seems satisfactory, and even Pelayo and Elisenda, whom the angel's presence has made wealthy, spend their money on a house "with iron bars on the windows so that angels wouldn't get in." When at last the old man flies away, Elisenda feels relief, "because then he was no longer an annoyance in her life but an imaginary dot on the horizon of the sea."

In discussing how he receives artistic inspiration, García Márquez says, "There's nothing deliberate or predictable in all this, nor do I know when it's going to happen to me. I'm at the mercy of my imagination." Without intending to limit the story's implications, one might associate the angel with this sort of unpredictable intrusion of the visionary and wonderful into everyday life. As an old man with wings, the angel recalls the mythical symbol of the artist, Daedalus, except that his wings are "so natural on that completely human organism that [the doctor] couldn't understand why other men didn't have them too." Bogged down in the mud, the angel seems less an allusion to Daedalus's son, the overreacher Icarus, than a representation of the difficulty of the artistic imagination in sustaining its flight through the unpleasant circumstances of this "sad" world. True artists are often misunderstood, ill treated, and rejected in favor of more practical concerns or of the creators of ersatz works that flatter established prejudices. Just so, nobody can understand the angel's "hermetic" language, and when he performs his aggressively unpractical miracles, no one is delighted. Exploited by his keepers, to whom he brings vast wealth, the angel receives as royalties only his quarters in the chicken coop and the flat side of the broom when underfoot. Popular for a time as a sideshow attraction, the angel is soon passed over in favor of the horrible "woman who had been changed into a spider for having disobeyed her parents," a grotesque and slapdash creation of the lowest order of imaginative synthesis, whose "human truth" gratifies both sentimentality and narrow-mindedness. But the artistic imagination lives happily on eggplant mush, possesses a supernatural patience, and though functionally blind to the bumping posts of ordinary reality, ever again takes wing. The angel has, perhaps rightly, appeared to his human observers "a cataclysm in repose", but near the end, as he sings his sea chanteys under the stars, he definitely comes to resemble "a hero taking his ease," preparing to navigate the high seas beyond the horizon.

WILLIAM E. SHEIDLEY

Questions for Discussion

1. Why are there crabs in the house? Is it for the same reason the old man with enormous wings has fallen in the courtyard? What other associations does the story make between the old man and the crabs?
2. Pelayo first thinks the old man is a nightmare. What other attempts are made to put this prodigy into a familiar category?
3. How does the old man differ from our usual conceptions of angels? What is the essential difference?
4. Explain Father Gonzaga's approach to the angel. What implications — about the angel and about the church — may be derived from his failure to communicate with him effectively?

5. Comment on the angel's career as a sideshow freak. Who receives the benefit of his success? Why does he fall? Compare what he has to offer with what the spider-woman has. What reasons might people have to prefer the latter?
6. Why do you think the angel tolerates the child patiently?
7. What are the implications of the angel's examination by the doctor?
8. How do we feel as the angel finally flaps away at the end? Does Elisenda's response adequately express the reader's?

Topics for Writing

1. Consider the ordinary and the enormous in "A Very Old Man with Enormous Wings." (Consider the etymological meaning of "enormous.")
2. Is García Márquez's fallen angel a fairy tale, a myth, or an allegory?
3. Recharging the sense of wonder: How does García Márquez make the reader believe in his angel?
4. Read the story aloud to a selected spectrum of people (at least three) of various ages and educational levels. Tabulate their responses and opinions, perhaps in an interview. Combining this evidence with your own response to the story, try to define the basis of its appeal.
5. Select a supernatural being from a fairy tale or other familiar source (the cartoons involving talking animals that wear clothes and drive cars might be worth considering), and imagine the being as a physical reality in your own ordinary surroundings. Write a sketch about what happens.
6. **CONNECTIONS** Compare "A Very Old Man with Enormous Wings" with other presentations of the supernatural. (Hawthorne's, for example.)

Suggested Readings

Bell-Villada, Gene H. *García Márquez: The Man and His Work.* Chapel Hill: U of North Carolina P, 1990.

Byk, John. "From Fact to Fiction: Gabriel García Márquez and the Short Story." *Mid-American Review* 6(2) (1986): 111–16.

Fau, Margaret Eustella. *Bibliographic Guide to Gabriel García Márquez 1979–1985.* Westport, CT: Greenwood, 1986.

García Márquez, Gabriel. *Collected Stories.* New York: Harper, 1984.

García Márquez, Gabriel. *Strange Pilgrims: Twelve Stories.* New York: Knopf, 1993.

McMurray, George R. *Gabriel García Márquez.* New York: Ungar, 1977. 116–19.

McNerney, Kathleen. *Understanding Gabriel García Márquez.* Columbia: U of South Carolina P, 1989.

Morello Frosch, Marta. "The Common Wonders of García Márquez's Recent Fiction." *Books Abroad* 47 (1973): 496–501.

Oberhelman, Harley D., ed. *Gabriel García Márquez: A Study of the Short Fiction.* Boston: Twayne 1991.

Ortega, Julio. *Gabriel García Márquez and the Powers of Fiction.* Austin: U of Texas P, 1988.

Williams, Raymond L. *Gabriel García Márquez.* Boston: Twayne, 1984.

Zhu, Jingdong. "García Márquez and His Writing of Short Stories." *Foreign Literatures* 1 (1987): 77–80.

Charlotte Perkins Gilman

The Yellow Wallpaper (p. 531)

Gilman wrote "The Yellow Wallpaper" between 1890 and 1894, during what she later recalled were the hardest years of her life. She had left her first husband and child to live alone in California after a nervous breakdown, and she was beginning to give lectures on freedom for women and socialism while she kept a boardinghouse, taught school, and edited newspapers. During this time, her husband married her best friend, to whom Gilman relinquished her child. The emotional pressures and economic uncertainties under which Gilman lived contributed to the desperate tone of this story.

Early readers of "The Yellow Wallpaper" compared it with the horror stories of Edgar Allan Poe (William Dean Howells said it was a story to "freeze our . . . blood" when he reprinted it in 1920 in *Great Modern American Stories*). Like Poe's homicidal narrators, Gilman's heroine tells her story in a state of neurotic compulsion. But she is no homicidal maniac. Unlike Poe, Gilman suggests that a specific social malady has driven her heroine to the brink of madness: the bondage of conventional marriage.

Her husband is her physician and keeper, the father of her beloved but absent child, the money earner who pays the rent on the mansion where she is held captive for her "own good." When she begs to get away, he replies practically, "Our lease will be up in three weeks, and I can't see how to leave before." Insisting that he knows what is best for her, he believes that the cure for her mysterious "weakness" is total rest. The husband is supported in his view by the opinion of the foremost medical authority on the treatment of mental illness, Dr. S. Weir Mitchell, a name explicitly mentioned in the story. Gilman had spent a month in Dr. Mitchell's sanitorium five years before. In her autobiography she later reported that she almost lost her mind there and would often "crawl into remote closets and under beds — to hide from the grinding pressure of that profound distress."

Gilman transferred the memory of her physical debilitation and "absolute incapacity" for normal (read "conventional") married life into her heroine's state in "The Yellow Wallpaper." The story dramatizes Gilman's fear while living with her first husband that marriage and motherhood might incapacitate her (as it apparently had Gilman's mother) for what she called "work in the world." She felt imprisoned within her marriage, a victim of her desire to please, trapped by her wedding ring. Gilman left her husband, but in "The Yellow Wallpaper" her heroine is sacrificed to the emotional turmoil she experiences.

As a symbolic projection of psychological stress, "The Yellow Wallpaper" has resemblances to Kafka's "The Metamorphosis," although it is more specific in its focus on social injustice to women. Like Gregor Samsa, Gilman's heroine is victimized by the people she loves. The yellow wallpaper surrounding her is "like a bad dream." It furnishes the central images in the story. The reader can use it like a Rorschach test to understand the heroine's experience of entrapment, confinement, and sacrifice for other family members. Like Gregor Samsa, she regresses to subhuman behavior as a self-inflicted punishment following her psychological rebellion — the wallpaper's bad smell, its bars and grid, its fungus and toadstools, and its images of the creeping (dependent, inferior) woman. But unlike Gregor

Samsa, Gilman's heroine thinks she is freed from the "bad dream" by telling her story, not to a "living soul," but to what she calls (nonjudgmentally) "dead paper."

Telling her story enables her to achieve her greatest desire — the symbolic death of her husband. The story ends, "Now why should that man have fainted? But he did, and right across my path by the wall, so that I had to creep over him every time!" The central irony of the story, however, is that by the time she realizes the twisted ambition fostered by obediently following "like a good girl" her passive role as a conventional member of the "weaker sex," she has been driven insane.

Questions for Discussion

1. Why have the narrator and her husband, John, rented the "colonial mansion"? What is its history, and what is the reaction of the heroine to this estate? Does she feel comfortable living in the house?

2. Give a description of John. Why does the heroine say that his profession is *"perhaps . . . one reason I do not get well faster"*? How does the narrator view her husband? Does she agree with John's diagnosis and treatment? Who else supports John's diagnosis? What effect does this have on the heroine?

3. What clue does the narrator's repeated lament, "what can one do?" give us about her personality? Describe other aspects of the woman's personality that are revealed in the opening of the story. What conflicting emotions is she having toward her husband, her condition, and the mansion?

4. How would you characterize the narrator's initial reaction to, and description of, the wallpaper?

5. Describe the narrator's state after the first two weeks of residence. Has John's relationship with his wife changed at all?

6. Who is Jennie? What is her relationship to the narrator, and what is her function in the story?

7. How has the narrator changed in her description of the wallpaper? Is it fair to say that the wallpaper has become more dominant in her day-to-day routine? Explain.

8. By the Fourth of July, what does the narrator admit about the wallpaper? What clues does Gilman give us about the education of the narrator and her increasingly agitated state? Is she finding it more and more difficult to communicate? Explain.

9. As the summer continues, describe the narrator's thoughts. What is her physical condition? Is there a link between her symptoms and psychological illness?

10. How does the narrator try to reach out to her husband? What is his reaction? Is this her last contact with sanity? Do you think John really has no comprehension of the seriousness of her illness?

11. Why do you think Gilman briefly changes the point of view from first person singular to the second person as the narrator describes the pattern of the wallpaper? What effect does the narrator say light has on the wallpaper?

12. Who does the narrator see in the wallpaper? How have her perceptions of John and Jennie changed from the beginning of the story?

13. Abruptly the narrator switches mood from boredom and frustration to excitement. To what does she attribute this change? How does John react to this? What new aspects of the wallpaper does she discuss?

14.   By the final section of the story, what is the narrator's relationship to her husband? to Jennie? to the wallpaper? How has the narrator's perspective changed from the start of the story? What change do we see in her actions?
15.   Identify what has driven the narrator to the brink of madness. How does she try to free herself from this element? What is her greatest desire? What is the central irony of the story?

Topics for Writing

1.   Compare and contrast the husband-wife relationship and its outcome in Gilman's "The Yellow Wallpaper" and Henrik Ibsen's play "A Doll's House."
2.   **CONNECTIONS**   Compare and contrast the monologue in Gilman's "The Yellow Wallpaper" with that in Poe's "The Cask of Amontillado" or "The Tell-Tale Heart."
3.   **CONNECTIONS**   Compare and discuss the concept of marriage in Gilman's "The Yellow Wallpaper," Carver's "What We Talk About When We Talk About Love," and Walker's "Roselily."

Related Commentaries

Sandra M. Gilbert and Susan Gubar, A Feminist Reading of Gilman's "The Yellow Wallpaper." p. 1420.
Charlotte Perkins Gilman, Undergoing the Cure for Nervous Prostration, p. 1423.

Suggested Readings

Bader, J. "The Dissolving Vision: Realism in Jewett, Freeman and Gilman." *American Realism; New Essays.* Ed. Eric J. Sundquist. Baltimore: Johns Hopkins UP, 1982. 176–98.
Delaney, Sheila. *Writing Women: Women Writers and Women in Literature, Medieval to Modern.* New York: Schocken, 1983.
Feminist Papers: From Adams to de Beauvoir. Ed. Alice S. Rossi. New York: Columbia UP, 1973.
Hanley-Peritz, J. "Monumental Feminism and Literature's Ancestral House: Another Look at 'The Yellow Wallpaper.'" *Women's Studies* 12.2 (1986): 113–28.
Hill, Mary A. "Charlotte Perkins Gilman: A Feminist's Struggle with Womanhood." *Massachusetts Review* 21 (1980): 503–26.
————. *Charlotte Perkins Gilman: The Making of a Radical Feminist, 1860–1896.* Philadelphia: Temple UP, 1980.
Lane, Ann J. "Charlotte Perkins Gilman: The Personal Is Political." *Feminist Theorists.* Ed. Dale Spender. New York: Pantheon, 1983.
Nies, Judith. *Seven Women.* New York: Viking, 1977. 127–45.
Shumaker, C. " 'Too Terribly Good to Be Printed': Charlotte Gilman's 'The Yellow Wallpaper.'" *American Literature* 57 (1985): 588–99.

Nikolai Gogol

The Overcoat (p. 544)

"The Overcoat," like Gogol's work in general, has been the subject of widely differing critical responses, some of which will surely be replicated in class discussion. A humanitarian view that sees the story as the vindication of a downtrodden little man coordinates fairly well with an interpretation that stresses the story's satiric attack on the rigid Czarist bureaucracy. Readers who note the grim joke with which the story ends, however, find its report on the destruction of a being too paltry even for contempt to be harrowingly cynical and heartless, while those who closely attend to the shifting narrative tone praise Gogol for producing a masterpiece of that combination of comedy and horror that we designate as the grotesque.

In some ways an obverse of romantic or Laforguian irony, which expresses a self-conscious revulsion from one's own emotional enthusiasms, the grotesque vision dissolves in grim laughter the appalled revulsion from a world devoid of any positive value. Neither Akaky Akakievich Bashmachkin (whose name in Russian alludes to dung on a shoe) nor the social and physical world with which he is at odds offers anything admirable, and the narrator's continuously shifting understatements, overstatements, verbal ironies, and bathetic juxtapositions repeatedly prevent the reader from any mistaken investment of esteem. Nonetheless, the possibility that Akaky Akakievich is our brother in ways not considered by his sentimental young colleague remains the source of the story's grip on our imagination.

Before time, which ages his coat, and the chill of the St. Petersburg winter combine to impose a need on him, Akaky Akakievich lives in a static and self-contained world of meaningless alphabetic letters, which he finds fulfillment and delight in replicating. He is a "writer" of sorts, but a writer who — like Gogol himself, according to Charles C. Bernheimer — hesitates to express himself in what he writes. With his fall from this undifferentiated condition into his struggle to acquire an overcoat, he is born into temporal human existence. His isolation breaks down, and so does his innocence: He makes a friend; he participates in a creative act; he experiences stirrings of sensuality; and he eventually manages to assert himself in words. He also becomes guilty of vanity, pride, lust, and deception. Having gained an identity as a man with a new coat, he becomes vulnerable to the destruction of that identity and consequently of the self it defines, which happens in three rapid stages.

Because we have seen him emerge from a state approximating nonexistence, Akaky Akakievich's brief history as a suffering human being does not appear to be much different from the radically reduced quintessence of the fate we imagine to be our own. That the retribution carried out by the shade of Akaky Akakievich — which suggests his vindication and the exaltation of his overcoat-identity to the stature of a myth — can finally be nothing more than a fantasy or a joke only serves to underline the inescapable dilemma that the story propounds between the meaninglessness of remaining locked within the circle of the self and the danger of aspiring beyond it.

William E. Sheidley

(text pp. 544–565)

Questions for Discussion

1. Characterize the narrative mode of the opening paragraphs. Can you define a consistent tone?
2. In what sense was it "out of the question" to give Akaky Akakievich any other name?
3. Does Gogol share the feelings of "the young man" who thinks Akaky Akakievich's complaints mean "I am your brother"?
4. Describe Akaky Akakievich's life before his coat wore out.
5. Why does Gogol bother to make Petrovich such an unsavory character?
6. Describe Akaky Akakievich's feelings about his new overcoat once he decides to acquire it.
7. What possible attitudes might one take toward Akaky Akakievich's experience at the party? about his visit to the "Person of Consequence"?
8. Near the end, the narrator speaks of how "our little story unexpectedly finishes with a fantastic ending." What is the effect of this and the narrator's other implicit acknowledgments of the fictionality of his story — made as implausible assertions of its veracity — on the reader?
9. Consider Nabokov's commentary on "The Overcoat." What "gaps and black holes in the texture of Gogol's style" seem to you to "imply flaws in the texture of life itself"?

Topics for Writing

1. Discuss satire as a diversionary tactic in "The Overcoat."
2. Consider the "Person of Consequence" and a person of little consequence: two sides of the same coin?
3. Write an essay arguing that disappointed expectation is the goal of Gogol's style.
4. Study the long sentence on page 547 that begins "Even at those hours..." and continues nearly to the end of the paragraph it opens. Write a similar sentence about a community with which you are familiar (e.g., college students on a campus; the residents of your neighborhood). Try to follow Gogol as closely as possible: clause for clause, phrase for phrase. How would you define the tone of what you have written? Is it the same as Gogol's tone?
5. Nabokov concludes his commentary on this story (p. 1469) by suggesting that "after reading Gogol one's eyes may become gogolized and one is apt to see bits of [Gogol's irrational] world in the most unexpected places." Write a sketch in which, by manipulating style and diction, you cause your reader to glimpse a darker world beyond the surface appearances of things.
6. **CONNECTIONS** Compare and discuss Gogol's Akaky Akakievich and Melville's Bartleby as versions of the artist.

Related Commentary

Vladimir Nabokov, Gogol's Genius in "The Overcoat," p. 1469.

Suggested Readings

Bernheimer, Charles C. "Cloaking the Self: The Literary Space of Gogol's 'Over-coat.' " *PMLA* 90 (1975): 53–61.

Erlich, Victor. *Gogol.* Yale Russian and East European Studies 8. New Haven: Yale UP, 1969. Esp. 143–56.

Karlinsky, Simon. *The Sexual Labyrinth of Nikolai Gogol.* Cambridge, MA: Harvard UP, 1976. 135–44.

Lindstrom, Thaïs S. *Nikolay Gogol.* Twayne's World Authors Series 299. New York: Twayne, 1974. Esp. 88–96.

NADINE GORDIMER

Town and Country Lovers (p. 567)

This tale includes two brilliant stories about race relations in South Africa, linked by theme. Two mixed-race couples, one from town, the other from the country, become lovers and are brutally separated by social conventions. The linking of the stories, identical in their unhappy endings yet dissimilar in their circumstances, suggests the power of the attraction between all lovers — intangible, mysterious, beyond description in words. It overcomes differences of background, education, job status, and race. Yet, as Gordimer shows in these two stories, it cannot survive the virulence of unjust social conventions.

Story I

The town lovers are grown-ups. He is Dr. Franz-Josef von Leinsdorf, a German geologist with an aristocratic background, dedicated to his work. She is a light-skinned cashier in a supermarket in Johannesburg, her nature as sweet as she is pretty. She is given no name, identified merely as "the girl," as if Gordimer wants to suggest she isn't quite human to the aristocratic Dr. von Leinsdorf, despite their intimacy. Perhaps his emotional distance from her has something to do with the gap between her teeth, which he doesn't find attractive, thinking of it as "a little yokel's or peasant's . . . gap." Their love affair is a matter of convenience for him. She seems content with the relationship, yet she is not unintelligent and dreams of one day helping him type his notes (he teaches her to type) and sitting beside him in his car "like a wife."

After some months, just before Christmas, three policemen invade the geologist's apartment, identify themselves, and search the place without benefit of a warrant. They force entry into the locked cupboard where the girl has hidden herself, and hustle the couple off to the police station. There the girl is physically examined for signs of intercourse by the district surgeon, a procedure that feels like rape to her: "[H]e [the doctor] placed her legs apart, resting in stirrups, and put into her where the other had made his way so warmly a cold hard instrument that expanded wider and wider." After a night in a cell, she is bailed out by the clerk of the lawyer engaged for her by Dr. von Leinsdorf. The "guilty" pair meet only once again, in court, where they do not greet or speak to each other.

Story II

The country lovers are children together and grow up to become lovers. He is Paulus Eysendyck, the white son of the farm owner employing the black girl's father. She is named Thebedi; she is pretty, and clever with her hands. Her affection for Paulus is returned, and their lovemaking — which he instigates — is lyrically described: "They were not afraid of one another, they had known one another always; he did with her what he had done that time in the storeroom at the wedding, and this time it was so lovely, so lovely, he was surprised . . . and she was surprised by it, too."

The outcome of this love affair is a mixed-blood colored baby with straight fine hair and Paulus's hazel eyes. When he sees his child, Paulus cries out of anger and self-pity. His life will be ruined, his family shamed (later his father says, "I will try and carry on as best I can to hold up my head in the district." Paulus murders the infant, Thebedi buries it, but the police come and dig it up. Someone has reported that it died mysteriously. Evidence in court is insufficient, so the verdict is "not guilty." The affair is over; as the black girl says to the newspaper reporter, "It was a thing of our childhood, we don't see each other anymore."

Both stories have a similar plot structure. Story I begins in the present tense, but switches to past narrative tense when Dr. von Leinsdorf first talks to the colored girl cashier at the supermarket and their story begins. Story II begins with a paragraph in the present tense, about social customs on the farm, but when Paulus and Thebedi are introduced in the next paragraph, the narrative goes into past tense. The personal stories come to an end and require the past tense. The social background continues on.

The volatile emotions potentially in any love affair are kept in careful control through Gordimer's expert handling of point of view in Story I and character in Story II. Dr. von Leinsdorf expresses his ingrained sense of social superiority verging on racial stereotyping when he sees the colored cashier outside the supermarket and notices, "She was rather small and finely-made, for one of them. The coat was skimpy but no big backside jutted." Gordimer gives the geologist's point of view without authorial comment, resulting in an emotional distancing on the part of a sensitive reader. Thus feelings are kept in check. In Story II, Thebedi marries a native boy who accepts her baby and treats it so well that the judge later commends his "honourable behaviour." By introducing this character, Gordimer keeps Thebedi from being a tragic or sentimental figure, abandoned by Paulus and left on her own. Gordimer's decency, compassion, and restraint are in marked contrast to the laws of the society she describes.

Questions for Discussion

1. What does the opening paragraph explain about Dr. Franz-Josef von Leinsdorf's character? How is this characterization achieved? Look at the diction; he's a geologist wrapped up, enfolded, swaddled in the layers and layers of his work. How do you interpret the information that "even as a handsome small boy he presented only his profile" to his mother? What does this paragraph tell you about the geologist's ability to love?

2. On page 568, the geologist describes the "coloured girl." List the parts of her body that make up his description. See page 570: "She had a little yokel's,

peasant's (he thought of it) gap between her two front teeth when she smiled that he didn't much like."

3. "He said, watching her sew, 'You're a good girl'; and touched her." Does the narrator give us access to the characters' minds? Does the geologist love the colored girl? Does she him? What are their motivations? Why might Gordimer keep the reader at such a psychological distance in this story?

4. How does the introductory phrase "On a summer night near Christmas" prepare the Western reader for the conclusion? Why do the policemen search the girl and the clothes and sheets "for signs of his seed"? What effect does Gordimer's graphic description of the girl's physical examination have on your understanding of the story's denouement: "He placed her legs apart, resting in stirrups, and put into her where the other had made his way so warmly a cold hard instrument that expanded wider and wider. Her thighs and knees trembled uncontrollably while the doctor looked into her and touched her deep inside with more hard instruments, carrying wafers of gauze."

5. Both part I and part II of "Town and Country Lovers" end with the protagonists in court. Why does Gordimer close both *stories* with the court scene? Why does she give, in both stories, the quotations carried by the Sunday papers? How would you compare the stories given to the public — both legal and journalistic — and the more private stories you have had access to through reading "Town and Country Lovers"?

6. After Paulus sees his baby for the first time, he says, "I feel like killing myself." Why does this make both Thebedi and Paulus sense a return of the "feeling between them that used to come when they were alone down at the river-bed"?

7. While Paulus is murdering the baby, Thebedi thinks she hears "small grunts ... the kind of infant grunt that indicates a full stomach, a deep sleep." She tells her husband the baby is sleeping. When she first testifies, she is hysterical, and says things that we know are not true. More than a year later she retestifies, and tells the truth. At no point does Gordimer give the reader any explicit commentary on Thebedi's feelings and actions. How do you interpret the flat description of events in these most highly charged moments in the story?

8. What themes are common to both parts of "Town and Country Lovers"? Are the protagonists in each part similar or not?

Topics for Writing

1. In Gordimer's essay "The Flash of Fireflies" in Part Two (p. 1425), she says that "the short story is a fragmented and restless form, a matter of hit or miss, and it is perhaps for this reason that it suits modern consciousness — which seems best expressed as flashes of fearful insight alternating with near-hypnotic states of indifference." Analyze the language and structure of "Town and Country Lovers" with reference to this definition.

2. Discuss the effects of apartheid on human relationships.

3. Discuss the effects of repressive policies on human rights in "Town and Country Lovers."

4. Consider other legislation that you feel violates human rights and write a short story illustrating its effects.

(text pp. 582–595)

Related Commentary

Nadine Gordimer, The Flash of Fireflies, p. 1425.

Suggested Readings

Clayton, Cherry, ed. *Women and Writing in South Africa. A Critical Anthology.* Marshalltown: Heinemann Southern Africa, 1989, 183ff.

Cooke, J. "African Landscapes: The World of Nadine Gordimer." *World Literature Today* 52 (1978): 533–38.

Eckstein, B. "Pleasure and Joy: Political Activism in Nadine Gordimer's Short Stories." *World Literature Today* 59 (1985): 343–46.

Gordimer, Nadine. *Jump and Other Stories.* New York: Farrar, 1991.

Gray, S. "Interview with Nadine Gordimer." *Contemporary Literature* 22 (1981): 263–71.

Heywood, Christopher. *Nadine Gordimer.* Windsor, ONT: Profile, 1983.

Hurwitt, J. "Art of Fiction: Nadine Gordimer." *Paris Review* 25 (1983): 83–127.

Jacobs, J. U. "Living Space and Narrative Space in Nadine Gordimer's 'Something Out There.'" *English in Africa* 14(2) (Oct. 1987): 31–43.

Lazar, Karen. "Feminism as 'Piffling'? Ambiguities in Some of Nadine Gordimer's Short Stories." *Current Writing* 2(1) (Oct. 1990): 101–16.

Mazurek, Raymond A. "Nadine Gordimer's 'Something Out There' and Ndebele's 'Fools' and Other Stories: The Politics of Literary Form." *Studies in Short Fiction* 26(1) (Winter 1989): 71–79.

Newman, Judie. *Nadine Gordimer.* New York: Routledge, 1988.

Ross, Robert L., ed. *International Literature on Major Writers.* New York: Garland, 1991. 762ff.

Smith, Rowland. *Critical Essays on Nadine Gordimer.* Boston: G. K. Hall, 1990.

Smyer, R. I. "Africa in the Fiction of Nadine Gordimer." *Ariel* 16 (1985): 15–29.

Trump, Martin. "The Short Fiction of Nadine Gordimer." *Research in African Literature* 17(3) (Fall 1968): 341–69.

NATHANIEL HAWTHORNE

My Kinsman, Major Molineux (p. 582)

The critic Lewis Leary has said that "in the hand of a master, [the short story] becomes consummately an art, suggesting more than it seems at first to reveal." This statement is certainly true about "My Kinsman, Major Molineux," which has attracted a massive number of critical interpretations. In Part Two, Simon O. Lesser brings a psychological approach to his reading of this classic tale (p. 1450).

One way to approach the story in the classroom is to compare and contrast it with "Young Goodman Brown." Both describe the experience of immature, arrogant young men who seek something outside the familiar circle of their experience; both underestimate the impediments in their paths as they search for enlightenment. Hawthorne's distance from both Robin and Brown allows him to present them ambivalently, displaying simultaneous contradictory attitudes toward their quests so that both stories suggest a good deal more than they seem "at first to reveal."

Robin sets a high value on himself, yet he is woefully ignorant of the political climate of his times; self-interest is his only concern. In the beginning paragraph of "My Kinsman, Major Molineux," Hawthorne tells us more about the hardships faced by colonial governors than Robin appears to know. Thus Robin lacks political savvy in the eyes not only of the townspeople but also of the reader. Hawthorne adopted this strategy, carried on in popular fiction writing in our own time, to give historical weight to his magazine tale. But few writers inject historical material this way, to tell the reader something the protagonist does not know. Thus Hawthorne ensures that the reader will also be emotionally distanced from Robin.

Why did the author make Robin such a bumpkin? The customary answer is that Hawthorne wrote tales of initiation, dramatizing male rites of passage in the New England community. A more politicized reading would suggest that in both "My Kinsman Major Molineux" and "Young Goodman Brown" Hawthorne is investigating the darker side of the American dream of self-fulfillment, putting personal ambition before community involvement. Material advancement drives Robin, spiritual ambition rules Brown; both are the products of a society whose traditions are so recent that its citizens hope to attain power just by asking for it. Hawthorne shows us that the road to hell is paved with good intentions: which way the road to heaven?

Questions for Discussion

1. What is the importance of the historical background in the opening paragraph of "My Kinsman, Major Molineux"?
2. What are Robin's good qualities? his limitations?
3. Trace Robin's search for his kinsman. What kind of picture does Hawthorne paint of pre-Revolutionary New England life?
4. What is your interpretation of the grotesque character with his face painted in two colors whom Robin meets in the inn and later sees on the street?
5. How does the description of the moonlight help to set the scene and prepare for the end of the story?
6. What is the importance of Robin's dreams of home just before he meets the "gentleman in his prime" who befriends him?
7. How do you react to the description of Major Molineux "in tar-and-feathery dignity" on the uncovered cart? Would you have reacted the way Robin did to the sight of his uncle? What does his reaction tell you about Robin?
8. Interpret the last words of the "gentleman in his prime" at the end of the story. Does he have good or bad intentions toward Robin?
9. Do you think Hawthorne intended "My Kinsman, Major Molineux" to be read as a realistic tale or as an allegory? Explain.

Topics for Writing

1. Rewrite the story making Robin a contemporary young man who goes to a state capital seeking political favor from a distant relative.

2. **CONNECTIONS**   Contrast and compare "My Kinsman, Major Molineux" and "Young Goodman Brown."

Related Commentaries

Edgar Allan Poe, The Importance of the Single Effect in a Prose Tale, p. 1488.
Simon O. Lesser, A Psychological Reading of Hawthorne's "My Kinsman, Major Molineux," p. 1450.

Suggested Readings

See page 112.

NATHANIEL HAWTHORNE

Young Goodman Brown (p. 595)

Teaching "Young Goodman Brown," you should encourage students to read "The Elements of Fiction" (p. 1608) carefully, since different aspects of Hawthorne's story are analyzed throughout the discussion of the elements of short fiction. "Writing about Short Stories" (p. 1621) also has student essays developing different ideas about "Young Goodman Brown."

Students often need help recognizing stories that are not intended to be read as realistic narrative. Some readers tend to take every word in the story literally; Hawthorne, however, meant "Young Goodman Brown" to be a moral allegory, not a realistic story. While most students will be able to recognize the use of symbolism, you might have to introduce them to the idea of allegory, in which the entire story is an extended metaphor representing one thing in the guise of another.

An allegory is a story that has a dual meaning — one in the events, characters, and setting; and the other in the ideas they are intended to convey. At first, "Young Goodman Brown" holds our interest on the level of the surface narrative. But the story also has a second meaning, which must be read beneath, and concurrent with, the surface narrative. This second meaning is not to be confused with the theme of the story — all stories have themes, but not all stories are allegories. In an allegory, the characters are usually personifications of abstract qualities (faith) and the setting is representative of the relations among the abstractions (Goodman Brown takes leave of his "Faith" at the beginning of the story).

A story is an allegory only if the characters, events, and setting are presented in a logical pattern so that they represent meanings independent of the action described in the surface story. Most writers of allegorical fiction are moralists. In this moral allegory, Hawthorne is suggesting the ethical principle that should govern human life. The *unpardonable sin* for Hawthorne is a "want of love and reverence for the Human Soul" and is typified by the person who searches the depths of the heart with "a cold philosophical curiosity." The result is a separation of the intellect from the heart, which is fatal in relationships among human beings, as shown in what happens to Goodman Brown when he returns to Salem village at the end of the story.

Questions for Discussion

1. When is a careful reader first aware that Hawthorne intends this story to be read as a moral allegory?
2. One of the characters in a Hawthorne story says, "You know that I can never separate the idea from the symbol in which it manifests itself." Hawthorne's flat characters — such as Deacon Gookin, Goody Cloyse, and the minister — represent social institutions. Why does Hawthorne include them in the story?
3. On pages 596–97 Hawthorne writes, "But the only thing about him that could be fixed upon as remarkable was his staff, which bore the likeness of a great black snake, so curiously wrought that it might almost be seen to twist and wriggle itself like a living serpent. This, of course, must have been an ocular deception, assisted by the uncertain light." What is the assertion contained in the first sentence? What effect do the words "might almost" have on that assertion? Why does Hawthorne immediately qualify the first sentence in the second? On page 602, Hawthorne writes: "Either the sudden gleams of light flashing over the obscure field bedazzled Goodman Brown, or he recognized a score of the church members of Salem village famous for their especial sanctity." Discuss the function of this sentence and find others like it throughout the story. What is their cumulative effect?
4. Why is it important that most of the action in this story takes place in the forest? Looking through Hawthorne's story, isolate the particular words that are associated with the woods. Consider the paragraph on page 600 that begins "And, maddened with despair." List the characteristics of forests that are responsible for this long literary tradition. Consider, too, whether the idea of wilderness remains static throughout history. In the late nineteenth century, with industrialization such a potent force, would people have conceived of the forest in the same way the early settlers did? Why or why not?
5. Where does this story take place (besides in the forest)? On page 596 a man addresses the protagonist saying, "You are late, Goodman Brown. . . . The clock of the Old South was striking as I came through Boston, and that is full fifteen minutes agone." What does this detail — that the traveler was in Boston fifteen minutes ago — mean to our interpretation of the story?
6. One page 603, "the dark figure" welcomes his listeners to "the communion of your race." What is usually meant by the word "communion"? How is it meant here? What does the speaker mean by the phrase in which he uses it? What kinds of powers does the "sable form" promise the crowd? Discuss the kinds of knowledge that will henceforth be accessible to his listeners' senses. Who is speaking in this passage on page 603: "Herein did the shape of evil dip his hand and prepare to lay the mark of baptism upon their foreheads, that they might be partakers of the mystery of sin, more conscious of the secret guilt of others, both in deed and thought, than they could now be of their own"? How does this sentence guide your judgment of Young Goodman Brown in the closing paragraph of the story? How does the sable figure's sermon comment on the closing paragraph?

7. How much time does this story cover? Where do the first seven paragraphs take place? How many paragraphs are set in the forest? What do the final three paragraphs address? What might be some reasons for the story to be built this way?

Topic for Writing

1. Show how a knowledge of seventeenth-century New England history and Puritan theology can enhance a reading of the story.

Related Commentaries

Herman Melville, Blackness in Hawthorne's "Young Goodman Brown," p. 1458.
Edgar Allan Poe, The Importance of the Single Effect in a Prose Tale, p. 1488.

Suggested Readings

Arvin, Newton. *Hawthorne.* Russell and Russell, 1961.
Bloom, Harold. *Nathaniel Hawthorne.* New York: Chelsea House, 1990.
Cowley, Malcolm, ed. *Portable Hawthorne.* New York: Penguin, 1977.
Crowley, J. Donald, ed. *Centenary Edition of the Works of Nathaniel Hawthorne.* Columbus: Ohio State UP, 1974. Vol IX, *Twice-Told Tales;* Vol. X, *Mosses from an Old Manse;* Vol. XI, *The Snow Image and Uncollected Tales.*
Ferguson, J. M., Jr. "Hawthorne's 'Young Goodman Brown.' " *Explicator* 28 (1969): Item 32.
Fetterley, Judith. *The Resisting Reader.* Bloomington: Indiana UP, 1978.
Gallagher, Edward J. "The Concluding Paragraph of 'Young Goodman Brown.' " *Studies in Short Fiction* 12 (1975): 29–30.
McIntosh, James, ed. *Nathaniel Hawthorne's Tales.* New York: Norton, 1987.
Newman, Lea Bertani. *A Reader's Guide to the Short Stories of Nathaniel Hawthorne.* Boston: G. K. Hall, 1979.
Robinson, E. Arthur. "The Vision of Goodman Brown: A Source and Interpretation." *American Literature* 35 (1963): 218–25.
Von Frank, Albert J., ed. *Critical Essays on Hawthorne's Short Stories.* Boston: G. K. Hall, 1991.
Whelan, Robert E. "Hawthorne Interprets 'Young Goodman Brown.' " *Emerson Society Quarterly* 62 (1971): 3–6.

BESSIE HEAD

Life (p. 605)

This story opens with a paragraph of explanation about its background, reminiscent of the beginning of "My Kinsman, Major Molineux." As Hawthorne tells us that the colonial governors appointed by the king of England often ran into trouble with their subjects in the New World, Head explains that the village people in Botswana rejected city habits that were harmful to them and that "the murder of Life had this complicated undertone of rejection." In their introductory paragraphs, both Head and Hawthorne eliminate a large measure of suspense in their stories by giving broad hints of both the plot and theme to come. What, then, makes the reader want to continue?

This question is a useful one to begin a discussion about "Life." For one thing, Head's protagonist has an unusual name, and most readers will entertain the possibility that Head is writing an allegory investigating the human situation, and that the specific twenty-seven-year-old woman named Life is a literary symbol in addition to being a realistic character.

This sense of a larger dimension to the character in Head's story — as in Hawthorne's depiction of Robin's adventures searching for his uncle — is strengthened by the author's description of the setting. In a very few pages, "Life" tells us a great deal about how people live in the villages of Botswana. We read about the traditional custom of continuing to offer a home in the village to members of families who left for Johannesburg, even as long as seventeen years after a family has departed. We learn of the village women's willingness to help Life by working to make her yard and house habitable. Traditional food, references to the feasting at weddings, the villagers' matter-of-fact attitude toward sex ("that it ought to be available whenever possible like food and water"), the division of labor between men and women, the careers available to educated women, the social differences between the respectable housewives and the beer-brewing women — all these details paint a rich picture and develop our awareness of the moral structure of village customs.

The narrator's point of view is close and balanced, not distant and ironic like Hawthorne's attitude toward Robin. Head is an omniscient storyteller; she tells us that "one evening death walked quietly into the bar" when she introduces Lesego, the cattleman who becomes Life's husband. Head succinctly defines their attraction for us: "[T]hey looked at each other from their own worlds and came to fatal conclusions." The tragedy of their marriage is the second half of the story, and what happens to them focuses the moral dimension of "Life."

Questions for Discussion

1. Is suspense lacking in the story because Head tells you the ending in her first paragraph? Explain.
2. What is attractive about Life? Is her "undertone of hysteria" attractive or unattractive?
3. Why is Lesego so confident that Life will change her promiscuous ways if he marries her?
4. Explicate the paragraph of commentary beginning "She hadn't the mental equipment to analyse what hit her" after Lesego tells Life that he will kill her if she is unfaithful to him.
5. Head's description of the activity of Life's yard — the blaring transistor radio, the people reeling around "dead drunk," the prostitution — is not presented in a judgmental way. How do you know what Head thinks of such behavior?
6. Is Head more sympathetic to the village women or to Life? Explain.

Topics for Writing

1. Analyze the function of food and drink in "Life."
2. Use a feminist critical strategy to analyze the ending of "Life," Lesego's action and his punishment.
3. In the final paragraph, Head suggests that the beer-brewing women have the last word "on the whole affair." Agree or disagree with this statement and explain your response.
4. **CONNECTIONS**   Compare and contrast "Life" with Zora Neale Hurston's "Spunk."

Suggested Readings

Head, Bessie. *The Collector of Treasures and Other Botswana Village Tales.* London: Heinemann, 1977.
———. *Tales of Tenderness and Power.* Portsmouth, NH: Neinemann International, 1990.

Ernest Hemingway

Hills Like White Elephants (p. 615)

Hemingway wrote this story in May 1927, while on his honeymoon in the Rhône delta with his second wife, Pauline. According to his biographer Kenneth Lynn, the story was a dramatization of a fantasy he had about his first wife, Hadley: "[I]f only the two of them had not allowed a child to enter their lives they would never have parted." Throughout his biography, Lynn interprets the fiction in terms of Hemingway's relationships. How much this approach sheds light on the fiction each reader must judge.

This story is an early example of a minimalist technique. Characterization and plot are mere suggestions, and it is possible for some young readers to finish the story for the first time with no idea that the couple are discussing an abortion. The setting Hemingway chooses for the couple's conversation is more richly developed. The symbolism of the "two lines of rails" at the station (the choice either to end the pregnancy or have the child); the fields of grain and trees along the Ebro River, which the girl sees on the other side of the station (fertility, a settled life) compared with the barren hills, long and white like white elephants (something considered unlucky, unwanted, and rejected); the bar and the station building (the temporary escape offered by alcohol, the sense of people in transit) — one can interpret these details in perfect harmony with the couple's emotional and physical dilemma.

The man's bullying of the girl drives the story. His ignorance about abortion and his insensitivity to what she is feeling or will have to endure physically ("It's not really anything. It's just to let the air in") are not presented as weakness. They are simply part of his insistence on persuading Jig to do what he wants her to do.

The girl is also worthy of discussion. Her vulnerability is idealized, yet she is not stupid. Without the suggestion of her intelligence, there would be no story.

Hemingway regarded "Hills Like White Elephants" as one of his best stories, reserving a prominent place for it in his second collection, *Men Without Women*, published in the fall of 1927. Lynn states that in choosing this title for the book, Hemingway meant to suggest "that the alienation of women from men (as well as vice versa) was one of his themes."

Questions for Discussion

1. In what ways could you categorize this story as a minimalist work?
2. What do we know about the man? About the girl? Why isn't Jig called "a woman" in the story?
3. What is a "white elephant"? How does this expression suit the story?
4. What do you think will happen to this couple after the story ends?
5. Read the story aloud in class, assigning two students the roles of the man and the girl. Is the story as effective read as dialogue as it is on the page as a literary text?

Topic for Writing

1. Rewrite the story in a different setting to discover the importance of the railroad station and the Spanish landscape in "Hills Like White Elephants."

Suggested Reading

Baker, Carlos, ed. *Ernest Hemingway: A Life Story.* New York: Macmillan, 1976.
———. *Ernest Hemingway: Selected Letters 1917–1961.* Scribner's, 1981.
Beegel, Susan F., ed. *Hemingway's Neglected Short Fiction: New Perspectives.* Ann Arbor, MI: UMI Research Press, 1989.
Benson, Jackson. *The Short Stories of Ernest Hemingway: Critical Essays.* Durham, NC: Duke UP, 1975.
———, ed. *New Critical Approaches to the Short Stories of Ernest Hemingway.* Durham, NC: Duke UP, 1990.
Brenner, Gerry, and Earl Rovit. *Ernest Hemingway, Revised Edition.* Boston: Twayne, 1990.
Flora, Joseph M. *Ernest Hemingway: A Study of the Short Fiction.* Boston: Twayne, 1989.
Hays, Peter L. *Ernest Hemingway.* New York: Continuum, 1990.
Lynn, Kenneth S. *Hemingway.* New York: Simon, 1987.
Martin, Terence. *Ernest Hemingway: Revised Edition.* Boston: Twayne, 1990.
Reynolds, Michael S., ed. *Critical Essays on Ernest Hemingway's* In Our Time. Boston: G. K. Hall, 1983.

ZORA NEALE HURSTON

The Gilded Six-Bits (p. 620)

An instructor presenting this story may find that it is difficult to reconcile some of the contemporary commentary on the work of Zora Neale Hurston with the realities of her short fiction. The tendency has been to idealize her and her work, overlooking the bitter realities that she describes. It may be that she grew up in an isolated community, and that a current writer could comment, as did scholar Mary Helen Washington, that the community was "neither ghetto, nor slum, nor black bottom, but a rich source of black cultural traditions . . .," but the violence and the near collapse of the strong familial tradition that Hurston describes in a story like *The Gilded Six-Bits* reflects a society that has been degraded by years of systematic racism and economic repression.

It is sometimes emphasized that Hurston learned much about her little community through her research into the oral folk tradition, but the story doesn't relate to any of the characteristics of the oral folktale. Despite the muted sentimentality of the ending, the story is a realistic description of a clumsy infidelity on the part of a young wife. Hurston described how she loved to listen to the men of the community vying with each other as they told the old folktales on the grocery steps, but the story certainly doesn't have anything to do with Brer Rabbit.

At a point in American social consciousness when there is much concern about the effect of negative images in the portrayal of minority groups, it is interesting that the story has recently enjoyed a widespread popularity. Perhaps this is because Hurston's opening descriptions of the young couple, Joe and Missie May, present them as childlike and innocent. What she describes in the short story is almost a child marriage. Joe is so delighted with Missie May's girlishness that, when she is seduced by a newcomer to town, he punishes her the way a child would be punished, with silence and withdrawal.

Joe is almost as childlike as Missie May in his eventual acceptance of her infidelity. The newcomer had impressed him the way an adult impresses a child, with his swagger, his pretense of sophistication and wealth. For Joe this is summarized by the gold piece the man wears on his watch chain. When Joe surprises the man in bed with Missie May there is a short fight, and Joe pulls loose the man's chain with the gold piece. When he looks at it later he finds that it's only a fifty cent piece that has been gilded to look like gold, and it's obvious all the man's claims were lies. After some weeks Joe and Missie May mend their marriage, and she bears him a son. A week after the child is born Joe tells the storekeeper that he was never fooled by the other man at all, and he uses the fifty cent piece to buy candy for his wife and son. When he returns home they play again the youthful game of their marriage that opened the story.

In the real world of the dirt road, tar-paper shack communities that Hurston is describing, adultery was much more harshly punished. Perhaps the story has earned some of its popularity with student readers by describing the world as we wish it were, instead of how it is.

Questions for Discussion

1. How would you describe the economic conditions of Joe and Missie May's life?
2. Would this description only be real for the community of Eatonville, Florida, where Hurston grew up, or would it apply to black rural communities everywhere in the South?
3. How does the author make us aware of Joe's lack of sophistication? Is this presented in a negative way?
4. Why does the author make a point of Joe's being excited that the newcomer has lived in a city?
5. How is the newcomer different from the other men in the small town?
6. Hurston never tells the reader what finally happens to Slemmons. Why isn't this important to her?
7. What is likely to happen to Missie May in the future?

Topics for Writing

1. Discuss the images of coins and money that occur in the story, beginning with the title.
2. Consider the possibilities that Joe and Missie May have to change their life for the better.
3. Analyze the economic factors that make a man like Slemmons fascinating to people in the small town.
4. Describe the elements of racism that have conditioned Joe and Missie May to accept their life as it is.

Related Commentaries

Robert Bone, A Folkloric Analysis of Hurston's "Spunk" and "The Gilded Six-Bits," p. 1389.
Zora Neale Hurston, What White Publishers Won't Print, p. 1430.
Alice Walker, Zora Neale Hurston: A Cautionary Tale and a Partisan View, p. 1505

Suggested Readings

See page 119.

ZORA NEALE HURSTON

Spunk (p. 628)

The title of Hurston's story has a double meaning. "Spunk" refers to Spunk Banks, the giant of a man who courts the married woman Lena and who "ain't skeered of nothin' on God's green footstool — *nothin'*!" But it also refers to the quality of "spunk" (courage) shown by Lena's timid husband, Joe, the sarsaparilla-drinking "round-shouldered figure in overalls much too large," who comes back from the grave after Spunk has shot him in order to take his revenge. It took spunk for Joe to try to get Lena back from her pistol-packing lover, and Joe's courage lasts until he succeeds at what he wanted to do.

Hurston has written a ghost story based on the revenge motif in the Florida black tradition of vernacular speech and folk superstition. Joe first comes back from the dead in the figure of a "big black bob-cat" (an unearthly color for a bobcat). In this animal form he frightens Spunk so much that Spunk can't shoot his army .45 pistol, a small revenge in itself. For the ultimate revenge, something pushes Spunk in the back onto the buzz saw. Spunk believes it's Joe's ghost and vows to get him in hell. As a storyteller, Hurston pulls out of the two men's quarrel at this point. She ends the narrative with Lena, the "small pretty woman" who is the object of the two men's affections and who holds a wake for her departed lover. Hurston's interest is firmly in this world, describing the scene with a poetic economy of detail:

> The cooling board consisted of three sixteen-inch boards on saw horses, a dingy sheet was his shroud.
> The women ate heartily of the funeral baked meats and wondered who would be Lena's next. The men whispered coarse conjectures between guzzles of whiskey.

Questions for Discussion

1. Why is the main part of the story told through the conversation between Elijah Mosley and Walter Thomas? They are, after all, outsiders to the intimate action, depending on hearsay for the bulk of their information.
2. Look at the final paragraph: "The women ate heartily of the funeral baked meats and wondered who would be Lena's next. The men whispered coarse conjectures between guzzles of whiskey." How does this paragraph, one of the few scenes related by the narrator, influence your interpretation of this story? Is "Spunk" about events that happen, or is it about the stories about events that happen? What's the difference?
3. This story is split into four parts, yet it's only five pages long. What is the effect of this structure? What is the narrative burden of each section?
4. In the opening paragraph of section II, Hurston writes, "Lena wept in a frightened manner." What are some other ways of saying this? What effect does this particular way have on your estimation of Lena's character? In the next paragraph Hurston writes, " 'Well,' Spunk announced calmly, 'Joe came out there wid a meat axe an' made me kill him.' " Is this statement factually true? Where does the language Spunk uses locate the responsibility for the killing?
5. What effect does the black Florida dialect have on the setting and characterization of the story? How much physical description is present in "Spunk"? How does the dialect convey the same ideas that physical detail might?
6. Analyze the final paragraph in section II: "A clear case of self-defense, the trial was a short one, and Spunk walked out of the court house to freedom again. He could work again, ride the dangerous log-carriage that fed the singing, snarling, biting circle-saw: he could stroll the soft dark lanes with

his guitar. He was free to roam the woods again; he was free to return to Lena. He did all of these things." Notice the sentence lengths: three long sentences followed by a short one. What sentence gains the emphasis in this arrangement and why? What effect does the repetition of both words and syntax create? Look at the list of adjectives that precedes "circle-saw." How would you describe the style of this paragraph? How does it relate to the kind of story Hurston is telling?

7. What do you make of the supernatural elements that are introduced into sections III and IV? What kinds of stories contain supernatural elements like this? What is a "h'ant"?

8. With whom does the narrator place her sympathies in this story: Spunk, Joe, Lena, Elijah, or Walter? Discuss the passages that support your conclusion.

Topics for Writing

1. Describe the country humor in "Spunk."
2. Discuss courage in "Spunk."
3. Write an essay analyzing the supernatural elements in "Spunk."
4. Rewrite the story from Lena's point of view.
5. **CONNECTIONS** Compare and contrast the folk elements in "Spunk" and Ellison's "Battle Royal."

Related Commentaries

Robert Bone, A Folkloric Analysis of Hurston's "Spunk" and "The Gilded Six-Bits," p. 1389.
Zora Neale Hurston, What White Publishers Won't Print, p. 1430.
Alice Walker, Zora Neale Hurston: A Cautionary Tale and a Partisan View, p. 1505.

Suggested Readings

Bone, R. A. "Three Versions of the Pastoral." *Down Home: A History of Afro-American Short Fiction from Its Beginnings to the End of the Harlem Renaissance.* New York: Putnam, 1975. 139–70.
Cooke, Michael. *Afro-American Literature in the Twentieth Century: The Achievement of Intimacy.* New Haven: Yale UP, 1984.
Hemenway, R. "Zora Neale Hurston and the Eatonville Anthropology." *The Harlem Renaissance Remembered.* Ed. A. W. Bontemps. New York: Dodd, 1972. 190–214.
Howard, L. P. "Marriage: Zora Neale Hurston's System of Values." *CLA Journal* 21 (1977): 256–68.
Hurston, Zora Neale. *The Gilded Six-Bits.* Minneapolis: Redpath, 1986.
———. *I Love Myself When I Am Laughing . . . and Then Again When I Am Looking Mean and Impressive.* Ed. Alice Walker. Old Westbury, NY: Feminist, 1979.
———. *Mules and Men.* Westport, CT: Greenwood, 1969.
Johnson, B. "Thresholds of Difference: Structures of Address in Zora Neale Hurston." *Critical Inquiry* 12 (1985): 278–89.

Love, T. R. "Zora Neale Hurston's America." *Papers on Language and Literature* 12 (1976): 422–37.

Lupton, M. J. "Zora Neale Hurston and the Survival of the Female." *Southern Literary Journal* 15 (1982): 45–54.

Sheffey, Ruth T., ed. *Rainbow Round Her Shoulders: The Zora Neale Hurston Symposium Papers*. Baltimore: Morgan State UP, 1982.

Washington, Mary Helen, ed. *Invented Lives: Narratives of Black Women 1860–1960*. Garden City, NY: Anchor Press, 1987.

SHIRLEY JACKSON

The Lottery (p. 634)

The interpretive suggestions in the headnote should guide students toward a recognition of the main themes of "The Lottery." The near universality of the ritual sacrifice of year gods and scapegoats in primitive cultures to ensure fertility, the continuation of life, and the purgation of society has been a common assumption since the publication of James G. Frazer's *The Golden Bough*. Jackson does not explore the transmutations of these old ceremonies in the accepted religious practices and psychological mechanisms of modern humanity; rather, she attempts to shock her readers into an awareness of the presence of raw, brutal, and superstitious impulses within us all. A fruitful approach for class discussion might involve exploring how the story achieves its impact. Jackson's comments (included in Part Two, p. 1434) provide incontrovertible documentation of the power of "The Lottery" to stir the dark instincts dwelling below the surface of the civilized psyche, perhaps the same regions from which the story emerged fully formed — as Jackson claims — in the mind of the writer. No wonder readers, from the author's agent on, have found "The Lottery" disturbing.

But they have also found it compelling, fascinating, and irresistible, and the reason may have partly to do with Jackson's technical skill. For the inattentive first reader, the natural suspense of any drawing, contest, or lottery provides strong motivation to hurry through to the ending, and when the realization of what is at stake comes, it strikes with redoubled force because of the reader's increased velocity. For the more careful reader, or for the reader already aware of the ending, the subtle foreshadowing — the boys are gathering stones, the box is black, Tessie Hutchinson "clean forgot what day it was" — triggers an uncomfortable double awareness that also urges haste, a haste like that which spurs Mr. Summers's final, horrible remark, "All right, folks. . . . Let's finish quickly," and the cries of "Come on" and "Hurry up" by other villagers.

For Jackson has succeeded in gaining the reader's vicarious participation in the lottery. Even the backwoods New England quaintness of the setting draws not the kind of condescending laughter that would distance the reader but the warm sentimental indulgence we reserve for the cutest Norman Rockwell illustrations. Little boys are being little boys as they pick up the stones, the villagers are walking clichés, and even Tessie Hutchinson, singled out from the rest by her tardiness, is tardy for the most housewifely of reasons. (How different the story would be if she appeared nervous and flustered, a few moments ahead of, say, a disheveled Steve Adams!) The reader is drawn to sink into this warm bath of comfortable stereotypes, illusions intact. Totally off guard against the possibility that the good hearts of these neighborly folks might beat in time with an ancient and brutal rhythm, that superstitious fears of hunger and death might easily outweigh feelings of friendliness and compassion, the reader may well recoil from any previous fascination and, in an effort to deny involvement, recoil from the story, too. Except that we do not reject it; "The Lottery" continues to exert such power over the imagination of its readers that it clearly must be providing a catharsis for instincts similar to those that move the villagers to pick up stones.

WILLIAM E. SHEIDLEY

Questions for Discussion

1. What associations does the word "lottery" have for you? Are they relevant to the story?
2. Comment on the ending of the first paragraph.
3. On what other occasions might the people of the village gather in the way they do for the lottery? Mr. Summers is in charge of "civic activities." Is the lottery one of these? Explain.
4. Discuss the degree to which the tradition of the lottery has been kept. Why does no one want to make a new box? Why is the whole institution not abandoned?
5. Examine the character of Tessie Hutchinson. She claims that her fate is not *fair*. Is there any reason why she should be singled out? Is she a tragic heroine? Consider her cry, "There's Don and Eva. . . . Make *them* take their chance!"
6. On your first reading, when did you begin to suspect what happens at the end of the story? How soon might it become evident? What are the most important hints?
7. One reason the ending can surprise a reader is that the villagers never speak directly of what they are about. Why not? Are they ashamed? afraid?
8. Comment on the conversation between the Adamses and Old Man Warner. What is the implication of Steve Adams's last appearance in the story?
9. Does the rhyme "Lottery in June, corn be heavy soon" adequately explain the institution of the lottery? What other reasons might people have for such behavior? What is the social function of a scapegoat?
10. After her family has received the black spot, Tessie complains, but Mrs. Delacroix tells her, "Be a good sport, Tessie." Comment on this choice of words.
11. Discuss the reaction of the Hutchinson family. Why does the lottery single out a family first, then a victim?
12. Old Man Warner says, "People ain't the way they used to be." Are they? What does he mean?
13. Why are the people in such a hurry to "finish"?
14. What is the implication of "someone gave little Davy Hutchinson a few pebbles"?

Topics for Writing

1. Discuss Jackson's techniques for building suspense in "The Lottery."
2. Write an essay exploring the usefulness of stereotypes in "The Lottery."
3. Examine the behavior of groups of people with which you are familiar. Can you find actual instances of formal or informal practices similar to the one described in "The Lottery" — even though they may not lead to such a brutal finale? Have you or has anyone you know been made a scapegoat? Write an essay showing how one such case reflects and confirms the implications of Jackson's story.
4. **CONNECTIONS** Compare and contrast Jackson's "The Lottery" and Le Guin's "The Ones Who Walk Away from Omelas."

Related Commentary

Shirley Jackson, The Morning of June 28, 1948, and "The Lottery," p. 1434.

Suggested Reading

Freidman, Lenemaja. *Shirley Jackson.* Twayne's United States Authors Series 253. Boston: G. K. Hall, 1975. 63–67.

HENRY JAMES

The Beast in the Jungle (p. 642)

James's commentary on "The Beast in the Jungle" (included in Part Two, p. 1437) acknowledges it as an "elaborated fantasy — which, I must add, I hold a successful thing only as its motive may seem to the reader to stand out sharp." This somewhat apologetic explanation concludes that the reader (as a "detached witness" to James's literary efforts) might not be successful at disengaging his "treated theme" from the labyrinth of sentences surrounding it. If James was so apprehensive about the obstacles to understanding his story that the leisured class of readers who bought his New York edition of *Collected Works* might encounter, teachers have good cause to proceed with care in discussing this text in the contemporary curriculum. After all, for most students James's long, complex story competes with assigned reading lists and problem sets in several other courses.

The critic Clifton Fadiman regards "The Beast in the Jungle" as the best of James's stories, "combining the utmost concentration of effect with the utmost inclusiveness of meaning." In Fadiman's explication, the story is pure myth, grounded in James's ironic treatment of the concept of the Faustian man that dominates our society: "Faust, we say, is ourselves, is Western man, the striver, the man to whom things happen, the man who makes things happen, the hero of experience." But the truth is that most people live modestly. We "live pitifully un-Faustian lives and die pitifully un-Faustian deaths." So James shows us how to present "the un-Faustian life in imaginative terms." According to Fadiman, the subject of "The Beast in the Jungle" is "not the life we have had but the life we have missed. . . . Most of us are only dimly aware that it never happens; but it is Marcher's horrifying fate to know it intensely."

Another more recent interpretation by the gender critic Eve Kosofsky Sedgwick, argues that John Marcher was a latent homosexual (see Part Two, p. 1491). Sedgwick, unlike most of the male critics who analyze "The Beast in the Jungle," considers May Bartram's desire as something more than a supplement to John Marcher's predicament. It is this kind of fresh approach to short-story classics that may show students the value of criticism, as well as the ability of great short fiction to survive its interpreters.

Questions for Discussion

1. Describe the main characters in the story and summarize their relationships.
2. What are the main events of the plot?
3. How would you characterize James's prose style?
4. How well do you think James succeeded in this story, in terms of what he said he wanted to do? (See his commentary in Part Two, p. 1437).

Topics for Writing

1. Assign each student in the class one sentence in the opening paragraphs of the story (the number of sentences assigned will depend on the class size). Ask students to paraphrase their sentences, using the clearest, simplest words that convey James's meaning. Collect these sentences and assemble them to correspond to the original. Distribute copies of the paraphrased text, and discuss what has been lost (or gained) in the translation.
2. Rewrite one of the major scenes of the book from the first-person point of view of John Marcher or May Bartram, or reimagine the whole story from May's point of view on her deathbed.
3. Read James's commentary (p. 1437) on "The Beast in the Jungle" and write an essay evaluating how successfully James achieved what he set out to do.
4. **CONNECTIONS** Compare John Marcher's progress through life to that of Tolstoy's Ivan Ilych in "The Death of Ivan Ilych" or Flaubert's Félicité in "A Simple Heart."

Related Commentaries

Henry James, The Subject of "The Beast in the Jungle," p. 1437.
Eve Kosofsky Sedgwick, The Beast in the Closet: A Gender Critic Reads James's "The Beast in the Jungle," p. 1491.

Suggested Readings

Aziz, Maqbool, ed. *The Tales of Henry James.* London: Oxford UP, 1984.
Dupee, Frederick W., ed. *Henry James: An Autobiography.* Westlake Village, NJ: Princeton UP, 1983.

Edel, Leon, ed. *The Complete Tales of Henry James.* 20 vols. Philadelphia: Lippincott, 1964.

——, and Lyall Powers, eds. *The Complete Notebooks of Henry James.* New York: Oxford UP, 1988.

Fadiman, Clifton, ed. "A Note on 'The Beast in the Jungle.'" *The Short Stories of Henry James.* New York: Random, 1945.

Hocks, Richard A. *Henry James: A Study of the Short Fiction.* Boston: Twayne, 1990.

Jones, Vivien. *James the Critic.* New York: St. Martin's, 1985.

Kappeler, Susanne. *Writing and Reading Henry James.* New York: Columbia UP, 1980.

Kraft, James. *The Early Tales of Henry James.* Carbondale: Southern Illinois UP, 1969.

Stowell, H. Peter. *Literary Impressionism, James and Chekhov.* Athens: U of Georgia P, 1980.

Wagenknecht, Edward. *The Tales of Henry James.* New York: Ungar, 1984.

Sarah Orne Jewett

A White Heron (p. 675)

Jewett portrays Sylvia, whose very name associates her with the woodland, as torn between the natural world in which she is so fully at home and the first stirrings of the "great power" of love in her "woman's heart." Her project of pleasing the young hunter and winning the treasure of his gratitude, in the form of ten dollars, leads her out of her shyness and into the heroic adventure of climbing the great pine tree. As a result of her efforts, Sylvia grows within herself. The reader worries that she may be tempted into betraying the white heron and thus into surrendering something essential to her own integrity, but Sylvia, in her vision from the top of the tree and her face-to-face meeting with the heron, has gained the perspective necessary to hold firm.

Jewett's rich evocation of the landscape and the emotional intensity with which she narrates the climactic action contribute to the story's deeper resonances. If Sylvia recalls the woodland goddess Diana — and similarly guards her chastity — she also resembles those heroes and heroines of myth and folklore who must go to some symbolic world-navel or towering height in quest of wisdom, or who must suffer an initiation that involves mastering their fear of the (sometimes phallic) *other* and reintegrating their identities in order to cope with it. Sylvia rejects the destructive gun and mounts the pine tree, "a great main-mast to the voyaging earth," electing the fecund life of a natural world she is still discovering over the destructive promises of the "ornithologist," whose grounds are populated with dead, stuffed birds. While the narrator ends fretting over Sylvia's having consigned herself to loneliness and love-longing, nothing in the story suggests that she would be better off having sold herself for ten dollars and a whistle.

Students may find it easier to approach the story through its autobiographical dimensions. According to Eugene Hillhouse Pool, who builds on F. O. Matthiessen's early study, Jewett remained childlike and single all her life, treasuring the love of her father, who used to take her on long rambles through the countryside when she was a girl. "As Sylvia elects to keep her private and meaningful secret, so is she choosing for Miss Jewett too. . . . She chooses, psychologically, to remain a child, with Sylvia." But if Jewett chose to remain a child, it is a child in terms she met in reading Wordsworth, whom she admired: as one privy to the indwelling spirit of the natural world.

The imagery that surrounds Sylvia is uniformly associated with *mother* nature until she ventures up the tree and meets the heron. Her adventure enables her to reject assertively the young man and the advancing modern world of science and machinery with which he is associated. This is a step forward from her original strategies of withdrawal and concealment. The antinomy, however, is not resolved. The only perfect marriage in the story is between the nesting herons; and Jewett offers no key to a satisfactory union between the world of nature and the civilization that threatens to despoil it.

WILLIAM E. SHEIDLEY

Questions for Discussion

1. Jewett is known as a local colorist. To what extent is the locale of this story its subject? To what extent does the story transcend its specific Maine setting?
2. Discuss the presentation of the cow Sylvia is driving as the story opens. What does her "loud moo by way of explanation" actually explain?
3. Comment on the men, apart from the hunter, mentioned in the story. Is the absence of men from Sylvia's world a significant factor in the story?
4. As a child in town, Sylvia has the reputation of being "afraid of folks." Is she? Does she have reason?
5. Explain Sylvia's reaction when she hears the hunter's whistle. Why does Jewett briefly switch to the present tense here? Does she do so elsewhere?
6. Comment on the omniscient-narrative point of view in this story. How is it controlled? What does the narrative voice contribute?
7. Describe the character and appurtenances of the young hunter, and contrast them with those of Sylvia. How important are his evident gentleness and good intentions?
8. How does Jewett charge the pine tree and Sylvia's climb to the top of it with special meaning? What does Sylvia see up there that she has never seen before?
9. What do Sylvia and the heron have in common?
10. Analyze the last paragraph. What has Sylvia lost? What has she preserved? What has she gained?

Topics for Writing

1. Research elements of folk and fairy tale in "A White Heron."
2. Analyze Sylvia's nighttime excursion as a journey into the self.
3. Examine maternal and sexual imagery in "A White Heron."
4. Consider "A White Heron" as a rejection of modern industrial society.

(text pp. 684–690)

Related Commentary

Sarah Orne Jewett, Looking Back on Girlhood, p. 1441.

Suggested Readings

Brenzo, Richard. "Free Heron or Dead Sparrow: Sylvia's Choice in Sarah Orne Jewett's 'A White Heron.' " *Colby Library Quarterly* 14 (1978): 36–41.

Cary, Richard. *Sarah Orne Jewett.* Albany, NY: New Collections UP, 1962.

Donovan, Josephine L. *Sarah Orne Jewett.* New York: Ungar, 1980.

Hovet, Theodore R. "America's 'Lonely Country Child': The Theme of Separation in Sarah Orne Jewett's 'A White Heron.'" *Colby Library Quarterly* 14 (1978): 166–71.

———." 'Once Upon a Time': Sarah Orne Jewett's 'A White Heron' as a Fairy Tale." *Studies in Short Fiction* 15 (1978): 63-68.

Keyworth, Cynthia, et al. *Master Smart Women: A Portrait of Sarah Orne Jewett.* Belfast, ME: North Country, 1988.

Nagel, Gwen. *Critical Essays on Sarah Orne Jewett.* Boston: G. K. Hall, 1984.

Pool, Eugene Hillhouse. "The Child in Sarah Orne Jewett." *Appreciation of Sarah Orne Jewett.* Ed. Richard Cary. Waterville, ME: Colby College P, 1973. 223–28, esp. 225. Originally published in *Colby Library Quarterly* 7 (1967): 503–09.

Westbrook, Perry D. *Acres of Flint: Sarah Orne Jewett and Her Contemporaries, Rev. Ed.* Metuchen, NJ: Scarecrow, 1981.

CHARLES JOHNSON

Menagerie, A Child's Fable (p. 684)

Despite the subtitle of "Menagerie" ("A Child's Fable"), Johnson's interest in psychology, philosophy, religion, history, and folk and popular culture contributes such a wealth of references to people, ideas, images, and events in this story that it jumps out of the category of Children's Literature to become a story for adults (or precocious children). Yet Johnson's writing is so clear, steady, and lucid that his references, far from seeming obscure, explain themselves with little fuss or fanfare. Of course a flighty aerobic dance teacher would own a flirtatious little female poodle. Of course a cruel pet shop owner with a heart condition would live alone and fail to show up one fine Monday Morning. By the time readers finish "Menagerie," there's a good chance they will have emphathized so closely with the narrator Berkeley, the German shepherd, that they will feel that they are also on his intellectual wavelength: "Not the smartest, but steady."

Children's stories with fabulous talking animals that dramatize a moral are not unusual (Aesop's fables come immediately to mind), but adult stories "peopled" with talking animals instead of human beings are rare indeed. Johnson's irrepressible sense of humor — and his unwavering moral sense — underpin the narrative, but it is his ability to create realistic "human" characters in the bodies of dog, monkey, turtle, fish, rabbit, and Siamese that holds our interest.

Take Monkey, for example. We're told right from the start that Berkeley didn't care "a whole lot" for him, and then we're shown his uninhibited wickedness: he is "a comedian always grabbing his groin to get a laugh, throwing feces, or fooling with the other animals." He's the Freudian amoral id in action, doing just as he pleases, totally devoid of any higher instincts of conscience, justice, or gratitude, entirely capable of biting the hand that feeds him. Tortoise, on the other hand, is at the other extreme, so repressed by his dizzying week of freedom after escaping from his cage that "he hadn't spoken in a year."

"Menagerie, A Child's Fable" is included in Johnson's collection of what he calls "tales and conjurations," *The Sorcerer's Apprentice*. (*Webster's Dictionary* defines "conjuration" as the act of conjuring, or practicing magic; the word also has a second meaning, "a solemn appeal.") Johnson uses as an epigraph a quotation from chapter XXIII of Herman Melville's *The Confidence Man:* "It is with fiction as with religion; it should present another world, and yet one to which we feel the tie." "Menagerie" presents a fictional world that has such clear ties to our own muddled state of humanity that students should understand the allegory without much explanation. If they need help interpreting the chaos of the last scene, a suggestion that they watch the evening news on television or read the front page of their local newspaper might help to illuminate Johnson's meaning for them.

Questions for Discussion

1. When do you become aware that the story will be narrated solely from the point of view of the animals in the pet shop?
2. What is the larger point Johnson is making when he tells us that Berkeley mistakes the gunfire on television for the real thing?
3. What is the basic conflict in the story?
4. How does Johnson make you sympathetic to some of the animals and hostile to others?
5. Is Monkey right in saying that Berkeley is being a fascist by keeping the animals locked up? In what ways is Monkey smarter than Berkeley? In what ways is Monkey less intelligent?
6. Why is Berkeley unsympathetic to Rabbit's organization of the females into a radical group hostile to the males? What does Berkeley suggest to smooth relations between the sexes? Why does his rational suggestion fall upon deaf ears?
7. Why does Berkeley fret over the idea that "truth was decided in the end by those who could be bloodiest in fang and claw"? How does this idea reflect Darwin's theory of evolution? Does Monkey's use of the store owner's gun challenge nineteenth-century evolutionary theory?
8. Why does Johnson give Tortoise the last grim word in the story?

Topics for Writing

1. Create a story in which animals who think and speak and interact are the only characters.
2. Write an essay in which you discuss the implications of Johnson's fable as a moral allegory.
3. Rewrite "Menagerie" as a comic strip.

(text pp. 692–696)

Suggested Reading

Johnson, Charles. *The Sorcerer's Apprentice.* New York: Penguin, 1987.

JAMES JOYCE

Araby (p. 692)

The rich texture of imagery and allusion that Joyce weaves into "Araby" may delight the sophisticated reader, but for the classroom instructor it represents a temptation comparable to the temptation that may be brought to mind by the apple tree in the "wild garden" mentioned in the second paragraph. Students should not be asked to contemplate the story's symbolism until they grasp its plot. To begin class discussion of "Araby" with the question What happens? may well be to discover that, for a novice reader, no meaningful action seems to have been completed. When the confusion arising from this sense of anticlimax is compounded by the difficulties presented by the unfamiliarity of florins, bazaars, hallstands, and other things old and Irish, "Araby" may strike students as pointless and unnecessarily obscure.

Once it is seen, however, that the narrator's disappointment at the bazaar resolves the tension built up by his attraction to Mangan's sister and his quest to fetch her a symbol of his love, the many specific contrasts between the sensuous and romantic world of the narrator's imagination and the banal and tawdry world of actual experience become meaningful keys to understanding what has happened. The opposition between fantasy and reality continues throughout: "Her image accompanied me even in places the most hostile to romance." The story's pivotal paragraph ends with the narrator cooling his forehead against the window in one of the empty upper rooms, staring out not really at Mangan's sister but at "the brown-clad figure cast by my imagination." Before this moment, his excited fancy has transformed the "decent" and somewhat dilapidated neighborhood of North Richmond Street into a fitting backdrop for such a tale as one might find in a yellow-leaved romance. Mangan's sister, kissed by lamplight, becomes in his view a work of art like a painting by Rossetti. The narrator's soul luxuriates in a dream of exotic beauty soon to be possessed by means of a journey to Araby: "I imagined that I bore my chalice safely through a throng of foes." But after the protracted visit from the tedious Mrs. Mercer and the even longer delayed return of the narrator's uncle with the necessary coin, the limitations of the romantic imagination begin to emerge. The "chalice" is replaced by a florin, held "tightly in my hand"; the quest is made by "third-class carriage"; and the bazaar itself, its potential visionary qualities defeated by failing illumination, turns out to be an ordinary market populated by ordinary shop girls from no farther east than England. At Araby, what matters is not purity of heart but hard cash.

The pitiful inadequacy of the narrator's two pennies and sixpence to master "the great jars that stood like eastern guards" at the door of the bazaar stall completes his painful disillusionment, but Joyce allows his hero one last Byronic vision of himself "as a creature driven and derided by vanity." When the lights go out in Araby, its delusive magic collapses, and the bazaar becomes as "blind" as North Richmond Street. Well might the narrator's eyes burn, for they have been working hard to create out of intractable materials a much more beautiful illusion than Araby. This imaginative power cannot be entirely vain, however, since in the mind that tells the story it is capable of evoking experiences like those described in the story's third paragraph, against which even the hoped-for transports of Araby would have paled.

WILLIAM E. SHEIDLEY

Questions for Discussion

1. Why does the narrator want to go to the bazaar?
2. Why does he arrive so late?
3. Why doesn't he buy anything for Mangan's sister?
4. Enumerate the activities taking place at Araby. To what extent do they sustain its "magical name"?
5. What had the narrator expected to find at Araby? What was the basis of his expectation?
6. Define the narrator's feelings for Mangan's sister. To what extent is she the cause of those feelings? What, as they say, does he *see* in her?
7. What purpose might Joyce have had in choosing not to mention the object of the narrator's affections until the middle of the third paragraph? Describe the context into which she is introduced. In what ways is she part of the world of North Richmond Street?
8. What is the role of the narrator's uncle in the story? What values and attitudes does he represent? Are they preferable to those of the narrator?

Topics for Writing

1. Make a study of light, vision, and beauty in "Araby."
2. Compare "Araby" and the quest for the Holy Grail.
3. Analyze the function of nonvisual sense imagery in "Araby."
4. Explore Joyce's control of tone in "Araby."
5. On a second reading of the story, keep two lists. In the first record ideas, images, and allusions that suggest contexts remote from the immediate situation, jotting down associations that they bring to mind. In the second list note anything mentioned in the story with which you are unfamiliar. Look some of these items up. Then write an informal paragraph or two showing to what extent tracking Joyce's mind in this fashion helped you to understand and enjoy the story.
6. Using the first three paragraphs of "Araby" as a model, write a recollection of the way you spent your evenings at some memorable period of your childhood. Use specific sensory images to evoke the locale, the activities, and the way you felt at the time.
7. Narrate an experience in which you were disappointed. First show how your erroneous expectations were generated; then describe what you actually encountered in such a way that its contrast with your expectations is clear.

(text pp. 696–725)

Suggested Readings

See page 132.

JAMES JOYCE

The Dead (p. 696)

"The Dead" is an apprehension of mortality. Joyce's carefully detailed scrutiny of the party, with all its apparent vivacity, serves only to reveal the triviality, transience, and emptiness of what passes for life in Dublin. The story involves a series of supersessions. Miss Ivors's friendliness is superseded by rigid politics, and she departs. Her kind of fervor is superseded by the "hospitality" of the dinner table that Gabriel feels so good about and that he celebrates in his speech. That conviviality, however, is exposed as mostly hypocritical, as each person reveals a selfish preoccupation — including Gabriel, who uses his oration to reassure himself after his self-esteem has been wounded by Miss Ivors. The long evening, however, generates in the heart of Gabriel a strong surge of love for Gretta that supersedes his selfishness. It is edged with jealousy and self-contempt, Gabriel's habitual weaknesses; nonetheless, the reader feels for a while that out of the waste of the soiree at least this rejuvenation has been salvaged. But Gabriel is longing for something just as dead as Michael Furey, and Gretta's devastating disclosure of a dead lover's power over her mind brings the "thought-tormented" Gabriel to his final recognition of the predominance of death. Like the monks of Mount Melleray, all people in Ireland, dead or alive — from the aged Aunt Julia on down — seem to be sleeping in their coffins.

While Gabriel's vision is triggered by the revelation of a dead man's sway over the emotions of his wife and of his consequent power to thwart Gabriel's desire, it is supported by the pervasive imagery of snow, chill, and death that comes to fulfillment in the last paragraph. The snow has been falling intermittently throughout the story. Gabriel is blanketed with it when he arrives on the scene, and images of cold and dampness pervade the narration. Last year "Gretta caught a dreadful cold"; Bartell D'Arcy has one this year. The girl in the song he sings holds her death-cold infant in a soaking rain. Not only are the physical descriptions of some characters so vivid that one almost sees the skulls beneath the flesh; even the warm, lively, cheerful elements of the story contribute to the final impression of morbidity. The Misses Morkan are giving what may be their final dance. The alcoholic antics of Mr. Browne and Freddy Malins consist only of ersatz good humor. And Gabriel himself, on whom everyone depends, can barely sustain his nerve and perform his function as master of the revels, keeper of order, and sustainer of life.

In the moribund and sterile world presided over by his three spinster aunts, Gabriel is called upon to play a role not unlike that of a year god at this Christmas season. (The party probably takes place on Epiphany, January 6.) From the outset he is willing, but in three sequential encounters he fails. Each failure strikes a blow at his naiveté, his self-confidence, and his sense of superiority. His first two defeats are followed by accomplishments (handling Freddy, his performance at dinner), but their effect on him is cumulative. Gabriel's cheerful banter with the pale, pale Lily does not suit her, as one who has been hurt in love, and his Christmas gift of a coin can do little to ease her "great bitterness." Afterward, his pretensions to take care of people are subjected to merciless ridicule in the "goloshes" passage. With Miss Ivors, Gabriel is more circumspect than with Lily, but that does not prevent him from being whipsawed between her political hostility and her personal affection. This confusing interaction not only causes Miss Ivors to abandon the company and Gabriel in his speech to reject the entire younger generation of Ireland, it also sets the stage for his ultimate failure with Gretta. Gretta's favorable response to Miss Ivors's plan for a trip to Galway now seems to Gabriel a betrayal, and the association of this trip with Gretta's love for the long-dead Michael compounds the feelings of alienation and self-contempt that Miss Ivors's disapproval fosters in him.

Gabriel's failures and self-doubts should not diminish him unduly in the reader's eyes: Joyce portrays him as aesthetically sensitive, charitable, and loving. The "generous tears" he sheds out of sympathy for Gretta's sorrow may not redeem anyone in a world devoted to death, but they are the distillation of a compassion quite opposite to the self-serving hypocrisy that has passed for friendly conversation at the Misses Morkan's ball. By the end of the story Gabriel no longer feels superior to his compatriots. He recognizes that when Aunt Julia dies his speechifying will be useless. He turns his mind away from the past and toward a future in which, as he feels his old identity fade and dissolve, at least the theoretical possibility of growth and change exists. The ambiguity of Gabriel's much-debated "journey westward" reflects the uncertainty of any future, but Gabriel's readiness to embrace it represents a major step forward from his rejection of Miss Ivors's proposition in favor of recycling of the European continent.

WILLIAM E. SHEIDLEY

Questions for Discussion

1. Contrast the mood of the first paragraph with that of the second. Why does Joyce move from anticipation to rigidity?
2. Why are the Misses Morkan so eager for Gabriel to arrive?
3. What is the basis of Gabriel's error with Lily?
4. Explain Gabriel's hesitation to quote Browning.
5. What does Gabriel's interest in galoshes reveal about him?
6. Comment on the men present at the dance besides Gabriel. Why does Joyce limit his cast so narrowly?
7. Discuss the reception of Mary Jane's "Academy piece."
8. What does Miss Ivors want from Gabriel? Why is he so upset by his conversation with her? Why does she leave early? Figuratively, what does she take with her when she goes?
9. Explain Gabriel's longing to be out in the snow. Is Gabriel "thought-tormented"?
10. Explain the irony of Julia's singing "Arrayed for the Bridal" to Mary Jane's accompaniment. What, in this regard, is the effect of the subsequent conversation?
11. Comment on the relevance of the dinner-table conversation to the themes of the story.

12. Why is Gabriel so cheerful when carving and when proposing his toast? Is he justified? Why does he imagine people standing in the snow before he begins to speak?

13. What is the effect of Joyce's ending the tribute to the Misses Morkan with a glimpse of Freddy conducting the singers with his fork?

14. Comment on Gabriel's anecdote about "the never-to-be-forgotten Johnny." Can it be read as a summation in a minor key of the party now ending? of the life of the Morkan family? of their society?

15. Discuss the scene in which Gabriel watches Gretta listening to D'Arcy. What is Gabriel responding to? What is Gretta responding to? What do they have in common? Trace their moods as they proceed to the hotel.

16. Why is Gabriel so humiliated when he learns that Michael Furey is dead? What other effects does this revelation have on him? Explain what he realizes in the last section of the story.

17. Discuss the final paragraph. What does its poetic beauty contribute to the story? What is our final attitude toward Gabriel?

Topics for Writing

1. Discuss the relationship between Gabriel Conroy and women in general.

2. Would you say "The Dead" is a Christmas story? Why or why not?

3. Comment upon Gabriel Conroy's death wish.

4. Consider Gabriel Conroy as a failed redeemer.

5. Explore habit and hypocrisy in "The Dead."

6. After your first reading of the story, scan it again, marking the following: all references to cold, dampness, and snow; all references to death, illness, or people dead at the time of the story; all references to warmth, light, fire, and the like; all references to youth, young people, children, and the like. Catalog your findings and write a paragraph on the importance of these elements in the story.

7. For a specific occasion, plan and compose an after-dinner speech with several headings like Gabriel's. Then analyze your speech, explaining what you were trying to accomplish for your audience — and for yourself. Compare your intentions with Gabriel's.

Related Commentaries

Richard Ellmann, A Biographical Perspective on Joyce's "The Dead," p. 1414.
Frank O'Connor, Style and Form in Joyce's "The Dead," p. 1482.

Suggested Readings

Anderson, Chester G. *James Joyce*. New York: Thames Hudson, 1986.

Attridge, Derek, ed. *The Cambridge Companion to James Joyce*. New York: Cambridge UP, 1990.

Beck, Warren. *Joyce's "Dubliners": Substance, Vision, and Art*. Durham, NC: Duke UP, 1969. 303–60.

Beckett, Samuel, et al. *An Examination of James Joyce*. Brooklyn: Haskell, 1974.

Benstock, Bernard, ed. *Critical Essays on James Joyce*. Boston: G. K. Hall, 1985.

Brugaletta, J. J., and M. H. Hayden. "Motivation for Anguish in Joyce's 'Araby.'" *Studies in Short Fiction* 15 (1978): 11–17.

Cronin, E. J. "James Joyce's Trilogy and Epilogue: 'The Sisters,' 'An Encounter,' 'Araby,' and 'The Dead.'" *Renascence* 31 (1979): 229–48.

Ellmann, Richard. *James Joyce. New and Revised Edition*. New York: Oxford UP, 1982.

Levin, Harry. *James Joyce: A Critical Introduction*. New York: New Directions, 1960.

Loomis, C. C., Jr. "Structure and Sympathy in 'The Dead.'" *Twentieth Century Interpretations of "Dubliners."* Ed. Peter K. Garrett. Englewood Cliffs, NJ: Prentice, 1968. 110–14. Originally published in *PMLA* 75 (1960): 149–51.

Mason, Ellsworth, and Richard Ellmann, eds. *The Critical Writings of James Joyce*. Ithaca, NY: Cornell UP, 1989.

Morrissey, L. J. "Joyce's Narrative Struggles in 'Araby.'" *Modern Fiction Studies* 28 (1982): 45–52.

Riqueline, John P. *Teller and Tale in Joyce's Fiction: Oscillating Perspectives*. Baltimore: Johns Hopkins UP, 1983.

Roberts, R. P. "'Araby' and the Palimpsest of Criticism, or Through a Glass Eye Darkly." *Antioch Review* 26 (1966–67): 469–89.

San Juan, Epifanio, Jr. *James Joyce and the Craft of Fiction: An Interpretation of "Dubliners."* Rutherford, NJ: Fairleigh Dickinson UP, 1972, 209–23.

Scott, Bonnie. *James Joyce*. Atlantic Highlands, NJ: Humanities Press International, 1987.

Stone, H. "'Araby' and the Writings of James Joyce." *Antioch Review* 25 (1965): 375–410.

FRANZ KAFKA

A Hunger Artist (p. 727)

This "brief but striking parable of alienation" (to quote Kafka's biographer Ernst Pawel) was probably written in February 1922, shortly before Kafka began *The Castle*. He had just returned to Prague after a four-week winter vacation prescribed by his doctor as a sort of "shock treatment" to arrest his advancing tuberculosis and deepening depression. Back at his desk, in his room in his parents' apartment, Kafka described his activities in a letter to a friend: "In order to save myself from what is commonly referred to as 'nerves,' I have lately begun to write a little. From about seven at night I sit at my desk, but it doesn't amount to much. It is like trying to dig a foxhole with one's fingernails in the midst of battle."

"A Hunger Artist" was among the few works Kafka allowed to be published in his lifetime. Ironically, he read the galley proofs only a few days before his death. Pawel describes the scene:

> On May 11, [his friend Max] Brod came for what he knew would be his last visit, pretending merely to have stopped off on his way to a lecture in Vienna so as not to alarm his friend. Kafka, by then quite unable to eat, was wasting away, dying of starvation [because of throat lesions] and immersed in the galley proofs of "A Hunger Artist." Fate lacked the subtle touch of Kafka's art.

The effort drained him. "Kafka's physical condition at this point," Klopstock [a medical student] later wrote, "and the whole situation of his literally starving to death, were truly ghastly. Reading the proofs must have been not only a tremendous emotional strain but also a shattering kind of spiritual encounter with his former self, and when he had finished, the tears kept flowing for a long time. It was the first time I ever saw him overtly expressing his emotions this way. Kafka had always shown an almost superhuman self-control."

As a parable, "A Hunger Artist" may be interpreted in as many ways as there are reader's finding words to describe their response to the text. Kafka created in his fiction a metaphorical language akin to music, touching emotions at a level beyond the denotations of the words he used to dramatize his imaginary characters' situations. The title is significant: "*A* Hunger Artist," not "*The* Hunger Artist." There are many kinds of hungers, and many kinds of artists expressing different needs for substance. Students may define the "hunger" as a desire for religious certainty and the "fasting" as the stubborn abstention from a faith without God. Or the key to the parable may lie in the Hunger Artist's statement at the end of the story: "I have to fast. I can't help it. . . . Because I couldn't find the food I liked. If I had found it, believe me, I should have made no fuss and stuffed myself like you or anyone else." Kafka was tormented by a failure of nourishment—from his faith, his family, his talent, his art.

Questions for Discussion

1. What is a parable? Is "A Hunger Artist" a parable?
2. Is it possible to read Kafka's story literally, as a realistic tale? What gives you the sense that there is more to "A Hunger Artist" than its plot and characters?
3. Is Kafka describing an unimaginable situation? Explain.
4. Gaping spectators, butchers, theatrical managers, circus people—the world of the Hunger Artist is mercenary and materialistic. He is described as a "martyr." A martyr to what?
5. As the Hunger Artist loses his popularity, he joins the circus, and his cage is put on display near the animal cages. What does this symbolize? What does this action foreshadow?
6. Explicate the last paragraph of the story. Analyze the function of the panther and his "noble body."

Topics for Writing

1. Write a parable of your own.
2. Agree or disagree with this statement by Primo Levi, the Italian author who translated Kafka's *The Trial*:

> Now I love and admire Kafka because he writes in a way that is totally unavailable to me. In my writing, for good or evil, knowingly or not, I've always strived to pass from the darkness into the light. . . . Kafka forges his path in the opposite direction: he endlessly unravels the hallucinations that he draws from incredibly profound layers, and he never filters them. The reader . . . never receives any help in tearing

through the veil or circumventing it to go and see what it conceals. Kafka never touches ground, he never condescends to giving you the end of Ariadne's thread.

> But this love of mine is ambivalent, close to fear and rejection: it is similar to the emotion we feel for someone dear who suffers and asks us for help we cannot give.... His suffering is genuine and continuous, it assails you and does not let you go.

3. **CONNECTIONS** "It was not the hunger artist who was cheating, he was working honestly, but the world was cheating him of his reward." Compare and contrast "A Hunger Artist" and "The Metamorphosis," taking this statement as the theme of both stories.

Related Commentary

Milan Kundera, Kafka and Modern History, p. 1444.

Suggested Readings

See page 137.

Franz Kafka

The Metamorphosis (p. 733)

This story admits the broadest range of explications — biographical, psychoanalytical, religious, philosophical. Here is one way it might be read: As the sole supporter of his family after the collapse of his father's business, Gregor Samsa has selflessly devoted himself to serving others. Bringing home "good round coin which he could lay on the table for his amazed and happy family" has given him great satisfaction, and his only ambition has been to send his sister, "who loved music, unlike himself," to study at the Conservatorium. After his metamorphosis, Gregor can no longer justify his existence by serving others. Instead, he must come to terms with himself *as* himself, an alien being whose own nature and needs are perhaps only by a degree more strange to Gregor than those of the human Gregor Samsa would have been, if somehow he had confronted them rather than deferring to the version of himself projected by the supposed needs of his family.

Kafka simultaneously traces Gregor's painful growth to self-willed individuality and the family's liberation from dependence upon him, for the relationship of dependence and exploitation has been crippling to both parties. Gregor learns what food he likes, stakes his sticky claim to the sexually suggestive picture of the woman with the fur muff (which may represent an objectification of his libido), and, no longer "considerate," at last *comes* out, intruding his obscene existence upon the world out of a purely self-assertive desire to enjoy his sister's music and to be united with its beauty. With this act Gregor has become fully himself; his death soon after simply releases him from the misery of his existence.

It is also a final release of the family from dependence and from the shame and incompetence that it entails. As an insect, Gregor becomes quite obviously the embarrassment to the family that they allowed him to be when he was human. Step by step they discover their ability to support themselves — taking jobs, coping with what is now merely the troublesome burden of Gregor, and learning finally the necessity of escaping from the prison that his solicitousness has placed them in. Gregor's battle with his father strangely transmutes the Oedipal conflict. It is triggered by Gregor's becoming a being for whom there is no longer room in the family, just as if he were a youth growing to sexual maturity, but the result is that the father, who has previously been reduced to a state of supine inertia by Gregor's diligent exertions, returns to claim his full manhood as husband and paterfamilias.

Emerging from their apartment, "which Gregor had selected," the family members grow into an independent purposiveness that Gregor himself is never able to attain. The story may be said to end with a second metamorphosis, focused in the image of Grete stretching her young body — almost like a butterfly newly emerged from her cocoon. Gregor, left behind like the caterpillar whose demise releases her, is denied all but a premonitory glimpse of the sexual and reproductive fulfillment for which his sister seems destined.

William E. Sheidley

Questions for Discussion

1. Describe the effect of Kafka's matter-of-fact assertion of the bizarre incident with which the story begins. Are you very interested in how it came to pass? How does Kafka keep that from becoming an issue in the story?
2. What are Gregor's concerns in section I? To what degree do they differ from what would matter to him if he had *not* been transformed into an insect?
3. When Gregor is trying to get out of bed, he considers calling for help but then dismisses the idea. Why?
4. What seems most important to the members of Gregor's family as he lies in bed? his health?
5. Describe the reaction of Gregor's parents to their first view of the metamorphosed Gregor. What circumstances in ordinary life might elicit a similar response?
6. Discuss the view from Gregor's window.
7. Trace Gregor's adaptation to his new body. In what ways do the satisfactions of his life as an insect differ from the satisfactions of his life as a traveling salesman?
8. When Gregor's father pushes him back into his room at the end of section I, Kafka calls it "literally a deliverance." Comment on the possible implications of that description.
9. Describe Grete's treatment of Gregor in section II. Is Gregor ill?
10. What are Gregor's hopes for the future? Is there anything wrong with those hopes?
11. For a time, Gregor is ashamed of his condition and tries to hide from everyone. In what way might this be called a step forward for him?
12. Discuss the conflicting feelings Gregor has about the furniture's being taken out of his room. Why does he try to save the picture? What might Kafka's intention be in stressing that it is on this occasion that Grete calls Gregor by his name for the first time since his metamorphosis?

13. "Gregor's broken loose." What does Gregor's father do? Why? Explain the situation that has developed by the end of section II.
14. How does the charwoman relate to Gregor? Why is she the one who presides over his "funeral"?
15. Compare the role of the lodgers in the family with that of Gregor. Have they supplanted him? Why does Gregor's father send them away in the morning?
16. Why does Gregor, who previously did not like music, feel so attracted to his sister's playing? What change has taken place in his attitude toward himself? What might Kafka mean by "the unknown nourishment he craved"?
17. Comment on Grete's use of the neuter pronoun "it" to refer to Gregor.
18. What is the mood of the final passages of the story?

Topics for Writing

1. Write an essay describing how Kafka gains the reader's "willing suspension of disbelief."
2. Consider Gregor Samsa's metamorphosis as a triumph of the self.
3. Analyze Kafka's "The Metamorphosis" as a study of sublimated incest.
4. Consider Kafka's use of apparently symbolic images whose complete meaning seems impossible to state in abstract terms — the apples, the fur muff, or the hospital beyond the window, for example. Write a vignette in which symbolic objects play a role without becoming counters in a paraphrasable allegory. Some examples of symbols: a candle, a cup, the sea, broken glass, ants.
5. **CONNECTIONS** Compare and discuss Tolstoy's "The Death of Ivan Ilych" and Kafka's "The Metamorphosis" as two studies of dying.

Related Commentaries

Gustav Janouch, Kafka's View of "The Metamorphosis," p. 1439.
Milan Kundera, Kafka and Modern History, p. 1444.
Jane Smiley, Gregor: My Life as a Bug, p. 1495.
John Updike, Kafka and "The Metamorphosis," p. 1502.

Suggested Readings

Anderson, Mark. *Reading Kafka*. New York: Schocken, 1990.
Canetti, Elias. *Kafka's Other Trial: Letters to Felice*. New York: Schocken, 1988.
Greenberg, Martin. "Kafka's 'Metamorphosis' and Modern Spirituality." *Tri-Quarterly* 6 (1966): 5–20.
Gross, Ruth V. *Critical Essays on Franz Kafka*. Boston: G. K. Hall, 1990.
Kafka, Franz. *The Diaries of Franz Kafka*. New York: Schocken, 1988.
———. *The Metamorphosis*. Trans. and ed. Stanley Corngold. New York: Bantam, 1972. (Contains notes, documents, and ten critical essays.)
Levi, Primo. "Translating Kafka," *The Mirror Maker*. New York: Schocken, 1989.
Moss, Leonard. "A Key to the Door Image in 'The Metamorphosis.'" *Modern Fiction Studies* 17 (1971): 37–42.

Nabokov, Vladimir. *Lectures on Literature.* New York: Harcourt, 1980. 250–83.

Pascal, Roy, *Kafka's Narrators: A Study of His Stories and Sketches.* New York: Cambridge UP, 1984.

Pawel, Ernst. *The Nightmare of Reason: A Life of Franz Kafka.* New York: Farrar, 1984.

Spann, Meno. *Franz Kafka.* Boston: G. K. Hall, 1976.

Tauber, Herbert. *Franz Kafka: An Interpretation of His Works.* Brooklyn: Haskell, 1969.

Taylor, Alexander. "The Waking: The Theme of Kafka's 'Metamorphosis.'" *Studies in Short Fiction* 2 (1965): 337–42.

Wolkenfeld, Suzanne. "Christian Symbolism in Kafka's 'The Metamorphosis.'" *Studies in Short Fiction* 10 (1973): 205–07.

Jamaica Kincaid

Girl (p. 769)

Kincaid's one-paragraph story is a dialogue between a mother and a daughter, consisting mostly of the mother's litany of advice about how to act in a ladylike manner. Students might enjoy reading it aloud. The West Indian prose rhythms are subtly beautiful, and the humor of the mother's advice is revealed in the audible reading process for anyone who has missed it by scanning too quickly. The conflict between the girl and her mother is evident in the mother's fears that her daughter will grow up to be a "slut." Everything the mother says is twisted in light of that fear. The daughter wonders, *"But what if the baker won't let me feel the bread ?"* And the mother replies, "You mean to say that after all you are really going to be the kind of woman who the baker won't let near the bread?" The following speech rhythm is reminiscent of James Joyce's interior monologues. In fact, we are not amiss to ask whether the mother is actually speaking to her daughter in the story, or whether the daughter has internalized her mother's voice and written it down for us to read to the accompaniment of our own laughter.

Questions for Discussion

1. What are the major subjects in this litany of advice? What kind of life do they describe?

2. The title of the story is "Girl," yet the girl seems to have only two lines of her own, one a protest and the other a question. Why might the author have decided to call the story "Girl" rather than "Mother" or "Woman" or "Advice" or "Memory"?

3. Identify and discuss Kincaid's use of humor in "Girl." What contribution does it make to the story?

4. What is the effect of fairly precise household rules alternating with comments such as "on Sundays try to walk like a lady and not like the slut you are so bent on becoming." String together the lines that admonish the potential slut. What do we think of the mother? What connection is there between the subjects the mother is speaking of and the idea of a slut? Why does it keep popping up from the most innocuous of items? What does this

refrain make us think of the daughter? Is the slut refrain a joke or is the author making a suggestion about the construction of self?

5. Some of the advice seems like it could never have been spoken, but only inferred: "this is how you smile to someone you don't like too much; this is how you smile to someone you don't like at all; this is how you smile to someone you like completely." Throughout the whole piece, do you think the mother is speaking to her daughter? What other possibilities could underlie the story's composition?

6. On page 769 the kind of advice changes: "this is how to make a good medicine to throw away a child before it even becomes a child," says the mother. Surely she's not speaking to a young girl here. In the final line, the mother calls her a "woman," the only direct address in the story; earlier the listener has been addressed as a potential slut and been told she's "not a boy." What's the difference between the advice that precedes and follows the reference to aborting a child? Which is more concrete? More abstract? Why does the advice change because of the listener's age? What kinds of knowledge is her mother able to offer?

Topics for Writing

1. Analyze Kincaid's use of humor to indicate conflict in "Girl."
2. Expand the story through the use of descriptive prose. Is the result more or less effective than Kincaid's original?
3. Write a short story in which you use only dialogue.

Suggested Readings

Kincaid, Jamaica. *At the Bottom of the River.* New York: Vintage, 1985.
———. Interview. *New York Times Book Review* 7 Apr. 1985: 6+.

Milan Kundera

The Hitchhiking Game (p. 772)

The unnamed young man and woman whose frightening adventure Kundera describes emerge from a vague backdrop as sharply defined personalities, but Kundera reserves his most detailed artifice for the purpose of making credible the process that calls the reality of these personalities into question. Because he carefully documents each evolving stage of the hitchhiking game as it is experienced by both characters, Kundera is able to convince the reader not only that this assault of fiction upon real life is motivated, plausible, and even likely, but also that it reveals an important truth applicable to us all.

Setting out on a long-awaited vacation from their burdensome and confining jobs the lovers are inclined toward experimentation and play. Each is also inclined, it turns out, to take a vacation from certain self-imposed and mutually imposed constraints on their relationship. The girl is cut off from full sensual awareness by being shy. Her ambition that her relationship with the young man should be *complete* ironically limits it: "The more she tried to give him everything, the more she denied him something: the very thing that a light and superficial love or a flirtation gives to a person." The young man likes the jealousy that arises from her worry on this score just as he likes the girl's shyness: "In the girl sitting beside him he valued precisely what, until now, he had met with least in women: purity." But by definition this relationship is thus limited for him by the lack of what he has found *instead* of purity in the women he has known before, and "he worshipped rather than loved her."

The hitchhiking game offers a way to break free from these constraints, and its result is to engage the two in a relationship antithetical to what has gone before. The young man puts the girl on a pedestal, all right, but in order to humiliate her rather than to worship her, and the perfect harmony of their bodies as they enjoy intercourse beyond "the forbidden boundary" comes at the expense of the unity of body and soul that they have previously known. Even near the beginning both participants have occasion to see that the game is getting out of hand, but each is so fascinated with the sensation of freedom inherent in acting out an alien role that neither is able to stop its progress.

In pretending to be someone other than themselves, the two not only find the freedom to turn off from the narrow road of their prescribed destiny but they also lose touch with what they have thought themselves to be. The young woman *vanishes* behind a little bush to emerge as a hitchhiker, and later, after *disappearing* with a wiggle behind a screen from the view of the man who propositions her in French, she seems to the young man to be crossing a "horrifying boundary" that changes the nature of the self just "as water ceases to be water beyond the boiling point."

At the end the meaning of their experience becomes clear in the recognition that the assertion of identity, "I am me," is a "pitiful tautology." The substitution of any nontautological content for "me" plunges one into a frightening indeterminacy that carries with it a power of decision more burdensome than the illusory confinement it supplants. As a result of having indulged in the freedom of playing their game, these lovers must now say, "I am a man who has demeaned and humiliated his lover," and "I am a woman who has acted like a whore and enjoyed it."

WILLIAM E. SHEIDLEY

Questions for Discussion

1. What purposes are served by the opening conversation about running out of gas?
2. Evaluate the young man's attitude toward the girl's shyness and his delight in making her blush.
3. What conflicts about her relationship with the young man trouble the girl?
4. Explain the implications of the paradox that the girl gets "the greatest enjoyment from the presence of the man she loved" when she is alone.
5. Why, do you think, does the girl start the hitchhiking game?
6. One of the first results of the game is that the lovers get angry at each other. Why do they keep playing? Does their anger contribute to the continuation of the game?

7. What kinds of freedom does the game bring to each player?
8. At what stage does the game begin to get out of control? Or has it ever been in the control of either participant? Explain.
9. Define the change of atmosphere that takes place at the beginning of section VI.
10. When does the girl fully enter into her role? What does that involve? What purposes does it serve for her? Answer the same questions about the young man.
11. Explain the insight about the girl that the young man reaches in section VII. Does she reach a similar conclusion at any stage?
12. "There's no escape from a game." Is that true? Explain both by reference to the story and in general.
13. What is the effect of the young man's forgetting that he is playing a game? Why does he do so?
14. Explain the last sentence of section XI.
15. Why is "I am me" a "pitiful tautology"?
16. How does what takes place in this story differ from organized theatrics? from daily role playing?
17. Why does the concluding line of the story sound like a sentence to punishment rather than the declaration of a holiday?

Topics for Writing

1. Examine the first paragraph of "The Hitchhiking Game" as a microcosm.
2. Consider Kundera's story as a philosophical parable.
3. Write an essay discussing what the lovers in "The Hitchhiking Game" gain and what they lose.
4. Explore Kundera's use of stock imagery in "The Hitchhiking Game" (for example, the road, the woods, the dark, dirty, and wandering city).
5. With a fellow student, act out the scenes of sections III, V, VII, and IX. Record your sensations and your awareness of the doubly fictitious persona with which you are conversing. How would you feel about acting out the rest of the story?
6. Write a sketch in which you portray yourself pretending to be someone very different. Perhaps you are habitually polite and deferential to waiters in restaurants. Imagine yourself behaving in an outrageously assertive manner. Or perhaps you are smooth and confident with members of the opposite sex. Describe an encounter in which you are tongue-tied and embarrassed. Follow your incident through to a conclusion that embodies the insight into your personality that writing it suggests.

Suggested Readings

Carlisle, Olga. "A Talk with Milan Kundera." *New York Times Magazine* 19 May 1985.

Lodge, David. "Milan Kundera and the Idea of the Author in Modern Criticism." *Critical Quarterly* Spring/Summer 1984.

D. H. LAWRENCE

Odour of Chrysanthemums (p. 786)

Because of its unusual vocabulary and emotional complexity, this can be a difficult story for many students to understand. Before they read it, their attention should be directed to the first paragraph of the headnote, which suggests an approach. Elizabeth Bates, the protagonist, is bitter because she feels trapped in her marriage. She is caught between her attempt to relate to her husband and her struggle to break free from her marital bondage. Her husband drinks away most of the meager wages he earns at the coal mine, leaving her to tend the children in a dark, squalid cottage she calls a "dirty hole, rats and all." She is fiercely protective of their two children — daughter, Annie, and young son, John. There is another baby on the way. Consumed with anger toward her husband, Elizabeth channels her love and tenderness toward her children. She feels herself "absolutely necessary for them. They were her business."

Recognizing the pattern of Lawrence's use of symbolism in the story may be one of the best ways to approach it. In the opening paragraph, Elizabeth's emotional situation is prefigured in the image of the nameless woman forced back into the hedge by the oncoming train. The female-male opposition in the story is symbolized here: marriage and home (the hedge) versus the mine and the pub (the train). A little later on, Lawrence has Elizabeth comment explicitly on the symbolism implied in the title of the story. When her young daughter is charmed to see her mother wearing the chrysanthemums — "You've got a flower in your apron" (pregnancy = flowering), Elizabeth tells her that she's speaking nonsense. To the mother, the flowers are not beautiful anymore. Most emphatically she does not treasure them as a hardy symbol of fertility in her otherwise bleak existence. To her, they are a symbol of death: "It was chrysanthemums when I married him, and chrysanthemums when you were born, and the first time they ever brought him home drunk, he'd got brown chrysanthemums in his button-hole."

Ironically, near the end of the story, when Elizabeth lays out her dead husband on the parlor floor, she smells "a cold, deathly smell of chrysanthemums in the room." One of the miners coming in with the stretcher knocks the vase of flowers to the floor, and she mops up the spilled water. In this action she is a servant of death, "her ultimate master" at the end of the story.

For most of the story, however, her master is her husband. The word "master" is the common name for husband among the village wives, but Elizabeth has refused to submit to her destiny. The line between female and male is clearly drawn in her world, where the sight of twelve children living at home on a miner's salary is not uncommon. But Elizabeth feels herself apart from the other housewives and miners. She judges everyone she comes in contact with, except herself. Then, as she begins to wash the naked body of her dead husband, she feels herself "countermanded. She saw him, how utterly inviolable he lay in himself. She had nothing to do with him. She could not accept it."

The final scene of "Odour of Chrysanthemums," the description of the mother and the wife laying out the body of the dead man, is one of the most unforgettable moments in Lawrence's fiction. The physicality of the dead man is unmistakable, and it affects the two women differently. Now Elizabeth fully accepts the reality of her individuality, her separate existence in the world. Before, she felt herself apart as an emotional defense against her disappointment with her marriage. Now she knows "the utter isolation of the human soul." The husband she hated existed only in her mind. With his death, she is free to ask, "Who am I? What have I been doing? . . . What wrong have I done? . . . There lies the reality, this man." The story ends with her horrified by the distance between them. Yet she is at peace.

Questions for Discussion

1. "Odour of Chrysanthemums" is set in the kind of mining village Lawrence grew up in. The first four paragraphs "pan in" on the social world of the story, establishing a relationship among the industrial landscape, wild nature, and human beings. Read the opening carefully, noting the diction of the passage, and try to state Lawrence's vision of the relationship among these elements.

2. Note how Elizabeth Bates appears on the scene merely as "a woman." How does the author go on to establish a closer relationship to her? What is she like when we first meet her? Describe the world she inhabits.

3. When Elizabeth sets out to find Walter, she notes "with faint disapproval the general untidiness" of the Rigleys. Consider the use of dialect in this passage. Who uses it? Can you determine Elizabeth's relationship to her neighbors and her class position? Might it be connected to her general satisfaction with her marriage?

4. In section I the family awaits Walter Bates's return from the mines — and yet his presence seems to haunt the family. What influence does even his absence exert on his wife and children?

5. Elizabeth's mother-in-law arrives, and the two women discuss Walter. How does Lawrence subtly and comically establish their relationship to each other and to Walter?

6. Miners stripped down to work underground; half-naked, white Walter is strangely beautiful as he is brought home. Her husband's body is a revelation to Elizabeth: "And she knew what a stranger he was to her." Try to explain the epiphany Elizabeth undergoes; what does she now understand about her marriage?

7. Lawrence said of literary symbols, "You can't give a symbol a meaning anymore than you can give a cat a 'meaning.' Symbols are organic units of consciousness with a life of their own, and you can never explain them away because their value is dynamic, emotional, belonging to the sense-consciousness of the body and soul, and not simply mental. An allegorical image has a *meaning*" (from an essay that appears in *Dragon of Apocalypse: Selected Literary Criticism,* ed. Anthony Beal [New York: Viking, 1966]). Trace the meaning that chrysanthemums take on in each stage of this story. Is it possible to give them a "full" meaning? According to Lawrence, are the flowers symbolic or allegorical?

8. Given the portrait of the social world in the story and the portrayal of this unhappy marriage, how might the two be related? Is Lawrence explicit about the relationship or might you like to argue with him about the causes of feeling in it?

9. One of the difficulties in understanding "Odour of Chrysanthemums" is its vocabulary. Consult a good dictionary to discover the meanings of words such as "gorse," "coppice," "hips," "spinney," "cleaved," "whimsey," "reedy," "pit-pond" "alders," "tarred," "pit-bank," "headstocks," and "colliery." How does this increase your understanding of Lawrence's story?

Topics for Writing

1. Analyze light and dark imagery in "Odour of Chrysanthemums."
2. Discuss the use of sound and silence in "Odour of Chrysanthemums."
3. **CONNECTIONS** Compare the isolation and alienation of marriage in Lawrence's "Odour of Chrysanthemums" and Mason's "Shiloh."

Suggested Readings

See page 146.

D. H. Lawrence

The Rocking-Horse Winner (p. 800)

Lawrence's masterful technical control wins the reader's assent to the fantastic premise on which the story is built; without that assent, the thematic statement the story propounds would lack cogency. Rather than confronting us boldly with his improbable donnée, as Kafka does in "The Metamorphosis," Lawrence edges up to it. The whispering voices in the house that drive Paul to his furious rocking begin as a thought in the mother's mind and then become a figure of speech that crystallizes imperceptibly into a literal fact — or rather, into an auditory hallucination heard by the children that expresses their perception of their mother's unquenchable need for funds. Paul's ability to pick a winner by riding his rocking horse to where he is lucky requires even more circumspect handling. Like the family members, we learn about it after the fact, putting together bits of information to explain a set of peculiar but at first not at all implausible circumstances — Paul's claim, "Well, I got there!", his familiarity with race horses, Bassett's reluctance "to give him away" to Oscar, Paul's giving Oscar a tip on a long shot that comes in a winner, and only then, with Oscar's skepticism always preempting that of the reader, the revelation of how much he has won. It is not until the very end that we, with his astonished mother, actually witness Paul in the act of receiving revelation — just as he slips beyond the world of everyday probability for good and into the uncharted supernatural realm from whence his "luck" seems to emanate.

Although no explanation, supernatural or otherwise, is necessary to account for good fortune at the race track, Lawrence persuades the reader that Paul's success is caused by his exertions and therefore has a moral meaning. In Paul's household the lack of love is perceived as a lack of money and the lack of money is attributed to a lack of luck. Since luck is by definition something that happens *to* one, to blame one's troubles on luck is to deny responsibility for them and to abandon any effort to overcome them. As the event makes clear, Paul's mother will never be satisfied, no matter how much money falls her way, because no amount of money can fill the emptiness left by the absence of love. The "hard little place" in her heart at the beginning of the story has expanded until, at the end, she feels that her whole heart has "turned actually into a stone." Paul sets out by the force of will to redefine luck as something one can acquire. He places belief before evidence and asserts, "I'm a lucky person.... God told me," and then makes good on his promise by riding his rocking horse to where luck comes from. " 'It's as if he had it from heaven,' " Bassett says, "in a secret, religious voice."

In his single-minded devotion to winning money for his mother at the racetrack by riding his rocking horse (which W. D. Snodgrass has likened to masturbation as Lawrence understood it), Paul diverts his spiritual and emotional forces to material aims, and Lawrence symbolically represents the effect of this *materialization* in the process of petrification by which the mother's heart and Paul's blue eyes, which have throughout the story served as an emblem of his obsession, turn to stone. At the end Oscar states the case with epigrammatic precision: Hester's son has been transformed into eighty-odd thousand pounds — a tidy sum, but of course it will not be enough.

WILLIAM E. SHEIDLEY

Questions for Discussion

1. How is Paul's mother portrayed at the outset? Does Lawrence suggest that she is blameworthy? Why or why not?
2. Explain the family's "grinding sense of the shortage of money." Why do the voices get even louder when some money becomes available? What would it take to still the voices?
3. Discuss the implications of Paul's confusing *luck* with *lucre*. How accurate is his mother's definition of luck? What would constitute true good luck for him?
4. Explain Paul's claim to be lucky. In what sense is he justified? In what sense is he very unlucky?
5. What function do Oscar and Bassett play in the story, beyond providing Paul with practical access to the racetrack and the lawyer?
6. "Bassett was serious as a church." Is this a humorous line? Does it suggest anything beyond the comic?
7. What is the effect on the reader of the episode in which Oscar takes Paul to the track and Paul's horse Daffodil wins the race?
8. Explain the mother's response to her birthday gift. What is its effect on Paul? Why?
9. Before the Derby, Paul does not "know" for several races. Can this dry spell be explained? What brings it to an end?
10. Analyze Paul's last words in the story. What does he mean by *"get there"*? Where, in fact, does he go? Is *absolute* certainty possible? How? Why is Paul so proud to proclaim that he is lucky to his mother? Finally, comment on her reaction.

11. Evaluate Oscar's remarks, which end the story. Was Paul a "poor devil"? In what senses?

Topics for Writing

1. Describe the handling of the supernatural in Lawrence's "The Rocking-Horse Winner."
2. Explore the religious theme of "The Rocking-Horse Winner."
3. Consider luck, will, and faith in "The Rocking-Horse Winner."
4. Analyze the realistic elements and the social theme of Lawrence's supernatural tale.
5. Consider luck, lucre, and love in "The Rocking-Horse Winner."
6. Look up a newspaper story about some unexplained phenomenon, ghost, or poltergeist, and work it into a narrative whose meaning is finally not dependent on an interest in the supernatural.

Related Commentary

Janice H. Harris, A Psychosocial Explication of Lawrence's "The Rocking-Horse Winner," p. 1428.

Suggested Readings

Boulton, J. T., ed. *The Letters of D. H. Lawrence.* New York: Cambridge UP, 1989.

Clayton, J. J. "D. H. Lawrence: Psychic Wholeness through Rebirth." *Massachusetts Review* 25 (1984): 200–21.

Harris, Janice. *The Short Fiction of D. H. Lawrence.* New Brunswick, NJ: Rutgers UP, 1984.

Hyde, G. M. *D. H. Lawrence.* New York: St. Martin's, 1990.

Jackson, Dennis, and Felda Jackson. *Critical Essays on D. H. Lawrence.* Boston: G. K. Hall, 1988.

Kalnins, M. "D. H. Lawrence's 'Odour of Chrysanthemums': The Three Endings." *Studies in Short Fiction* 13 (1976): 471–79.

Lawrence, D. H. *Portable D. H. Lawrence.* New York: Penguin, 1977.

Meyers, Jeffry. *D. H. Lawrence: A Biography.* New York: Knopf, 1990.

Olson, Charles. *D. H. Lawrence and the High Temptation of the Mind.* Santa Barbara, CA: Black Sparrow, 1980.

Rice, Thomas Jackson. *D. H. Lawrence: A Guide to Research.* New York: Garland, 1983.

Rose, S. "Physical Trauma in D. H. Lawrence's Short Fiction." *Contemporary Literature* 16 (1975): 73–83.

Sager, Keith. *D. H. Lawrence: Life into Art.* Athens: U of Georgia P, 1985.

San Juan, E., Jr. "Theme versus Imitation: D. H. Lawrence's 'The Rocking-Horse Winner,'" *D. H. Lawrence Review* 3 (1970): 136–40.

Schneider, Daniel J. *The Consciousness of D. H. Lawrence: An Intellectual Biography.* Lawrence: U of Kansas P, 1986.

———. *D. H. Lawrence, The Artist as Psychologist.* Lawrence: UP of Kansas, 1984.

Shaw, M. "Lawrence and Feminism." *Critical Quarterly* 25 (1983): 23–27.

Snodgrass, W. D. "A Rocking Horse: The Symbol, the Pattern, the Way to Live." *D. H. Lawrence: A Collection of Critical Essays.* Ed. Mark Spilka. *Twentieth Century Views.* Englewood Cliffs, NJ: Prentice, 1963. Originally published in *Hudson Review* 11 (1958).

Squires, Michael, and Keith Cushman. *The Challenge of D. H. Lawrence.* Madison: U of Wisconsin P, 1990.

Widmer, Kingsley. *The Art of Perversity: D. H. Lawrence's Shorter Fictions.* Seattle: U of Washington P, 1962. 92–95, 213.

David Leavitt

Braids (p. 812)

"We all had our little tricks," Ellen asserts at the close of Leavitt's story, emphasizing the connection between herself and all the "scared women, crawling home alone" whose lives are, if only through their memories, braided together: Holly Reardon (the schizophrenic friend from childhood), Natalie (the schizophrenic tablemate), and Diana (the repentant lesbian). All the women live lives devoid of true union with another, despite, or perhaps because of, the "conspiracy to protect the privacy of the angelic married couple," which is the equivalent of the heterosexual ideal.

By the end of the story, Ellen claims that she can no longer muster anger at a social system weighted in favor of heterosexuality and aggressively antagonistic toward lesbianism. The tension between the socially acceptable (and thus advantageous) and the deviant (and thus disadvantageous) is comically, if bitingly, rendered in the mother of the bride's cattiness; Diana's symbolic "flushing" away of her lesbian past; Ellen's relegation to the table of misfits, minorities, kooks, and oddities; the jaded, vapid rituals of the stereotypical wedding; and Ellen's life within her "remorse and secret-pleasure house."

Despite Diana's embracing of the sexual norm, she finds her life to be a parallel of Ellen's, and she feels out of place and isolated from the world at large. Ellen and Diana are as isolated, separate, and invisible as Ellen's childhood playmate or the schizophrenic girl stabbing melon balls in the darkest corner of the reception hall. Forced to live within themselves, and forced to make concessions to a society indifferent to or hostile to their true natures, the women exhibit impotent rage, or a symbolic violence, aimed at their abstracted or projected enemies. Ellen is unable to maintain her rage at Diana, and is left with the hopeless realization that human relationships are of two types: "a whole life of mistakes spinning out from one act of compromise" or "one which was harder but better."

"Braids" is an interesting story to teach alongside Jane Smiley's "Long Distance," since both stories have as central characters persons who have a distaste for the compromises (or sacrifices) necessary to form lasting relationships. Yet unlike the protagonist of "Long Distance," Ellen's refusal to compromise is presented in more positive terms even if the end result is a painful isolation.

Questions for Discussion

1. Ellen says that the braids Diana gives her were "clipped easily as toenail pairings, offered like a dozen roses." What is the significance of these comparisons?
2. Does Ellen's attitude toward Diana's wedding differ from what you would imagine any badly treated ex-lover of the bride would feel (whether male or female)?
3. Ellen has a wonderful sense of humor and a clear understanding of how others view her. How does this affect you and your sympathy with her position?
4. Is Diana a lesbian? How is the narrative constructed so as to leave this issue not entirely resolved?
5. What is the significance of *Night Gallery* to Ellen's life? How does it relate to Leavitt's view of the short story?

Topics for Writing

1. Analyze the impulse behind Ellen's wish to perform acts of violence and her resistance to that impulse.
2. Does the fact that a man is writing about a lesbian's reaction to her lover's wedding affect the way you read the story? Does being male give Leavitt any special insight into Ellen's relationship with Diana? Does knowing that Leavitt is homosexual aid or hinder your appreciation of Ellen as a character?
3. **CONNECTIONS** Discuss the nature of Ellen's love for Diana as compared to Roselily's love for the man she is marrying in Alice Walker's "Roselily."

Related Commentary

David Leavitt, The Way I Live Now, p. 1447.

Suggested Readings

Leavitt, David. *Family Dancing: Stories.* New York: Knopf, 1984.
Leavitt, David, and M. Mitchell, eds. *The Penguin Book of Gay Short Stories.* New York: Viking, 1984.
"The New Lost Generation." *Esquire* 103 (1985): 85–88.
"New Voices and Old Values." *New York Times Book Review* 12 May 1985: 1+.

Ursula K. Le Guin

The Ones Who Walk Away from Omelas (p. 827)

The tone of Le Guin's story deserves special mention, because it supports the humane wisdom of her theme. Rational, unhurried, calm, and composed, her words flow in long paragraphs like the deep bed of a river. She subtitles her story "Variations on a theme by William James." Read her explanation of the source of her story in Part Two (p. 1449), where she quotes two paragraphs by James, the American philosopher and experimental psychologist (1842–1910) and older brother of the writer Henry James. Students will recognize that Le Guin's tone is similar to James's in his philosophical discourse, which she so admires.

The tone of Le Guin's story is animated by her choice of narrator. Simultaneously certain and uncertain, she is both assured and tentative in her description of the happy, peace-loving community. (Remember *Omelas* means "O-peace," as well as Salem, Oregon, spelled backward.) Le Guin is too modest in her assertion of writing about "fortune cookie ideas." She possesses great authority in her definitions: "Happiness is based on a just discrimination of what is necessary, what is neither necessary nor destructive, and what is destructive." Perhaps students need to discuss this philosophical point to make sure they understand it. Major themes of the story — that ideals are the probable causes of future experience, and that what you touch, touches you — are based on this definition of happiness. The ones who walk away from Omelas have used it in formulating their decision to leave the utopian community.

Le Guin is also wise in matters of human psychology. She purposely leaves the details of the good life in Omelas vague, so that readers can imagine their own utopias, complete with as many or as few drugs and as much or as little sex as they are comfortable with. She also knows that her readers will find her vision of the good life more believable after her description of the tormented child on whom everything depends. For human beings, the ideal becomes real only with the introduction of pain and loss, "the terrible justice of reality." The destination of those who leave Omelas is less imaginable than the city of near-perfection. The ones who leave are unwilling to be bound by the terrible laws of this "utopia"; they must create their own futures. Le Guin's fantasy isn't escapist literature. It's as real and inescapable as life itself.

Questions for Discussion

1. What is the tone of this story?
2. What is the point of view in the story? Who is the narrator? Briefly discuss the dual attitudes of the narrator.
3. How accurate is Le Guin's contention that "happiness is based on a just discrimination of what is necessary, what is neither necessary nor destructive, and what is destructive"? How central is this idea to the themes of the story?
4. What type of society is Omelas? Did you find the narrator's description substantive or vague? Discuss possible reasons the author constructed the story in this manner.

5. What role does the tormented child play in the story? How does it affect the citizens of Omelas?
6. Why do some citizens desert Omelas? What is the place that is "even less imaginable to most of us than the city of happiness"?
7. What is the source of conflict in the story? Who is the protagonist? the antagonist?
8. Discuss the major themes of the story.
9. How would you characterize Le Guin's narrative style? Do you feel her use of the short question is effective? Why?
10. What is your reaction to the story?

Topics for Writing

1. Analyze the idea of the utopian society in "The Ones Who Walk Away from Omelas."
2. **CONNECTIONS** Compare and contrast the societies and philosophies in Omelas and in the small town in Jackson's "The Lottery."

Related Commentary

Ursula K. Le Guin, The Scapegoat in Omelas, p. 1449.

Suggested Readings

Cogell, E. C. "Setting as Analogue to Characterization in Ursula Le Guin." *Extrapolation* 18 (1977): 131–41.
Manlove, C. N. "Conservatism in the Fantasy of Le Guin." *Extrapolation* 21 (1980): 287–97.
Moylan, T. "Beyond Negation: The Critical Utopias of Ursula K. Le Guin and Samuel R. Delany." *Extrapolation* 21 (1980): 236–53.
Wood, S. "Discovering Worlds: The Fiction of Ursula K. Le Guin." *Voices for the Future: Essays on Major Science Fiction Writers.* Ed. J. D. Clareson. Bowling Green: Bowling Green U Popular P, 1976–79. 2: 154–79.

DORIS LESSING

Debbie and Julie (p. 833)

Lessing's story is chiefly concerned with abandonment: Debbie's abandonment of Julie, Julie's abandonment of her baby, and the parents' emotional abandonment of Julie. The story indicts those who seek to live solely on their own terms as much as it indicts those who lead others to attempt such lives of mistaken self-sufficiency. Debbie, who has her own secrets, attempts to reduce men to "customers" in the hope that turning relationships into business ventures will free her from the reality of female dependence upon males, but this approach fails. Not only does she remain dependent upon men to sustain her in her role as prostitute, but her hope of attracting the steady customer leads to her abandonment of Julie and thus constitutes a denial of her own victimization. Julie realizes that Debbie's motto, "Take what you want and *don't* pay for it," is a delusion, yet it is precisely to this level of denial, and the emotional repression it requires, that Julie inevitably sinks.

Julie's pregnancy is a thing to be "managed," and she mistakenly believes she has managed it well by avoiding much of the "cost" of revealing it to her parents. However, like Debbie, Julie has managed only to alter the outward form of her victimization by disguising it. Julie can hide her pregnancy beneath a sky blue coat, but she cannot as easily dismiss her feelings for her child and the remorse she feels in giving it up.

The reader also becomes aware of how Julie has been taught to see herself in the way she stresses that her own daughter's "enormous cunt" is her most distinguishing feature. After the delivery, Julie quickly attempts to sever any emotional tie she has to the child, and this act is mirrored by her impatience to cut the umbilical cord, "the twisted rope of flesh, full of life, hot and pulsing in her hand." Later, she represses her feelings for the child, giving vent to them only in the form of a wish for owning a dog, or by clutching her toy panda, until, eventually, she satisfies herself that Rosie is in a safe place and that she herself is "all right."

The story is not only horrific in its graphic depiction of a naive girl's struggle to "manage" her unwanted pregnancy alone, but also a horrifying depiction of Julie's inability to escape the destructive patterns of behavior inherited from her parents and present in Debbie's hollow sisterhood. Ostensibly a family, Julie and her parents each exist independently and incompletely, each enveloped in the same sense of loss, bitterness, and emptiness that Julie feels at the abandonment of her baby. Abandoned emotionally by her parents, Julie's abandonment of her baby is just a continuation of the pattern and part of her evolution into a person like her mother and father, who sit "each in a chair well apart from the other, not comforting each other, or holding her, or wanting to hold each other, or to hold her." This denial of tenderness and honest feeling is Julie's initial response to her own child, and it serves not only as the foundation for her interaction with her parents upon her homecoming, but also as the basis for her belief that she is, after all, all right.

Questions for Discussion

1. Julie describes the people who shared the train platform on the night she left home as "baddies" and "goodies." What do these terms say about Julie? Within the context of the story, are these two groups so easily differentiated?
2. What is the role of the dog that shares the shed where Julie gives birth? How does Julie react to it? Does her treatment of the dog change? If so, what does that change represent?
3. Julie remembers that Debbie called her "honey" on the phone and says that Debbie used the term for her lover's benefit, not Julie's. Why is this significant?
4. Julie is amazed by how different her father appears after she returns home. To what can this change be attributed?

5. Why does Julie mention her parents' sleeping in separate beds? How does this situation compare to Julie's having a bed at Debbie's?
6. Julie claims that after her bath she rids herself of the birth, the dirty shed, the damp dog smell, and the blood. Does she entirely? If so, what does that say about her?
7. How does the father's revelation about Aunt Jessie affect your view of Julie's decision?
8. Julie asserts she has managed her pregnancy well. Has she? Can she do anything she wants, as she suggests?

Topics for Writing

1. Julie is a somewhat naive narrator. How does Lessing use this to reveal deep and disturbing truths about the characters in this story and the ways in which they live?
2. **CONNECTIONS** Compare Julie's indictment of her parents' lives with Kirby Cristianson's dissatisfaction with his brothers' families in Smiley's "Long Distance."

Suggested Readings

Dembo, L. S., and Anis Pratt, eds. *Doris Lessing: Critical Essays.* Ann Arbor, MI: Books Demand UMI, 1988.

Fishburn, Katherine. *The Unexpected Universe of Doris Lessing: A Study in Narrative Technique.* Westport, CT: Greenwood, 1985.

Hanson, Clare. "Each Other: Images of Otherness in the Short Fiction of Doris Lessing, Jean Rhys, and Angela Carter." *Journal of the Short Story in English* 10 (Spring 1988): 67–82.

———, ed. *Re-Reading the Short Story.* New York: St. Martin's, 1989.

Knapp, Mona. *Doris Lessing.* New York: Ungar, 1984.

Lessing, Doris. *The Doris Lessing Reader.* New York: Knopf, 1989.

Pickering, Jean. *Understanding Doris Lessing.* Columbia: U of South Carolina P, 1990.

Pruitt, Virginia. "The Crucial Balance: A Theme in Lessing's Short Fiction." *Studies in Short Fiction* 18(3) (Summer 1981): 281–85.

Sprague, Claire, and Virginia Tiger, eds. *Critical Essays on Doris Lessing.* Boston: G. K. Hall, 1986.

Whittaker, Ruth. *Doris Lessing.* New York: St. Martin's, 1988.

NAGUIB MAHFOUZ

Half a Day (p. 849)

For many readers "Half a Day" will be a reminder that one of the oldest uses of storytelling is to relate a moral or philosophical truth. As in an allegory, the events of the story correspond symbolically to the events of another subject that is the writer's real concern. The most famous allegorical narrative in English literature is Bunyan's *Pilgrim's Progress,* which presents the way to salvation as a long, burdensome journey. In classical literature, the most famous allegory is Plato's Myth of the Cave, in which human knowledge is presented as the pattern light and shadow cast by a fire onto the walls of a cave.

In modern literature the use of this kind of substitution is more complicated, and perhaps the term "allegory" is not as strictly applicable, but it could be argued that other stories the student may have read also use this technique. For example, there is a basic similarity between the methods of this story and those of stories such as Gilman's "The Yellow Wallpaper," which presents the condition of women of her time as entrapment in a room, or Kafka's "The Metamorphosis," which, among many other things, presents withdrawal from family as a metamorphosis into an insect.

Although few of the references in Mahfouz's story are Christian, there is something parabolic in his presentation of human life as a half day in school. Life, in Christian allegory, is often compared to a day or to a moment, and the conclusion to be drawn from this image is that one should either make use of the time in order to enjoy it fully or use it to fulfill some kind of duty. The difference in Mahfouz's allegory is that what happens is already decided. It is the Moslem concept of preordination that differentiates this story from stories with a Christian treatment of the same theme. Here there is no suggestion that there is anything to be done. As Mahfouz describes the relationships of the school yard, "from the first moments my heart made friends with boys as were to be my friends and fell in love with such girls as I was to be in love with."

For most readers this will be the first suggestion that the story is not the simple description of a boy's first half-day at school. Still, it is a surprise to the reader when the gate is opened and the boy leaves the school to find that the world is changed and that he is now an old man. His life has passed in what he thought were a few hours at school.

Clearly Mahfouz is using his story to say things about the present state of his country, Egypt, that he would have had difficulty saying more openly. The world the old man finds outside the gate is violent and disturbing; a fire is raging, there are trucks carrying soldiers on the street, there are quarrels and shouting. What is even more complicated is Mahfouz's use of school as an allegory for life rather than as preparation for life, as it is usually considered. Even though he leaves the reader with complex questions, in the sweep and sure skill of his story Mahfouz convinces us that life can be thought of as a kind of sheltered dream, a dream from which we must sometime awaken.

Questions for Discussion

1. What things about the story will be familiar to students who remember their own first day at school? What things will be different?
2. There are many references in the story to the Moslem concept of predestination. How many of these references can you find?
3. Mahfouz is a well-known writer in his own country, and his use of one area of Cairo is well known to his readers. Is it because of this familiarity that he has to present his comments on present-day Egypt in allegorical terms?

4. Can the reader learn from the text what the author means when he describes the fire or the circus the old man discovers in the streets outside the school?
5. Would these things have a more specific meaning to Mahfouz's Egyptian readers?

Topics for Writing

1. Compare the Moslem concept of predestination with the Christian concept of individual self-determination.
2. Discuss the ways allegory can be used to illustrate an idea.
3. Discuss the ways allegory can be used as a means of protective self-concealment by a writer.
4. Using events in recent Egyptian history, try to identify some of the references in the story's last paragraph.
5. Mahfouz has often had difficulties with fundamentalist Moslem groups in his own country. Suggest some of the reasons why these groups have found his work troubling.

Suggested Readings

Malak, Amin. "The Private and the Universal: The Fiction of Naguib Mahfouz." *Toronto South Asian Review* Summer 11:1 (1992): 1–8.

Mahfouz, Naguib. *God's World: An Anthology of Short Stories.* Trans. Akef Abadir and Roger Allen. *Studies in Middle Eastern Literature* 2 (1973).

———. *Time and the Place and Other Stories.* New York: Doubleday, 1991.

BERNARD MALAMUD

Black Is My Favorite Color (p. 852)

Malamud characteristically mixes comedy and tragedy in his fiction, and this story is no exception. Nat Lime, the forty-four-year-old narrator of "Black Is My Favorite Color" is the Jewish owner of a liquor store in Harlem. He employs two black men to help out in his business and a black cleaning lady to clean his apartment once a week, and he has fallen in love with and proposed marriage to an attractive black woman living in Harlem named Ornita, who refuses to marry him after they are taunted and roughed up by three black men on 115th Street: "Shut your mouth, Jewboy. No more black pussy for you."

If, as the plot summary makes clear, race relations in the United States are tragic, since Lime's good-natured efforts to bridge the color gap lead only to hostility, violence, and alienation for both whites and blacks, then what is comic about "Black Is My Favorite Color"? The answer is Nat Lime, who remains an optimist despite the fact that throughout his life his attempts to make friends with black people have soured every time.

His experiences begin with his boyhood attempt to befriend Buster Wilson, the skinny neighborhood kid with an abusive father who lived a block away. Nat tells the reader that he picked Buster because he liked Buster's "type," that is, he sensed that Buster, like himself, was a loner. Nat treated Buster to movies and candy and was rewarded with a smack in the teeth. When Nat asks, "What did you hit me for? What did I do to you?," Buster answers much as the three hoods in Harlem do thirty years later: "Because you a Jew bastard."

For the protagonist in Gogol's "The Overcoat," there is a kind of life after death, but there is no afterlife for this Jewboy, and therefore no justice. Even after the people he's tried to befriend have refused him, Nat Lime still hasn't learned the rules of the game. The story begins and ends with his efforts to eat lunch with his black cleaning lady Charity Quietness, whom he sees as "a small person with a flat body, frizzy hair, and a quiet face that the light shines out of, and Mama had such eyes before she died." Nat hasn't learned that most African Americans, like Buster, Charity, and Ornita, have learned from their experience of racism in the United States to follow the rules. They reflect what has been done to them and see Nat as a type — a "white Jewish bastard" — rather than as a kind-hearted individual.

Buster's hateful remarks reflect the brutality of his life at home with a drunken father, whom the boy has seen severely beaten by white police. Ornita's love affair with Nat cannot withstand the social pressures against mixed-race couples (the story takes place in the 1960s). Charity Quietness relates to Nat as her employer, and a cleaning lady doesn't sit down to eat with the boss. Nat cannot break through the barriers of social conditioning with his protest that "Black is my favorite color," much as he tries.

Malamud has said in his memoir, "Long Work, Short Life," that in the late 1940s he "spent a year teaching in Harlem, incidentally picking up ideas for short stories like 'Black Is My Favorite Color.'"

Questions for Discussion

1. "Black Is My Favorite Color" takes place in the United States in the 1960s. What was happening in the Civil rights movement at this time?
2. Why is Nat Lime so sympathetic to African Americans?
3. In what ways does he fit the stereotype of a Jewish businessman in Harlem? In what ways does he not?
4. What is Malamud saying about the operation of stereotypes in our society when Nat Lime says, "You have a good idea now and then, but in the end what do they come to? After all, it's a strange world."
5. Why does Ornita agree to marry Nat Lime? What makes her change her mind?
6. Why does Charity Quietness refuse to eat lunch at his table?
7. How does Malamud play on the word "ghetto" in the opening paragraph of the story?

Topic for Writing

1. Analyze Nat Lime's distinctive speech and thought patterns, and discuss how they contribute to the humor in "Black Is My Favorite Color."

(text pp. 860–870)

Suggested Readings

Bell, P. K. "Heller and Malamud, Then and Now." *Commentary* 67 (1979): 71–75.

Bellman, Samuel I. "Women, Children, and Idiots First: The Transformation Psychology of Bernard Malamud." *Critique* 7 (1965): 131–32.

Benedict, H. "Bernard Malamud: Morals and Surprises." *Antioch Review* 41 (1983): 28–36.

Malamud, Bernard. "Long Work, Short Life." *Writers and Their Craft.* Ed. Nicholas Delbanco and Laurence Goldstein. Detroit: Wayne State UP, 1991.

———. *The Stories of Bernard Malamud.* New York: Farrar, 1983.

Pinsker, S. "Achievement of Bernard Malamud." *Midwest Quarterly* 10 (1969): 379–89.

Raffel, B. "Bernard Malamud." *Literary Review* 13 (1969–70): 149–55.

Shrubb, P. "About Love and Pity — The Stories of Bernard Malamud." *Quadrant* 9 (1965): 66–71.

Stern, D. "Art of Fiction: Bernard Malamud." *Paris Review* 16 (1975): 41–64.

KATHERINE MANSFIELD

Bliss (p. 860)

The life that blooms in Bertha Young presses against the restraints of "idiotic civilization" like a blossom bursting out of its bud case. Through all the incidents leading up to the devastating revelation of the liaison between Harry and Pearl, Mansfield develops Bertha's flowerlike vulnerability. We are attracted by her tolerant and amused appreciation of her husband and guests, the delight she takes in her "absolutely satisfactory house and garden," and her love for Little B. But at the same time we must feel a growing anxiety for this young woman, who herself knows that she is "too happy — too happy!" She is so little in command of her life that she must beg Nanny for a chance to feed her own daughter; her catalog of the wonderful things in her life dwindles off into trivia ("their new cook made the most superb omelettes"); and her husband and "modern, thrilling friends" look to the skeptical eye of the reader more like *poseurs* and hypocrites than the charming and sincere eccentrics Bertha takes them for.

Mansfield defines Bertha's condition and the danger to which it exposes her in the explicit symbol of the pear tree in bloom, to which Bertha likens herself, and in the unsettling glimpse of the cats, a gray one and its black shadow, that creep across the lawn beneath it. On the telephone to Harry, Bertha tries and fails to communicate her state of bliss, but she hopes that her fascinating new "find," Pearl Fulton, with whom she feels a mysterious kinship, will somehow be able to understand. In the moonlight the pear tree resembles the silvery Pearl, just as in the daylight it matched Bertha's green and white apparel, and as the two women gaze at it together, Bertha feels that the ecstatic communion she has desired is taking place. And in a sense it is, for the moment seems to release in Bertha for the first time a passionate sexual desire for her husband that, as she too soon learns, is likewise shared by Pearl.

The reader winces as the long-anticipated blow falls at last, and Eddie Warren intones the line that might end a more cynical version of the story: "'Why Must it Always be Tomato Soup?' It's so *deeply* true, don't you feel? Tomato soup is so *dreadfully* eternal." But Mansfield will not leave it there. As the gray cat Pearl and the black cat Eddie slink off into the night, Bertha returns to the window to find the pear tree, an embodiment of the same energy and beauty that wells up within herself, standing "as lovely as ever and as full of flower and as still."

WILLIAM E. SHEIDLEY

Questions for Discussion

1. Define the impression of Bertha given by the opening section. What is the source of her bliss?
2. What is the function of the scene in which Bertha feeds Little B? Comment on the way the section ends.
3. What does Bertha try and fail to say to Harry on the telephone?
4. What explains Pearl Fulton's limited frankness?
5. Do you agree that Harry's use of phrases like "liver frozen, my dear girl" or "pure flatulence" is an endearing, almost admirable quality? Why or why not?
6. Comment on the juxtaposition of the cats and the pear tree.
7. Can one be "too happy"? Explain.
8. Evaluate Bertha's summary of her situation. Does she indeed have "everything"?
9. Explain the line "Her petals rushed softly into the hall."
10. What techniques does Mansfield use to characterize the Knights and Eddie Warren? What do you think of these people?
11. Comment on the possible implications of Harry's delayed arrival, followed shortly by that of Pearl Fulton.
12. Why is Bertha eager for Pearl to "give a sign"?
13. What transpires as Bertha and Pearl look at the pear tree?
14. Explain Harry's way of offering a cigarette to Pearl and Bertha's interpretation of it.
15. Why does Bertha feel "that this self of hers was taking leave of them forever" as she bids farewell to her guests?
16. What is the effect of Eddie Warren's quoting a poem about tomato soup while the climax of the story takes place?
17. What *is* going to happen now?

Topics for Writing

1. Comment on the names in "Bliss."
2. Discuss the rebirth of Bertha Young.
3. Write an essay analyzing Mansfield's use of light and color in "Bliss."
4. The story is divided by white spaces into a number of sections. On your first reading, stop at each one of these spaces and write a few sentences addressed to Bertha Young. What would you say to her at each of those moments? When you have finished the story, review your previous advice and write one more letter to Bertha in response to her concluding question.

5.   Study the way Mansfield characterizes Harry, the Knights, Eddie, and Pearl. Then write a character sketch of your own using some of the same techniques and devices.

Related Commentary

Willa Cather, The Stories of Katherine Mansfield, p. 1398.

Suggested Readings

See page 160.

KATHERINE MANSFIELD

The Garden-Party (p. 870)

"The Garden-Party," like its protagonist, Laura Sheridan, is brimming with life. Mansfield's lush, sensual descriptions of the sights, sounds, smells, and tastes that are observed by Laura throughout the party preparations help to create a vibrant character filled with a childlike wonder and anticipation. Posed on the brink of adulthood, Laura sees and feels everything so intensely that we feel uneasy for her, sensing that some calamity, or at the very least some major disappointment, is waiting to shake her innocent dream of life's perfection.

For all her sensitivity and good nature, Laura appears, in the opening scenes, to be a typical upper-class young woman, delighted by the prospect of a party, and rather egocentric in her vision of such things as the cooperation of the weather and the blooming of the roses, and of the "absurdity" of the class distinction between herself and the workmen. She naively imagines that taking a bite of her bread-and-butter in front of these men makes her "just like a workgirl." but, as she will be reminded before the end of the story, there is a much greater difference between her life and that of a workgirl than a simple relaxation of stuffy manners and conventions. Laura is clearly glamorizing the lives of the working class in these imaginings, although it seems that she should know better. Later on, we discover that she and her brother have walked many times through the lane of cottages just below their home, where the poor live, because "one must go everywhere; one must see everything." While this is a perfect description of Laura's enthusiastic willingness to embrace life, we have to wonder what these excursions have really shown her, if she is so easily able to envision herself as a "workgirl."

It is the fate of the cottages that brings Laura's awakening to some of life's realities. The news of the accidental death of a young man from the lane intrudes on Laura's beautiful day. She reacts with characteristically intense emotion to the news, insisting that the party "must be called off." But she quickly discovers that she is the only one of her family and friends who is at all disturbed by the knowledge of the young man's death. In her exchanges with her sister and mother, she begins to discover just how deep are the class distinctions that she had scoffed at earlier. Her mother calmly states "people like that don't expect sacrifices from us," and that she "can't understand how they keep alive in those poky little holes" (as if they had any choice). Laura's sensitivity, which allows her to imagine the pain of the widow, and to recoil at the impropriety of the band playing and people laughing just yards from where a tragedy is occurring, is obviously not shared by her family. She is shaken and confused by the vast difference between her own instinctive sympathy and the cold lack of concern displayed by her mother and sister, but concludes that her mother "must be right," that it would be selfish and silly for her to "spoil the party" for everyone else, and decides to "think about it all later."

After the party, when Laura's mother, Mrs. Sheridan, is reminded of the unpleasant subject of the dead man by her husband, she has the "brilliant idea" of sending some of the leftover party food to the widow. Laura is repelled by this idea, which she finds too patronizing. But, after her own "extravagant" display of sympathy, she can't refuse when she is chosen to take the basket to the dead man's house. There, she has her first unromanticized view of the lives of the lower class, and an acutely painful realization of her own difference from them, as well as her first close-up view of death. However, it is in Laura's "encounter" with the dead man that the truly remarkable strength and beauty of her character emerges. For she is even able to empathize with the dead, to feel death from the man's point of view, a "marvelous" state of peace, rest, and beauty. Laura sees death, in a very realistic but highly unusual way for one so young, as just another aspect of the wondrous, overwhelming beauty and mystery of life.

Questions for Discussion

1. How would you characterize Laura after reading the scene where she "supervises" the workmen?
2. Does your vision of Laura change as the story progresses? Trace the development of her character through the major incidents of the story.
3. How do you think Laura's mother and sisters see her? What do you think creates the close bond between her and her brother Laurie?
4. What is the effect of the detailed, highly sensual description of the setting? How does it contribute to your understanding of Laura as a character?
5. Do you think the party should have been cancelled? Why or why not?
6. How do you react to Laura's mother and sister Jose as characters? Compare them to Laura.
7. How do you think the mourners feel about Laura's visit to deliver the food basket? Is the sense that she was "expected" all in Laura's mind? Do the people show any resentment?
8. Were you surprised by Laura's reaction to the dead man? Discuss her attitude toward death. Is it consistent with other things that you have learned about her character?

Topics for Writing

1. Analyze "The Garden-Party" as a story of maturation and development.
2. Discuss Laura's desire to be just like "a workgirl."

(text pp. 883–886)

3.   **CONNECTIONS**   Compare and discuss the imagery in "The Garden-Party" and "Bliss."

Related Commentary

Willa Cather, The Stories of Katherine Mansfield, p. 1398.

Suggested Readings

Boddy, Gill. *Katherine Mansfield: The Woman and the Writer.* New York: Penguin, 1988.

Fullbrook, Kate. *Katherine Mansfield.* Muskogee: Indiana UP, 1986.

Hanson, Clare, ed. *The Critical Writings of Katherine Mansfield.* New York: St. Martin's, 1987.

Kobler, Jasper F. *Katherine Mansfield: A Study of the Short Fiction.* Boston: G. K. Hall, 1990.

Mansfield, Katherine. *Journal of Katherine Mansfield.* New York: Ecco, 1983.

O'Sullivan, Vincent, and Margaret Scott. *The Collected Letters of Katherine Mansfield.* New York: Oxford UP, 1987.

Rohrberger, Mary H. *The Art of Katherine Mansfield.* Ann Arbor, MI: UMI, 1977.

Saadat Hasan Manto

The Dog of Titwal (p. 883)

War is such an all-encompassing event, and it involves so many moral and ethical dilemmas, that writers again and again have used a single wartime incident to illustrate the whole experience. In *The Red Badge of Courage,* for instance, Stephen Crane uses a single day in one soldier's experience to tell the story of the whole conflict. In the same way, Manto presents his reaction to the war between India and Pakistan in "The Dog of Titwal," his story of a small dog caught between two fighting forces.

In its description of the weather and the beauty of the natural scenery, the story may remind some students of the scene in the film *All Quiet on the Western Front* when the hero exposes himself to an enemy sharpshooter and is killed as he reaches from his shelter to pluck a spring flower. In a similar vein, Manto uses his story to show his disgust at the meaninglessness of a hillside skirmish that has dragged on for many months. The dog is an obvious symbol of war's helpless victims, caught up in events they don't understand. As Manto wrote in response to the bloodshed following the 1947 partition of India and Pakistan, "Who was responsible for the blood which was being mercilessly shed every day?" For him the answer is that the men on both sides are responsible. Through history Manto addresses both sides in the war, Pakistani and Indian, Muslim and Hindu: "You are the murderers." By describing their prejudice and their cruelty toward a small dog he strips their skirmish of heroism and indeed of meaning.

Students may find the concept of an "inside" and "outside" stylistic method helpful in understanding a story like this one, in which the point of view is outside the consciousness of the protagonists. There is no epiphany, no sudden moment of consciousness or understanding for the characters themselves. The consciousness of what is happening in the story is in the mind of the writer.

To further emphasize this aspect of the story, Manto has given the soldiers no distinctive personal characteristics. He has purposely described the two groups as being similar in their attitudes, anger, and sentimentalities. Each side has a singer, each side a gruff leader. They are symbolic of war's stupidity and brutality, just as the dog is symbolic of war's victims. There is no heroism or idealism in Manto's war, and he gives his soldiers no reason for their actions. As he said of all the reasons that were being given for the war: "Every question had an answer, but when you tried to look for truth, they were no help."

Questions for Discussion

1.   Why did the author make a small dog the victim of the shooting? Could he have used a child or a woman in the same way?
2.   Why does the author describe the singer from each side?
3.   Does the author describe any real differences between the two groups of men who are trying to kill each other?
4.   Is there anything in the story that presents the Pakistanis as more heroic or less cruel than the Indians? Consider the fact that the author is writing as a Pakistani.
5.   Does the author predict any kind of victory in this skirmish?
6.   Does the author suggest anywhere in the story that there is ever victory in war?

Topics for Writing

1.   In his description of the hillside where the men are fighting, the author describes the beauty of the flowers and the clouds: "It seemed as if summer and winter had made their peace." How does he contrast the natural world, which is also the world of the small dog, with the actions of the soldiers?
2.   Authors such as Manto, who bring a moralistic point of view to their writing, are often considered subversive or dangerous to society in a time of war or national crisis. Why is this?
3.   In wartime many of a society's basic freedoms are severely limited. Could a story like "The Dog of Titwal" be considered subversive by the Pakistani government? Describe why or why not.
4.   **CONNECTIONS** Compare and contrast Manto's vision of war with O'Brien's in "The Things They Carried" and Okri's in "In the Shadow of War."

Suggested Readings

Hasan, Khalid. "Saadat Hasan Manto: Not of Blessed Memory." *Annual of Urdu Studies* 4 (1984): 85–95.

Manto, Saadat Hasan. *Kingdom's End & Other Stories.* Trans. Hasan Khalid. New York: Routledge, 1988.

Bobbie Ann Mason

Shiloh (p. 888)

The trip to Shiloh is supposed to be a second honeymoon for Leroy and Norma Jean Moffitt, a chance for them to start their marriage all over again, as Leroy says, "right back at the beginning." The trouble is, as Norma Jean is quick to point out to her husband, they had already started all over again after his tractor-trailer accident brought him home for good, and "this is how it turned out."

It's a topsy-turvy world in Mason's story. Husbands are hurt so they take up needlepoint; housewives are self-reliant so they study composition at community college when they aren't working at the drugstore. Thirty-four-year-old "girls" like Norma Jean irrationally turn on their mothers after years of obedience just because their mothers catch them smoking cigarettes. And yet it's a familiar world to readers of fiction by women authors about women's domestic rebellion these past fifteen years: Erica Jong's *Fear of Flying,* Sue Kauffman's *Diary of a Mad Housewife,* and Lisa Alther's *Kinflicks,* for example. Norma Jean might scoff at her husband's suggestion that she has been influenced by the feminist movement — he asks her, "Is this one of those women's lib things?" — but he's no fool. She probably wouldn't have told him she was going to leave him if Betty Friedan hadn't published *The Feminine Mystique* and helped bring a feminist consciousness back to America about the time Norma Jean married her high school sweetheart, Leroy Moffitt.

The old patriarchal consciousness still permeates the story, of course, since this consciousness has a tight hold on the mate and the older fictional characters. Norma Jean is introduced in the first sentence as "Leroy Moffitt's wife, Norma Jean." The story is told in the present tense, making the reader aware of the slow passage of time for the characters caught in a static way of life, as mother Mabel says, "just waiting for time to pass." But Norma Jean feels the need for change. The opening of "Shiloh" is one of the most exhilarating first sentences in contemporary American short fiction. "Leroy Moffitt's wife, Norma Jean, is working on her pectorals." Used to be only boys lifted weights to build up their muscles. Now opportunity beckons even for a thirty-four-year-old married woman who bakes cream-of-mushroom casseroles. She doesn't want to be known as somebody's wife, a hackneyed first name between two commas evoking the more famous "real" name of a departed sex goddess from an era before Betty Friedan.

We don't know much about what she's thinking, this fictional Norma Jean, because Mason has structured the story so that her husband's consciousness and feelings are in the forefront. Through his confusion about what's happening with his wife, the reader senses that probably at this point Norma Jean doesn't know exactly what she wants herself, beyond wanting to break free. On their trip to Shiloh she walks rapidly away from Leroy to stand alone on a bluff by the river. He sees her waving her arms, and he can't tell if she's beckoning him or doing another exercise for her pectorals. One thing they both know is that she won't be needing the dust ruffle his mother-in-law made for their marital bed. If this Wonder Woman has her way, she won't be pushing her jogging shoes under her husband's couch or hiding the dust under his bed one day longer than she has to.

Questions for Discussion

1. After reading the story, look back at the first five paragraphs. What do they say about Norma Jean and Leroy's relationship? Does the rest of the story bear out the opening moment?

2. On the first page we discover that, through building an array of kits, "Leroy has grown to appreciate how things are put together." How does his fascination with building comment on Leroy's marriage? What is the impulse behind building the log cabin? How would you compare Leroy's hobby with Norma Jean's interests?

3. In this passage Mason introduces the background of the Moffitts' marriage: "Perhaps he reminds her too much of the early days of their marriage, before he went on the road. They had a child who died as an infant, years ago. They never speak about their memories of Randy, which have almost faded, but now that Leroy is home all the time, they sometimes feel awkward around each other, and Leroy wonders if one of them should mention the child. He has the feeling that they are waking up out of a dream together — that they must create a new marriage, start afresh. They are lucky they are still married. Leroy has read that for most people losing a child destroys the marriage." The figure of a dead child might be expected to haunt the couple in this story. Does the child control their present actions? We discover later that Randy would be sixteen now, so Leroy has been away from home, basically, for sixteen years. What difference does his sudden presence make to the marriage?

4. "When the first movie ended, the baby was dead. . . . A dead baby feels like a sack of flour." Usually, a subject like the death of infants evokes a particular kind of rhetoric, laden with sentimentality and tragedy. How would you describe these two sentences? Why doesn't the narrator use some euphemisms for death? What effect do these perceptions create? How do these sentences influence your assessment of Leroy's character?

5. Although the title emphasizes the importance of "Shiloh," we don't hear anything about it until page 891, when Mabel Beasley says, "I still think before you get tied down y'all ought to take a little run to Shiloh." What does Shiloh represent for Mabel? What does history itself mean to Leroy and Norma Jean? Can they articulate their shared history? Consider the passage about the baby on pages 893–94.

6. When Norma Jean tells Leroy she's leaving him, he asks her, "Is this one of those women's lib things?" Is this a story about feminism? Consider the point of view; discuss the ideology apparent in the opening line of the story. What do we know about Norma Jean's feelings? Consider how a descriptive sentence such as "She is doing goose steps" gives us some access into her emotional life. How would you describe Mabel Beasley within a feminist framework?

7. How does Leroy's opinion that "nobody knows anything. . . . The answers are always changing" comment on the themes of this story?

8. Leroy concludes that "the real inner workings of a marriage, like most of history, have escaped him." This seems like a poignant realization in the face of Norma Jean's departure. Does Leroy assign blame for the dissolution of his marriage? Does this knowledge imply that he will be able to forge a new, vital marriage with Norma Jean? Is the final paragraph hopeful? What do you make of Leroy's inability to distinguish between Norma Jean's exercise and her signals?

Topics for Writing

1. In an interview Bobbie Ann Mason had with Lila Havens, she said she's more interested in the male characters in her stories than in the females. How has she selected the details of "Shiloh" to portray Norma Jean's husband, Leroy Moffitt, with compassion?
2. Discuss Mason's use of details to enrich the story's reality.
3. **CONNECTIONS** Compare and contrast the theme of alienation in Mason's "Shiloh" and Lawrence's "Odour of Chrysanthemums."

Suggested Readings

Reed, J. D. "Postfeminism: Playing for Keeps." *Time* 10 Jan. 1983: 61.

Ryan, Maureen. "Stopping Places: Bobbie Ann Mason's Short Stories." *Women Writers of the Contemporary South*. Ed. Peggy Whitman Prenshaw. Jackson: UP of Mississippi, 1984. 283–94.

Smith, W. "Publisher's Weekly Interviews." *Publisher's Weekly* 30 Aug. 1985: 424–25.

Guy de Maupassant

The Necklace (p. 900)

"The Necklace" has long been one of the most popular of Maupassant's stories, and one of the most interesting aspects of the story is this popularity, since artistically it is far from his best. The story is little more than an anecdote. Mme. Loisel, a woman from the lower middle class, is deeply dissatisfied with her station in life. As she sits down to dinner with her husband — a "little clerk at the Ministry of Public Instructions" — she thinks of "dainty dinners, of shining silverware, of tapestry which peopled the walls with ancient personages and with strange birds in the middle of a fairy forest."

Her husband, sensing her unhappiness, gets a ticket for a grand ball, and, when she is miserable at not having a fine dress, he gives her money he has been saving for a gun and a shooting holiday with his friends. When she is still unhappy at not having jewels, he suggests she borrow some from a wealthy friend, Mme. Forestier. Mme. Loisel borrows what she thinks is a diamond necklace, is a great success at the ball, but loses the necklace on the way home.

Too ashamed to tell the friend what has happened, the couple borrow money to buy a diamond necklace like the one that was lost. They return the necklace and slowly repay the loan. After ten years, during which the wife has become "the woman of impoverished households — strong and hard and rough," she accidentally meets Mme. Forestier and learns that she had lent her only a paste copy of a diamond necklace. Mme. Loisel and her husband have destroyed their lives for nothing.

Unlike in his finest stories, Maupassant here stays on the surface of the characters. Mme. Forestier and Mme. Loisel's husband are only faintly sketched; they seem to exist merely to act out roles. The anecdote itself is so implausible that a single question — why didn't Mme. Forestier notice that a different necklace had been returned to her? why did M. Loisel allow his life to be destroyed without a protest? — would bring it to earth. But most readers are willing to suspend their disbelief.

When we place the story in the time it was written, its themes stand out even more sharply. On its most obvious level this is one of the tales of moral instruction that were so widespread in nineteenth-century popular literature. Mme. Loisel's dreams of clothes and jewels represent the sin of vanity, and someone who has such dreams must be punished. The punishment inflicted on the woman and her husband is memorably out of proportion to their sin, the better to serve as a warning to those reading the story for moral instruction.

A second theme, which may be less obvious to the contemporary reader, is that Mme. Loisel has dreamed of moving to a higher social level. French society was rigidly structured, and Mme. Loisel's ambitions represented a threat, however vague, to the story's privileged audience. They would, of course, want to see her punished for this ambition.

These facts help to explain why the story was so widely read when it was written — but for today's readers other factors seem to be at work. For example, to one young student the necklace became the symbol for everything the world of adults represents. Perhaps it is the story's weaknesses — its implausible simplicities, the lack of definition of its minor characters, the trite obviousness of Mme. Loisel's yearning, and the pious cruelty of her punishment — that make it possible for other generations to give "The Necklace" their own interpretation.

Questions for Discussion

1. Do we use anecdotes like "The Necklace" to point out moral lessons today? What other examples of this kind of moral instruction can you think of in popular literature?
2. How did an evening at a ball offer Mme. Loisel a chance to present herself in a new guise?
3. What do we learn from the story about the structure of French society at the time "The Necklace" was written?
4. What symbols for wealth and station could be used in a story like this written for today?

Topics for Writing

1. Analyze the symbolic implications of the necklace.
2. Consider the contrast between the lives of Mme. Loisel and her friend Mme. Forestier.

Related Commentaries

Kate Chopin, How I Stumbled upon Maupassant, p. 1407.
Guy de Maupassant, The Writer's Goal, p. 1456.

Suggested Readings

Fusco, Richard A. "Maupassant and the Turn of the Century American Short Story." *Dissertation Abstracts International* 51(5) (Nov. 1990): 1612A.

James, Henry. *Tales of Art and Life*. Schenectady, NY: Union College P, 1984.

Lohafer, Susan, ed. *Short Story Theory at a Crossroads*. Baton Rouge: Louisiana State UP, 1989. 276–98.

Los Angeles Public Library Staff. *Index to the Stories of Guy de Maupassant*. Boston: G. K. Hall, 1970.

McCrory, Donald. "Maupassant: Problems of Interpretation." *Modern Languages: Journal of the Modern Language Association* 70(1) (March 1989): 39–43.

Poteau-Tralie, Mary L. "Voices of Authority: The Criminal Obsession in Guy de Maupassant's Short Works." *Dissertation Abstracts International* 52(4) (Oct. 1991): 1353A.

Traill, Nancy Helen. "The Fantastic for the Realist: The Paranormal Fictions of Dickens, Turgenev, and Maupassant." *Dissertation Abstracts International* 50(9) Mar. 1990): 2891A.

Troyat, Henri. *Maupassant*. Paris: Flammarion, 1989.

HERMAN MELVILLE

Bartleby, the Scrivener (p. 908)

Many students have trouble reading this story because they cannot accept what they consider the weirdness of Bartleby's character. On first reading, the story seems to yield this interpretation. Shortly after it appeared in the November and December issues of *Putnam's Monthly Magazine* in 1853, for example, Richard Henry Dana, Sr., wrote to Melville's friend Evert Duyckinck saying that he admired the skill involved in creating the character of Bartleby because "the secret power of such an inefficient and harmless creature over his employer, who all the while has a misgiving of it, shows no common insight." Dana's interpretation will probably also be the way 99 percent of present-day college students will respond to the story, sharing his lack of sympathy for Bartleby.

The question is: Did Melville intend the readers of his story to feel this way? Why did he conclude his tale with the lines "Ah, Bartleby! Ah, humanity!"?

Most sympathetic literary critics see this story as Melville's attempt to dramatize the complex question of an individual's obligation to society. Like the dead letters that Bartleby burned in his previous job after they were no longer needed, his life ends when he is no longer useful to his employer. What standards should we use to judge someone's worth? How should we view those who no longer accept the world they are offered?

Questions for Discussion

1. How does the narrator's viewpoint affect your feelings toward Bartleby? What details particularly influence you one way or the other?
2. Do your feelings toward Bartleby change when the narrator reveals Bartleby's previous job in the Dead Letter Office?
3. How does Melville's humorous description of the two other clerks in the law office relieve his heavy presentation of the Wall Street setting? How do these minor characters set off each other, the lawyer, and Bartleby?
4. Do you ever feel like saying "I prefer not to" in reply to figures of authority? What do you do when you feel a bit of Bartleby in you?

Topics for Writing

1. Explicate the paragraph beginning "For the first time in my life a feeling of overpowering stinging melancholy seized me." A close reading of this passage may bring you closer to realizing the complexity of Melville's portrayal of the lawyer's relationship to Bartleby.
2. Analyze the conclusion of the story. How can Bartleby's life be compared to a dead letter?
3. This story has an unusually prolonged and discursive exposition before the title character is introduced. Also, Melville doesn't motivate his behavior until the end of the story, after he is dead and the lawyer finds out about his previous job. Breaking the customary rules of starting a short story with a brief exposition and motivating the characters as they are introduced, Melville might be accused of writing a poorly structured tale. Argue for or against this accusation, remembering that the short-story genre was in its infancy when Melville wrote "Bartleby, the Scrivener."
4. Read the excerpt from Melville's review of Hawthorne's *Mosses from an Old Manse* (p. 1458), discussing what Melville calls "the power of blackness" in Hawthorne's tales. Can you find the same "power of blackness" in Melville's description of Bartleby's situation?

Related Commentary

J. Hillis Miller, A Deconstructive Reading of Melville's "Bartleby, the Scrivener," p. 1460.

Suggested Readings

Boswell, Jeanetta. *Herman Melville and the Critics: A Checklist of Criticism.* Metuchen, NJ: Scarecrow, 1981.

Budd, Louis J., and Edwin H. Cady, eds. *On Melville.* Durham, NC: Duke UP, 1988.

Dillingham, W. B. *Melville's Short Fiction, 1853–1856.* Athens: U of Georgia P, 1977.

Fogle, R. H. *Melville's Shorter Tales.* Norman: U of Oklahoma P, 1960.

Freeman, John. *Herman Melville.* Brooklyn, NY: Haskell, 1974.

Higgins, Brian. *Herman Melville: A Reference Guide, 1931–1960.* Boston: G. K. Hall, 1987.

Inge, M. Thomas, ed. *Bartleby the Inscrutable: A Collection of Commentary on Herman Melville's Tale "Bartleby the Scrivener."* Hamden, CT: Shoe String, 1979.

McCall, Dan. *The Silence of Bartleby.* Ithaca, NY: Cornell UP, 1989.

Melville, Herman. *Correspondence.* Evanston, IL: Northwestern UP, 1991.

———. *Pierre, The Piazza Tales and Uncollected Prose.* New York: Library of America, 1984.

Vincent, H. P., ed. *"Bartleby the Scrivener": Melville Annual for 1965.* Kent, OH: Kent State UP, 1967. Includes Henry Murray's "Bartleby and I," 3–24.

Whitehead, Fred A. "Melville's 'Bartleby the Scrivener': A Case Study." *New York State Journal of Medicine* 90 (Jan. 1990): 17–22.

Yukio Mishima

Fountains in the Rain (p. 935)

Mishima begins the story "Cigarette" in *Acts of Worship* by describing the kind of adolescent mood that is the background of "Fountains in the Rain" in the same volume:

> It's odd how one's memories of youth turn out so bleak. Why does the business of growing up — one's recollections of growth itself — have to be so tragic. . . . Day follows day, nothing is ever really resolved: in adolescence, even this perfectly ordinary fact of life can seem intolerable. . . . From the outset of adolescence I couldn't, for one thing, bring myself to believe in "comradeship." My contemporaries seemed to me all insufferably dim. . . . And, dimly enough as yet, I had an intimation of women as something intensely unattractive.

Mishima's translator John Bester, in his introduction to *Acts of Worship*, describes "Fountains in the Rain" as a story that exhibits Mishima's "ability to organize a small form." Bester continues:

> A slight, humorous account of a tiff between a very ordinary young man and his girl, it skillfully portrays the instability, lack of confidence, and above all the self-centeredness that often characterize youth. With great skill, the imagery set forth in the title is worked into the fabric of the story; in a central set piece of description, the fountains reveal themselves as a symbol of the shifting impulses — ambition, aggression, sexuality — to which the hero is prey, and which are liable at any moment to be negated by the monotony of everyday life — the

rain — and its obligations. The girl is barely sketched in, but the suggestion of an firmer grasp of immediate realities provides a good foil to the boy's instability.

Questions for Discussion

1. Why doesn't Mishima give good reasons for the boy's decision to break up with his girlfriend?
2. Describe the different ways in which he behaves cruelly toward her.
3. Why does he decide to go to look at the fountains?
4. Why does the girl tag along with him after they leave the restaurant?
5. How does the boy's mood change as he looks at the fountains?
6. What is Mishima trying to suggest when the boy looks beyond the fountains to the sky and the rain?
7. In what way could it be said that the girl has the last word in the quarrel?

Topics for Writing

1. Analyze how the fountains in Mishima's story act as the "objective correlative" of the emotions of both the girl and the boy.
2. Write a story in which a description of rain or water is central to the action of the story.

Suggested Readings

Boardman, Gwenn R. "Greek Hope and Japanese Samurai: Mishima's New Aesthetic" *Critique* 12 (1970): 103–15.
Enright, D. J. "Mishima's Way." *Encounter* 36 (1971): 57–61.
Falk, Ray. "Yukio Mishima." *Saturday Review* 16 May 1959: 29.
Mishima, Yukio. *Acts of Worship.* Trans. and with an introduction by John Bester. Tokyo: Kodansha International, 1989.
Seidensticker, Edward. "Mishima Yukio." *Hudson Review* 24 (1971): 272–82.
Spurling, J. "Death in Hero's Costume: The Meaning of Mishima." *Encounter* 44 (1975): 56+.
Ueda, Makoto. "Mishima Yukio." *Modern Japanese Writers and the Nature of Literature.* By Ueda. Stanford: Stanford UP, 1976. 219–59.

LORRIE MOORE

How to Become a Writer (p. 942)

Students reading this humorous story may regard it as a mirror reflecting a "sitcom" version of themselves. It is as familiar as an empty Diet Coke can. The setting of the story is both nonexistence and omnipresent: parents on the verge of divorce, a son in the armed services, a kid sister who's good with little kids. Life swirls around, full of plot action, and what's a crazy girl who wants to become a writer to do? The answer for this affluent family: Advance one painless step — go on to college.

The girl attends college as a child psychology major. Nothing much happens there except a fateful accident: A computer erroneously assigns the girl to a creative writing class instead of "The Ornithological Field Trip" on Tuesdays and Thursdays at 2 P.M. So begins her apprenticeship to her craft, for which she shows more enthusiasm than talent. She apparently never reads short fiction, yet she tries very hard to write it. After graduation, she flirts briefly with the idea of law school before settling for slow starvation at home. Her kind, divorced mother is resigned: "Sure you like to write. Of course. Sure you like to write."

Moore's decision to tell the story in the second person gives her narrative its sense of immediacy. Her sense of humor does the rest, as she carves and serves up her tender victim, a sacrifice to the creative spirit that lives within us all.

Questions for Discussion

1. What is the irony involved in the girl's inability to find good plots for her stories, in the light of her parents' troubled marriage and her brother's military service in Vietnam?
2. Judging from the girl's behavior in her writing classes, does she slow any talent? Are creative writing classes in college a good place to find out if one can write?
3. What does Moore gain by organizing her story chronologically?
4. Do you think that the fragments the girl keeps in a folder can be developed into good stories?
5. How does the detail the girl notices about her date at the end of the story suggest that she might have the talent to become a writer after all?

Topic for Writing

1. Moore's story is a goldmine of possibilities for writing other stories. For example, experiment with the point of view of her narrative — rewrite it in the first or the third person. Or, develop her fragments into short stories of your own, humorous if possible, tragic if not.

Suggested Reading

Moore, Lorrie. *Self-Help.* New York: Knopf, 1985.

Es'Kia Mphahlele

Mrs. Plum (p. 948)

A few details about Mphahlele's background may suggest an approach to his story about Karabo, a twenty-two-year-old black South African woman from the country who works as a housemaid and cook for a white liberal South African employer, Mrs. Plum, in Greenside, a suburb of Johannesburg, in the 1960s.

Twelve years after publishing his first book of short stories, *Man Must Live,* Mphahlele published his autobiography, *Down Second Avenue* (1959), describing his life under apartheid and his work in the 1950s editing the pioneering black South African literary journal *Drum.* This autobiography was such a radical statement that it and Mphahlele's books of short stories were subsequently banned in South Africa, forcing the author into exile for many years. In a later book, *The African Image* (1962), Mphahlele wrote that he and other black South African writers had provoked the government because they had begun to fashion

> an urban literature on terms that are unacceptable to the white ruling class. They are detribalized or Coloured (of mixed blood), not accepted as an integral part of the country's culture (a culture in a chaotic state). But, like every other non-white, they keep on, digging their feet into an urban culture of their own making. This is a fugitive culture: borrowing here, incorporating there, retaining this, rejecting that. But it is a virile culture. The clamour of it is going to keep beating on the walls surrounding the already fragmented culture of the whites until they crumble.

Reading "Mrs. Plum," students with a good background in American literature may sense in the opening pages of Mphahlele's narrative a similarity to the style of Gertrude Stein's story about the black girl Melanctha in *Three Lives* (1909). The conversational lilt to the prose resulting from the idiosyncratic syntax that Karabo employs as she begins to tell her story, her simple vocabulary and constant repetitions, as in "she says to me she says" and "I ask her I say," may sound to these readers like a faint echo of Stein's use of language in her experimental, pioneering book.

But of course Mphahlele's story is the statement of a political activist with a very sharp message encoded in his narrative. The first time one reads "Mrs. Plum," the story may seem humorously exaggerated. This may be seen, for example, in the opening sentences: "My madam's name was Mrs. Plum. She loved dogs and Africans and said that everyone must follow the law even if it hurt. These were three big things in Madam's life." From these words the reader surmises that the speaker is not an educated person and may unintentionally have gotten the sequence of "dogs and Africans" wrong or put the two nouns in this order for humorous effect. Coming back to this opening paragraph after finishing the story, the reader immediately notices the past tense — "My madam's name *was* Mrs. Plum" — which might have slipped by as conventional narrative past tense usage the first time around. The second time, it's apparent that Karabo no longer works for Mrs. Plum and that her employer really did prefer dogs to Africans. Furthermore, the storyteller isn't trying to be funny. The scene toward the end of the story where Karabo peeks through the keyhole into Mrs. Plum's bedroom and sees her employer in bed in her nightgown, holding one of her dogs and masturbating, makes it clear that she "loved dogs and Africans," in that order.

The reasons why Karabo doesn't like Mrs. Plum aren't hard to find. Before the story gets under way, the young woman expresses her emotional reserve about her employer when she says carefully in the first section that after working for three years in the household, "I have been quite happy with Mrs. Plum and her daughter Kate. By this I mean that my place as a servant in Greenside is not as bad as that of many others." Like her friend Chimane, who works in the house next door and who got her the job, Karabo is a good daughter, sending her wages home to help support her aging parents and provide for the education of younger siblings. The system of apartheid in South Africa has stripped people of color of any opportunities for advancement, and Karabo is eager to learn all that Mrs. Plum can teach her. Karabo and her black friends (such as Dick the gardener) are systematically deprived of education, good wages, and stable employment. The story dramatizes their victimization in everything pertaining to their race, social class, and gender.

And yet Karabo holds her ground. She is a good friend, a good daughter, a good servant. The reader admires her and dislikes Mrs. Plum and her spoiled daughter Kate. Mrs. Plum, for all her liberal sentiments about helping the blacks (so long as the legal system of apartheid is not challenged), is so ripe that she's ready to fall from the tree. Oblivious to the injustice of the life inflicted upon Karabo by people like herself, she doesn't see her servant as a person but rather as a representative of a "downtrodden" race. Yet she is bereft without her housemaid. At the end of the story Mrs. Plum asks Karabo to return to work for her and agrees to increase her wages and vacation time. "You know," she tells Karabo, "I like your people . . . the Africans." And the girl wonders, "And Dick and Me?"

Questions for Discussion

1. What was Karabo's background before she came to work for Mrs. Plum?
2. What did Karabo and Kate have in common? How were they different?
3. What kind of people were the white and black friends of Mrs. Plum? How do you know that she treated Karabo not as an individual but as the representative of a "downtrodden race?"
4. What was the Black Crow Club, and what did Karabo learn there on her Thursday afternoons off?
5. After going to the Black Crow Club, why did Karabo think of Mrs. Plum as "a dark forest which one fears to enter, and which one will never know"? How does Karabo begin to express her growing sense of independence?
6. What is the point of Karabo's anecdote about seeing Moruti K. and his little dog in front of the Black Crow Club?
7. Why do Karabo and Dick dislike Mrs. Plum's two dogs?
8. Why does Mrs. Plum object to Kate's marrying the black doctor? What are Karabo's objections to the marriage?
9. The servant's illicit party at the big house in the owner's absence and Chimane's desperate abortion are two of the main events in Karabo's life. How do they suggest the limitations placed on the blacks' lives under apartheid?
10. What does Mphahlele add to his narrative by including the scene of Mrs. Plum in bed with her dog Malan?

Topic for Writing

1. **CONNECTIONS** Compare and contrast Mphahlele's handling of the interaction of whites and blacks in South Africa with Nadine Gordimer's in the
linked stories in "Town and Country Lovers." Which author conveys a more
vivid impression of the suffering of the south African people under apartheid?

Suggested Readings

Barnett, Ursula A. *Ezekiel Mphahlele*. Boston: Twayne, 1976.
Mphahlele, Ezekiel, *Renewal Time*. London: Readers International, 1990.

BHARATI MUKHERJEE

The Management of Grief (p. 975)

Bharati Mukherjee cites Moghul miniature painting, with "its insistence that
everything happens simultaneously, bound only by shape and color," as a model
for her fiction. This "sense of the interpenetration of all things" informs "The
Management of Grief," which initially situates the reader among a rather bewil-
dering array of characters and actions. Gradually we become aware that Shaila
Bhave, who narrates the story, has recently lost her husband and two sons in a
plane crash. The disoriented quality of her narrative ("A woman I don't know is
boiling tea the Indian way in my kitchen") mirrors the state of her mind as she
struggles to make sense of her loss, focusing on memories and odd details. The
abruptness of our entry into the story suggests the abruptness of tragedy itself.
Kusum, the similarly bereaved neighbor, voices the question that might occur to
anyone afflicted with such loss: "Why does God give so much if all along He
intends to take it away?"

Mukherjee asks us to consider the manner in which various characters cope
with grief. The community looks toward Mrs. Bhave as "a pillar" because she has
"taken it more calmly," but she is troubled by her inability to grieve outwardly,
referring to herself as "a freak." Her equanimity, we learn, is due as much to
Valium as to inner strength. With the help of the drug she is able to "manage" her
grief in a way that may be ultimately less healthy than that of the relatives who
express their grief more openly. While in Ireland waiting to identify bodies, she
admits, "I haven't eaten in four days, haven't brushed my teeth." By the end of the
story Shaila experiences a visitation on the streets of Toronto by her departed
husband and sons, who urge her, "Go, be brave." While the experience may be
interpreted in a positive light, a transition in her grieving process, it also may be
seen as an aural hallucination, the result of her mixing tranquilizers in her
distraught emotional state. Her dropping her package and directionless walking
suggest purposelessness and lack of direction.

While personal tragedy commands center stage in this story, cultural vectors
play out across the background. The crash may have been caused by a Sikh bomb.
Judith Templeton, the culturally naive social worker, persuades Shaila to try to

convince a grieving Sikh couple to take advantage of available aid. Templeton, while meaning well, has little sensitivity to the cultural and political complications of the situation, and she overlooks the difficulty of the position for which she recruits Shaila — that of helping a potential enemy. The plane crash pulls the relatives, now well assimilated into Canada, back to India and the old ways, which cling with more tenacity than they may have realized.

Questions for Discussion

1. At one point, Shaila observes, "Like my husband's spirit, I flutter between worlds." What does she mean?
2. Review the India section of the story. In what ways have the characters changed in moving from India to Canada?
3. Do you detect a pattern of inhibited emotional response in Shaila? If so, to what extent may this pattern be culturally induced?

Topic for Writing

1. Discuss the grieving processes and coping mechanisms of the various characters. Is Shaila as healthy and calm as she outwardly appears to be? What does Dr. Ranganathan mean when he says, "We've been melted down and recast as a new tribe"? Do the relatives experience successive stages of grief?

Related Commentary

Bharati Mukherjee, A Four-Hundred-Year-Old Woman, p. 1465.

Suggested Readings

Boxill, Anthony. "Women and Migration in Some Short Stories of Bharati Mukherjee and Neil Bissoondath." *Literary Half Yearly* July 32:2 (1991): 43–50.
Mukherjee, Bharati. *The Middleman and Other Stories.* New York: Grove, 1988.
Nelson, Emmanuel S. *Bharati Mukherjee: Critical Perspectives.* New York: Garland, 1993.
———. "Kamala Markandaya, Bharati Mukherjee and the Indian Immigrant Experience." *Toronto South Asian Review* Winter 9:2 (1991): 1–9.

ALICE MUNRO

Walker Brothers Cowboy (p. 987)

"Walker Brothers Cowboy" is set during the Depression, and it is the Depression itself that determines and motivates the lives in Tuppertown Munro describes. The father in the story has lost his fox farm, and the family has been forced to move into an unfriendly neighboring town while the father works as a door-to-door salesman of household items manufactured by a company called Walker Brothers.

Munro's story is specifically in a time, and her narrator devotes much of the early part of the story to describing the setting. Details of her mother working on a dress made of the family's old clothes and the description of the encounter with the tramp reinforce the sense of economic hardship, but some of the strongest details are the names of the shops and the description of neighbors sitting out, "men in shirt-sleeves and undershirts and women in aprons — not people we know but if anybody looks ready to nod and say 'Warm night,' my father will nod too and say something the same."

The events of the story are slight. The narrator and her younger brother go with their father as he sells his products. At one of the houses he visits, someone empties a chamber pot on him from a second-story window. Although he laughs about it in front of his children, the father is obviously disturbed. Then he takes the children off his route to visit a woman he knew and loved when he was younger.

The slight events of the story are conveyed with poignant restraint and affection by the narrator, an adult who represents the incidents of that afternoon through the eyes of her younger self. The author's intent is to fix a life at a moment and in a place, and her story brilliantly succeeds.

Questions for Discussion

1. When did the Depression take place, and what was its effect on the lives of people such as those the author portrays?
2. Describe some of the details and incidents of the walk the narrator takes with her father that set the story in its time and place.
3. Why does the father describe himself as a "Walker Brothers Cowboy"?
4. Do men like this father still travel the backroads of the United States selling products like Walker Brothers medicines and household supplies? What has happened to this kind of job?
5. What does Munro tell us of the lives of women like the friend the father takes his children to visit?

Topics for Writing

1. Find another example of writing about the Depression years and compare it with "Walker Brothers Cowboy."
2. Comment on the following passage from the story, which describes the girl's mother and her attitude toward their new life:

> No bathroom with a claw-footed tub and flush toilet is going to comfort her, nor water on tap and sidewalks past the house and milk in bottles, not even the two movie theatres and the Venus Restaurant and Woolworths so marvellous it has live birds singing in its fan-cooled corners and fish as tiny as finger nails, as bright as moons, swimming in its green tanks. My mother does not care.

3.   The critic Michiko Kakutani writes that Munro's characters "never com-
      pletely dispose of their pasts. Unlike so many characters in contemporary
      fiction, they do not assume that they can continually reinvent themselves,
      that they can always start over tabula rasa. They tend to stay in touch with
      ex-lovers, distant family members, childhood friends; they acknowledge,
      however reluctantly, the ways in which their pasts have shaped their
      futures." How does this comment apply to "Walker Brothers Cowboy"?

Suggested Readings

Bardolph, Jacqueline, ed. *Short fiction in the New Literature in English: Proceedings of
    the Nice Conference of the European Association for the Common Wealth Literature
    and Language Studies*. Nice: Faculté des Lettres et Sciences Humaines de Nice,
    1989. 141–51.
Blodgett, E. D. *Alice Munro*. Boston: Twayne, 1988.
Carrington, Ildiko de Papp. *Controlling the Uncontrollable: The Fiction of Alice
    Munro*. DeKalb: Northern Illinois UP, 1989.
Hanson, Clare, ed. *Rereading the Short Story*. New York: St. Martin's, 1989. 65–85.
Jansen, Reamy. "Being Lonely: Dimensions of the Short Story." *Crosscurrents* 39(4)
    (Winter 1989–90): 391–401, 419.
MacKendrick, Louis K., ed. *Probable Fictions: Alice Munro's Narrative Acts*.
    Downsview, ONT: ECW, 1983.
Martin, W. R. *Alice Munro: Paradox and Parallel*. Edmonton: U of Alberta P, 1987.
Miller, Judith. *The Art of Alice Munro: Saying the Unsayable: Papers from the Waterloo
    Conference*. Madison: U of Wisconsin P, 1984.
Nischik, Reingard M., ed. *Modes of Narrative: Approaches to American, Canadian, and
    British Fiction*. Wurzburg: Konigshausen, 1990. 110–18, 141–52.
Rasporich, Beverly J. *Dance of the Sexes: Art and Gender in the Fiction of Alice Munro*.
    Edmonton: U of Alberta P, 1990.
Stich, K. P., ed. *Reflections: Autobiography and Canadian Literature*. Ottawa: U of
    Ottawa P, 1988. 176.

JOYCE CAROL OATES

Heat (p. 1000)

In Oates's introduction to this story, she states that the "formal challenge of
'Heat' was to present a narrative in a seemingly acausal manner, analogous to the
playing of a piano sans pedal; as if each paragraph, or chord, were separate from
the rest. For how otherwise can we speak of the unspeakable, except through the
prism of technique?"

The "unspeakable," the sex crime involving the murder of the twins Rhea
and Rhoda Kunkel by their simpleminded nineteen-year-old neighbor Roger
Whipple, is never directly described, but Oates understands that leaving it to
readers' imaginations is the most effective way to handle the scene. The tension in
Oates's narrative gains intensity from her indirection as a storyteller. Always clear,

her voice brings the reader to the edge of the suggested gothic horror depiction —
she believes that the gothic genre is "a fairly accurate assessment of modern life"
— and then she steps carefully back: "What had been done to them, the lower parts
of them, didn't show in the caskets."

Rhea and Rhoda join the other portraits of adolescent girls that Oates has
created; as the critic Ellen G. Friedman has recognized, Oates "has perhaps the
largest gallery of adolescent girls of any contemporary writer." Their doubling as
twins reflects Oates's interest in the themes of twins and the double as developed
in the series of thrillers she has written under the pseudonym Rosamond Smith. In
"Heat," the doubling of the victims subtly informs the reader that the situation is
somehow askew, as suggestive as a portrait from the 1950s by the brilliant
American photographer Diane Arbus.

"Heat" is narrated in the first person by one of the twins' schoolmates, about
eleven years old, like the twins. Her perspective is limited by her age, but it is
similar to the twins, so we learn a good deal about their families and games,
including the twins' pleasure in stealing six dollars from their grandmother's
purse. The narrative jumps to the future, when the narrator is in the tenth grade,
and then to a description of her adultery after her marriage, before returning in the
final paragraphs to the twins' murders. Oates's skillful control of the progression
of her story highlights the obsessive quality of the narrator's memory, surfacing
after all these years in the story: "I wasn't there, but some things you know."

Questions for Discussion

1. What part does the heat of the summer play in the story?
2. Would the story be less effective if it had been about the murder of one girl
   and not twin sisters? What dimension does Oates add by making the sisters
   twins?
3. Why did the twins steal six dollars from their grandmother? What did they
   intend to do with the money?
4. Were the twins likeable girls?
5. What is the relationship of the narrator to the twins?
6. How does the incident under the Kunkels' veranda help to foreshadow the
   murders?
7. What is added to the story by the narrator's description of her adultery years
   after the murders?
8. Why does she obsess about the murders?

Topics for Writing

1. In *On Writers and Writing*, John Gardner wrote that in her fiction Oates
   "avoids analysis in a way that seems intentional, fragmenting the world . . .
   by a use of close, almost myopic examination followed by startling cuts —
   to another character, another era — that disorient the reader like the kick of
   a mule. . . . [She produces] an image of history, personal or public, as a track
   of machine-gun wounds. Value affirmations are as fleeing as destructions,
   and often as grotesque." Analyze the narrative structure of "Heat" in
   relation to Gardner's description.

2.   **CONNECTIONS**   Compare and contrast "Heat" with Katherine Anne Porter's story "He." (The link between them is suggested by Oates's use of the surname "Whipple," the surname of the family in Porter's story.)
3.   **CONNECTIONS**   Compare and contrast "Heat" with Sherwood Anderson's "Death in the Woods," relating both stories to Anderson's idea that a writer should emphasize "form, not plot" in a short story.

Suggested Readings

See page 181.

JOYCE CAROL OATES

Where Are You Going, Where Have You Been? (p. 1009)

Pointing to Oates's remark that she usually writes "about real people in a real society" should help to keep discussion away from premature allegorization or mythologizing, which — for all its eventual value and interest — smothers the story's impact by diverting attention from its realism. Her further observation that she understands Connie to be "struggling heroically to define personal identity in the face of incredible opposition, even in the face of death itself," may suggest how to go about answering the main question the story poses when considered in naturalistic terms: Why does Connie go out to Arnold Friend?

Connie's life as Oates depicts it takes place in two realms. Within her home and family Connie feels condemned and rejected, and she returns the disapproval. Outside these familiar precincts lies a world defined by movies, the drive-in restaurant, and the ever-present popular music. It is *not* the music of Bob Dylan, as Tom Quirk assures us, but the comparatively mindless, sentimental, and romantic music against which in the early 1960s Dylan stood out in such bold contrast. Connie's idea of the world into which, at the age of fifteen, she is beginning to make her first tentative forays is shaped by these songs and occupied by *boys*: boys who can be snubbed with impunity, boys who merge into one undifferentiated and safe blur in her mind, boys who offer hamburgers and "the caresses of love." And that love is "not the way someone like June would suppose but sweet, gentle, the way it was in movies and promised in songs." To these boys Connie presents herself as undifferentiated *girl*, and she is concerned that she look attractive to them.

The world, however, is occupied not only by frank and tentative boys but also by determined and deceitful men, by evil as well as by innocence, by hypocrisy, perversion, and violence — an exponent of all of which Connie attracts in Arnold Friend. Although in the course of their interview Connie sees through his disguise, the impoverishment of her world provides her no way to resist his advances. Her home offers no refuge, her father does not come when she needs him (he has always been essentially absent anyway), and she is unable to manipulate the telephone because of her panic. Meanwhile, Arnold, who presents himself in the guise of a movie hero, a teenage "boy," and her lover, offers to take charge of her. He places his mark upon her and gives her a role to play in a world of his devising. Because she is cut off from her past and has no idea of a future, she is at his mercy in determining what to do in the present. Like her cultural cousin, Vladimir Nabokov's Lolita, sobbing in Humbert's arms, she simply has nowhere else to go. Not only does Arnold show Connie that she is desired, he also provides her a way to be "good": By going with him she will save her undeserving family from getting hurt. Connie does not so much decide to go out to Arnold as she watches an alien being that Arnold has called into existence in her body respond to his desires. The final ironic horror, of course, is that she will be raped and murdered and buried in the desert not as brown-eyed Connie but as the imaginary "sweet little blue-eyed girl" of Arnold's sick imagination.

Oates acknowledges that her inspiration for the story came in part from reading about an actual case, and Tom Quirk has demonstrated at length the degree to which the circumstances of "Where Are You Going, Where Have You Been?" seem to be derived from an article in *Life* (4 Mar. 1955) by Don Moser entitled (in a reference to some lyrics from a popular song) "The Pied Piper of Tucson." Even some of the most apparently allegorical details, such as Arnold's trouble with his boots, which has been attributed to his having cloven hooves or wolf paws, reflect the facts about Charles Schmid, a wiry gymnast of twenty-three who stuffed things in his boots, wore makeup, and drove around Tucson in a gold car playing the hero to a group of high-school kids until he was arrested for the rape and murder of three young girls. Quirk's argument that Oates followed the magazine article's theme in relating this horror in the "golden west" to the emptiness of "the American dream" points out an important dimension of the story, and his emphasis keeps the real horror of the incident in focus.

Gretchen Schulz and R. J. R. Rockwood are aware of the *Life* article, but they focus instead on another acknowledged source of Oates's inspiration, the folktale. Their discussion of the story's allusions to and affinities with "The Pied Piper of Hamelin," "Cinderella," "Little Red Riding Hood," and other tales suggests why "Where Are You Going, Where Have You Been?" is such a disturbing work. Their article offers detailed interpretations of the psychological crises Connie passes through, based on psychoanalytic interpretations of the meaning and developmental function of the analogous tales. (They use Bruno Bettelheim as their chief authority.) But whereas folktales most often smooth the passage of their readers through Oedipal conflicts and reintegration of the childhood identity into the adult by working through to a happy ending, "Where Are You Going, Where Have You Been?" taps these powerful psychic forces in the reader only to pour them out on the sand.

WILLIAM E. SHEIDLEY

Questions for Discussion

1. Define Connie's relationships with her mother, sister, and father. What is missing from this family? Why does Connie wish "her mother was dead and she herself was dead and it was all over"?

2. What are Connie's "two sides"? In your opinion, is Connie's case unusual for a girl her age in our society? In what ways is she atypical? What about June?

3. The girls enter the drive-in with "faces pleased and expectant as if they were entering a sacred building," and the popular music in the background seems

"like music at a church service." Explore the drive-in religion further. What are its creeds, its mysteries? Is it a true religion? a guide to the good life? Does Connie believe in anything else?

4. Discuss the similarities between Eddie, who rotates on a counter stool and offers "something to eat," and the emblem of the drive-in on its bottle-top roof. What else does Eddie offer? Compare Eddie with Arnold Friend as we first see him at the drive-in.

5. What does Oates accomplish by returning briefly to Connie's relationship with her family before narrating what happens "one Sunday"?

6. Discuss Connie's daydreams, in which "all the boys fell back and dissolved into a single face that was not even a face, but an idea, a feeling, mixed up with the urgent insistent pounding of the music," and in which she associates sunbathing with the "sweet, gentle" lovemaking "in movies and promised in song." What is the source of the sexual desire reflected in these dreams? What is its object?

7. Asbestos was formerly used as a noninflammable insulating material. Trace the images of heat and fire associated with it in the story.

8. Compare Connie's gentle breathing as she listens to the "XYZ Sunday Jamboree" with her breath "jerking back and forth in her lungs" when she tries to use the telephone at the climax of the story.

9. Why does Connie whisper "Christ. Christ" when she hears a car coming up the driveway? Does the effort to see Arnold Friend as a Christ figure find further substantiation in the text? Does it yield any meaningful insights?

10. Where does Connie stand during the first part of her conversation with Arnold? Is Oates's blocking of the scene realistic? symbolic?

11. Describe Arnold's car and clothing. What purpose is served by his transparent disguise? Why does it take Connie so long to penetrate the disguise?

12. Does Arnold have supernatural knowledge about Connie, her family, and her friends? Can his apparent clairvoyance about the barbecue be explained in naturalistic terms?

13. Account for Connie's idea that Arnold "had driven up the driveway all right but had come from nowhere before that and belonged nowhere and that everything about him and even the music that was so familiar to her was only half real." Explain the importance of that idea for understanding what happens to Connie.

14. Why does Connie's kitchen seem "like a place she had never seen before"? How has Arnold succeeded in making Connie feel cut off from her past and unprotected in her home? What is the implication of "the echo of a song from last year" in this context?

15. What is the role of Ellie in Arnold's assault on Connie?

16. Arnold implies that Connie can protect her family from harm by coming with him. How important a factor is this in his winning her over to his will?

17. Examine the passage in which Connie tries to telephone her mother and then collapses in panic and hysteria. Notice its associations with sex and birth. What is taking place in Connie at this moment?

18. Arnold asks rhetorically, "What else is there for a girl like you but to be sweet and pretty and give in?" In what sense is this true?

19. Explain Connie's feeling that she is watching herself go out the door. What has caused this split in her consciousness?

Topics for Writing

1. Discuss Arnold Friend's obvious masquerade, and why it succeeds.
2. Comment on popular music and religion in "Where Are You Going, Where Have You Been?"
3. Read the story once while bearing in mind that it is "based on fact" — something very much like this is known to have actually happened. After finishing the story, write a personal essay giving your reaction. What does this account imply about human nature? About the society reflected in the story?
4. Reread the story with an eye to its allusions to folktales and fairy tales with which you are familiar. Arnold's "coach" has a pumpkin on it; Connie is nearly asleep when he awakens her; he has big teeth; and so forth. What are the tales alluded to about? Is this story a fairy tale, too?
5. Select an item from the news that grips your imagination, and ask yourself why it does. Does it have affinities with folktales or myths? Does it suggest disturbing ideas about human nature and society? Write a narrative of the event, perhaps from the point of view of one of the participants, that incorporates these larger implications.
6. **CONNECTIONS** Compare technique and theme in Oates's "Where Are You Going, Where Have You Been?" and Jackson's "The Lottery."
7. **CONNECTIONS** Compare and contrast Arnold Friend and Flannery O'Connor's Misfit.
8. **CONNECTIONS** Study the allusions to religion in the story. How would Flannery O'Connor have handled this material?

Related Commentary

Joyce Carol Oates, *Smooth Talk:* Short Story into Film, p. 1477.

Suggested Readings

Bloom, Harold. *Joyce Carol Oates.* New York: Chelsea House, 1981.

Friedman, Ellen G. "Joyce Carol Oates." *Modern American Women Writers.* Ed. Elaine Showalter. New York: Macmillan, 1991.

Gardner, John. *On Writers and Writing.* Reading, MA: Addison-Wesley, 1994. 75.

Gillis, Christina Marsden. " 'Where Are You Going, Where Have You Been?': Seduction, Space, and a Fictional Mode." *Studies in Short Fiction* 18 (1981): 65–70.

Johnson, Greg. *Understanding Joyce Carol Oates.* Columbia: U of South Carolina P, 1987.

Oates, Joyce Carol. *New Heaven, New Earth.* New York: Vanguard, 1974.

———. *(Woman) Writer: Occasions and Opportunities.* New York: NAL-Dutton, 1989.

Milazzo, Lee. *Conversations with Joyce Carol Oates.* Jackson: UP of Mississippi, 1989.

Pearlman, Mickey, ed. *American Women Writing Fiction: Memory, Identity, Family, Space.* Lexington: U of Kentucky P, 1989. 9–44.

Plimpton, George. *Women Writers at Work: The Paris Review Interviews.* New York: Penguin, 1989.

Quirk, Tom. "A Source for 'Where Are You Going, Where Have You Been?' " *Studies in Short Fiction* 18 (1981): 413–19.

Rozga, Margaret. "Threatening Places, Hiding Places: The Midwest in Selected Stories by Joyce Carol Oates." *Midwestern Miscellany* 18 (1990): 34–44.

Schulz, Gretchen, and R. J. R. Rockwood. "In Fairyland, without a Map: Connie's Exploration Inward in Joyce Carol Oates's 'Where Are You Going, Where Have You Been?' " *Literature and Psychology* 30 (1980): 155–67.

Urbanski, Marie Mitchell Olesen. "Existential Allegory: Joyce Carol Oates's 'Where Are You Going, Where Have You Been?' " *Studies in Short Fiction* 15 (1978): 200–03.

Wegs, Joyce M. " 'Don't You Know Who I Am?': The Grotesque in Oates's 'Where Are You Going, Where Have You Been?' " *Journal of Narrative Technique* 5 (1975): 66–72.

Wesley, Marilyn Clarke. "Transgression and Refusal: The Dynamic of Power in the Domestic Fiction of Joyce Carol Oates." *Dissertation Abstracts International* 49(11) (May 1989): 3365A.

Winslow, Joan D. "The Stranger Within: Two Stories by Oates and Hawthorne." *Studies in Short Fiction* 17 (1980): 263–68.

Tim O'Brien

The Things They Carried (p. 1022)

In "The Things They Carried," O'Brien has found a brilliant solution to one of the most common problems a writer faces: how to find a new way to approach a subject that has been written about many times before. His subject is men at war, a topic that has occupied writers since remotest antiquity. The earliest epic in the European tradition is Homer's account of the siege of Troy, and the earliest griot narratives from the empires of Africa recount battles fought along the banks of the Niger River.

The Vietnam War has been treated in a stream of stories, books, articles, studies, and debates. O'Brien's innovation is to tell us directly not about the soldiers, or about the meaningless war they find themselves in, but about the things they are carrying on their shoulders and in their pockets. This simple device is startling and effective. The things his "grunts" are carrying are one way to identify them, to bring them to life, and the author also tells us about the things they carry under different circumstances.

This use of the small detail to illuminate the whole picture would not be as effective if it were limited to a simple description of what each of the men is carrying. But as he discusses the items — their use, their importance to the assignment the men are carrying out, and the significance of each thing to each man — O'Brien tells us about the war itself, and the soldiers' attitudes toward what they are doing. By presenting each of these objects as a microcosm of the reality of the war, the author makes the experience more comprehensible. He has found a dimension that shows us the soldiers as human beings, and that is the most important task for a writer who wants to make us face this cruel reality again.

Questions for Discussion

1. What is the effect of O'Brien's use of abbreviations and acronyms: R & R, SOP, M & Ms, USO, Psy Ops, KIA?
2. When the author writes, "Afterward they burned Than Khe," what is he telling us about the attitude of the men toward the people in the villages around them?
3. Why is it important to specify the weight of the equipment each man is carrying?
4. Does the language of the soldiers sound "real"? Do the descriptions of the weapons have the feeling of reality?
5. Why does the lieutenant burn the letters he has been carrying?

Topics for Writing

1. Soldiers from both sides are fighting the war, but the author only tells us about the men from one side. Why doesn't he describe the North Vietnamese soldiers?
2. Discuss the attitudes toward the war in the United States as they are reflected in the attitudes of the soldiers in "The Things They Carried."
3. Stories about men at war usually emphasize heroism and heroic acts; these are completely absent in this story. What has caused this change in attitude?
4. **CONNECTIONS** Compare O'Brien's depiction of soldiers with Manto's in "The Dog of Titwal" and Okri's "In the Shadow of War." Do their depictions of soldiers indicate anything about how they view war?

Suggested Readings

Bonn, Maria S. "A Different World: The Vietnam Veteran Novel Comes Home." *Fourteen Landing Zones: Approaches to Vietnam War Literature*. Ed. Philip K. Jason. Iowa City: U of Iowa P, 1992.

Calloway, Catherine. "Pluralities of vision: Going After Cacciato and Tim O'Brien's Short Fiction." *America Rediscovered: Critical Essays on Literature and Film of the Vietnam War*. Ed. Owen W. Gilman, Jr. New York: Garland, 1990.

———. "Tim O'Brien (1946–): A Primary and Secondary Bibliography." *Bulletin of Bibliography* Sept. 50:3 (1993): 223–29.

Flannery O'Connor

Everything That Rises Must Converge (p. 1037)

"Everything That Rises Must Converge" is one of O'Connor's most powerful stories. Although they are emotionally linked as closely as Siamese twins, Julian and his mother are in such fundamental disagreement that only death can bring their souls together, since "everything that rises must converge." O'Connor goes to great lengths to spell out the differences between mother and son. They are so extreme that humor is the one thing that makes them bearable to the sensitive reader. Julian asserts that "true culture is in the mind." His mother says, "It's in the heart." He insists that "nobody in the damn bus cares who you are." She replies, "I care who I am." She always looks on the bright side of things. He glories in scenting out impending disasters. He tells himself he isn't dominated by his mother. She knows he's both financially and emotionally dependent on her, and she gets him to do whatever she asks.

Contrasts and opposites rule this unlikely pair, but the world they inhabit is also in a state of opposition to their sense of themselves. Blacks no longer know their place in the back of the bus; mother and son are exiled from the destroyed family mansion; Julian wants to be a writer after his college education, but he's selling typewriters instead. The only constant is his mother's ridiculous hat. It reappears on the head of the black lady sitting with her little son next to Julian and his mother on the bus. This sight amuses his mother, who hasn't lost her sense of humor, her spirit refusing to be worn down by the remarks and behavior of her critical, hostile son. As a character she is partially redeemed (despite her racial bigotry) by her humor and her fundamental generosity. In contrast, Julian is damned by his sense of pride.

O'Connor makes certain of this damnation by subtly shifting the point of view to Julian's mental outlook during his journey on the bus, when he withdraws "into the inner compartment of his mind where he spent most of his time." He will be alone there, feeling smugly superior to his mother, until he realizes that he has lost her, at which time he will be forced to include her in his emotional state by entering "the world of guilt and sorrow."

Students may enjoy discussing the humor in this story as well as O'Connor's sublime ear for the ridiculous in her characters' speech. "Everything That Rises Must Converge" also lends itself well to different critical perspectives. Since O'Connor wrote from a Christian orientation, the religious implications of the narrative can be traced: the references to Saint Sebastian, or the Negro mother's threat to her little boy, "Quit yo' foolishness . . . before I knock the living Jesus out of you!" Or O'Connor's quiet comment about "guilt and sorrow" at the end. Students who are budding social historians, psychologists, or feminists can also find abundant material in this story to explore from their orientations.

Questions for Discussion

1. O'Connor writes that Julian's mother's eyes, "sky-blue, were as innocent and untouched by experience as they must have been when she was ten." Again, when she turns her eyes, now a "bruised purple," on Julian, he gets an "uncomfortable sense of her innocence." What are we to make of her innocence? How do we reconcile this attribute with her racism?
2. Julian seems to hate almost everything about his mother. Does she hate anything about her son? Why does he despise her? Why does she love him?
3. The idea of family mansion implies family ties. How do family ties appear in this story? Does the "decayed mansion" mean more to Julian or to his mother? What does it mean to him? to her?
4. What point of view controls "Everything That Rises Must Converge"? At which points in the story do we have the most intimate access to Julian's thoughts?

5. Describe Julian's relationships with people other than his mother. Consider the paragraphs beginning "He began to imagine" and "He imagined his mother." Who would he like to be friends with and why? Does his acknowledgment of his mother's racism imply positive things about Julian's own character?

6. On page 1042 we discover that Julian's mother doesn't think Julian knows "a thing about 'life,' that he hadn't even entered the real world" yet. Does the narrator agree with her? Discuss this sentence and the closing sentence of the story together. What does this imply about the characteristics that belong to "real life"?

7. After his mother's stroke, Julian looks "into a face he had never seen before." What is different about her face now? What metaphor is O'Connor sustaining behind the description of the literal differences brought on by neurological devastation?

8. O'Connor, a devout Catholic, said her stories were meant to be more like parables than true to life. What elements of this story are Christian? Is the preoccupation central to this story available only to Christians?

Topics for Writing

1. Compare and contrast the two mothers and the two sons in the story.
2. Analyze the symbolism of the hat at the convergence of two apparent opposites — the two mothers.
3. Discuss the role of pride and the response to charity in Julian and the black mother.
4. Write an examination of the changing social order between the generations of Julian's mother and Julian.
5. Explore the role of irony in "Everything That Rises Must Converge."

Related Commentaries

Wayne, C. Booth, A Rhetorical Reading of O'Connor's "Everything That Rises Must Converge," p. 1563.
Robert H. Brinkmeyer, Jr., Flannery O'Connor and Her Readers, p. 1554.
Anthony Di Renzo, A Dialogical Reading of "Everything That Rises Must Converge," p. 1567.
Flannery O'Connor, From *Letters 1954–1955*, p. 1542.
Flannery O'Connor, Writing Short Stories, p. 1544.
V. S. Pritchett, Flannery O'Connor: Satan Comes to Georgia, p. 1552.

Suggested Readings

See page 191.

Flannery O'Connor

Good Country People (p. 1048)

In the world of Flannery O'Connor's fiction, characters are seldom who we think they are or even who they think they are. "Good Country People" provides an intriguing twist on the archetypal theme: Events and people are seldom as simple as they seem.

O'Connor revels in the idiosyncrasies of personality, peopling this story with three strong characters in Joy (Hulga), Mrs. Hopewell, and Manley Pointer, as well as an interesting subsidiary character, Mrs. Freeman, with her "special fondness for the details of secret infections, hidden deformities," and "assaults upon children." O'Connor's choice of names figures prominently. Joy changes her name to Hulga to symbolize her sense of her own ugliness. Mrs. Hopewell continually hopes well of things, blathering a stream of banal platitudes that reveal her own lack of depth. The name Manley Pointer strikes the reader as almost humorously phallic and predatory-sounding, given the surprising turn of events in the storage barn.

We don't see how "right" the details of this story are until we reach its sardonic conclusion, Pointer going Hulga's intellectual atheism one better, disappearing with her leg in his "Bible" valise, Mrs. Hopewell in her ignorance commenting on "that nice dull young man." Looking back, we see the clever meticulousness of Pointer's con — the feigned heaviness of his satchel, his feigned simplicity (as in mistaking the name of the house for its owner), the rube suit. It turns out that this specimen of "good country people" reads people better than the highly educated Hulga or the self-aggrandizing Mrs. Hopewell.

The experience of losing her artificial limb to the perverted Manley Pointer is the loss of a certain kind of virginity for Hulga, and however harrowing the experience, we sense that it will be a valuable one. Prior to her victimization, we feel mainly revulsion for Joy-Hulga. We sympathize with her hunting accident, but O'Connor highlights the unpleasant abrasiveness of her personality; clearly Hulga's psyche, as well as her body, has been damaged. Hulga's low self-esteem is exacerbated by her mother's implications of Hulga's abnormality, which focus on her intellectualism as much as on her disfigurement. For all Mrs. Hopewell's assertions that "it takes all kinds to make the world go 'round," she resents her daughter's interest in philosophy (female education is for a "good time") as well as Hulga's individuation: "It seemed to Mrs. Hopewell that every year she grew less like other people and more like herself."

In this multifaceted story of moral blindness, Hulga experiences a physical intimacy with Pointer that forces her into a new mode of reacting and out of her customary detached intellectualism: "Without the leg she felt entirely dependent on him. Her brain seemed to have stopped thinking altogether and to be about some other function that it was not very good at." However dastardly Pointer's actions, he forces Hulga to feel and acknowledge her emotions for the first time. We go away from the story feeling that Hulga will be a changed — and humbled — person less presumptuous and closer to psychic wholeness.

Questions for Discussion

1. What does Mrs. Hopewell mean by "good country people"?
2. Why does Joy change her name to Hulga?
3. In what ways do you expect Joy/Hulga will change after her experience in the barn with Manley Pointer?
4. Discuss O'Connor's choice of names for the characters in this story.
5. Is Manley Pointer a believable character? Have you in your own experience encountered people who are entirely other than they seem? What is Pointer really interested in? Why does he carry off Hulga's leg?
6. Discuss the dramatic function of Mrs. Freeman and her two daughters.
7. Discuss the effects on characterization of O'Connor's choosing to give Joy a Ph.D. in philosophy and an artificial leg. How do these details predispose our expectations?

Topics for Writing

1. Discuss the function of Christianity in "Good Country People."
2. **CONNECTIONS** Compare "Good Country People" with "Everything That Rises Must Converge." What similarities and differences do you find among mother, son or daughter, and stranger in these stories? What can you infer from this comparison about Flannery O'Connor's attraction to certain types of characters?

Related Commentaries

Robert H. Brinkmeyer, Jr., Flannery O'Connor and Her Readers, p. 1554.
Dorothy Tuck McFarland, On "Good Country People," p. 1559.
Flannery O'Connor, From *Letters 1954–1955*, p. 1542.
Flannery O'Connor, Writing Short Stories, p. 1544.

Suggested Readings

See page 191.

FLANNERY O'CONNOR

A Good Man Is Hard to Find (p. 1063)

O'Connor's comments (included in Part Three, p. 1549) direct attention to the climax of her story and suggest how she intended the central characters to be viewed and what she meant the story to imply. Students may benefit, however, from struggling at first to interpret the text unassisted by authorial explanation.

The effort should reveal dimensions of O'Connor's art that might otherwise be overlooked.

The grandmother's reawakening to reality, which leads to her gesture of grace as she reaches out to The Misfit as one of her own children, may be triggered by the violence of the murders going on just offstage and the extremity of her own case, but her conversion has been carefully prepared for. Throughout the story this old woman longs in various ways to go back *home* — to Tennessee, to the days of her youth, to the mansion with the imaginary secret panel, which is as much in heaven as it is down a hilly back road in Georgia. Death is seldom far from her thoughts, though for a long time she does not apprehend its reality. Her initial worries about The Misfit are disingenuous, but encountering him or returning to east Tennessee come to the same thing in the end. On the road, the grandmother dresses up in nice clothes so that "anyone seeing her dead on the highway would know at once that she was a lady," observes a graveyard, and remembers her mansion at a town named Toombsboro. The Misfit and his men approach in a "hearse-like automobile"; the family awaits them in front of the woods that "gaped like a dark open mouth." The grandmother is at odds with present times. She squabbles with the children (whose behavior even the reader may find unusually improper), easily upstages the cabbage-headed, slacks-wearing woman who is their mother, joins Red Sammy in deploring the state of world affairs, and disastrously deludes Bailey by smuggling the cat into the car. But she loves the world as well, in a selfish, childish way. She *will* have the cat along; she admires the scenery (including a picturesque "pickaninny" for whose poverty she is not yet ready to feel compassion); she wishes she had married Mr. E. A. Teagarden, who courted her with watermelon and would have supplied all her worldly needs from the proceeds of his Coca-Cola stock; and she even makes a play for Red Sammy, the only tycoon in sight.

These desires may be misdirected, but just as it takes very little to upset the valise, release the cat, flip the car off the road, and carry the story into an entirely new set of circumstances, so, under the intensifying presence of death, it takes only a moment for the grandmother's selfish love for and alienation from the world to flip over into the selfless love that leads her to open her heart to The Misfit. After all, she at least rationalizes bringing the cat to protect it; she supportively asserts that Red Sammy is "a good man" in face of his own cynicism and despair; and she offers the same praise to The Misfit from the moment she recognizes him. Without a doubt the grandmother's motive in insisting that The Misfit is "a good man" and in urging him to pray is to divert him from his evident intention and so to save her skin. But as the bullets ring out in the background and the grandmother's maternal instincts burst forth in her repeated cries of "Bailey Boy!" she begins to act charitably in spite of herself. She offers The Misfit one of Bailey's shirts, listens to his confession (although she is the one who is about to die), and when he *is* wearing Bailey's shirt, she reaches out to him in his anguish. A good man *is* hard to find; Jesus may have been the only one who was intrinsically good. But when she loves and pities the radically fallen Misfit, the grandmother becomes for the moment a *good woman* through her Christlike action, as The Misfit himself acerbically recognizes.

As O'Connor mentions in her commentary, The Misfit has evoked widely differing responses from readers and critics, who have associated him with the devil, the modern agnostic existentialist, or "the prophet he was meant to become," in O'Connor's own phrase. Perhaps The Misfit's daddy provides the best way of distinguishing him from the rest of the characters with his remark "It's some that can live their whole life out without asking about it and it's others has to know why it is, and this boy is one of the latters." Unlike O'Connor, whose vision of the world was grounded in *belief*, The Misfit wants to *know*. With Faustian presumption, he seeks to comprehend the divine mysteries in terms of his own intellect and demands a kind of justice in life that he can understand. When he cannot find the answers to his questions, but only the implication of inexplicable guilt (like Original Sin) in the punishment he receives, The Misfit sees the world not as the charming place it has appeared to the grandmother but as a prison whose empty sky resembles the blank walls of his cell in the penitentiary. In his own calculus of guilt, The Misfit feels he has been excessively punished, and he seems to be going about the world committing crimes in order to right the balance. His most perverse principle, "No pleasure but meanness," is sustained surprisingly well by the world O'Connor portrays. (Is *this* the reason for the story's lack of anything or anyone to admire and its unremittingly ironic tone?) But it gives way after he has been touched by the grandmother to his first true prophecy: "It's no real pleasure in life" — no *real* pleasure in *this* life, though true goodness sometimes appears in those made conscious of death.

WILLIAM E. SHEIDLEY

Questions for Discussion

1. What is the grandmother's reason for bringing up The Misfit at the beginning of the story?
2. Describe "the children's mother." Why does O'Connor make her such a nonentity?
3. What about John Wesley and June Star? What would have been the result had O'Connor characterized them as something other than totally obnoxious?
4. Discuss the grandmother's reasons for her fatal decision to bring Pitty Sing on the trip.
5. Why does the grandmother dress so nicely for the trip?
6. Compare the grandmother's response to the scenery and the trip with that of the children. What does O'Connor accomplish by means of this distinction?
7. Just before the stop at The Tower, the grandmother reminisces about her old suitor, Edgar Atkins Teagarden. Specify the connections between the two episodes.
8. What tower might O'Connor have had in mind in choosing the name for Red Sammy's establishment? Why is there a monkey in a chinaberry tree feasting on fleas posted outside The Tower? What do we learn about the world at Red Sammy's?
9. Contrast The Tower with the mansion the grandmother awakens to remember "outside of Toombsboro."
10. What factors cause the accident? Consider its meaning as a consequence of the grandmother's choices and desires.
11. Describe the manner in which The Misfit arrives on the scene. What effect does his appearance have on the reader?

12. The grandmother's response to The Misfit's remark "it would have been better for all of you, lady, if you hadn't of reckernized me," is "You wouldn't shoot a lady, would you?" Evaluate her question.
13. To what extent is the grandmother correct in her praise of The Misfit? In what ways is he a gentleman?
14. Describe the grandmother's reaction to Bailey's departure. Is her response consistent with her previous behavior?
15. Define The Misfit's experience of the world. To what extent can his criminality be blamed on the conditions of his life? Does The Misfit feel any more free outside the penitentiary than in it?
16. How can the logic of The Misfit's position that "the crime don't matter. . . . because sooner or later you're going to forget what it was you done and just be punished for it" be attacked? To what extent does The Misfit's description of himself apply to everyone? Bear in mind that the whole family is being punished with death for no ascertainable crime.
17. Explain how, to The Misfit, "Jesus thown everything off balance."
18. What is the effect of O'Connor's comparing the grandmother to "a parched old turkey hen crying for water"?
19. Does The Misfit do or say anything to deserve the grandmother's gesture of concern?
20. Explain The Misfit's final evaluation of the grandmother: "She would of been a good woman . . . if it had been somebody there to shoot her every minute of her life."
21. Contrast The Misfit's remark "No pleasure but meanness" with his last words in the story.

Topics for Writing

1. What is the function of tone in O'Connor's story?
2. Describe techniques of characterization in "A Good Man Is Hard to Find."
3. Write a parable or short tale designed to illustrate a religious or philosophical truth. Following O'Connor's example, portray your characters ruthlessly as embodiments of what you want them to represent.
4. **CONNECTIONS** Compare and contrast O'Connor's "A Good Man Is Hard to Find" and Tolstoy's "The Death of Ivan Ilych."
5. **CONNECTIONS** Comment upon the relationship between the grandmother and the Misfit in "A Good Man Is Hard to Find" and the relationship between Connie and Arnold Friend in Oates's "Where Are You Going, Where Have You Been?"

Related Commentaries

Robert H. Brinkmeyer, Jr., Flannery O'Connor and Her Readers, p. 1554.
Flannery O'Connor, The Element of Suspense in "A Good Man Is Hard to Find," p. 1549.
Flannery O'Connor, From *Letters 1954–1955*, p. 1542.
Flannery O'Connor, Writing Short Stories, p. 1544.

Suggested Readings

Asals, Frederick. *Flannery O'Connor: The Imagination of Extremity.* Athens: U of Georgia P, 1982. 142–54.

Brinkmeyer, Robert H., Jr. *The Art and Vision of Flannery O'Connor.* Baton Rouge: Louisiana State UP, 1989.

Browning, Preston M., Jr. *Flannery O'Connor.* Crosscurrents/Modern Critiques. Carbondale: Southern Illinois UP, 1974. 54–59.

Burke, John J. "Convergence of Flannery O'Connor and Chardin." *Renascence* 19 (1966): 41–47, 52.

Church, Joseph. "An Abuse of the Imagination in Flannery O'Connor's 'A Good Man Is Hard to Find.'" *Notes on Contemporary Literature* 20(3) May 1990): 8–10.

Clark, Beverly Lyon, and Melville J. Friedman. *Critical Essays on Flannery O'Connor.* Boston: G. K. Hall, 1985.

Esch, Robert M. "O'Connor's 'Everything That Rises Must Converge.' " *Explicator* 27 (1969): Item 58.

Feeley, Sister Kathleen. *Flannery O'Connor: Voice of the Peacock.* New Brunswick, NJ: Rutgers UP, 1972.

Gatta, John. "*The Scarlet Letter* as Pre-Text for Flannery O'Connor's 'Good Country People.'" *The Nathaniel Hawthorne Review* 16(2) (Fall 1990): 6–9.

Giannone, Richard. *Flannery O'Connor: A Study of the Short Fiction.* Boston: Twayne, 1988.

Grimshaw, James A. *The Flannery O'Connor Companion.* Westport, CT: Greenwood, 1981.

Hendin, Josephine. *The World of Flannery O'Connor.* Ann Arbor, MI: Books Demand UMI, 1986.

Kane, Patricia. "Flannery O'Connor's 'Everything That Rises Must Converge.' " *Critique: Studies in Short Fiction* 8 (1965): 85–91.

McDermott, John V. "Julian's Journey into Hell: Flannery O'Connor's Allegory of Pride." *Mississippi Quarterly* 28 (1975): 171–79.

Maida, Patricia Dinneen. "Convergence in Flannery O'Connor's 'Everything That Rises Must Converge.' " *Studies in Short Fiction* 7 (1970): 549–55.

Martin, W. R. "The Apostate in Flannery O'Connor's 'Everything That Rises Must Converge.' " *American Notes and Queries* 23 (1985): 113–14.

Nisly, P. W. "Prison of the Self: Isolation in Flannery O'Connor's Fiction." *Studies in Short Fiction* 17 (1980): 49–54.

Ochshorn, Kathleen G. "A Cloak of Grace: Contradictions in 'A Good Man Is Hard to Find.'" *Studies in American Fiction* 18(1) (Spring 1990) 113–17.

O'Connor, Flannery. *The Habit of Being.* Letters edited and with an introduction by Sally Fitzgerald. New York: Farrar, 1979.

———. *Mystery and Manners.* New York: Farrar, 1969.

Orvell, Miles. *Invisible Parade: The Fiction of Flannery O'Connor.* Philadelphia: Temple UP, 1972.

Paulson, Suzanne. *Flannery O'Connor.* Boston: G. K. Hall, 1988.

Petry, Alice Hall. "Miss O'Connor and Mrs. Mitchell: The Example of 'Everything That Rises.'" *The Southern Quarterly: A Journal of the Arts in the South* 27(4) (Summer 1989): 5–15.

Pyron, V. "'Strange Country': The Landscape of Flannery O'Connor's Short Stories." *Mississippi Quarterly* 36 (1983): 557–68.

(text pp. 1076–1084)

FRANK O'CONNOR

Guests of the Nation (p. 1076)

O'Connor's story draws exceptional power from its concern with a betrayal of the most primitive basis of human society, the host-guest relationship. The English prisoners, billeted with their guards in a cottage so thoroughly rooted in the land that its occupant still bears traces of indigenous paganism, earn the status of guests and come to feel at home. Belcher's contributions to the household chores call attention to the simple satisfactions of the peaceful, cooperative labor that is disrupted by the war, and Hawkins's learning Irish dances implies the underlying brotherhood of men, in contrast to which the scruples of "our lads" who "at that time did not dance foreign dances on principle" seem absurd — and ominous. The futility of Hawkins's debates with Noble on theology calls further into question the reality of the issues that divide the English from the Irish, and his international socialist politics provide a hint that there are issues of at least equal importance that would not polarize the two pairs of men but unite them against a common enemy.

The inhumanity of the conflict that orders Belcher and Hawkins to be executed by their "chums," their brothers, appears clearer for O'Connor's skillful portrayal of the prisoners as distinct from each other, individualized and consistent in their personalities. Further, by opening the story with a plunge into what seems an ongoing state of affairs, O'Connor shows that it is the war that interrupts the natural friendly interaction among the men rather than their fellowship interrupting a "normal" condition of bitter hostility between the English and the Irish. Even Jeremiah Donovan, who eventually brings down the cruel warrant and carries it out, forms part of the circle around the card table and scolds Hawkins for poor play "as if he were one of our own."

Bonaparte, the narrator, embraces the Englishmen as comrades and chafes at his official duties as their guard. With Noble, he imagines that the brigade officers, who also "knew the Englishmen well," will treat them as men rather than as enemies. But when the moment of decision arrives, Noble's resistance only extends to accepting the secondary role of gravedigger, and Bonaparte, though he hopes the prisoners will run away, finds himself powerless to aid them. Belcher and Hawkins are most fully themselves at the moment of their deaths, Hawkins talking on about his larger cause, Belcher finally revealing the fullness of his loving and generous nature. To Bonaparte and Noble the execution conveys a shock of revelation that changes the world for them. As Noble prays with the old woman in the doorway of the cottage — now become a shrine to the communion that took place within it, the only holy place in a world that seems to Noble composed entirely of the grave of his friends — Bonaparte, made profane in the literal etymological sense ("outside the shrine") and figuratively as well by his participation in the killing, feels himself cast out, alone, cut off from all atonement.

WILLIAM E. SHEIDLEY

Questions for Discussion

1. Describe and explain the pacing of the story. Contrast the movement of sections II and III with that of section IV.

2. What is the effect of the abrupt beginning of the story? Why does O'Connor introduce the characters before specifying that they are prisoners and guards in a war?
3. Why does O'Connor trouble to introduce the message from Mary Brigid O'Connell about her brother's socks?
4. Distinguish between the two Englishmen. Are they more different from the Irishmen or from each other?
5. Explore the significance of the old woman's superstitions about Jupiter Pluvius and "the hidden powers." Compare her interest in religion with that of Noble and Hawkins.
6. Why is Bonaparte so shocked when he learns what may happen to the hostages?
7. What is the relevance to the story of Hawkins's political beliefs? Do we think less of him when he volunteers to become a traitor and join the Irish cause?
8. What is the effect of Belcher's last-minute confidences? of his apparently sincere repetition of the word *chum* throughout his ordeal?
9. Discuss Bonaparte's role in the execution. Is he culpable? Does he feel guilty?
10. Define the symbolic implications of the final scene. Why do Noble and Bonaparte have contrasting visions? Do their visions have anything in common? Why does Bonaparte burst out of the cottage where Noble and the old woman are praying?

Topics for Writing

1. What is the meaning of the old woman and her cottage in "Guests of the Nation"?
2. Summarize the conflict and the action of this story on personal, public (national, historical, political), and eternal (philosophical, religious, mythical) levels. Could these levels be reconciled so that the polarities of value would be parallel?
3. **CONNECTIONS** Compre and contrast O'Connor's "Guests of the Nation" and Babel's "My First Goose" — introductions to war.
4. **CONNECTIONS** Compare and contrast executions in O'Connor's "Guests of the Nation" and Borowski's "This Way for the Gas, Ladies and Gentlemen."

Related Commentary

Frank O'Connor, The Nearest Thing to Lyric Poetry Is the Short Story, p. 1481.

Suggested Readings

Bordewyk, Gordon. "Quest for Meaning: The Stories of Frank O'Connor." *Illinois Quarterly* 41 (1978): 37–47. esp. 38–39.

Matthews, James. *Voices: A Life of Frank O'Connor.* New York: Atheneum, 1983.

O'Connor, Frank. *The Lonely Voice: A Study of the Short Story.* Cleveland: World, 1963.

Prosky, Murray. "The Pattern of Diminishing Certitude in the Stories of Frank O'Connor." *Colby Library Quarterly* 9 (1971): 311–21, esp. 311–14.

(text pp. 1086–1089)

Steinman, Michael. *Frank O'Connor at Work.* Syracuse, NY: Syracuse UP, 1990.
Tomory, William. *Frank O'Connor.* Boston: Twayne, 1980.

BEN OKRI

In the Shadow of War (p. 1086)

Okri has said that his stories about daily life in war-torn Nigeria are realistic narratives, not surrealistic fantasies. By using the perspective of the young boy Omovo to describe the events dramatized in "In the Shadow of War," Okri skillfully introduces an element of unreliability into the story and heightens its nightmarish aspect. Omovo is so young that he asks his father to explain the meaning of the word "eclipse," which they hear on the radio news broadcast. His father's definition, "That's when the world goes dark and strange things happen," suggests the condition of life for the people left to the mercy of the soldiers patrolling their village and foreshadows the conclusion of the story.

Omovo's attempt to follow the mysteriously appealing woman in the yellow smock (a maternal figure suggesting the nurturing quality of the sun) who is reputed to "have no shadow" is the plot of "In the Shadow of War." She leads him from his home into a landscape devastated by war, as barren as the moon. They pass deserted, crumbling buildings, contorted trees, the skeleton of a large animal, and a slithering snake. At first all that Omovo sees is described straightforwardly, but an element of uncertainty enters his experience after the woman disappears into a cave and reappears without her basket, followed by the thankful, starving wretches in hiding to whom she has brought food.

Then Omovo's description of his setting begins to blur, a sign of his tension and fatigue. Still following the woman, who moves "as if an invisible force were trying to blow her away," the boy comes to a dark river in which mysterious items float. When the three soldiers in the village suddenly reappear, violence erupts. The night landscape is so threatening to Omovo that the little boy loses his sense of reality. While hiding in the shadows he watches the soldiers capture the woman and shoot her. In terror the boy runs for home, the soldiers tramping after him, but he trips and falls unconscious. When sound and sight return, he finds himself back with his father, who is drinking palm wine with the three soldiers. Delirious, Omovo is unable to obey his father and thank the men for having brought him home from the forest, and the story ends as he is carted off to bed. The forest world of shadows and darkness has eclipsed the familiar world of home, and Omovo is imprisoned in the nightmare of war.

Questions for Discussion

1. Why is it appropriate that Omovo and his father hear that an eclipse is about to take place?
2. Why is Omovo's mother absent from his home?
3. How can "In the Shadow of War" be read as an allegory?

Topics for Writing

1. Analyze the importance of the setting of "In the Shadow of War" as a reflection of Omovo's state of mind.
2. **CONNECTIONS** Compare and contrast Okri's story with Chinua Achebe's "Civil Peace."

Suggested Reading

Okri, Ben. *Stars of the New Curfew.* New York: Penguin, 1988.

TILLIE OLSEN

I Stand Here Ironing (p. 1091)

One way to begin discussing this story is to look at the ending. "I will never total it all," the narrator affirms and then pronounces the summary whose inadequacy she has already proclaimed. The summarizing passage clarifies and organizes the impressions the reader may have gleaned from the preceding monologue. It is so clear that if it stood alone or came first in the story the validity of its interpretation of Emily could hardly be doubted. But since it follows her mother's "tormented" meditations, the summary seems incomplete in its clinical precision and must give way to a final paragraph of comparatively obscure and paradoxical requests focused in the startling but brilliantly adept image of the "dress on the ironing board, helpless before the iron," which links the story's end to its beginning and directs attention to the true central character.

What is mainly missing from the summary is the love and understanding that Emily's mother feels for her daughter as a result of living through the experiences bracketed by the orderly generalizations. Just as much as Emily, her mother has been the victim "of depression, of war, of fear." By virtue of having had to cope with those circumstances, she can respect Emily's response to them. Doing so enables her to counter the suggestion that "she's a youngster who needs help" with "Let her be." A good deal of the help Emily and her mother have received so far has put them in separate prisons — as when Emily was incarcerated at the convalescent home — and cut them off from love. To let Emily alone is at least to allow her some freedom to grow at her own slow pace.

Her mother is tempted to blame herself for the deficiencies in Emily's childhood, since she learned things about being a mother with her second family that she did not know with Emily. But her consideration of a characteristic incident early in the narrative suggests a crucial qualifying factor: When she parked Emily at nursery school at the age of two, she did not know what she was subjecting her daughter to, "except that it would have made no difference if I had known. . . . It was the only way we could be together, the only way I could hold a job." As much a victim of rigid and unfavorable economic and historic circumstances as her daughter, Emily's mother can speak her concluding line with feeling. In pleading that Emily somehow be made to know "that she is more than this dress on the ironing board, helpless before the iron," Emily's mother asks that her daughter be spared a condition to which she herself has been subjected. But Emily's mother, unlike Whistler's, does not sit for her portrait passively in a rocking chair; she stands there wielding the iron, controlling the very symbol of the circumstances that have not yet flattened her, painting her own self-portrait, and calling for help not in adjusting Emily to the world but in making the world a place in which Emily can thrive.

William E. Sheidley

Questions for Discussion

1. Who is "you" in the first sentence? What is the mother's first response to the request to unlock the mystery of Emily? Does her position change?
2. Does Emily's mother feel guilty about how she has cared for Emily? Why? What factors have affected her dealings with her daughter?
3. Why is the passage in which Emily throws the clock so effective?
4. Discuss the "help" Emily gets at the convalescent home. How does it compare with the help her mother calls for at the end?
5. Emily has suffered from the absence of her father, the exhaustion of her mother, poverty, asthma and other diseases, sibling rivalry, and unpopularity, among other complaints. What is the effect of these hardships on the young woman she has become? What is the effect of her discovery of a talent?
6. What has her mother learned from Emily?
7. Does Emily's mother love her daughter? How can we tell?

Topics for Writing

1. Compare and contrast Emily's talent and her mother's.
2. Discuss the function of the interruptions in "I Stand Here Ironing."
3. Consider "I will never total it all" — the importance of indeterminacy in Olsen's analysis of Emily.
4. Analyze the politics of "I Stand Here Ironing."
5. Write a summary statement in general terms about the personality of a sibling, relative, or friend you have known closely for a long time. Put it aside and cast your memory back to three or four specific incidents involving your subject. Narrate them briefly but in specific and concrete terms. Read over your sketches and compare the personality of your subject as it emerges with what you wrote in your generalized summary. Do you still think your summary is accurate? What are its limitations?

Suggested Readings

Frye, Joanne S. "'I Stand Here Ironing': Motherhood as Experience and Metaphor." *Studies in Short Fiction* 18 (1981): 287–92.

O'Connor, William Van. "The Short Stories of Tillie Olsen." *Studies in Short Fiction* 1 (1963): 21–25, esp. 21–22.

CYNTHIA OZICK

The Shawl (p. 1098)

The yellow Star of David sewn into Rosa's coat identifies the people on the march as Jews whose destination is a Nazi concentration camp. The prosaic details of Ozick's story are horrible. Rosa's inability to save her baby, Magda, when the prison guard throws her against the electric fence is the grim conclusion to a hopeless situation. Ozick's poetic language and skillful pacing of her narrative transform the nightmarish details of her fiction into art.

The title of the story suggests its blend of fact and poetry. "The Shawl" is on the one hand a prosaic linen shawl that Rosa uses to wrap her baby and carry her under her coat during the forced march to the camp. On the other hand, Ozick tells us that "it was a magic shawl." It nourishes Magda after Rosa's breast milk dries up. It hides the baby in the women's barracks in the camp for many months. It smothers Rosa's scream after she sees Magda thrown against the fence. The shawl appears to have a life of its own, drying like Rosa's breasts; yet before drying it nourishes Rosa: "Rosa drank Magda's shawl until it dried." That is, perhaps, until the memory of her baby's death is bearable.

The narrative develops through two conflicts, the Jewish-Aryan conflict dramatized through the camp setting and the personal conflict between the two sisters, the baby Magda and the fourteen-year-old Stella. The resolution of Stella's jealousy toward the baby — when Stella takes the shawl to cover herself against the cold and Magda totters outside the women's barracks looking for it — precipitates the climax of the story. There is no resolution to the larger Jewish-Aryan conflict, except that Rosa's will endures. She smothers her screams and survives the death of her baby.

The blend of fact and poetry is reinforced by Ozick's use of sound and silence in "The Shawl." Most of the time, the events described are unvoiced, evoking the eerie echo of silence in the black-and-white documentary films shot by the Allies liberating the concentration camps. Many students will have seen these films on TV programs about the Holocaust and will remember the images of the prison barracks, the hundreds of emaciated prisoners, the mounds of skeleton corpses.

Ozick suggests these familiar images by her use of poetic language to describe the malnutrition of her characters in "The Shawl." Stella's knees are "tumors on sticks, her elbows chicken bones." For the baby, death is a kind of deliverance. She makes a noise for the first time since her scream on the road. But the noises of the baby's scream and her cry "Maaaa" are subhuman, like the chicken-bone elbows. They reinforce the terror of the situation, people degraded into subhuman forms. In a way, silence is a relief. Rosa swallows the shawl to smother her howl so the prison guard won't shoot her. Silence is a means of survival in this story. Ironically, the silence of Ozick's words on the printed page is a testimony to the endurance of her people.

Questions for Discussion

1. How does Ozick use details to allude to the plot situation without naming it specifically? What mood does she create by her method of introducing details?
2. What two conflicts are evident throughout the story? How is the shawl central to these oppositions?
3. In what ways is the shawl "magic"? Whom does it nourish? How?
4. Discuss Ozick's use of poetic language to present the images of the story. Give examples of this use.
5. Who is the protagonist of the story? the antagonist? Is there more than one possible answer to these questions? Explain.
6. Sound and silence are integral to the total effect of the story. Discuss.
7. What is the climax of the story? Are any of the conflicts resolved? What is Ozick protesting? What human qualities does the story commemorate?

Topics for Writing

1. Discuss Ozick's use of sensory images and their contribution to the overall story.
2. Rewrite the story from the point of view of Stella.
3. **CONNECTIONS** Compare and contrast the quality of endurance in O'Brien's "The Things They Carried" and Ozick's "The Shawl."
4. **CONNECTIONS** Compare and discuss the theme of quiet desperation in Ozick's "The Shawl," Gilman's "The Yellow Wallpaper," and Steinbeck's "The Chrysanthemums."

Suggested Readings

Berg, Stephen, ed. "Cynthia Ozick: Lesson of the Master." *In Praise of What Persists.* New York: Harper, 1983. 181–87.
Epstein, J. "Fiction: Cynthia Ozick, Jewish Writer." *Commentary* 77 (1984): 64–69.
Ottenberg, E. "Rich Visions of Cynthia Ozick." *New York Times Magazine* 10 Apr. 1983: 46–47.
Rosenberg, R. "Covenanted to the Law: Cynthia Ozick." *MELUS* 9 (1982): 39–44.
Strandberg, V. "Art of Cynthia Ozick." *Texas Studies in Language and Literature* 25 (1983): 266–312.

GRACE PALEY

A Conversation with My Father (p. 1103)

The story the narrator writes in response to her father's request is so interesting that it is easy to forget for a while that it is only an element within the larger story Paley has to tell. Confronted with the inescapable fact of the father's imminent death, the narrator and her father respond in differing ways because of their differing needs. Both use gallows humor to make the situation less intolerable, as when the father remarks, "It so happens I'm not going out this evening"; but the narrator seeks that refuge much more often, and her father chides her repeatedly for doing so. Things *matter* to a dying man, and it is not surprising that he should prefer the straight line of tragedy — in which failure and defeat are compensated for by a perception of the real value of what has been lost — to the idea of "the open destiny of life," which, by holding out hope of recovery from any disaster, implies that there is nothing indispensable, no absolute loss. A man on his deathbed knows better.

The narrator's first attempt to write a story that suits her father's taste reflects her discomfort with the assignment. Her "unadorned and miserable tale" remains so sketchy that it lacks verisimilitude and conviction, like meaningless statistics on highway deaths or counterinsurgency body counts. Challenged to try again, she partly confirms her father's complaint that "with you, it's all a joke" by writing a brilliantly comic and incontrovertibly realistic version of the story, whose merits even her father has to recognize: "Number One: You have a nice sense of humor." In a few deft strokes, Paley renders an incisive satiric portrait of two contemporary "life-styles," their hypocrisy, and their destructiveness, focused neatly in the competing periodical titles, *Oh! Golden Horse!* (heroin) and *Man Does Live by Bread Alone*. The narrator knows as well as her father how thorough a perversion of true spiritual values is embodied in each of these titles, and she dramatizes her understanding in the destruction of the mother in her story. But she cannot quite "look it in the face," and she ends her tale with one last grim joke: "terrible, face-scarring, time-consuming tears." Her father spies her desperate evasion: "Number Two: I see you can't tell a plain story. So don't waste time." Ironically, the clarity of his disillusioned vision enables the dying man to feel a purer sympathy for the mother in the story than does the narrator herself, although she claims to care so much about her characters that she wants to give them all a second chance. "Poor woman," he says. "Poor girl, born in a time of fools, to live among fools. The end. The end. You were right to put that down. The end." Not necessarily, the narrator argues, and goes on to invent the kind of future for her character that we always imagine for the dying, in the probably misguided effort to ease their anxiety. But her father, as usual, knows better: " 'How long will it be?' he asked. 'Tragedy! You too. When will you look it in the face?' "

WILLIAM E. SHEIDLEY

Questions for Discussion

1. Describe the medical condition of the narrator's father. How important is it to understanding his position in the conversation?
2. Explain the phrase "despite my metaphors" in the first paragraph. What other writerly tactics of the narrator does her father ignore?
3. The narrator says she *would* like to tell a story with the kind of plot she has always despised. Analyze her conflict.
4. What is the point of the first version of the story? What is wrong with it as a piece of fiction?
5. When her father asks for details, the narrator comes up with things he calls jokes. Are they? What makes them jokes rather than facts?

6. Why does the narrator's father consider that "it is of great consequence" whether the woman in the story is married? Is he simply old-fashioned?
7. What does the narrator add to her story in the second version? Does the point of the story remain the same? Does her father get the point?
8. The woman in the story "would rather be with the young." Consider that motivation and its results from the point of view of the narrator and of her father.
9. What techniques does Paley use to satirize the woman's son and his girl-friend?
10. Explain the term "time-consuming" at the end of the inset story.
11. The narrator's father makes three separate responses to the story. Account for each of them. Do they cohere?
12. What does the narrator's father mean by the statement he makes in various forms culminating in his final question?

Topics for Writing

1. Analyze "A Conversation with My Father" as a story about writing.
2. Evaluate the qualities of tragedy versus satire in "A Conversation with My Father."
3. Write your own version of the narrator's story. Start from her first version and elaborate on it as you choose, without necessarily using the material the narrator includes in her second version and subsequent commentary.
4. **CONNECTIONS** Compare and contrast attitudes toward death and life in Paley's "A Conversation with My Father" and Tolstoy's "The Death of Ivan Ilych."

Related Commentary

Grace Paley, A Conversation with Ann Charters, p. 1484.

Suggested Readings

Aarons, Victoria. "Talking Lives: Storytelling and Renewal in Grace Paley's Short Fiction." *Studies in Jewish Literature* 9(1) (Spring 1990): 20–35.

Arcana, Judith. "Grace Paley: Life and Stories." *Dissertation Abstracts International* 50(7) (Jan. 1990): 2271A.

Baba, Minako. "Faith Darwin as Writer, Heroine: A Study of Grace Paley's Short Stories." *Studies in American Jewish Literature* 7(1) (Spring 1988): 40–54.

Halfman, Ulrich, and Philipp Gerlach. "Grace Paley: A Bibliography." *Tulsa Studies in Women's Literature* 8(2) (Fall 1989): 339–54.

Isaccs, Neil David. *Grace Paley: A Study of the Short Fiction.* Boston: Twayne, 1990.

Logsdon, Loren, and Charles W. Mayer, ed. *Since Flannery O'Connor: Essays on the Contemporary American Short Story.* Macomb: Western Illinois U, 1987. 93–100.

Lyons, Bonnie. "Grace Paley's Jewish Miniatures." *Studies in American Jewish Literature* 8(1) (Spring 1989): 26–33.

Paley, Grace. *Long Walks and Intimate Talks. Stories and Stories by Grace Paley.* New York: Feminist Press and the City U of New York, 1991.

Taylor, Jacqueline. *Grace Paley: Illuminating the Dark Lives.* Austin: U of Texas P, 1990.

———. "Grace Paley on Storytelling and Story Hearing." *Literature in Performance: A Journal of Literature and Performing Art* 7(2) (April 1987): 46–58.

Wilde, Alan. "Grace Paley's World, Investing Words." Wilde, *Middle Grounds.* Philadelphia: U of Pennsylvania P, 1987.

OCTAVIO PAZ

My Life with the Wave (p. 1108)

Although the Mexican poet Octavio Paz has published few short stories, "My Life with the Wave," which first appeared in *Arenas movedizas* (1949), established him as a master of the genre. Images of water and the sea abound in Paz's poetry, so it is not surprising that his handling of these images in a work of short fiction should also exhibit his customary brilliance and virtuosity.

Students reading "My Life with the Wave" will need no help understanding it as a work of fantasy verging on the surreal. The atmosphere and events in the story take on the intense irrational reality of a dream. Paz's incongruous imagery begins immediately, when we learn that the "tall and light" wave is a "she" dressed in "floating clothes" who leaves "that sea" to go off with the narrator. He protests, but by the author's ingenious ploy of changing a pronoun (delivered with grave finality as in a dream), the narrator's fate is sealed: "No, your decision is made. You can't go back." (A rational if uncooperative response by the wave to the narrator would have been, "No, my decision is made. I can't go back.")

How do readers understand that this unusual story is about a "she" and a "he"? The female nature of the wave is given to us in the second sentence: "She was tall and light." We don't learn the sex of the narrator until we see him on a train a short time later, when one of the passengers tells the conductor, "This man put salt in the water." At first the narrator calls the wave his "friend," but after they live together, they become lovers. For four paragraphs they share a blissful happiness, until the wave turns moody and willful. She befriends certain "repulsive and ferocious" fishes, he throws them out of the house. She attacks him, he nearly drowns and begins to hate her. In the cold of winter, the wave turns into a block of ice, and the narrator knows what he must do: in order to get rid of her, he sells her to a "waiter friend," who chops the wave into bits of ice and put them into buckets to chill bottles.

In this fantasy story Paz presents a romantic view of woman as the goddess of love — always capricious, mysteriously unknowable, eternally beautiful, and ultimately destructive.

Questions for Discussion

1. Despite the unhappy ending of the love affair, "My Life with the Wave" is often humorous. Give examples in the story of the narrator's (and the author's) sense of humor.
2. Does this story have a reliable or an unreliable narrator? Is the narrator meant to be the same person as Octavio Paz, or a fictional character in the story?
3. In what ways does the wave resemble a human woman? What problems occur in the love affair because the narrator's lover is a wave?
4. What aspects of the story suggest the narrator's fantasies about women? To what extent are these fantasies stereotypical qualities that men often attribute to women?

Topic for Writing

1. **CONNECTIONS** Compare and contrast the fantasy story "My Life with the Wave" by Octavio Paz with "Axolotl" by Julio Cortázar or "The Erl-King" by Angela Carter.

Suggested Reading

Paz, Octavio. *Eagle or Sun.* Trans. Eliot Weinberger. New York: New Directions, 1976.

EDGAR ALLAN POE

The Cask of Amontillado (p. 1113)

Poe is the great master of the contrived suspense story, and "The Cask of Amontillado" is a model of narrative compression toward a single effect. Students should understand that Poe had a theory on the short story; its essential points are suggested in his review of Hawthorne's tales in Part Two (p. 1488).

Despite Poe's rational explanation of how a writer should compose a story, his own fiction is directed toward eliciting irrational emotions. Poe's literary style aims at using as many extravagances of character, setting, and plot as he could invent, exploiting the reader's emotional vulnerability to disturbing images of darkness and chaos. The hectic unpredictability of the carnival season, the creepy subterranean wine cellar, and the ancient family crypt with its molding skeletons all challenge us emotionally and make us want to read further.

In the reading, our own fears become the true subject matter. As in a nightmare, Fortunato finds himself being buried alive, one of the most basic human fears. On a more conscious level, we rely on a social contract to bind us together as a human family, and Montresor's lawlessness plays on our fear that any person can take the law into his or her own hands without being checked by conscience. Poe doesn't have to give us a great number of details about his characters; our imagination draws from the depths of the common human psyche to supply all that we need.

This story is a good example to use in stressing the importance of the students' close reading of a text. It's easy for readers to miss, in the last paragraph, the sentence "My heart grew sick — on account of the dampness of the catacombs." Yet upon this sentence rests the interpretation of Montresor's character: Can we excuse his action on grounds of insanity? Was he insane at the time he buried Fortunato alive, or did he go insane in the half century during which, he tells us, his crime has remained undetected? If the reader has not paid careful attention to that sentence, he or she will have missed an essential detail in understanding the story.

The book *Mysterious New England,* edited by A. N. Stevens (1971), suggests that Poe first heard the anecdote upon which he might have based this story when he was a private in the army in 1827. Supposedly, only ten years before, a popular young lieutenant named Robert F. Massie had also been stationed at Fort Independence in Boston Harbor; when Poe was serving there, he saw a gravestone erected to the memory of Lieutenant Massie, who had been unfairly killed in a duel by a bully named Captain Green.

> Feeling against Captain Green ran high for many weeks, and then suddenly he vanished. Years went by without a sign of him, and Green was written off the army records as a deserter.
>
> According to the story that Poe finally gathered together, Captain Green had been so detested by his fellow officers that they decided to take a terrible revenge on him for Massie's death.
>
> Visiting Captain Green one moonless night, they pretended to be friendly and plied him with wine until he was helplessly intoxicated. Then, carrying the captain down to one of the ancient dungeons, the officers forced his body through a tiny opening that led into the subterranean casemate. His captors began to shackle him to the floor, using the heavy iron handcuffs and footcuffs fastened into the stone. Then they sealed the captain up alive inside the windowless casemate, using bricks and mortar that they had hidden close at hand.
>
> Captain Green shrieked in terror and begged for mercy, but his cries fell on deaf ears. The last brick was finally inserted, mortar applied, and the room closed off, the officers believed, forever. Captain Green undoubtedly died a horrible death within a few days.

WILLIAM E. SHEIDLEY

Questions for Discussion

1. How does Poe motivate the behavior of Montresor? Does the story provide any hints as to the "thousand injuries" he has suffered? Are any hints necessary?
2. Why is the setting of the story appropriate?
3. What does Montresor's treatment of his house servants tell us about his knowledge of human psychology, and how does it prepare us for his treatment of Fortunato?

4.   How does Poe increase the elements of suspense as Fortunato is gradually walled into the catacombs?

Topics for Writing

(Remind the class that there is a student paper in "Writing about Short Stories," p. 1621 in the anthology, comparing and contrasting this story with Hawthorne's "Young Goodman Brown.")

1.   Montresor doesn't tell his story until a half century after the actual event. Analyze how Poe adapts the flashback technique to affect the reader of "The Cask of Amontillado."
2.   Explicate the passage in the story in which Montresor entices Fortunato into the crypt.

Related Commentaries

D. H. Lawrence, The Lust of Hate in Poe's "The Cask of Amontillado," p. 1446.
Edgar Allan Poe, The Importance of the Single Effect in a Prose Tale, p. 1488.

Suggested Readings

See page 205.

Edgar Allan Poe

The Tell-Tale Heart (p. 1118)

"The Tell-Tale Heart" is a story about what has been called "the demonic self" — a person who feels a compulsion to commit a gratuitous act of evil. Poe wrote explicitly about what he calls this "spirit of perverseness" in his story "The Black Cat," published in 1843, two years before "The Tell-Tale Heart":

> Of this spirit [of perverseness] philosophy takes no account. Yet I am not more sure that my soul lives, than I am that perverseness is one of the primitive impulses of the human heart — one of the indivisible primary faculties, or sentiments, which give direction to the character of Man. Who has not, a hundred times, found himself committing a vile or a silly action, for no other reason than because he knows he should *not*? Have we not a perpetual inclination, in the teeth of our best judgment, to violate that which is *Law*, merely because we understand it to be such?

According to the critic Eric W. Carlson, "The Tell-Tale Heart" was one of Poe's favorite stories. In addition to dramatizing the "spirit of perverseness" in his narrative, Poe combines other elements of the gothic tale (the evil eye, the curse), the psychorealistic (the narrator's paranoia), the dramatic (concentrated intensity of tone, gradually heightened series of dramatic events), and the moral (the compulsion to confess).

Questions for Discussion

1. How would you describe the narrator of the story? How does your description compare or contrast with what he would like to have you believe about him?
2. What disease is the narrator referring to in the first paragraph?
3. What caused the narrator to murder the old man? Was his reason valid?
4. What narrative devices does Poe use to heighten the suspense of the tale? Give examples.
5. Poe believed in the existence of the "spirit of perverseness" within every man. How is this revealed in the story?
6. Do you feel the confession at the end of the tale is necessary? Why? What is Poe's purpose in presenting this confession?

Topics for Writing

1. Discuss the significance of the light and dark imagery in "The Tell-Tale Heart."
2. Consider the effect of premeditation in "The Tell-Tale Heart."
3. Discuss the use of sight and sound as dramatic devices in "The Tell-Tale Heart."
4. Write an essay analyzing the dichotomy between the narrator's view of himself and our view of him in "The Tell-Tale Heart."
5. Explore reality versus illusion in "The Tell-Tale Heart."
6. Rewrite the story from the point of view of the police officers or from the point of view of the old man.
7. Consider the events that might result from the action of this story, and write a sequel presenting these developments.

Related Commentary

Edgar Allan Poe, The Importance of the Single Effect in a Prose Tale, p. 1488.

Suggested Readings

Adler, Jacob H. "Are There Flaws in 'The Cask of Amontillado'?" *Notes and Queries* 199 (1954): 32–34.
Buranelli, Vincent. *Edgar Allan Poe.* 2nd Ed. Boston: G. K. Hall, 1977.
Baudelaire, Charles P. *Baudelaire on Poe: Critical Papers.* University Park: Pennsylvania State UP, 1952.
Carlson, Eric W., ed. *Critical Essays on Edgar Allan Poe.* Boston: G. K. Hall, 1987.
Carlson, Eric W. *Introduction to Poe: A Thematic Reader.* Glenville, IL: Scott, 1967.

Dillon, John M. *Edgar Allan Poe*. Brooklyn, NY: Haskell, 1974.

Fletcher, Richard M. *The Stylistic Development of Edgar Allan Poe*. New York: Mouton, 1974.

Gargano, J. W. "'The Cask of Amontillado': A Masquerade of Motive and Identity." *Studies in Short Fiction* 4 (1967): 119–26.

———. *The Masquerade Vision in Poe's Short Stories*. Baltimore: Enoch Pratt, 1977.

Hammond, J. R. *An Edgar Allan Poe Companion: A Guide to Short Stories, Romances and Essays*. Savage: B and N Imports, 1981.

Knapp, Bettina L. *Edgar Allan Poe*. New York: Ungar, 1984.

Levin, Harry. *The Power of Blackness: Hawthorne, Poe, Melville*. Columbus: Ohio UP, 1980.

Mabbott, Thomas Olivle, ed. *Collected Works of Edgar Allan Poe*. Cambridge, MA: Harvard UP, 1978.

May, Charles E., ed. *Edgar Allan Poe, A Study of Short Fiction*. Boston: Twayne, 1990.

Muller, John P., and William J. Richardson, eds. *The Purloined Poe: Lacan, Derrida and Psychoanalytic Reading*. Baltimore: Johns Hopkins UP, 1988.

Pitcher, E. W. "Physiognomical Meaning of Poe's 'The Tell-Tale Heart.' " *Studies in Short Fiction* 16 (1979): 231–33.

Robinson, E. A. "Poe's 'The Tell-Tale Heart.' " *Nineteenth Century Fiction* 19 (1965): 369–78.

Symons, Julian, ed. *Selected Tales*. New York: Oxford UP, 1980.

Tucker, B. D. "Tell-Tale Heart and the Evil Eye." *Southern Literary Journal* 13 (1981): 92–98.

KATHERINE ANNE PORTER

He (p. 1122)

"He" is the earliest of three stories in this anthology that are related by subject—the plot is about what happens to a boy or man of subnormal intelligence. The other two stories are "Heat" by Joyce Carol Oates and "Night" by Tatyana Tolstaya.

The similarity of the characters' surnames suggests that Porter's story served as the direct inspiration for Oates's narrative. "He" was included in Porter's collection *Flowering Judas*, published in 1930. Like the photographs from the 1930s taken in the American South by Dorothea Lange and Walker Evans for the Works Progress Administration, which can serve as eloquent illustrations of the lives of poor families, it describes the poverty-stricken lives of many rural Americans like the Whipple family in Porter's story.

The Whipples' struggle to feed and clothe their family is made more difficult by the fact that their second son is mentally defective. (They have two normal children, their daughter Emly and their son Adna.) This boy doesn't have a name. He is referred to as "He" or "Him" or "His," always with a capital "H," signifying His special status in the family. The extraordinary quality of the story is the result of the way it is told. The third-person-singular narration is channeled through the point of view and characteristic language of Mrs. Whipple, who is her son's primary caretaker and who is deeply emotionally involved in his welfare. "His" interior life is blocked to us, because he never talks, but Mrs. Whipple tells us everything she thinks and feels and elicits comments from family and neighbors around her; we participate in the tragedy of the boy's life through her responses.

With such a subject, it would be extremely easy for Porter's story to slip into sentimentality given the reader's direct access to Mrs. Whipple's feelings. What makes the story effective is Porter's unflinching honesty in dramatizing the social and economic background of the characters and her brilliant use of Mrs. Whipple's language, both of which keep the narrative solidly positioned on the hard nub of truth. (A generation later Flannery O'Connor took Porter's work as a model for her use of colloquial speech rhythms and dialogue in her short fiction.)

For example, the Whipples' neighbors say behind their backs that it would be much better for the family if the second son died ("'A Lord's pure mercy if He should die,' they said"), yet to their faces "everybody said, 'He's not so bad off. He'll be all right yet. Look how He grows!'"

Mrs. Whipple does the best she can to love and protect her second son. Taking care of Him becomes a way to repel the bad luck visited upon the family. His well-being is a sign that she and the family will survive this bad luck so long as He keeps going. She also believes that no matter how badly things go for the family, her good care of her second son is a way to show the world that the Whipples may be whipped, but not beaten. The neighbors who speak ill of her boy really are judging her entire family. As Mrs. Whipple says, "I get sick of people coming around saying things all the time."

Even a visit from her brother's family, whom she loves, isn't a happy occasion. Mr. Whipple resents the fact that they must kill a suckling pig for them in order to put on the appearance of doing well. He ruins his wife's pleasure in recollecting the visit by suggesting that the guests were critical of the family: "Who knows what they had in their minds all along?" Mrs. Whipple's response is to defend the way she has cared for her second son: "They can't say He wasn't dressed every lick as good as Adna — oh, honest, sometimes I wish I was dead!"

The family's fortunes continue to slide during the development of the story. Mrs. Whipple says, "We're losing our hold. Why can't we do like other people and watch for our best chances? They'll be calling us poor white trash next." Adna and Emly leave home to take jobs to earn much-needed money, and He gets sick. Even after four months' worth of medical bills, Mrs. Whipple manages to remain optimistic. Her refusal to accept the reality of the situation continues nearly until the end, when He begins to cry as the wagon leaves the Whipple residence on the way to the County Home. When He breaks down, she begins to cry too, and Porter lets us share her internal anguish as she relinquishes her boy: "There was nothing she could do to make up to Him for His life. Oh, what a mortal pity He was ever born."

Questions for Discussion

1. What is Mr. Whipple's educational background? Mrs. Whipple's? How much better educated will Emly and Adna be?
2. What opportunities do the Whipples have to make money and prosper?

3. Why does Mrs. Whipple take her brother's visit so seriously? Why didn't Mr. Whipple want to kill the suckling pig?
4. Why does Mrs. Whipple box His ears? How does she feel afterwards?
5. What is the relationship between Mr. and Mrs. Whipple?
6. Why is Mrs. Whipple so nervous when she sees Him leading the bull? Is this a foreshadowing of His sickness later in the story?

Topics for Writing

1. Describe Mrs. Whipple's personality. Is she a good or an overprotective mother?
2. Analyze how Porter dramatizes the economic hardship of the Whipple family in "He" and makes it an integral part of the story.
3. **CONNECTIONS** Compare and contrast the narrative point of view in "He" with Oates's treatment of the same aspect in "Heat" and Tolstaya's choice of point of view in "Night."

Suggested Readings

Bayley, Isabel. *Letters of Katherine Anne Porter.* New York: Atlantic Monthly Press, 1990.

Bruccoli, Matthew J., ed. *Understanding of Katherine Anne Porter.* Columbia: U of South Carolina P, 1988.

Demouy, Jane Krause. *Katherine Anne Porter's Women: The Eye of Her Fiction.* Austin: U of Texas P, 1983.

Hendrick, Willene, and George Hendrick. *Katherine Anne Porter.* Boston: Twayne, 1988.

Mooney, Harry J. *The Fiction and Criticism of Katherine Anne Porter. Rev. ed.* Pittsburgh: U of Pittsburgh P, 1990.

Plimpton, George, ed. *Women Writers at Work: The Paris Review Interviews.* New York: Penguin, 1989.

Porter, Katherine Anne. *The Collected Essays and Occasional Writings.* New York: Harcourt Brace, 1970.

———. *Flowering Judas.* New York: Harcourt Brace, 1930, 1958.

Stout, Janis P. *Strategies of Reticence: Silence and Meaning in he Works of Jane Austen, Willa Cather, Katherine Anne Porter and Joan Didion.* Charlottesville: UP of Virginia, 1990.

Tanner, James T. F. *The Texas Legacy of Katherine Anne Porter.* Denton: U of North Texas P, 1990.

Unrue, Darlene H. *Truth and Vision in Katherine Anne Porter's Fiction.* Athens: U of Georgia P, 1985.

Frank Sargeson

A Great Day (p. 1131)

"A Great Day," like all of Sargeson's writing, shows an almost obsessive involvement with the New Zealand landscape and the English dialect spoken there. The incident that Sargeson relates begins with disarming simplicity. Two men are going fishing on a beautiful day. As they row out to the place where they think they will find fish, it becomes clear from their conversation that both of them are in love with the same woman. One of the men, Ken, bigger and casually handsome, has a clear advantage over the other man, Fred, who is smaller, older, and weaker. As the story evolves, Sargeson tells us that Fred has lost his job, that he's feeling his age, and that the woman, Mary, who was going out with him before she met Ken, has been forced by her family's circumstances to go to work as a servant in the home of Ken's aunt.

Using guile and cunning as weapons against the younger man, Fred kills Ken, so that he can have Mary to himself. He does this by tricking Ken into getting out of their dinghy to gather mussels for bait on a shallow reef that is covered by the tide. When Ken turns his back, Fred, knowing that Ken can't swim, rows away and leaves him to drown. (Fred had earlier stuffed his ears with cotton wool, using the excuse that getting salt spray in his ears gives him an earache.)

The setting in the first pages is so tranquil and sunny — a "great day" — that the violent ending catches the reader by surprise. Many students may find that they have been so surprised by the ending that they will want to read the story a second time. As they reread it they will find all the clues that Sargeson placed in his seemingly innocent narrative, and almost from the beginning will see the forboding tone of the story. What the story describes is not a pleasant day of fishing that ends tragically, but a carefully planned murder.

Questions for Discussion

1. Is this essentially a story of New Zealand, or are there aspects of the narrative that could allow it to be set in the United States?
2. What do we know about the economic situation in which the two men find themselves?
3. The first overt clue the writer gives us that the story is about more than a day's fishing is Fred's remark that Ken doesn't know how to swim. What clues in the next pages increase the reader's suspicions?
4. What is the significance of the cotton wool Fred puts in his ears, and why does he close his eyes as he pulls away from the reef in the dinghy?
5. Is this a story that could happen today?

Topics for Writing

1. One of the most famous modern short narratives that has fishing as its theme is Ernest Hemingway's *The Old Man and the Sea.* How do the two stories compare in their views of human nature?

(text pp. 1138–1144)

2. **CONNECTIONS** Compare and contrast Sargeson's technique of foreshadowing with Jackson's in "The Lottery."

Suggested Readings

Copland, R. A. *Frank Sargeson.* New York: Oxford UP, 1976.

Dass, Veena Noble. "Human Relationships in the Stories of Frank Sargeson." *New Zealand Literature Today.* New Delhi: Indian Society for Commonwealth Studies, 1993.

Dresing, H. "New Zealand Society in the Imaginative Writings of Frank Sargeson." *Dissertation Abstracts International* August 42:2 (1981): 1546C.

During, Simon. "Reading New Zealand Literature." *Southern Review: Literary and Interdisciplinary Essays, South Australia* Mar. 18:1 (1985): 65–85.

New, W. H. "Joining and's and Butting Out: On Reading Sargeson." *Commonwealth Essays and Studies* Spring 12:2 (1990): 1–6.

Sargeson, Frank. *I Saw in My Dream.* Aukland: Auckland UP, 1974.

———. *More Than Enough: A Memoir.* London: Martin Brian and O'Keefe, 1975.

LESLIE MARMON SILKO

Lullaby (p. 1138)

Silko placed "Lullaby" as the second story in her collection *Storyteller*, between "Storyteller" and "Yellow Woman." "Lullaby" is closely related to the poem that precedes it, which tells the story of two little girls abandoned by their parents during a flood in their haste to get to high ground. The children manage to catch up with the others in their tribe and are briefly reunited before they look around and see that their parents are nowhere to be found. The older sister takes the younger on her lap and soon, writes Silko, "they all [turned] to stone." At the very end of her poem, Silko adds that many of the stories she was told end like this — inconclusively, mysteriously, with no explanation.

Should there be an explanation for "Lullaby"? Like "Storyteller," it is told in the third person and seems to reflect a historical immediacy rather than an image of tribal mythology newly reimagined. Ayah, the old Navajo woman who has lost her three children to war and BIA (Bureau of Indian Affairs) education, has been emotionally estranged from her husband Chato, whom she blames for the loss of her two younger children (her older son Jimmie died in the war). The plot of "Lullaby" is very sad: Silko describes Ayah's emotional reconciliation with her husband and the inner strength she reveals when she watches over him as he freezes to death. Waiting out the night, she sings to him a lullaby that she remembers that her grandmother and mother have sung.

The destruction of Native American lives in the western United States by the Anglo ranchers who have usurped their land and exploited their labor is the theme of this story. Silko gives "no explanations" but shows how the women in Ayah's family have passed on to her an oral tradition of poetry and song that helps her to survive life's blows by offering sustenance and support in difficult times.

Questions for Discussion

1. Why were Ayah's younger children taken away from her?
2. Why did Chato's employer let him go?
3. Why didn't the bar owner like Indians in his place, "especially Navajos"?
4. How has Ayah's age helped her survive her troubles?
5. Has Silko created round or flat characters in her depiction of Ayah and Chato?

Topics for Writing

1. Read Silko's *Storyteller* and report on the mixture of poetry and prose in the book.
2. **CONNECTIONS** Compare and contrast Silko's portrayals of the lives of older Native American women in "Lullaby" and "Storyteller."

Related Commentaries

Kim Barnes, An Interview with Leslie Marmon Silko, p. 1578.
Jim Ruppert, Storytelling: The Fiction of Leslie Silko, p. 1587.
Leslie Marmon Silko, Language and Literature from a Pueblo Indian Perspective, p. 1573.

Suggested Readings

See page 215.

LESLIE MARMON SILKO

Storyteller (p. 1145)

This story is one of Silko's most complex works. Its title is also the title of her book *Storyteller* (1981), a collection of poems and prose narratives in which it appears as the leading story, followed by "Lullaby" and "Yellow Woman."

According to a traditional Eskimo poem, words once had the power to

come alive
and what people wanted to happen could happen —
all you had to do was say it.

"Storyteller" is a revenge narrative with a very intricate plot. The main story, told as a flashback, is about a young Eskimo woman who wants to avenge the deaths of her parents after they drank poisoned liquor sold to them by a "Gussuck," a white man keeping a store for Eskimos in the far north of Alaska. The young woman plots the murder of the Gussuck storekeeper with calm deliberation. Her story unfolds parallel to another story being told by the old man with whom she lives. He is close to death, and is occupying himself during his final days with the telling of a traditional legend about a brave hunter's confrontation with a great bear. "All night she listened to him describe each breath the man took, each motion of the bear's head as it tried to catch the sound of the man's breathing, and tested the wind for his scent."

The young woman is initiated into sex by the old man during the long winter nights in the north. She is educated by listening to the stories told by the old man and by her grandmother, who also lives in the house, and these stories focus the girl's resolve to dedicate her life to avenging her parents. Silko has often remarked on "the power which the stories [of her tribe, the Laguna] still have, to bring us together, especially when there is loss and grief."

Loss and grief are the protagonist's inheritance in "Storyteller," until she herself becomes the actor in a story, planning and executing revenge for her parents' deaths. She is as brave a hunter as the hero of the great bear story told by the old man. From the hunting story she learns the necessity for careful planning, patience, and endurance. But unlike the legendary hunter, exhausted by cold, whose hand is unable to hold his knife, the girl is victorious in the end, luring the Gussuck storekeeper onto the ice to his death and insisting on telling her story to the Gussuck attorney.

Questions for Discussion

1. Why did the Eskimo jailer refuse to speak his native language, Yupik, to the girl?
2. Why does the girl hate the way the BIA (Bureau of Indian Affairs) has constructed buildings like the jail in town?
3. How does the girl know when it is fifty below zero? Why is this temperature important?
4. What was the girl's experience with the BIA education offered to her?
5. Who is the old man in her house? What is his relationship to the girl's grandmother? How does the girl feel about him?
6. What has the girl learned from her grandmother?
7. Why does the girl have sex with the Gussuck oil drillers?
8. What does the photograph the oil driller puts over his bed tell you about Silko's attitude toward him?
9. What is the relation between the old man's story about the hunter and the bear and the girl's plan for revenge?
10. What was the "something red in the grass" that the girl saw the morning after her parents died? Why is this detail important to her?

Topics for Writing

1. Write a summary of any one of the commentaries in the Silko casebook in the anthology.
2. Compare Silko's portrayals of the Gussuck and the Native American interactions with the natural world. What is the author's attitude about Gussuck technology?

3. How many stories are told within "Storyteller"? What is the significance of storytelling in the Native American culture?
4. Explain the connection between the old man's story of the hunter and the polar bear and the girl's story about killing the Gussuck.

Related Commentaries

Kim Barnes, An Interview with Leslie Marmon Silko, p. 1578.
Linda L. Danielson, A Feminist Reading of "Storyteller": Grandmother Spider's Web, p. 1590.
Jim Ruppert, Storytelling: The Fiction of Leslie Silko, p. 1587.
Leslie Marmon Silko, Language and Literature from a Pueblo Indian Perspective, p. 1573.

Suggested Readings

See page 215.

LESLIE MARMON SILKO

Yellow Woman (p. 1157)

This story is told in the first person and presented episodically in several sections. It takes place over two days, beginning the morning Yellow Woman wakes up beside the river with Silva, the stranger she has spent the night with. The story ends at sundown the next day, when she returns to her family in the Pueblo village.

"Yellow Woman" is built on different traditions from those in the cultural background of most American students. Silko writes fiction that preserves her cultural heritage by re-creating its customs and values in stories that dramatize emotional conflicts of interest to modern readers.

As Yellow Woman narrates the story of her abduction and return to her family, the reader comes to share her mood and her interpretation of what has happened. As a girl she was fascinated by the stories her grandfather told her about Silva, the mysterious kachina spirit who kidnaps married women from the tribe, then returns them after he has kept them as his wives. These stories were probably similar to the imaginary tales passed down in an oral tradition whose origins are lost to contemporary American folklorists. Silko has created their modern equivalent, her version of how they might be reenacted in today's world. The overweight, white Arizona rancher is familiar to us, as is the Jell-O being prepared for supper, and we have no difficulty imagining the gunnysacks full of freshly slaughtered meat bouncing on the back of Yellow Woman's horse.

The dreamlike atmosphere Silko creates in "Yellow Woman" makes such realistic details protrude sharply from the soft-focus narrative. Yellow Woman doesn't think clearly. She seems bewitched by the myths her grandfather told her, and her adventure following the man she calls Silva holds her enthralled. At the end she says, "I thought about Silva, and I felt sad at leaving him; still, there was something strange about him, and I tried to figure it out all the way back home." We are not told what — if anything — she does figure out.

Instead, action takes the place of thought in the story. Yellow Woman looks at the place on the riverbank where she met Silva and tells herself that "he will come back sometime and be waiting again by the river." Action moves so swiftly that we follow Yellow Woman as obediently as she follows her abductor, mesmerized by the audacity of what is happening. There is no menace in Silva, no danger or malice in his rape of Yellow Woman. The bullets in his rifle are for the white rancher who realizes he has been killing other men's cattle, not for Yellow Woman — or for us.

Questions for Discussion

1. Why is Yellow Woman so eager to believe that she and Silva are acting out the stories her grandfather told her?
2. How does Silko structure the opening paragraphs of the story to help the reader suspend disbelief and enter the dreamlike atmosphere of Yellow Woman's perceptions?
3. Why does Silko tell the story through the woman's point of view? Describe the Pueblo Indian woman we know as Yellow Woman. Is she happy at home with her mother, grandmother, husband, and baby? Why is Yellow Woman's father absent from the story?
4. Are there any limitations to Silko's choice to tell the story through Yellow Woman's point of view? Explain.
5. Why doesn't the narrator escape from Silva when she discovers him asleep by the river as the story opens? What makes her decide to return home the next day?

Topics for Writing

1. Tell the story through a third-person omniscient narration.
2. Compare "Yellow Woman" with an Indian folktale about the kachina spirit who kidnapped married women.
3. **CONNECTIONS** Compare Silko's "Yellow Woman" and Oates's "Where Are You Going, Where Have You Been?" as rape narratives.

Related Commentaries

Paula Gunn Allen, Whirlwind Man Steals Yellow Woman, p. 1586.
Kim Barnes, An Interview with Leslie Marmon Silko, p. 1578.
Cochiti Pueblo Story, Sun Steals Yellow Woman, p. 1585.
Jim Ruppert, Storytelling: The Fiction of Leslie Silko, p. 1587.
Leslie Marmon Silko, Language and Literature from a Pueblo Indian Perspective, p. 1573.

Suggested Readings

Allen, Paula Gunn. *The Sacred Hoop: Recovering the Feminine in American Indian Traditions*. Boston: Beacon, 1986.

———, ed. *Spider Woman's Granddaughters: Traditional Tales* and *Contemporary Writing by Native American Women*. Boston: Beacon, 1989.

Graulich, Melody, ed. *"Yellow Woman."* Women, Text and Contexts Series. New Brunswick, NJ: Rutgers UP, 1993.

Hoilman, Dennis. "The Ethnic Imagination: A Case History." *Canadian Journal of Native Studies* 5:2 (1985): 167–75.

Nelson, Robert M. *Place and Vision: The Function of Landscape in Native American Fiction*. New York: P. Lang, 1993.

Sands, Kathleen Mullen. "Indian Women's Personal Narrative: Voices Past and Present." *American Women's Autobiography: Fea(s)ts of Memory*. Ed. Margo Culley. Madison: U of Wisconsin P, 1992.

Silko, Leslie Marmon. *Almanac of the Dead*. New York: Simon, 1991.

ISAAC BASHEVIS SINGER

The Spinoza of Market Street (p. 1165)

Singer suggests the theme of this story in the quotation from the writing of the Dutch philosopher Baruch Spinoza (1632–1677) at the beginning of the narrative: "A free man thinks of nothing less than of death and his wisdom is a meditation not of death, but of life" *(Ethics)*.

Dr. Nahum Fischelson, the protagonist of the story, *is* the Spinoza of Market Street in Warsaw. He has spent thirty years reading and annotating the *Ethics,* but his commentary is incomplete because the more he studied, "the more puzzling sentences, unclear passages, and cryptic remarks he found." In a sense, he has spent his life working himself into a blind alley.

He has been meditating on death, rather than on life, because his years of study of the great Dutch philosopher have been unproductive. Not only has Dr. Fischelson not been able to write and publish his commentary for other scholars to read, but also in the process of his work he has gradually withdrawn from human society, living in self-imposed isolation and poverty in his garret in Warsaw's Jewish ghetto. From his rooftop window at night he views the heavens through his telescope or observes the crowd in the marketplace below, existing in what he regards as a "half-lit bedlam" of passion and emotion. The years pass uneventfully for him until the outbreak of World War I, when his regular pension from Berlin fails to reach him. Penniless and alone, fearing his stomach cramps are a symptom of cancer, he prepares to die.

Then, in the fifth of the story's seven parts, the plot takes a new turn. As Singer says, "The eternal laws, apparently, had not yet ordained Dr. Fischelson's end." A spinster named Dobbe lives in the attic room next to the Spinoza scholar, and she finds him lying unconscious on his bed. Under her care, he regains his health, and the pair decide to marry. After the rabbi performs the ceremony, the couple return to Dr. Fischelson's room, and "what happened that night could be called a miracle. . . . Powers long dormant awakened in him. . . . He embraced Dobbe, pressed her to himself, was again a man as in his youth. Dobbe was faint with delight; crying, she murmured things to him in a Warsaw slang which he did not understand." Later, as Dobbe snores, Dr. Fischelson goes to his attic window, enjoys the cool night breeze, and says, "Divine Spinoza, forgive me. I have become a fool."

This summary of the plot suggests how Dr. Fischelson turns from his fruitless meditation on death to a much wiser meditation on life. Dobbe represents the life force to him, and through her Dr. Fischelson finds the strength to continue his life. If he thinks himself a fool for marrying, he has become a wise fool: in joining the human community, he comes much closer to Spinoza, who taught him that "the most moral deed a man could perform was to indulge in some pleasure which was not contrary to reason."

How does the reader know that Singer's story is a "meditation not of death, but of life"? By the imaginative details of the storyteller's brilliant recreation of the Warsaw ghetto and the Spinoza scholar's life, which for many years satisfied his spirit and comforted him in the knowledge that he was "a part of the cosmos, made of the same matter as the celestial bodies; to the extent that he was a part of the Godhead, he knew he could not be destroyed." Spinoza's faith is also Singer's faith, expressed through the thoughts of "weak, puny" Dr. Fischelson.

Questions for Discussion

1. Who was Spinoza? Why does Dr. Fischelson feel compelled to spend his life studying this philosopher's work?
2. What is Dr. Fischelson's educational background? Why does he return to Poland after his studies?
3. How does he support himself? Why is he a respected member of the community despite his poverty?
4. Describe life in the ghetto. How do the Jews interact with the Poles in Warsaw?
5. What are Dr. Fischelson's recreations? What do they tell us about his personality?
6. In what ways is "The Spinoza of Market Street" a comic story?
7. What does America represent to Dobbe? Why isn't Dr. Fischelson interested in that country?
8. Why is the crowd surprised by Dobbe's appearance at the wedding ceremony?
9. What is Dobbe's feeling for her husband?

Topics for Writing

1. Research the life and work of Spinoza and relate this information to Singer's story.
2. Describe the comment on Singer's description of traditional Jewish life in Poland in the early years of this century.

Suggested Readings

Alexander, Edward. *Isaac Bashevis Singer.* World Authors Series. Boston: Twayne, 1980.

Singer, Isaac Bashevis. *Collected Stories.* New York: Farrar, 1981.

JANE SMILEY

Long Distance (p. 1178)

The title of Smiley's story has many possible meanings, from the long distance call that serves as the story's beginning to the long distance that Kirby Christianson still must go to acquire the discipline and will to forge familial relationships. Kirby feels the inadequacy of his individual existence, yet is unable to make the sacrifices necessary to maintain a lasting relationship. He is relieved that Mieko cannot come to visit, because he is aware that he would eventually disappoint her if she did. As Leanne tells him at the story's close, he has always attempted to engage in relationships without paying some cost, some surrendering of his values. But while he constantly craves something better, he settles for much worse; he views his two brothers' lives with disdain though he knows his life is more worthy of reproach.

Kirby sees no options that would allow him to escape this dilemma, since there is nothing that he loves deeply enough to embrace, and he lacks the discipline to live with what he holds in contempt. As a result, Kirby is a self-contained individual whose "being does not extend past his fingertips and toes to family, real estate, reputation." Alone and guideless, Kirby moves by "inertia," and in social relationships lacks not only the self-discipline necessary to maintain those relationships but also a partner to help restrain his more destructive tendencies.

Kirby's long drive back to his family, like "a marble that has rolled, only by luck, into a safe corner," sets up the possibility of Kirby's connecting with others for the first time, even if it means that he must bear the boredom that comes with good fellowship or make the sacrifices that are necessary to remain in safe corners.

Questions for Discussion

1. What theme unifies Kirby's relationship with Mieko, the nature of his long drive, and Leanne's appraisal of Kirby?
2. Do you agree with Leanne's view that some knowledge is not learned but realized? What implications does this hold for Kirby?
3. Explain Kirby's relationships with his two brothers. How do they help you to better understand his character?

Topics for Writing

1. The despair Kirby feels, Smiley tells us, "presents itself aesthetically." Write a short paper examining Kirby's aesthetic judgments of his brothers' homes and what these judgments reveal about Kirby.

2. Analyze what isn't said during conversations in "Long Distance."
3. **CONNECTIONS** In the story "Braids," the main character, Ellen, undergoes what she calls "accident panic." How does her fear relate to that felt by Kirby during his drive? Would you characterize his fear as accident panic?
4. **CONNECTIONS** Gregor Samsa in "The Metamorphosis" and Kirby Christianson are both individuals who are isolated within a family. Write an essay examining the causes of their separation from their families.

Suggested Readings

Smiley, Jane. *The Age of Grief: A Novella and Stories.* New York: Knopf, 1987.
————. *Ordinary Love; And Goodwill: Two Novellas.* New York: Knopf, 1989.

Susan Sontag

The Way We Live Now (p. 1191)

Most stories by contemporary authors in this anthology are told from a limited-omniscient point of view. Leslie Marmon Silko narrates her story through the perceptions of Yellow Woman; Jane Smiley shows us the difficulty of relationships as experienced by an emotionally detached man in "Long Distance." James Baldwin uses first-person narration in "Sonny's Blues." Susan Sontag does something very different in "The Way We Live Now." The story chronicles the last months of a man dying of AIDS, but we never learn directly what he sees or feels. Instead, we hear what he is suffering through the comments of his many friends. The end result is a work that deliberately treats its subject the way most people treat AIDS itself — at a distance, through hearsay, with mingled fascination and horror, as something terrible that can only happen to other people.

We never learn the name, occupation, or physical description of the AIDS victim in Sontag's story. Instead, we are told the responses of his friends, like a roll call of potential victims of the virus. These friends — more than twenty-five of them — are also not described, only presented by name as they talk to one another about the sick man. Their names follow one another so rapidly we are not given any explanation of their relationships: Max, Ellen, Greg, Tanya, Orson, Stephen, Frank, Jan, Quentin, Paolo, Kate, Aileen, Donny, Ursula, Ira, Hilda, Nora, Wesley, Victor, Xavier, Lewis, Robert, Betsy, Yvonne, Zack, and Clarice. The first-name basis is fitting, since the majority of the people know one another and inhabit the same world. We are never told what city they all live in, but we assume from the way they talk and their large numbers that they live in New York and are part of its cliques of people active in the arts, literature, and cultural journalism.

The first-name basis of the conversations is also aesthetically appropriate, because for the most part the characters are using the telephone. They repeat the latest gossip they have learned from one another; for all their sophistication, they pass along news of the stages of their friend's illness like the voices of tribal drums alerting the inhabitants of villages in Africa. The reader has the same sense of a closely knit community joined by common interests and means of livelihood. Because the community is left unspecified, the setting and the characters become mythologized into "Anyplace" and "Everyone." Sontag's implication is that we are all participants in this human tragedy. AIDS can happen to anyone.

As we read "The Way We Live Now," our rational impulses function despite the lack of specificity about the central character. The short conversational exchanges function as a literary code that we try to unlock. We attempt to trace relationships (Quentin, Lewis, Paolo, and Tanya have all been lovers of the AIDS victim); we categorize important information about lives outside the main story (Max gets AIDS too, as does Hilda's seventy-five-year-old aunt); we highlight generalizations that suggest a broader social and moral significance to this individual tragedy (the age of "debauchery" is over).

Close readers may even be able to interpret the fragments of conversations to gain psychological insights of use in other contexts. For example, Kate tells Aileen that the sick man is "not judging people or wondering about their motives" (when they come to see him in the hospital); rather, "he's just happy to see his friends." By presenting the numbers of people linked to a specific AIDS victim who appears to be well known and highly regarded in his community, Sontag is making an ironic comment about the isolation of all AIDS victims. Her story is an attempt to write about a taboo subject and encourage compassion toward those suffering from the disease.

Questions for Discussion

1. The story is developed chronologically, from the news of the patient's illness, through his first hospitalization, to his return home and rehospitalization. How does this progression give coherence to the story?
2. How do the relationships suggested among the twenty-five characters in the story give you a sense of the occupation and lifestyle of the central character?
3. Hilda says that the death of the pianist in Paris "who specialized in twentieth-century Czech and Polish music" is important because "he's such a valuable person . . . and it's such a loss to the culture." Do you think Sontag shares Hilda's opinion? Do you? Why or why not?
4. Agree or disagree with Ursula's idea at the end of the story.

Topics for Writing

1. Write a review of Sontag's nonfiction work *AIDS and Its Metaphors*.
2. Choose any five characters in "The Way We Live Now" and invent backgrounds for them.
3. Rewrite the story from the point of view of the AIDS patient, perhaps in the form of his diary.

Related Commentary

David Leavitt, The Way I Live Now, p. 1447

Suggested Reading

Sontag, Susan. *AIDS and Its Metaphors*. New York: Farrar, 1989.

JOHN STEINBECK

The Chrysanthemums (p. 1206)

The instinctive life that Elisa Allen loves as she tends her chrysanthemum plants lies dormant under her fingers. She is good with flowers, like her mother before her. Elisa says, "She could stick anything in the ground and make it grow." But it is December, and Steinbeck tells us it is "a time of quiet and of waiting." The Salinas landscape lies peacefully, but Elisa is vaguely unfulfilled. She begins to transplant her little chrysanthemum shoots, working without haste, conscious of her "hard-swept" house and her well-ordered garden, protected with its fence of chicken wire. Everything in her little world is under control. The tension in the scene is in herself, something she vaguely senses but refuses to face: the difference between her little world and the larger one encompassing it. Elisa is strong and mature, at the height of her physical strength. Why should she lie dormant? She has no fit scope for her powers. Steinbeck suggests the contradiction between her strength and her passivity in his description of the landscape: "The yellow stubble fields seemed to be bathed in pale cold sunshine, but there was no sunshine in the valley now in December." Like Hemingway, Steinbeck uses physical and geographical details to suggest the *absence* of positive qualities in his fictional characters. There is no sunshine in the valley, and the chrysanthemum plants aren't flowering, but what is natural in the annual vegetation cycle is out of kilter in Elisa. She experiences the world as a state of frustration.

Steinbeck has written an understated Chekhovian story in which ostensibly nothing much happens. It is a slice of life as Elisa lives it, sheltered and comfortable, yet — in Henry David Thoreau's words — life lived in a state of "quiet desperation."

The two male characters feel none of Elisa's lack of fulfillment. They live in a male world and take their opportunities for granted. Her husband, Henry Allen, is having a fine day. He's sold his thirty head of steer for a good price, and he's celebrating this Saturday night by taking his wife out to dinner and the movies in town. The traveling man is a trifle down on his luck, but it's nothing serious. He's found no customers this day so he lacks the money for his supper, but he knows a mark when he sees one. He flatters Elisa by agreeing with her and handing her a line about bringing some of her chrysanthemums to a lady he knows "down the road a piece." Elisa springs into action, delighted to be needed. Her tender shoots need her too, but she is not sufficiently absorbed by her gardening. The men do the real work of the world in this story. Gardening is a hobby she's proud of, and her husband encourages her to take pride in it, but she needs to feel of use in a larger dimension. Elisa mistakes this need for the freedom she imagines the transient knows on the road. Steinbeck gives her a clue as to the man's real condition in the state of his horse and mule, which she as a good gardener shouldn't have missed: "The horse and donkey drooped like unwatered flowers."

Instead, Elisa is caught up in her romantic fantasy of his nomadic life. Her sexual tension reduces her to a "fawning dog" as she envisions his life, but finally she realizes the man doesn't have the money for his dinner. "She stood up then, very straight, and her face was ashamed." Ashamed for what reason? Her lack of sensitivity to his poverty? her sexual excitement? Her sense of captivity in a masculine world, where apparently only motherhood would bring opportunities for real work? Elisa brings the man two battered pots to fix and resumes talking, unable to leave him or her fantasy about the freedom she thinks he enjoys. He tells her outright that "it ain't the right kind of a life for a woman." Again she misreads the situation, taking his comment as a challenge. Her response is understandable, since she's never had his opportunity to choose a life on the road. She defends her ability to be his rival at sharpening scissors and banging out dents in pots and pans.

When the man leaves, Elisa is suddenly aware of her loneliness. She scrubs her body as rigorously as she's swept her house, punishing her skin with a pumice stone instead of pampering it with bubble bath. Then she puts on "the dress which was the symbol of her prettiness." An odd choice of words. Without understanding her instinctive rebellion against male expectations, Elisa refuses to be a sex symbol. Again she loses, denying herself pleasure in soft fabrics and beautiful colors. When Henry returns, he is bewildered by her mood and unable to reach her. She sees the chrysanthemums dying on the road, but she still can't face the truth about her sense of the repression and futility of her life. Wine at dinner and the idea of going to see a prize fight briefly bring her closer to the flesh and the instinctive life she has shunned outside her contact with her flowers, but they don't lift her mood. She feels as fragile and undervalued as her chrysanthemums. She begins to cry weakly, "like an old woman," as Henry drives her down the road.

Like Lawrence's heroine in "The Odour of Chrysanthemums," Elisa is frustrated, cut off from the fullness of life by her physical destiny as a woman in a man's world. Does Steinbeck understand the sexual bias that undermines Elisa's sense of herself? He makes Henry as considerate a husband as a woman could wish for — he takes Elisa to the movies instead of going off to the prize fight himself. Like Hemingway, Steinbeck was sensitive to women's frustration, depicting it often in his fiction, even if he didn't look too closely at its probable causes in the society of his time.

Questions for Discussion

1. Based on Steinbeck's description in the first three paragraphs, how would you characterize the initial tone of the story? What do you associate with Steinbeck's image of the valley as "a closed pot"? In what way does this initial description foreshadow the events of the story?
2. What kind of character is Elisa Allen? What are the physical boundaries of her world? What is Elisa's psychological state at the beginning of the story?
3. Characterize the two men who are part of Elisa's world. In what ways are they similar and different? How does their way of life compare and contrast with the life Elisa leads?
4. What is the role of the chrysanthemums in Elisa's life? What do they symbolize?
5. How does Elisa delude herself about the life of the tinker? What other fantasies does this lead her to indulge in?
6. In what way does the tinker manipulate Elisa to accomplish his goals?
7. When the tinker leaves, a change comes over Elisa. What has she suddenly realized, and what course of action does she adopt?
8. As Elisa, both realistically and symbolically, goes out into the world, has she achieved any resolution of her problem? Why does she end the story "crying weakly — like an old woman"?

Topics for Writing

1. Discuss Steinbeck's use of setting to establish theme in "The Chrysanthemums."
2. Consider the isolation of Elisa Allen.
3. Analyze Elisa's illusions about the tinker and his interest in her as contrasted with reality.
4. Recall a time when you felt threatened and frustrated by events that isolated you. Write a narrative recounting this experience from a third-person point of view.
5. **CONNECTIONS** Compare male versus female societal and sexual roles in Lawrence's "Odour of Chrysanthemums" and Steinbeck's "The Chrysanthemums."
6. **CONNECTIONS** Discuss woman in a man's world: Steinbeck's Elisa and Silko's Yellow Woman.

Suggested Readings

Marcus, Mordecai. "The Lost Dream of Sex and Children in 'The Chrysanthemums." *Modern Fiction Studies* 11 (1965): 54–58.

McMahan, Elizabeth. "'The Chrysanthemums': Study of a Woman's Sexuality." *Modern Fiction Studies* 14 (1968-69): 453–58.

Miller, William V. "Sexual and Spiritual Ambiguity in 'The Chrysanthemums.'" *Steinbeck Quarterly* 5 (1972): 68–75.

Renner, S. "The Real Woman behind the Fence in 'The Chrysanthemums.'" *Modern Fiction Studies* 31 (1985): 305–17.

Sweet, Charles A. "Ms. Elisa Allen and Steinbeck's 'The Chrysanthemums.'" *Modern Fiction Studies* 20 (1974): 210–14.

AMY TAN

Two Kinds (p. 1215)

"Two Kinds," which was first published in the February 1989 issue of *The Atlantic Monthly*, is an excerpt from Amy Tan's best-selling book, *The Joy Luck Club*. It is a skillfully written story that will probably pose no difficulty for most students; plot, characters, setting, and theme are immediately clear. The narrator states what she's "learned" from her experience in her final paragraph: she has come to realize that "Pleading Child" and "Perfectly Contented" are "two halves of the same song."

Looking back to her childhood, the narrator appears to be "perfectly contented" with her memories. Her interpretation of her relationship with her mother is presented in a calm, even self-satisfied way. After her mother's death, she tunes the piano left to her in her parents' apartment. "I played a few bars [of the piano piece by Robert Schumann], surprised at how easily the notes came back to me." The painful memory of her fiasco as a piano student has dissipated. Now she is her own audience, and she is pleased with what she hears. There is no real emotional stress in "Two Kinds"; the girl has had a comfortable life. She has survived her mother and can dispose of her possessions as she likes. She is at peace with her past, fulfilling her mother's prophecy that "you can be best anything."

The mother earned her right to look on the bright side of life by surviving tremendous losses when she left China. Her desire to turn her daughter into a "Chinese Shirley Temple" is understandable but unfortunate, since it places a tremendous psychological burden on the child. A discussion about this story might center on parents' supporting children versus "pushing" them to succeed in tasks beyond their abilities or ambitions.

Still, the narrator doesn't appear to have suffered unduly from her mother's ambitions for her. By her own account she was more than a match for her mother in the contest of wills on the piano bench. After her wretched performance at the recital, the daughter refuses to practice anymore. When her mother shouts, "Only two kinds of daughters. . . . Those who are obedient and those who follow their own mind! Only one kind of daughter can live in this house. Obedient daughter! . . . The girl answers by saying the unspeakable: "I wish I'd never been born! I wish I were dead! Like them [the mother's twin baby girls lost in China]." This ends the conflict but the narrator goes on to tell us that she was unrelenting in victory: "In the years that followed, I failed her many times, each time asserting my will, my right to fall short of expectations. I didn't get straight As. I didn't become class president. I didn't get into Stanford. I dropped out of college." She tells us that only after her mother's death can she begin to see things in perspective, when she is free to create her version of the past.

Since most students in class will be of the age when they are also asserting their will against parents in a struggle to take control of their lives, they will probably sympathize with Tan's narrator and accept her judgments uncritically. Will any reader take the mother's side?

Questions for Discussion

1. Why is the setting of this story important? What do you learn from it about the experience of Asian immigrants in their first years in the United States?
2. What advantages are offered to the child? What disadvantages?
3. How typical is Tan's story of the mother-daughter conflict? Explain.
4. Explain the meaning of the last paragraph of the story.

Topics for Writing

1. **CONNECTIONS** Compare and contrast the theme of initiation in Ellison's "Battle Royal" and Tan's "Two Kinds."
2. **CONNECTIONS** Analyze the use of dialect in Wright's "The Man Who Was Almost a Man" and Tan's "Two Kinds."
3. **CONNECTIONS** Compare and contrast the mother in Tan's "Two Kinds" with Olenka, the protagonist of Chekhov's "The Darling."
4. **CONNECTIONS** Compare and contrast Tan's "Two Kinds" with Munro's "Walker Brothers Cowboy," in which the narrator does *not* try to justify her actions or her feelings for a parent.

(text pp. 1225–1228)

Suggested Readings

Tan, Amy. *The Joy Luck Club.* New York: Ballantine, 1989.
————. "The Language of Discretion." *The State of the Language.* Ed. Christopher Ricks. Berkeley: U of California P, 1990.

JAMES THURBER

The Secret Life of Walter Mitty (p. 1225)

Like a good joke, a successful comic story may be easy to enjoy but hard to explain. Thurber has rendered his hero so convincingly that "Walter Mitty" has long since entered the popular vocabulary as a shorthand term for a certain personality type. The triumph of the story does not come, however, at the expense of the henpecked and bullied daydreamer. Stephen A. Black rightly points out that Mitty's escapism risks a denial of the self in its retreat from reality, but it is important to note that Mitty's fantasy life, despite its dependence on pulp fiction clichés, is just as real on the page as his (equally stereotypical) impatient and condescending wife, the officious policeman, and the insolent parking-lot attendant. Thus the reader may respond with admiration to Mitty's imaginary competence, courage, and grace under pressure.

Throughout the story Thurber uses things from the real environment to trigger Mitty's fantasies, but he also shows that the fantasies can have an impact on his actual life. The phrase "You miserable cur" reminds Mitty of the forgotten puppy biscuit. Near the end, after the sergeant tells "Captain Mitty" that "It's forty kilometers through hell, sir," Mitty has his life in Connecticut in mind when he musingly replies, "After all, . . . what isn't?" In his fantasy, "the box barrage is closing in," but Mitty is just as courageous in standing up to the salvo of questions and criticism launched moments later by his wife, which elicits his vague remark, "Things close in." As he stands against the drugstore wall in the Waterbury rain to face the imaginary firing squad, the reader can agree that he *is* "Walter Mitty the Undefeated" — because his inner life remains, for his banal tormentors, "inscrutable to the last."

WILLIAM E. SHEIDLEY

Questions for Discussion

1. What is Walter Mitty actually doing in the first paragraph of the story?
2. Explain Mitty's attitude toward his wife. Why does she insist that he wear gloves and overshoes?
3. How familiar is Walter Mitty with medical terminology? What is the purpose for Mitty of his medical fantasy?
4. Do Mitty's fantasies help or hinder him in dealing with reality?
5. Explain Mitty's words "Things close in."
6. Where do you think Walter Mitty gets his ideas of heroism? Is there any sense in which his real life can be called heroic?

Topics for Writing

1. Describe Walter Mitty's final wish.
2. Discuss the romantic and the banal: the basis of Thurber's humor in "The Secret Life of Walter Mitty."
3. Find as many connections as possible between Mitty's actual experiences and his fantasies. How are they related? What do you think will be the consequence, if any, of Mitty's imaginary execution?

Suggested Readings

Black, Stephen A. *James Thurber — His Masquerades: A Critical Study*. The Hague: Mouton, 1970. 15, 18–19, 32, 42–43, 49–50, 54, 56, 119.

Morseburger, Robert E. *James Thurber*. Twayne's United States Authors Series 62. New York: Twayne, 1964. 18–19, 44–48, 123, 151–52.

TATYANA TOLSTAYA

Night (p. 1229)

Even in translation from the original Russian, Tolstaya's story has an extraordinarily luminosity, its language shimmering on the page. The events of the story are slight: a simple-minded man named Alexei Petrovich, in the care of his eighty-year-old mother, wakes up, eats breakfast, works all day gluing boxes in the kitchen of their apartment, goes with his mother to deliver the boxes to a pharmacy, comes home, steals some money and goes out by himself into the night to buy ice cream, gets lost and frightened and found again, and is taken home by his mother.

The story is told in the third person from Alexei Petrovich's point of view, so that its dazzling poetic quality seems a reflection of his scrambled stream of consciousness. Because his mother takes such good care of him, he is basically a happy fellow, unaware of his intellectual limitations. In fact he aspires to be a writer like the great Russian poet Alexander Sergeyevich Pushkin, and he is encouraged in this ambition by his good-hearted mother. Judging from the way Tolstaya conveys his thoughts, he could become a poet, and the joke of the story is in its last line, when Alexei Petrovich takes a sharp pencil in hand writes in big letters on white paper what he has learned from his adventure: "Night. Night. Night. Night. Night. Night . . ."

Questions for Discussion

1. How many pounds is 135 kilos, the weight of Alexei Petrovich's mother? (Hint: multiply by 2.2 to transform kilograms into pounds.)
2. How does Tolstaya suggest that her characters associate a nightmarish quality with nighttime?

3. Why is Alexei described as "nature's blunder" as a late child? Is this his idea, or the narrator's? Describe his relationship with his mother.
4. Who is the brazen Sea Girl?
5. Where do the characters in the story live?
6. What picture of living conditions in Russia do you get from this story?
7. How do you know that Alexei is interested in words and letters from his response to his work gluing boxes?
8. Why does hearing his mother read poetry aloud make Alexei happy?
9. What does Alexei do when he becomes frightened when by himself outside at night?
10. Why is the word "Night" a "newly acquired truth" for him?

Topics for Writing

1. Research the Russian poet Pushkin and explain his importance in Tolstaya's story.
2. **CONNECTIONS** Compare and contrast the mother-son relationship in "Night" and in Katherine Anne Porter's "He."

Suggested Reading

Tolstaya, Tatyana. *Sleepwalker in a Fog*. New York: Knopf, 1992.

LEO TOLSTOY

The Death of Ivan Ilych (p. 1237)

No one who comes to "The Death of Ivan Ilych" from a direction other than that of *War and Peace* and *Anna Karenina* is likely to share the opinion of some Tolstoy scholars that it is parable-thin in its evocation of life, providing only a transparent surface of detail through which Tolstoy's allegorical intentions are exposed. The story is studded with brilliantly realistic representations of experiences that the reader encounters with a twinge of sometimes embarrassed recognition — Peter Ivanovich's struggle with the pouffe, for example. But it is nonetheless a product of the period following Tolstoy's religious crisis and a story written by one whose explicit theory of art rested on a utilitarian moral didacticism.

The story's effectiveness depends on Tolstoy's avoiding, until the last possible moment, preaching the sermon that, as the headnote suggests, he eventually means to preach. The opening section places us in the shoes of Peter Ivanovich, causing us to sympathize with the desire to look away from death, at the same time that it subjects that desire to a devastating satiric attack. Then, by returning to a long chronological survey of Ivan Ilych's life, Tolstoy forces us to do exactly the opposite of what Peter Ivanovich does: to confront death and its meaning in an extended and excruciatingly matter-of-fact account. What we see is not a life, but a death — or a life viewed as death. For Ivan Ilych's life, as he eventually comes to realize, is a slow but accelerating process of dying. The narration, however, decelerates, so that the reader may expect it to be nearly over around section VI, whereas in fact there are six more (albeit shorter) sections to come, containing a series of painful revelations that burst through the screen Ivan Ilych has built up to hide himself from reality.

Tolstoy tortures the reader just as Ivan Ilych is tortured, so that the precept finally advanced by the story arrives as the answer to the reader's fervent need. Ivan Ilych is not a particularly bad man; and — bad or good — all men, as Gerasim remarks, come to the same spot. Tolstoy makes this recognition virtually intolerable by his vivid rendering of Ivan Ilych's suffering. Then he offers a way out by proposing that one simple motion of the soul toward charity can release the sufferer from his mortal anguish. Tolstoy prepares us for this revelation by stressing the relief Ivan Ilych finds in the kindness of Gerasim, whose health, strength, and repose are bound up with his simple acceptance of sickness and death as necessary parts of life. Some critics have claimed that Tolstoy's art fails to encompass the illumination Ivan Ilych receives at the end, which rests on doctrines extrinsic to the text; but at least it can be said that he avoids sentimental piety by providing for an ironic interpretation when he caps Ivan Ilych's triumphant assertion "Death is finished. . . . It is no more!" with the paradoxical conclusion "He drew in a breath, stopped in the midst of a sigh, stretched out, and died."

The preoccupations and activities of Ivan Ilych and his peers during Ilych's lifetime in the society portrayed by Tolstoy contrast sharply with those of the unselfish peasant Gerasim. They are directed to no constructive end, serving only to gratify the ego with a sense of power and to hide the fear of death under a surface awareness of pleasure and propriety. Ivan Ilych is never more content than when manipulating the inert objects which are so plentiful in the story — as when decorating his new house — and he does his best to relate to people as he relates to things, insulating himself from true human contact. After he has received his death blow from the quite inert knob of a window frame, however, Ivan Ilych experiences a similar dehumanizing treatment by the doctors, his wife, and his friends, none of whom can bear to face the implications of his evident mortality. As his sickness steadily reduces him to a state of infantile dependency, Ilych comes to recognize first his own powerlessness and then the error in his strategy of living. Finally, as the coffin-womb he has built for himself falls away and he is reborn into the light of spiritual understanding, he sees the fundamental truth he has worked so hard to deny: the feelings of others are as real as his own. At this moment, moved by pity for his wife and son, he at last finds something worthwhile to do; and, in doing it, he attains the sense of ease and "rightness" that has previously eluded him. That the single positive act of Ivan Ilych's life is to die may be seen as either a grim irony or an exciting revelation, depending on the perspective from which the reader views it. But either way the conclusion of the story embodies the kernel of Tolstoy's social theme. As Edward Wasiolek puts it, "Death for Tolstoy now, as the supremely shared experience, is the model of all solidarity, and only the profound consciousness of its significance can bring one to the communion of true brotherhood."

WILLIAM E. SHEIDLEY

Questions for Discussion

1. How does the authorial voice qualify our view of Ivan Ilych's survivors' reactions to his death in section I?
2. Evaluate Peter Ivanovich's view of Ivan Ilych's son when he meets him near the end of section I.
3. Comment on the implications of Ivan Ilych's hanging a medallion bearing the motto *respice finem* (consider your end) on his watch chain.
4. What is wrong with Ivan Ilych's marriage? with his work? with his ambitions?
5. By examining the authorial comments in sections III and IV, define the attitude toward Ivan Ilych that Tolstoy asks the reader to share. Does this attitude change?
6. Consider the opening sentence of section VI. Is this section a low point in the story? If so, what kind of rise ensues?
7. Why does Ivan Ilych find relief in having his legs supported by Gerasim?
8. What is the effect of the shift to the present tense about one-third of the way through section VIII?
9. In section IX, Ivan Ilych complains to God in language similar to that of Job. Compare and contrast their plights.
10. What is the meaning of Ivan Ilych's reversion to childhood shortly before his death?
11. How might Ivan Ilych's dream of the black sack be interpreted?

Topics for Writing

1. Stop after reading section I and write a paragraph or two on the theme and tone of the story as you understand them so far. After reading the rest of the story, write a paragraph evaluating your original response. Write an essay examining the opening section as a story in itself, but one fully understood only after reading sections II–XII.
2. Consider bridge as an epitome of the life Ivan Ilych and his friends try to live.
3. Discuss Tolstoy's use of symbolic, descriptive details in "The Death of Ivan Ilych."
4. Using "The Death of Ivan Ilych" as the basis of your knowledge of society, write a manifesto calling for revolution or reform.
5. Write a sermon, using the demise of Ivan Ilych Golovin as your occasion.

Suggested Readings

Christian, R. F. *Tolstoy: A Critical Introduction.* Cambridge: Cambridge UP, 1969. 236–38.

Greenwood, E. B. *Tolstoy: The Comprehensive Vision.* New York: St. Martin's, 1975. 118–23.

Simmons, Ernest J. *Introduction to Tolstoy's Writings.* Chicago: U of Chicago P, 1968. Esp. 148–50.

Wasiolek, Edward. *Tolstoy's Major Fiction.* Chicago: U of Chicago P, 1978. Esp. 165–79.

JOHN UPDIKE

A & P (p. 1280)

Although Updike was a precociously successful writer who spent his apprenticeship living in New York City and writing for *The New Yorker* magazine, much of the strength of his writing stems from his ability to take the reader back to the atmosphere of the small town where he grew up. "A & P" showcases this ability. This story about a nineteen-year-old at a checkout counter in an A & P supermarket skillfully sustains the point of view of a teenage boy from a small-town working-class family.

The incident the story describes is slight. What gives "A & P" its substance is the voice of the narrator. He is obviously what the author thinks of as an ordinary teenager, impatient with old people, not interested in his job, and deeply aroused by girls. The longest descriptive passage — almost a third of the story itself — dwells on the body of one of the girls; as the story's slight action unfolds, the bodies of that girl and one of her friends are mentioned several times again. The narrator's adolescent desire and adoration are amusingly played off his clumsy bravado and the idiom of sexist stereotypes he is trying to master. "You never know for sure how girls' minds work (do you really think it's a mind in there or just a little buzz like a bee in a glass jar?)." His view of adult women is no less callow: "We're right in the middle of town, and the women generally put on a shirt or shorts or something before they get out of the car into the street. And anyway these are usually women with six children and varicose veins mapping their legs and nobody, including them, could care less."

It is probably true that when the story was written, in the late 1950s, its attitudes were not considered unusual. Today we have to ask ourselves whether the deplorable sexism is redeemed by the artfulness of the story, the technique Updike brings to constructing his narrator's voice.

Questions for Discussion

1. What does the language of the story tell us about the narrator's social background?
2. Are there any details in the story that place it in a specific part of the United States, or could it be happening anywhere within a few miles of a beach? Explain.
3. Is the boy's discomfort with older people limited to women, or is he also uncomfortable with men? Is there anyone in the store he *is* comfortable with? Explain.
4. Do you think Updike shares the narrator's attitudes?

Topics for Writing

1. Analyze the strengths and limitations of the first-person narrative in "A & P."

2. **CONNECTIONS** Consider "acting like a man": Updike's bag boy in "A & P," and Wright's Dave in "The Man Who Was Almost a Man."
3. **CONNECTIONS** Compare and contrast adolescent narrators in Updike's "A & P" and Joyce's "Araby."
4. **CONNECTIONS** Compare this story with Munro's "Walker Brothers Cowboy." How do the descriptive details in the two stories establish a specific time and place?

Suggested Readings

Cantor, Jay. "On Giving Birth to One's Own Mother." *TriQuarterly* 75 (Spring–Summer 1989): 78–91.

Detweiler, Robert. *John Updike. Rev. ed.* Boston: G. K. Hall, 1987.

Fleischauer, John F. "John Updike's Prose Style: Definition at the Periphery of Meaning." *Critique: Studies in Contemporary Fiction* 30(4) (Summer 1989): 277–90.

Greiner, Donald J. *The Other Updike: Poems, Short Stories, Prose, Play.* Columbus: Ohio UP, 1981.

Luscher, Robert M. "John Updike's Olinger Stories: New Light among the Shadows." *Journal of the Short Story in English* 11 (Autumn 1988): 99–117.

Lyons, E. "John Updike: The Beginning and the End." *Critique* 14.2 (1972): 44–59.

Newman, Judie. *John Updike.* New York: St. Martin's, 1988.

Samuels, C. T. "Art of Fiction: John Updike." *Paris Review* 12 (1968): 84–117.

Seib, P. "Lovely Way through Life: An Interview with John Updike." *Southwest Review* 66 (1981): 341–50.

Taylor, Charles C. *John Updike, A Bibliography.* Ann Arbor, MI: Books Demand UMI, 1989.

Thorburn, David, and Howard Eiland. *John Updike: A Collection of Critical Essays.* New York: Prentice-Hall, 1979.

Updike, John. *Hugging the Shore.* New York: Random House, 1983.

———. *Picked-Up Pieces.* New York: Knopf, 1976.

———. *Too Far to Go.* New York: Ballantine, 1979.

Wilhelm, Albert E. "Rebecca Cune: Updike's Wedge Between the Maples." *Notes on Modern American Literature* 7(2) (Fall 1983): Item 9.

———. "The Trail-of-Bread-Crumbs Motif in Updike's Maples Stories." *Studies in Short Fiction* 25(1) (Winter 1988): 71–73.

ALICE WALKER

Roselily (p. 1286)

This is the story of a black woman, Roselily, on her wedding day. Contrary to what we might expect, however, the tone is not joyful, but tense and apprehensive. Roselily is full of doubts, about herself and the man who will soon be her husband. Her motivation to marry this man is not love of him as an individual. In fact, she admits she "does not even know if she loves him." What she does love are some of his qualities and properties, "his sobriety," "his pride," "his blackness," "his gray car," "his understanding of her *condition*," and, most important, his ability to "free her" from her current life. And what of his love for her? Roselily is realistic enough to know that he loves her, but again, she admits, he does not love her because of who she is. She acknowledges that "he will make [an effort] to redo her into what he truly wants." We are left with a picture of a woman trying to escape her past by marrying a man who will "free her" to "be respectable and respected and free" and a man marrying out of an apparent desire to reform.

"Roselily" has as its seminal concept the number *two*. It presents two opposite individuals at a crucial moment in their lives. Yet, as they symbolically fuse their lives into a single relationship, each brings very different experiences and backgrounds to the marriage. Roselily knows only the southern, small town, country way of life, complete with its provincial religious beliefs and its sense of connectedness with family and community. Her husband is "against this." A northerner from Chicago, his ways are city ways, his religious beliefs are alien and restrictive. Rather than a feeling of community, he knows independence and anonymity.

Roselily wants freedom: "She wants to live for once. But doesn't know quite what that means. Wonders if she has ever done it. If she ever will." She spends the entire ceremony rationalizing that this marriage is the right thing to do, despite the fact that she "feels shut away from" this man. By the last paragraph she is finally able to formulate her feelings: "She feels ignorant, *wrong*, backward." By then, however, it is too late. The ceremony is complete, and "her husband's hand is like the clasp of an iron gate."

The structural framework for "Roselily" is the Christian marriage ceremony. It provides form as well as forward movement for a story that is essentially a stream-of-consciousness remembrance and narrative of the lead character, Roselily, from a third person point of view. Contrast is the subject of the story. Conflict is the theme.

The title, "Roselily," does more than introduce the heroine. It also foreshadows the scope of the story. The rose becomes a lily. By means of the marriage vows, Roselily changes from a woman who is passionate, natural, and, in the eyes of society, impure and immoral to one who is resurrected and reborn, but passionless and dead. For a price, she gains respectability. Now she must decide whether or not the cost is equal to the value. The conflict has not been resolved; it has only been postponed.

Questions for Discussion

1. Walker uses the marriage service to break up Roselily's reflections. What does this particular structure emphasize? What effect does it create?
2. Roselily's first passage opens with her dreaming of "dragging herself across the world. A small girl in her mother's white robe and veil, knee raised waist high through a bowl of quicksand soup." What subjects in these sentences persist throughout this story? Describe the qualities of this girl that reflect Roselily's own representation of herself in this story. Is she helpless, vulnerable, childish, struggling, or playacting?
3. Why does Roselily spend so much time thinking about her fourth child's father? Do we know as much about the man she is marrying as we do about

her ex-lover? What do Roselily's reflections on his character tell us about hers?

4. What does Roselily's fourth child, the one she gave to his father, represent? What kind of a connection does she feel to the child? Can she imagine his future?

5. Part of Roselily's reflections are devoted to wondering "what one does with memories in a brand-new life." What alternatives are open to her? Can she just shut her memories away, or break them off and start again? Consider the question of memory and the burden of the past against her sudden dream of having no children. Roselily's own mother is dead, yet Roselily still feels a connection to her. What are the "ghosts" that Roselily believes in?

6. Much of this story depends on oppositions. "Her husband's hand," Roselily thinks, "is like the clasp of an iron gate." What are the positive and negative qualities of an iron gate? Roselily thinks of "ropes, chains, handcuffs, his religion." What other images does she associate with this man she is marrying? He's going to "free her." How do you reconcile the images of bondage and freedom? Consider the diction in this passage: "A romantic hush. Proposal. Promises. A new life! Respectable, reclaimed, renewed. Free! In robe and veil." Yet suddenly, Walker presents "a rat trapped, concerned, scurrying to and fro in her head, peering through the windows of her eyes." What is the difference in the language in both examples? Is one kind of diction stronger than the other? Why?

7. What do you infer about Roselily's feelings from these sentences: "The rest she does not hear. She feels a kiss, passionate, rousing, within the general pandemonium. Cars drive up blowing their horns. Firecrackers go off. Dogs come from under the house and begin to yelp and bark." Look first at the syntax of these sentences. Why do you think they are all short and unconnected to one another? What effect does that create? What is the subject of each sentence? Why might Roselily only be able to receive certain kinds of impressions?

8. How do you interpret the final paragraph of this story? Does this paragraph control your understanding of the story retrospectively? How did you weigh the oppositions until this paragraph? Were Roselily's hopes and fears in equilibrium? Which words carry the heaviest burden of meaning for you? Would the paragraph — and your judgment — be very different without them?

Topics for Writing

1. Contrast Roselily's culture and environment and those of her husband-to-be.

2. Discuss the disparity between Roselily's dreams and her situation.

3. Describe the point of view in "Roselily."

4. Think back in your own life to a time when your thoughts received stimulation from an outside event but were not totally controlled by that event. Try to re-create your thought patterns and structure them into an interesting narrative account.

5. **CONNECTIONS** Compare and contrast the concept of marriage in Walker's "Roselily" and Lawrence's "Odour of Chrysanthemums."

Suggested Readings

Banks, Erma Davis, and Keith Byerman. *Alice Walker: An Annotated Bibliography 1968–1986.* New York: Garland, 1989.

Bell, Roseann P., Bettye J. Parker, and Beverly Guy-Sheftall, eds. *Sturdy Black Bridges: Visions of Black Women in Literature.* New York: Anchor, 1979.

Bloom, Harold. *Alice Walker.* New York: Chelsea House, 1990.

Byerman, Keith, and Erma Banks. "Alice Walker: A Selected Bibliography, 1968–1988." *Callaloo: An Afro-American and African Journal of Arts and Letters* 12(2) (Spring 1989): 343–45.

Byrne, Mary Ellen. "Welty's 'A Worn Path' and Walker's 'Everyday Use': Companion Pieces." *Teaching English in a Two-Year College* 16(2) (May 1989): 129–33.

Cooke, Michael. *Afro-American Literature in the Twentieth Century: The Achievement of Intimacy.* New Haven: Yale UP, 1984.

Davis, T. M. "Alice Walker's Celebration of Self in Southern Generations." *Women Writers of the Contemporary South.* Ed. Peggy Whitman Prenshaw. Jackson: UP of Mississippi, 1984. 83–94.

Erickson, P. "Cast Out Alone/To Heal/and Re-create/Ourselves: Family Based Identity in the Work of Alice Walker." *College Language Association Journal* 23 (1979): 71–94.

Evans, Mari, ed. *Black Women Writers (1950–1980): A Critical Evaluation.* New York: Anchor, 1984. 453–95.

Mariani, Philomena, ed. *Critical Fictions: The Politics of Imaginative Writing.* Seattle: Bay Press, 1991.

Petry, Alice Hall. "Alice Walker: The Achievement of the Short Fiction." *Modern Language Studies* 19(1) (Winter 1989): 12–27.

Stade, G. "Womanist Fiction and Male Characters." *Partisan Review* 52 (1985): 265–70.

Winchell, Donna Haisty. *Alice Walker.* Boston: Twayne, 1990.

EUDORA WELTY

Why I Live at the P.O. (p. 1291)

This story may be troublesome to some readers, especially if they have been sensitized to racial issues in short fiction through a discussion of Achebe's criticism of Conrad's "Heart of Darkness." The word "nigger" used as a racial slur occurs three times in Welty's story. The narrator who uses the word is clearly an uneducated bigot, but her contempt for people of color living in her community is underscored by her assumption that they are fit only for the lowest kind of work. Here are the passages concerned:

> So I merely slammed the door behind me and went down and made some green-tomato pickle. Somebody had to do it. Of course Mama had turned both the niggers loose; she always said no earthly power could hold one anyway on the Fourth of July, so she wouldn't even try. It turned out that Jaypan fell in the lake and came within a very narrow limit of drowning.

There was a nigger girl going along on a little wagon right in front. "Nigger girl," I says, "come help me haul these things down the hill, I'm going to live in the post office." Took her nine trips in her express wagon. Uncle Rondo came out on the porch and threw her a nickel.

In both cases, African-Americans are assumed to be stupid workhorses, barely tolerated as human beings and undeserving of respect. In the first instance the two house servants are "turned loose" (like animals?) on the Fourth of July, but they are so immature and irresponsible that they go wild on their chance to celebrate Independence Day (irony?); they get drunk, and one of them, Jaypan, nearly drowns. In the second case, African Americans are presumed to be so stupid that a black child won't mind stopping her play with a wagon to help move a white woman; the child will also be satisfied being paid a pittance for working so hard. Welty is writing a humorous story, of course, told from the point of view of a Mississippi cracker, but humor doesn't negate the racism, any more than Marlowe's naiveté condones his judgments about Africans in "Heart of Darkness." Racist jokes aren't any more tolerable because they are meant to be "funny."

Insensitive literary critics discussing "Why I Live at the P.O." usually comment on "the exasperation and frustration, loneliness and near-madness" of the narrator, trapped in a provincial Mississippi town. Or they view her as "a solid and practical person struggling to keep her self-possession and balance in the midst of a childish, neurotic, and bizarre family." In Welty's commentary on the story, she stresses the normalcy of characters like Sister (the narrator) and her family in the South. Thrown against one another with limited social resources, they bicker and feud but usually reconcile their differences, because family solidarity is important to them. At the end of the story we learn that Sister's outburst has been provoked after five days of living by herself in the post office; Welty has said that once the character's anger has cooled, she'd move back home. She writes, "I was trying to show how, in these tiny little places such as where they come from, the only entertainment people have is dramatizing the family situation, which they do fully knowing what they are doing. They're having a good time. They're not caught up; it's not pathological. It's a Southern kind of exaggeration."

Questions for Discussion

1. Can we equate Sister's voice with Welty's opinions? Explain.
2. Does the humor in the story soften or increase the tension between the members of the family? Why or why not?
3. Why do the two sisters fight so much?

Topics for Writing

1. Retell the story through the eyes of the house servant Jaypan or the little girl with the express wagon.
2. **CONNECTIONS** Compare Mississippi small towns as backgrounds for Welty's "Why I Live at the P.O." and Faulkner's "A Rose for Emily."

Suggested Readings

See page 237.

EUDORA WELTY

A Worn Path (p. 1300)

Try not to force the Christian or mythological schemes of allegory the story supports until you encourage students to savor the beauty of the literal narration. Phoenix Jackson is an embodiment of love, faith, sacrifice, charity, self-renunciation, and triumph over death in herself, quite apart from the typological implications of her name or the allusions to the stations of the cross in her journey. Phoenix transcends her merely archetypal significance just as she transcends the stereotype of old black mammies on which she is built. Welty accomplishes this act of creation by entering fully into the consciousness of her character. There she discovers the little child that still lives within the old woman and causes her to dream of chocolate cake, dance with a scarecrow, and delight in a Christmas toy. Phoenix is right when she says, "I wasn't as old as I thought," but she does not merit the condescension of the hunter's exclamation, "I know you old colored people! Wouldn't miss going to town to see Santa Claus!" Even in her greatest discomfort, lying in the weeds, losing her memory, getting her shoes tied, "stealing" a nickel, or taking one as a handout, Phoenix retains her invincible dignity, an essential component of the single glimpse we receive of her triumphant homeward march, bearing aloft the bright symbol of life she has retrieved through her exertions.

In her comments on the story (included in Part Two, p. 1507), Welty implies that the meaning of Phoenix's journey is that of any human exertion carried out in good faith despite the uncertainty of the outcome: "The path is the thing that matters." In keeping with this theme, Welty repeatedly shows Phoenix asserting life in the face of death. Her name itself, taken from the mythical bird that periodically immolates itself and rises reborn from its ashes, embodies the idea. (She even makes a noise like "a solitary little bird" in the first paragraph.) Phoenix makes her journey at the time of the death and rebirth of the year; her own skin color is like the sun bursting through darkness; she overcomes discouragement as she tops the hill; she extricates herself from a thorn bush (of which much may be made in a Christian allegorical interpretation); she passes "big dead trees" and a buzzard; she traverses a field of dead corn; she sees a "ghost" that turns out to be a dancing scarecrow; she is overcome by a "black dog" but rescued by a death-dealing hunter whose gun she faces down and whom she beats out of a shiny nickel; and she emerges from a deathlike trance in the doctor's office to return with the medicine her grandson needs to stay alive. Phoenix's strength lies in the purpose of her journey, and her spirit is contagious. The hunter, the woman who ties her shoes, and the doctor's attendant all perform acts of charity toward her, and lest the reader overlook the one word that lies at the heart of Welty's vision, the nurse says "Charity" while "making a check mark in a book."

Questions for Discussion

1. Notice Phoenix's identification with "a solitary little bird." What other birds does she encounter on her journey? Explain their implications.
2. What techniques does Welty use to suggest the laboriousness of Phoenix's trip?
3. Before she crosses the creek, Phoenix says, "Now comes the trial." Does she pass it? How? To what extent is this event a microcosm of the whole story? Are there other microcosmic episodes?
4. What effect do Phoenix's sequential reactions to the scarecrow, the abandoned cabins, and the spring have on the reader's view of her?
5. What is your opinion of the hunter? What conclusion might be drawn from the fact that even though he kills birds and patronizes Phoenix, he helps her in a way he does not know?
6. Interpret the passage that begins with Phoenix bending for the nickel and ends with her parting from the hunter.
7. Describe Natchez as Phoenix perceives it. Is it a worthy culmination for her journey?
8. In her comments reprinted in Part Two (p. 1507), Welty remarks that Phoenix's victory comes when she sees the doctor's diploma "nailed up on the wall." In what sense is this moment the climax of the story? What is different about the ensuing action from the action that leads up to this moment? Are there any similarities?
9. How does Phoenix describe her grandson? What is Welty's reason for using these terms?
10. Explain the irony in the way the nurse records Phoenix's visit.

Topics for Writing

1. Explain why many readers think that Phoenix Jackson's grandson is dead.
2. Discuss the symbolism of birds in "A Worn Path."
3. After your first reading of "A Worn Path," write a paragraph giving your opinion of Phoenix Jackson. Then study some symbolic interpretations of the story (such as those by Ardelino, Isaacs, and Keys, cited in Suggested Readings). Reread the story and write another assessment of the central character. Does she bear up under the freight of symbolic meaning the critics ask her to carry? Does her relation to these archetypes help to account for your original response?
4. Read Welty's account of how she came to write "A Worn Path" (Part Two, p. 1507). Following her example, write an account of what you imagine to be the day's experience of someone you catch a glimpse of who strikes your fancy. Use the intimate interior third person limited-omniscient point of view that Welty employs for Phoenix Jackson.

Related Commentary

Eudora Welty, Is Phoenix Jackson's Grandson Really Dead? p. 1507.

Suggested Readings

Ardelino, Frank. "Life out of Death: Ancient Myth and Ritual in Welty's 'A Worn Path.' " *Notes on Mississippi Writers* 9 (1976): 1–9.

Bloom, Harold. *Eudora Welty.* New York: Chelsea House, 1986.

Desmond, John F. *A Still Moment: Essay on the Art of Eudora Welty.* Metuchen, NJ: Scarecrow, 1978.

Isaacs, Neil D. "Life for Phoenix." *Sewanee Review* 71 (1963): 75–81.

Keys, Marilynn. " 'A Worn Path': The Way of Dispossession." *Studies in Short Fiction* 16 (1979): 354–56.

Kieft, Ruth M. *Eudora Welty.* Rev. ed. Boston: G. K. Hall, 1987.

MacNeil, Robert. *Eudora Welty: Seeing Black and White.* Westport, CT: Greenwood, 1990.

Phillips, Robert L., Jr. "A Structural Approach to Myth in the Fiction of Eudora Welty." *Eudora Welty: Critical Essays.* Ed. Peggy Whitman Prenshaw. Jackson: UP of Mississippi, 1979. 56–67, esp. 60.

Preenshaw, Peggy W., ed. *Eudora Welty: Thirteen Essays.* Jackson: UP of Mississippi, 1983.

Schmidt, Peter. *The Heart of the Story: Eudora Welty's Short Fiction.* Jackson: UP of Mississippi, 1991.

Turner, W. Craig, and Lee Harding, eds. *Critical Essays on Eudora Welty.* Boston: G. K. Hall, 1989.

Welty, Eudora. *The Eye of the Story.* New York: Vintage, 1990.

———. *One Writer's Beginnings.* New York: Warner, 1984.

EDITH WHARTON

Roman Fever (p. 1308)

Nearly every detail of this seemingly meandering narration that leads up to the final sequence of three dramatic revelations has a function in preparing for the climax. Wharton knits better than Grace Ansley, and her story does not fully unravel until the last words are spoken. When the secret is finally out, the reader experiences a flash of ironic insight that Wharton has been preparing from the beginning through her masterful delineation of the characters and their situation.

Face to face with "the great accumulated wreckage of passion and splendor" that spreads before them, and deserted in their advancing age by the pair of daughters who are now their sole concerns, the two widows may evoke the reader's condescending pity. They seem as small and pale as the images of one another each sees, in Wharton's metaphor, "through the wrong end of her little telescope." But as the two characters become differentiated, Alida Slade takes on depth and coloration. As the story of her flashy but parasitic life and of the jealousy and guilty resentment she has harbored toward her friend gradually emerges, the reader can no longer pity her but can hardly admire her either. Her revelation that it was she, not Delphin Slade, who wrote the letter inviting Grace to a tryst in the Colosseum may be unexpected, but it follows perfectly from her character as Wharton has established it. Its blow to Mrs. Ansley is severe, and it seems the more cruel to the reader, who has no reason as yet to revise the original estimate of her as merely pitiable. Mrs. Ansley staggers, but to the reader's surprise and gratification she gradually recovers herself. Impelled by the shock for once to assert herself, she caps Mrs. Slade's revelation with an even more dramatic one of her own.

Grace Ansley's reticence, and the quietness of her life in contrast to Alida Slade's, expresses neither emotional pallor nor weakness of character. She had the spunk to take what she wanted from Delphin Slade twenty-five years before, and she has been content with her memory ever since, not needing, as Alida Slade would have (and indeed *has*) needed, to get reassurance by parading her conquest in public. Thus, it is Mrs. Ansley who manifests greater independence and vitality. Mrs. Slade, by contrast, has been conventional and dependent. Widowhood is such an uncomfortable lot for her because she can no longer shine with the reflected brilliance of her husband. Barbara may be unlike Horace Ansley because Delphin Slade was really her father, but her differences from Jenny derive from the fact that Grace Ansley, not Alida Slade, is her mother.

Wharton has constructed her plot with a precision O. Henry would have admired, but she has based it less on contrivances of circumstance than on an understanding of her characters. By placing them in a setting that spans millennia — from ancient Rome to the airplane — she implies the universality of the passions, triumphs, and defeats that make up the lives of even these New York society ladies, whose wealth and status do not protect them from the human condition after all.

WILLIAM E. SHEIDLEY

Questions for Discussion

1. What do Barbara and Jenny think of their mothers? How accurate is their estimate?
2. Why does Grace Ansley place an "undefinable stress" on "me" and "I" in replying to Alida Slade's questions about her reaction to their view of the Roman ruins?
3. Why does Alida Slade consider Grace and Horace Ansley "two nullities"?
4. Compare and contrast the two ladies' responses to widowhood and advancing age. Who takes them harder? Why?
5. Alida Slade remembers that "Mrs. Horace Ansley, twenty-five years ago, had been exquisitely lovely." Explain the importance of this fact to Mrs. Slade, to Mrs. Ansley, and to the structure of the plot.
6. What is "Roman fever" — literally and figuratively?
7. Why has Alida Slade "always gone on hating" Grace Ansley?
8. What reaction does Alida Slade seem to have expected from Grace Ansley in response to her confession that she forged the letter? Why?
9. Alida Slade remarks, "Well, girls are ferocious sometimes." What about ladies?
10. Near the end of the story, why does Grace Ansley pity Alida Slade? Why does Mrs. Slade at first reject that pity?
11. Comment on the meaning of the way the ladies walk offstage.

Topics for Writing

1. Analyze the importance of setting in "Roman Fever."
2. Show how Wharton manipulates point of view in "Roman Fever."
3. Explain how "Roman Fever" conforms to Wharton's principles of the short story as stated in the excerpt from her book *The Writing of Fiction* (included in Part Two, p. 1514).
4. On your first reading of the story, mark passages whose significance is not entirely clear — such as Grace Ansley's peculiar intonations when acknowledging her memory of a former visit to Rome. After reading the story to the end, return to the marked passages and write explanations of them.
5. Which of the two ladies is more guilty of reprehensible behavior? Consider arguments on both sides, or organize a debate.
6. Write a story of your own about a secret that comes out or a misunderstanding that is resolved. Try to make both the perpetuation of the error or deception and the emergence of the truth dependent on character rather than circumstance.

Related Commentary

Edith Wharton, Every Subject Must Contain within Itself Its Own Dimensions, p. 1514.

Suggested Readings

Flynn, Dale Bachman: "Salamanders in the Fire: The Short Stories of Edith Wharton." *Dissertation Abstracts International* 45(12) (June 1985): 3638A.

Hollbrook, David. *Edith Wharton.* New York: St. Martin's, 1991.

Howe, Irving, ed. *Edith Wharton: A Collection of Critical Essays.* New York: Prentice-Hall, 1962.

Lewis, R. W. B. *Edith Wharton: A Biography.* New York: Harper, 1985.

McDowell, Margaret B. *Edith Wharton.* Boston: Twayne, 1991.

Petry, Alice Hall. "A Twist of Crimson Silk: Edith Wharton's 'Roman Fever.'" *Studies in Short Fiction* 24(2) (Spring 1987): 163–66.

Vita-Finzi, Penelope. *Edith Wharton and the Art of Fiction.* New York: St. Martin's, 1990.

Wharton, Edith. *The Collected Letters of Edith Wharton.* New York: Macmillan, 1987.

White, Barbara A. "Neglected Areas: Wharton's Short Stories and Incest, Part II." *Edith Wharton Review* 8(2) (Fall 1991): 3–10, 32.

JOHN EDGAR WIDEMAN

The Beginning of Homewood (p. 1319)

Perhaps the best way to approach John Edgar Wideman's virtuostic story "The Beginning of Homewood" is to think of a kaleidoscope, changing its images and its tonalities as it is turned in the light. Within the kaleidoscope of the story, however, the images are carefully sorted, so that each set of images shows a different facet of the same theme: Wideman's attempt to fuse the different aspects of his experience as an African American in contemporary society.

In order to organize the material he wishes to present in his kaleidoscope, Wideman sets the story throughout different historical periods: the present, as he addresses an unnamed person (who may be his brother) who has been imprisoned for a violent crime; the distant past of the escaping slave who was his great-great-great-grandmother; and the more recent past, when his Aunt May tells the story of his ancestor's escape. Wideman also shifts voices: he writes in his own voice, which has a modern consciousness and a political motive; his Aunt May's, which is the older African-American speech of the church and of oral narration; and the voice of his ancestor, as he follows her thoughts and emotions when she escapes with the young white man who is saving her and their children from being sold to a new owner.

The complex point of view that the story presents is similar to the multileveled consciousness of other African-American writers, from Langston Hughes to Ralph Ellison and Toni Morrison, who also balance their own consciousness (which has been shaped by the educational system and culture of a European American society) against their emotional commitment to their own African American identity. The opening sentence of the story, which sets the writer on a Greek island, is evocative of writing by Richard Wright or James Baldwin, as they turn to their American experience from the perspective of their lives in Europe. The central part of the story, his Aunt May's long narration of her memory of Sybela, is a brilliant evocation of African American speech and has the same power and authenticity as Ellison's recall of the same speech patterns in his novel *Invisible Man*.

In addition to setting his story within the tradition of African American writing, Wideman also sets his story during the emotionally charged 1960s and 1970s, as he describes the person to whom the story is addressed and another black prisoner as they are led through the crowd outside a courtroom. The final turn of Wideman's kaleidoscope is his account of a Supreme Court case that concerns the rights of prisoners in a prison system that he perceives as clearly racist. In the shifting images of his story Wideman has presented much of himself, and at the same time he has given the reader a series of images that present a moment in our shared history.

Questions for Discussion

1. How would you tell in a few words the story of the person to whom "The Beginning of Homewood" is addressed?
2. How would you tell the story of Sybela Owens?
3. How would you tell the story of Aunt May?
4. Why does Wideman use these different points of view to tell the story?
5. What elements of the story give it a political focus in the 1960s and 1970s?
6. Why does Wideman locate Aunt May's narrative within the framework of her church and her religion?
7. Although the writer makes it clear that the young white man who brings Sybela to freedom continues to live with her in Homewood, his experience doesn't enter into the story. Why doesn't it?

Topics for Writing

1.   The story presents a narrative within a narrative in Aunt May's telling of her meeting with Sybela. What is the difference between an oral narration and a written narration as represented by the story?
2.   **CONNECTIONS**   How does Wideman's use of oral narrative compare to similar uses by other African American writers in this anthology (e.g., Ellison)?

Suggested Readings

Wideman, John Edgar. *All Stories Are True.* New York: Vintage, 1993.
———. *The Collected Stories of John Edgar Wideman.* New York: Pantheon, 1992.

CHRISTA WOLF

Exchanging Glances (p. 1329)

The German author Christa Wolf was ten years old when Hitler's army invaded Poland and World War II, and she has summarized her memories of her response to the war in her essay "My Work as a Writer":

> I cannot forget how, at the start of the war, when the children of my generation were ten years old, the attempt was made to inject us with false grief, false love, false hate; how it almost succeeded; what effort it cost to break out of that net; how much help we needed from so many people; how much reflection, how much serious work, how many heated debates, how we also had to think back to the old dreams we had known as children.
>
> I grew up in a medium-sized town — more small than medium, really — east of the Oder. I was attached to my surroundings, to the view out my window, from which I could see the whole town and the river; to the lakes, the pine woods, to the landscape, which perhaps was barren, overall. I could not picture any other background for my life. As a child I never traveled as far as I did at the age of fifteen turning sixteen, during the evacuation. I had never seen the war so close up before. I learned that watching dead, mangled "enemies" on a movie screen is different from personally holding an infant who has frozen stiff and having to hand him over to his mother; that hearing the word "Communist" — always in a whisper and always combined with the word "criminal "— is different from sitting by a fire one cold night next to a German Communist in concentration-camp clothing, after many weeks on the road and after seeing many images one would never have believed possible.
>
> In the next few years we found out how much easier it is . . . to be ashamed of one's people when one has learned the whole truth than it is to learn to love them again.

In the story "Exchanging Glances," Wolf refers to several of the details of the evacuation that she mentions in her essay. She organizes her story chronologically as a deliberate attempt to remember the painful time when it had become apparent to loyal civilians like Wolf and her family that Germany had lost the war, and she suggests her state of shock at the time by describing how helpless she felt as a teenager before the onset of hysterical laughter, "the impropriety of which I find deeply offensive."

Yet there is nothing stiff or false in Wolf's narrative. She despises the American soldiers to whom she and her family must "surrender," and she does not hide this fact. The incident in which the Americans take the wristwatches from the Germans is a symbolic act as well as a calculated act of dominance. Wolf hides her watch, suggesting her refusal to be dominated, just as she later refuses to fraternize with the American sergeant like the "squealing German girl hanging on each arm."

It is unusual for Americans to get a "window" on themselves from writers to whom they have appeared as an enemy. Wolf writes honestly of her feelings as a loyal German subject. As the story opens, she remembers how frightened her grandmother was of the Russians, whom she regarded as "Asians" or barbarians, and how matter-of-factly she accepted the services of the SS officer who had been with them in the air-raid shelter. American pilots flew the fighter planes that strafed and killed unarmed German civilians like Wilhelm Grund on the road in the midst of his horrified family. Wolf recalls being "stunned" at the everyday tone of voice in which a German soldier beside the road called out, "The Führer is dead." She feels that his words should "have echoed frightfully between Heaven and earth," and she remembers how as a patriotic ten-year-old at the beginning of the war she had "thrown cigarette packs" to soldiers in "the dusty convoys which rolled eastward past our house" as the German army proceeded to occupy Poland during the summer of 1939.

On May 5, 1945, the Day of Liberation, the Jews and Communists are released from the nearby concentration camp and line the road, ragged and starving. For just "a fraction of a second," Wolf allows herself to recognize them and feel guilty, but a few minutes later, Wolf finds them "completely foreign." But an even bigger shock is seeing a Polish worker rebel against a German farmer: "Now the world had truly turned topsy-turvy." Before the war, she and her family were "settled, proper, respectable people" who suddenly felt like characters in a Grimm fairy tale after Hitler came to power. In retrospect, she understood that they were trapped like the modest fisherman married to the greedy Ilsebil. In the folktale, when the fisherman catches the magic flounder, who grants him his wishes, the insatiable wife first asks for a bigger house and then asks to become emperor, pope, and then God. At this last wish, all collapses and the fisherman returns to find his wife back in the little house in which they started. "Exchanging Glances" is no fairy tale. There is no going back for Christa Wolf, only tears and the haunting question asked by the released communist prisoner who shares their open fire: "Where, then, have you lived all these years?"

Questions for Discussion

1. Why does the SS officer call the Russians "those Asian hordes"?
2. Describe Wolf's settled family life before the war.

3. Why was she so shaken by the thought "You'll never see this again" when she left her hometown the previous January?
4. In section two of the story, how does Wolf reflect on the process of remembering the Spring of 1945? What were her feelings at the age of sixteen about accepting the fact of Germany's defeat? What was she "liberated from" on the Day of Liberation?
5. After Herr Grund was killed by the American fighter pilot, why did Wolf feel that his death "deviated from the ideal of death for Führer and Reich," despite hearing Herr Volk tell Grund's son that his father "died a soldier's death"?
6. What has Wolf learned from the experience of the evacuation?

Topics for Writing

1. Analyze Wolf's portrait of the Americans in "Exchanging Glances."
2. Report on the events of the Day of Liberation in Germany from your research on World War II.

Suggested Readings

Wolf, Christa. *What Remains and Other Stories.* Trans. Heike Schwarzbauer and Rich Takvorian. London: Virago, 1993.
———. *The Writer's Dimension: Selected Essays.* Trans. Jan Van Heurck. Introduction by Grace Paley. London: Virago, 1993.

TOBIAS WOLFF

Say Yes (p. 1340)

Tobias Wolff narrows the scope of "Say Yes" to zoom in on a seemingly ordinary evening in the life of a long-married couple. The unremarkable sequence of events nevertheless leads to the erotically charged atmosphere of the final paragraph. Through the routine domestic gestures of washing and drying dishes, attending to a cut finger, taking out garbage, mopping the floor, and magazine reading, Wolff manages to reveal much about the inner lives of these people. Their namelessness emphasizes their ordinariness.

A conversation about interracial marriage sets the story in motion. Early in the dialogue, after suggesting that interracial marriage is a bad idea (without being able to fully articulate his reasons), the husband, observing his wife's expression, realizes he should back off from the subject but instead presses forward. These two know each other intimately — know how to needle, cajole, hurt, and apologize in subtle and not-so-subtle ways. In fact, this very intimacy — as with most marriages — carries negative as well as positive meanings. The husband's insistence that "a person from their culture and a person from our culture could never really know each other" reflects back on the couple's own relationship, leading the reader to question the extent to which *any* two people can know each other. Taking out the garbage and observing the night stars, the husband reflects on his marriage. Ashamed of fighting, he realizes the depth of the intimacy he shares with his wife as well as the transitoriness of their relationship with an intensity that affects him physically. This epiphany transforms at least his short-term behavior. Where normally he would "heave rocks" at the two dogs that topple his garbage, in this instance he lets them go unharmed.

Back in the house, he apologizes in the terms of the earlier discussion of interracial marriage, which now becomes a fantasy when he affirms that he'd marry her even if she were black. This openness to unexplored possibilities recharges the erotic life of the couple. When his wife enters the room in the darkness, "his heart pound[s] the way it had on their first night together," as if they were strangers.

Questions for Discussion

1. Why doesn't the husband "keep his mouth shut" when he knows he should?
2. What do you think the husband means when he says, "A person from their culture and a person from our culture could never really know each other"? Do you agree? What are some advantages and disadvantages of intracultural versus intercultural romantic relationships?
3. Why does the husband not "heave rocks" at the dogs that topple his garbage on this occasion, as he normally would?
4. In the final paragraph, why is the husband so excited? Does he experience a positive, erotic excitement, or does he realize that he doesn't know his wife as well as he thought he did?
5. Why is the question "Would you have loved me if I had been black?" so important to the wife?
6. To whom does the title apply? Who is expected to say yes?

Topic for Writing

1. Discuss the role of domestic details in advancing characterization in "Say Yes." What do these details reveal about this couple and their marriage?

Suggested Readings

Wolff, Tobias. *Back in the World: Stories.* Boston: Houghton, 1985.

———. *The Barracks Thief and Other Stories.* New York: Bantam, 1984.

———. *In the Garden of the North American Martyrs: A Collection of Short Stories.* New York: Ecco, 1981.

Woodruff, Jay, ed. "In the Garden of the North American Martyrs." *A Piece of Work: Five Writers Discuss Their Revisions.* Iowa City: U of Iowa P, 1993.

Virginia Woolf

Kew Gardens (p. 1345)

This sketch might puzzle some students, since its point of view (clearly dictated by Woolf) seems so unusual. No particular person is having his or her story told. Rather, Woolf seems to be telling the story of a snail in a plot of flowers in Kew Gardens. "Cosmic" rather than "omniscient" might be the best word to describe Woolf's perspective, which blends blue sky and green earth so closely as to exclude the people strolling the garden paths between the two elements.

Woolf's story is experimental, and her concentration as she attempts to record "the essential life" of the creatures in the garden is almost palpable. According to the critic Susan Dick, in 1919 Woolf learned from studying Chekhov that "inconclusive stories are legitimate." Dick goes on to say that the narrator in a typical story by Woolf functions "as a perceptive observer of the external scene. . . . [or] the narrator dramatizes from within the minds of the characters . . . their perceptions of themselves and their world." In "Kew Gardens," Woolf moves seamlessly in and out of her characters' minds, recording their thoughts and feelings more substantially than the actual words they exchange.

The thoughts and words of the first couple, a married pair with two children, shape the reader's expectations for the rest of the story. Simon, the husband, thinks of Lily, an earlier love, to whom he'd proposed marriage in Kew Gardens when he was young. He remembers the shoe she wore, "with the square silver buckle at the toe," which symbolized her attractiveness and her lack of interest in his proposal. His wife, Eleanor, when he asks her if she ever thinks of the past, answers him bluntly, perhaps jealous that he is thinking of the beautiful Lily. Eleanor's memory of past love in Kew Gardens is the kiss given to her by "an old grey-haired woman with a wart on her nose, the mother of all my kisses all my life." We hear no more of this old woman (Eleanor's art teacher?), and we are not told why the kiss was so unsettling that Eleanor's "hand shook all the afternoon so that I couldn't paint." The married couple leave with their children, as much strangers to us as when they appeared.

The snail is the next character, and his conflict is a physical problem: how should he get around a dead leaf? This shift to the nonhuman prepares the reader for Woolf's shift to a cosmic view. The couples on the garden paths are reduced to colors as she lets the descriptive elements of the scene dissolve "like drops of water in the yellow and green atmosphere." The heat of the summer afternoon overcomes everything, reducing the "gross and heavy bodies" to a drowsy torpidity, but their voices continue as a manifestation of their spiritual essence, "as if they were flames lolling from the thick waxen bodies of candles." The silence is found to be composed of pure sound, the sound of buses, people, and the petals of flowers, whose colors seem to Woolf to be heard in the air.

Questions for Discussion

1. How does Woolf organize her sketch so that her description seems continuous and coherent?

2. Describe the people in the scene. What other living elements in the garden are treated as characters?
3. What is Woolf's tone? To which social class does she belong? Comment on her treatment of the two "elderly women of the lower middle class." How are they described? What can you tell about Woolf's attitude toward them from the words they exchange?
4. What is Woolf's attitude toward romantic love? old age? Do these two elements serve as the extremes of dramatic human conflicts in her sketch? Explain.

Topics for Writing

1. Rewrite "Kew Gardens" as it might be the following afternoon, when it's raining.
2. Analyze Woolf's range of vocabulary in this sketch. How does she suggest a poetic atmosphere in her descriptions of the garden and its inhabitants and visitors?

Related Commentary

Katherine Mansfield, Review of Woolf's "Kew Gardens," p. 1454.

Suggested Reading

Baldwin, Dean. *Virginia Woolf: A Study of the Short Fiction.* Boston: Twayne, 1986.
Beja, Morris, ed. *Critical Essays on Virginia Woolf.* Boston: G. K. Hall, 1985.
Bishop, Edward L. "Pursuing 'It' Through 'Kew Gardens.'" *Studies in Short Fiction* Summer 19:3 (1982): 269–75.
Homans, Margaret. *Virginia Woolf: A Collection of Critical Essays.* Englewood Cliffs, NJ: Prentice-Hall, 1993.
Marcus, Jane, ed. *New Feminist Essays on Virginia Woolf.* Lincoln: U of Nebraska P, 1981.
Oakland, John. "Virginia Woolf's *Kew Gardens.*" *English Studies: A Journal of English Language and Literature* June 68:3 (1987): 264–73.
Woolf, Virginia. *The Complete Shorter Fiction of Virginia Woolf.* San Diego: Harcourt, 1985.
———. *The Essays of Virginia Woolf.* San Diego: Harcourt, 1988.

RICHARD WRIGHT

The Man Who Was Almost a Man (p. 1351)

Dave Saunders dislikes being laughed at, and his discomfort at becoming an object of amusement for accidentally shooting old Jenny, the mule, precipitates his final step into manhood. Although the anecdote around which Wright builds the story is comical enough, the reader probably should accede to Dave's wish to be taken seriously, for the fate that lies ahead of this young man as he rolls toward his unknown destination atop a boxcar with nothing in his pocket but an unloaded gun is likely to be grim.

At the same time, however, Dave's self-esteem and independence deserve respect. At the beginning of the story he dissociates himself from the field hands and fixes on his ambition to declare his manhood by owning a gun. Throughout the story the idea that *boys* do not have guns recurs, and Dave not only wants a gun but also chafes at being call "boy" by his parents and at being treated as a child. Just before he goes out to master the gun and hop a freight, Dave grumbles, "They treat me like a mule, n then they beat me." His resolution to escape his inferior status will involve not only leaving home but taking potshots at the facade of white society just as he wants to shoot at "Jim Hawkins' big white house" in order "to let him know Dave Saunders is a man." The question Wright leaves hanging for the reader as his story trails off into ellipses is whether Dave has killed the mule in himself or whether he himself, like Jenny, may become the victim of his own wild shots.

WILLIAM E. SHEIDLEY

Questions for Discussion

1. Explain the pun in the last sentence of the first paragraph.
2. Define our first impression of Dave. What reasons do we have to admire him? to laugh at him? to pity him?
3. What does it take to be a man in the world of the story? Is a gun enough? How does one get a gun?
4. What is ironic about the way Dave gets the money to buy his gun?
5. How is Dave treated by his father? Why does Ma say of the gun, "It be fer Pa"?
6. With the gun under his pillow, Dave feels "a sense of power. Could kill a man with a gun like this. Kill anybody, black or white." What does Dave still have to learn before he can be called a man? How does the story bring it home to him?
7. Explain what happens the first time Dave fires the gun. What does he do differently the next time?
8. Why does Wright describe the death of the mule in such detail?
9. Explain why being laughed at is so painful for Dave. What might enable him to join in and laugh at himself?
10. Comment on the possible implications of Dave's remark "They treat me like a mule, n then they beat me," both within the story and in a broader social and historical context. Does Dave's killing the mule have a symbolic significance?
11. Where might Dave be headed as he hops the Illinois Central? What might he find at the end of his journey?
12. Why is the title not "The Boy Who Was Almost a Man"?

Topics for Writing

1. Examine the tone of Wright's story.
2. Discuss the treatment of Wright's social themes in "The Man Who Was Almost a Man." (See the story's headnote.)
3. Write a sequel to Wright's story, another episode in the life of Dave Saunders — something that happens on the train ride or when he arrives in New Orleans or Chicago or wherever. Try to sustain and develop as many themes and motives already present in Wright's story as you can, but make the material your own by imagining what you think happens, not necessarily what you guess Wright would have written. Decide whether to adopt Wright's style and point of view or employ a different mode of narration. Remember that the story is set during the Great Depression.

Related Commentary

Richard Wright, Reading Fiction, p. 1516.

Suggested Readings

Felgar, Robert. *Richard Wright.* Boston: Twayne, 1980.
Hakutani, Yoshinobu, ed. *Critical Essays on Richard Wright.* Boston: G. K. Hall, 1982.
Margolies, Edward. *The Art of Richard Wright.* Carbondale: Southern Illinois UP, 1969.
McCall, Dan. *The Example of Richard Wright.* New York: Harcourt, 1969.
Reilly, John M. *Richard Wright: The Critical Reception.* New York: Burt Franklin, 1978.
Wright, Richard. *Uncle Tom's Children.* New York: Harper, 1989.

HISAYE YAMAMOTO

The Eskimo Connection (p. 1361)

A casual reading of "The Eskimo Connection" may leave students wondering what the point of the story is. Not much happens in the plot except an exchange of letters over a period of more than a year between an "aging Nisei widow in Los Angeles" whose "main avocation was not writing poetry but babysitting the grandchildren" and a twenty-three-year-old Yupik (Eskimo) man imprisoned on unspecified charges who asks the widow to critique his essay (later a short story) about Alaska. She finds the writing "not enough to set her teeth on edge as sometimes happened, but almost."

This last phrase, placed at the end of the second paragraph of the story, can perhaps serve as a key to unlock Yamamoto's puzzle. As a gentle, deftly humorous attempt to defuse cultural stereotypes, "The Eskimo Connection" examines several aspects of current mythologies about minorities in the United States. In particular, the story poses and answers the question, Does an "Eskimo connection" (or any common ground) automatically exist between two supposedly "fellow" Asian Americans?

Yamamoto makes Emiko Toyama, the "aging Nisei widow," the protagonist of the story. She appears to be at the center of a stable family unit, still supporting her family on her widow's pension while offering a home to three of her children and babysitting their children, presumably so they can have the opportunity to continue their educations and careers. In contrast, young Alden Ryan Walunga hasn't taken much responsibility for himself or helped in the support of his family: In addition to the unspecified crime that has brought him to the federal penitentiary, he has been an alcoholic, he takes "massive doses of Thorazine" to relieve his depression, and he has become such a keen convert to Christianity that the study of Christ's word occupies most of his time.

Obviously Alden believes in an "Eskimo connection"; it is the reason he contacts Emiko after reading one of her poems in an Asian American publication. But Yamamoto makes clear that Emiko's response has little to do with any feelings of loyalty to her ethnic background or sense of solidarity with other Asian Americans. Rather, she responds to Alden's essay as a fellow poet, soft-pedaling her criticism so as not to discourage him. In return, she gets a chilling sense of prison life when a magazine she sends Alden is returned: "[T]hat was what being in prison was, was it, the relinquishment of every liberty that those on the outside took for granted"? The correspondence confirms her liberal outlook on punishment for criminals: "[T]here must be some system to temporarily segregate those who persisted in preying on others," but she "was not sure that prisons were the answer to crime." Yamamoto's story reflects the social turbulence of the United States in the mid-1970s, when Nixon was forced to resign his presidency after Watergate and the police were "pigs" to anti-Vietnam protestors.

Emiko's secular liberalism is not shared by Alden, whose Christian fundamentalism leads him to write a story about a Yupik family in Alaska whose oldest son is a rapist and murderer who becomes a new man, "washed clean of his sins" after his death by being "reborn in Christ." The brutality and bigotry expressed in the story stun Emiko, but she characteristically responds with gentle criticism and praise for "the poetry of the stark landscape with the snowbirds" that Alden knows so well near the Bering Sea.

If students accept Emiko as a stereotypical Nisei woman (responsible, intelligent, kind), will they accept Yamamoto's portrait of Alden as a stereotypical Yupik (alcoholic, depressed, criminal)? Or has Yamamoto challenged our perception of racial stereotypes by telling us that Alden is also somewhat educated (two semesters at the University of Alaska) and interested in the wider world of Japanese writers (he knows about Yukio Mishima's suicide) as well as passionately Christian? Yamamoto has written a story that reaches far beyond her account of an exchange of letters and manuscripts between two Asian Americans. Emiko gets the last word in the story, and she humorously descends to stereotype in her conclusion that Alden has stopped writing her after his transfer to a prison in Alaska because he was "probably much too busy back there on his home ground to continue to be the pen pal of some old woman way down there in California."

Questions for Discussion

1. Why does Emiko decide to write to Alden after he sends her an essay he has written?
2. How has she learned to be careful in her criticism of the work of other writers?
3. What is the "camp" she lived in as a young woman?
4. How serious was Alden's study of writing at the University of Alaska?
5. What is the significance of the similarity of Emiko's name to the word "Eskimo"?
6. Why is Emiko so tolerant of people who have spent time in prison? What newsworthy event does she refer to when she mentions "the horror of the year before, the mousetrapping and cooking alive of five young men and women who have gotten disillusioned with the establishment and taken matters into their own hands"? (Recall that in 1974 twenty-year-old Patty Hearst was kidnapped in California by members of the Symbionese Liberation Army, whom Hearst later assisted in robbing a bank in what she described as their "war for the freedom of oppressed people.")
7. Why wasn't Emiko allowed to visit Alden in prison?
8. What do you think of the writing style in Alden's short story?
9. Why is it in character for Alden to have told prison authorities "what he had seen of a homosexual rape in prison"?
10. Why is he unhappy in the Seattle City Jail? How does his last letter to Emiko help her to imagine his life after his return to Alaska?

Topics for Writing

1. **CONNECTIONS** Compare and contrast Yamamoto's description of Alden Ryan Walunga's background in Alaska as a Yupik in "The Eskimo Connection" with Silko's portrayal of Yupik life in "Storyteller," taking into account that Yamamoto wrote a realistic story and Silko created a fantasy. Which story is more convincing?
2. **CONNECTIONS** Compare and contrast Yamamoto's presentation of Alden's writing in "The Eskimo Connection" with Paley's story-within-a-story in "A Conversation with My Father."

Suggested Reading

Yamamoto, Hisaye. *Seventeen Syllables and Other Stories.* Latham, NY: Kitchen Table, 1988.

CHRONOLOGICAL LISTING OF AUTHORS AND STORIES

Nathaniel Hawthorne (1804-1864)
My Kinsman, Major Molineux
(1832)
Young Goodman Brown (1835)

Nikolai Gogol (1809–1852)
The Overcoat (1840)

Edgar Allan Poe (1809–1849)
The Tell-Tale Heart (1843)
The Cask of Amontillado (1846)

Herman Melville (1819–1891)
Bartleby, the Scrivener (1853)

Gustave Flaubert (1821–1880)
A Simple Heart (1877)

Leo Tolstoy (1828–1910)
The Death of Ivan Ilych (1886)

Ambrose Bierce (1842–1914?)
*An Occurrence at Owl Creek
Bridge* (1891)

Henry James (1843–1916)
The Beast in the Jungle (1903)

Sarah Orne Jewett (1949–1909)
A White Heron (1886)

Guy de Maupassant (1850–1893)
The Necklace (1884)

Kate Chopin (1851–1904)
Désirée's Baby (1892)
The Story of an Hour (1894)

Joseph Conrad (1857–1924)
Heart of Darkness (1902)

Charles Chesnutt (1958–1932)
The Sheriff's Children (1899)

Anton Chekhov (1860–1904)
The Darkling (1899)
The Lady with the Pet Dog (1899)

Charlotte Perkins Gilman (1860–
1935)
The Yellow Wallpaper (1892)

Edith Wharton (1862–1937)
Roman Fever (1936)

Stephen Crane (1873–1947)
The Open Boat (1897)

Willa Cather (1873–1947)
Paul's Case (1905)

Sherwood Anderson (1876–1941)
Hands (1919)
Death in the Woods (1933)

James Joyce (1882–1941)
Araby (1916)
The Dead (1916)

Virginia Woolf (1882–1941)
Kew Gardens (1919)

Franz Kafka (1883–1924)
A Hunger Artist (1924)
The Metamorphosis (1915)

Isak Dinesen (1885–1962)
The Sailor-Boy's Tale (1942)

D. H. Lawrence (1885–1930)
Odour of Chrysanthemums (1909)
The Rocking-Horse Winner (1926)

Katherine Mansfield (1888–1923)
Bliss (1920)
The Garden-iParty (1922)

Katherine Anne Porter (1890–1980)
He (1927)

Isaac Babel (1894–1939?)
My First Goose (1925)

James Thurber (1894–1961)
The Secret Life of Walter Mitty
(1942)

F. Scott Fitgerald (1896–1940)
Babylon Revisited (1935)

William Faulkner (1897–1962)
A Rose for Emily (1931)
that Evening Sun (1931)

Ernest Hemingway (19898–1961)
Hills Like White Elephants (1927)

Jorge Luis Borges (1899–1986)
The Garden of Forking Paths
(1941)

Zora Neale Hurston (1901?–1960)
  Spunk (1927)
  The Gilded Six-Bits (1933)

Kay Boyle (1902–1992)
  Black Boy (1932)

John Steinbeck (1902–1968)
  The Chrysanthemums (1938)

Frank O'Connor (1903–1966)
  Guests of the Nation (1931)

Frank Sargeson (1903–1982)
  A Great Day (1940)

Isaac Bashevis Singer (1904–1991)
  The Spinoza of Market Street (1961)

Richard Wright (1908–1960)
  The Man Who Was Almost a Man (1961)

Eudora Welty (b. 1909)
  Why I Live at the P.O. (1941)
  A worn Path (1941)

Paul Bowles (b. 1910)
  The Eye (1981)

Naguib Mahfouz (b. 1911)
  Half a Day (1989)

John Cheever (1912–1982)
  The Swimmer (1964)

Saadat Hasan Manto (1912–1955)
  The Dog of Titwal (1949)

Albert Camus (1913–1960)
  The Guest (1957)

Tillie Olsen (b. 1913)
  I Stand Here Ironing (1961)

Julio Cortázar (1914–1984)
  Axolotl (1963)

Ralph Ellison (1914–1994)
  King of the Bingo Game (1944)
  Battle Royal (1952)

Bernard Malamud (1914–1986)
  Black Is My Favorite Color (1963)

Octavio Paz (b. 1914)
  My Life with the Wave (1949)

Es'Kia Mphahlele (b. 1919)
  Mrs. Plum (1967)

Shirley Jackson (1919–1965)
  The Lottery (1948)

Doris Lessing (b. 1919)
  Debbie and Julie (1987)

Hisaye Yamamoto (b. 1921)
  The Eskimo Connection (1983)

Tadeusz Borowski (1922–1951)
  This Way for the Gas, Ladies and Gentlemen (1948)

Grace Paley (b. 1922)
  A Conversation with My Father (1974)

Italo Calvino (1923–1985)
  The Feathered Ogre (1956)

Nadine Gordimer (b. 1923)
  Town and Country Lovers (1980)

James Baldwin (1924–1987)
  Sonny's Blues (1957)

Mavis Gallant (b. 1924)
  1933 (1987)

Yukio Mushima (1925–1970)
  Fountains in the Rain (1963)

Flannery O'Connor (1925–1964)
  A Good Man Is Hard to Find (1955)
  Good Country People (1955)
  Everything That Rises Must Converge (1965)

Alice Adams (b. 1926)
  The Last Love City (1991)

Gabriel García Márquez (b. 1928)
  A Very Old Man with Enormous Wings (1955)

Cynthia Ozick (b. 1928)
  The Shawl (1980)

Milan Kundera (b. 1929)
  The Hitchhiking Game (1969)

Ursula K. Le Guin (b. 1929)
  The Ones Who Walk Away from Omelas (1976)

Christa Wolf (b. 1929)
  Exchanging Glances (1993)

THEMATIC INDEX

Story Pairs

On Writing

Fantasy and the Supernatural

Love, Marriage, and Infidelity

Parents and Children

War and Revolution

Looking at the Wall

SHORT STORIES ON FILM AND VIDEO

Babylon Revisited (F. Scott
Fitzgerald)
Movie Title: *The Last Time I Saw
Paris*
116 min., color, 1954
Cast: Elizabeth Taylor, Van
Johnson, Donna Reed, Eva
Gabor
Directed by Richard Brooks
Distributed by: Films, Inc.

Bartleby, the Scrivener (Herman
Melville)
Movie title: *Bartleby*
28 min., color, 1969
Distributed by: Encyclopaedia
Britannica

Movie title: *Bartleby*
29 min., b&w, 1965
Videotape from the American Short
Stories Classics Series
Distributed by: Michigan Media

The Cask of Amontillado (Edgar
Allan Poe)
19 min., color, 1979
Directed by Bernard Wilets
Distributed by: BFA Educational
Media

29 min., b&w, 1965
Videotape from the American Short
Stories Classics Series
Distributed by: Michigan Media

15 min., b&w, 1955
Cast: Monty Woolley
Distributed by: Audio Brandon

The Dead (James Joyce)
82 min., color, 1988
Cast: Anjelica Huston, Donal
McCann, Helena Carroll,
Cathleen Delany
Directed by: John Huston
Distributed by: Vestron Video, Inc.

The Death of Ivan Ilych (Leo
Tolstoy)
29 min., color, 1978
Part of the Begin with Goodbye
Series
Distributed by: Mass Media
Ministries

The Garden-Party (Katherine
Mansfield)
24 min., color, 1974
Available on videotape
Winner of the Red Ribbon at the
1974 American Film and Video
Association Awards
Distributed by: AIMS Media

Movie title: *Katherine Mansfield's
'The Garden Party'*
24 min., color, 1973
Available on film
Distributed by: Gurian-Sholder,
Garden Party Company
Kent State University

Heart of Darkness (Joseph Conrad)
Movie title: *Apocalypse Now*
153 min., color, 1979
Cast: Martin Sheen, Marlon Brando
Directed by Francis Ford Coppola
Distributed by: Paramount Home
Video

The Lady with the Pet Dog (Anton
Chekhov)
Movie title: *The Lady with the Dog*
86 min., b&w, 1960
In Russian with English subtitles
Cast: Iya Savvina, Alexei Batalov,
Alla Chostakova
Directed by Joseph Heifitz
Distributed by: Audio Brandon

The Lottery (Shirley Jackson)
18 min., color, 1969
Distributed by: Encyclopaedia
Britannica

The Man Who Was Almost a Man
(Richard Wright)
Movie title: *Almos' a Man*
39 min., color, 1977
Available on film or videotape
Cast: Levar Burton
Directed by Stan Lathan
Distributed by: Perspective Films

The Necklace (Guy de Maupassant)
23 min., color, 1979
Available on film
Distributed by: FilmFair Communications

22 min., color, 1981
Available on film and video
Distributed by: Barr Films

Movie title: *The Necklace by Guy de Maupassant*
20 min., color, 1980
Available on film
Distributed by: Encyclopedia Britannica Educational Corp.

An Occurrence at Owl Creek Bridge (Ambrose Bierce)
27 min., b&w, 1962
Cast: Roger Jacquet, Anne Cornaly, Anker Larsen
Directed by Robert Enrico
Winner at Cannes and American Film Festivals
Distributed by: Films, Inc.

30 min., b&w, 1964
Same as 1962 version, with prologue for its showing as an episode of *The Twilight Zone*
Distributed by: Classic Film Museum, Inc.
McGraw-Hill Films
Northwest Film Study Center
Viewfinders, Inc.

The Open Boat (Stephen Crane)
29 min., b&w, 1965
Distributed by: Michigan Media

Paul's Case (Willa Cather)
55 min., color, 1980
Available on film or videotape
Distributed by: Perspective Films

The Rocking-Horse Winner (D. H. Lawrence)
30 min., color, 1977
Cast: Kenneth More
Adapted by Julian Bond
Directed by Peter Modak
Distributed by: Learning Corp. of America

91 min., b&w, 1950
Cast: John Mills, Valerie Hobson
Directed by Anthony Pelessier
Distributed by: Films, Inc.
Budget Films

90 min., b&w, 1949
Cast: John Mills, Valerie Hobson
Available on videotape
Distributed by: Films for the Humanities, Inc.

A Rose for Emily (William Faulkner)
27 min., color, 1983
Distributed by: Pyramid Film and Video

The Secret Life of Walter Mitty
(James Thurber)
110 min., color, 1947
Cast: Danny Kaye, Virginia Mayo
Directed by Norman Z. MacLeod
Distributed by: Arcus Films
Audio-Brandon
ROA Films
Twyman Films, Inc.
Westcoast Films

The Swimmer (John Cheever)
94 min., color, 1968
Cast: Burt Lancaster, Janet Landgard
Directed by Frank Perry

The Tell-Tale Heart (Edgar Allan
   Poe)
26 min.
Cast: Alex Corde, Sam Jaffe
Distributed by: Churchill Films

**Where Are You Going, Where Have
   You Been?** (Joyce Caol Oates)
Movie title: *Smooth Talk*
92 min., color, 1985
Cast: Laura Dern, Treat Williams
Directed by Joyce Chopra
Distributed by: Vestron Video, Inc.

A White Heron (Sarah Orne Jewett)
26 min., color, 1978
Distributed by: Learning Corp. of
   America

The Yellow Wallpaper (Charlotte
   Perkins Gilman)
15 min., color, 1978
Produced by: International Institute
   of Television
Distributed by: Indiana University

Young Goodman Brown (Nathaniel
   Hawthorne)
30 min., color, 1973
Directed by Donald Fox
Distributed by: Pyramid Film and
   Video

Directory of Film Distributors

AIMS Media
9710 DeSoto Ave.
Chatsworth, CA 91311-4409

Arcus Films
1225 Broadway
New York, NY 10001

Audio Brandon
45 MacQuesten Parkway S.
Mt. Vernon, NY 10550

Barr Films
1201 Schabarum Ave.
P.O. Box 7878
Irwindale, CA 91706

BFA Educational Media
2211 Michigan Ave.
Santa Monica, CA 90404

Budget Films
4590 Santa Monica Blvd.
Los Angeles, CA 90029

Churchill Films
662 Oral Roberts Blvd.
Los Angeles, CA 90060

Classic Film Museum, Inc.
4 Union Sq.
Dover-Foxcroft, ME 04426

Encyclopaedia Britannica Educational
Corp.
425 North Michigan Ave.
Chicago, IL 60611

FilmFair Communications
10621 Magnolia Blvd., North
Hollywood, CA 91601

Films, Inc.
Film and Tape Division
733 Greenbay Rd.
Wilmette, IL 60091

Films for the Humanities, Inc.
P.O. Box 2053
Princeton, NJ 08540

Indiana University
Audio Visual Center
Bloomington, IN 47405

Kit Parker Films
P.O. Box 227
Carmel Valley, CA 93924

Learning Corp. of America
1350 Avenue of the Americas
New York, NY 10019

Mass Media Ministries
2116 N. Charles St.
Baltimore, MD 21218

McGraw-Hill Films
1221 Avenue of the Americas
New York, NY 10020

Michigan Media
University of Michigan
400 Fourth St.
Ann Arbor, MI 48109

Paramount Home Video
5555 Melrose Ave.
Hollywood, CA 90038

Perspective Films
65 East South Water St.
Chicago, IL 60601

Phoenix Films
470 Park Ave. S.
New York, NY 10016

Pyramid Film and Video
P. O. Box 1048
Santa Monica, CA 90406

ROA Films
1696 N. Astor St.
Milwaukee, WI 53202

SL Film Productions, Inc.
P. O. Box 41108
Los Angeles, CA 90041

Twyman Films, Inc.
329 Salem Ave.
Dayton, OH 45401

Vestron Video, Inc.
P.O. Box 4000
Stamford, CT 06907

Westcoast Films
25 Lusk St.
San Francisco, CA 94107

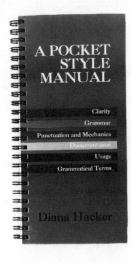

CRITICAL THINKING, READING, AND WRITING
A Brief Guide to Argument

Sylvan Barnet and **Hugo Bedau,** both of *Tufts University*

■ brief and inexpensive guide to critical thinking and writing — comprising the text and appendices of *Current Issues and Enduring Questions* ■ an ideal text for bringing critical thinking into a writing course ■ 21 model arguments for critical analysis ■ thorough coverage of research and documentation including MLA and APA style ■ 4 unique appendices on different argumentative perspectives, including Toulmin and Rogerian models

1993/paper
230 pages/$10 net
Instructor's Manual

"A marvel of concision…the techniques of argumentation come to life."
— John G. Hanna, *University of Southern Maine*

THE STRUCTURE OF ARGUMENT
Annette T. Rottenberg

■ comparatively brief and very affordable text ■ comprises the text of the best-selling argument text and reader, *Elements of Argument*, Fourth Edition ■ based on the Toulmin model of argumentation ■ covers writing and research ■ 36 readings for analysis ■ includes exercises for critical thinking

"The treatment of the Toulmin model is excellent — one of the most lucid available."
— Stanley S. Blair, *Marquette University*

1994/paper
325 pages/$10 net
Instructor's Manual

"An excellent introduction to the elements of argument."
— Richard Ruppel, *Viterbo College*

WRITING WORTH READING
A Practical Guide
Paperback Second Edition

Nancy Huddleston Packer, *Stanford University*
John Timpane, *Lafayette College*

■ paperback edition reprints the highly-praised rhetorical chapters of *Writing Worth Reading*, Second Edition, without the handbook section ■ emphasis on critical thinking and reading ■ in-depth treatment of specific writing assignments across the curriculum ■ extensive coverage of the research process and documenting sources for various disciplines ■ thorough Instructor's Manual

1993/paper
504 pages/$9.50 net
Instructor's Manual

"Lively, informative, practical and accessible."
— Marci Lingo, *Bakersfield College*

Bedford Books *of* St. Martin's Press
For exam copies, call 1–800–446–8923